FLOCKS OF BIRDS

FLOCKS OF BIRDS

Virginia Colonialism into Native Country, 1670–1776

ANTHONY S. PARENT JR.

THE UNIVERSITY OF SOUTH CAROLINA PRESS

© 2025 University of South Carolina

Published by the University of South Carolina Press
Columbia, South Carolina 29208

uscpress.com

Printed in the United States of America

Library of Congress Cataloging-in-Publication Data can be found at
http://catalog.loc.gov/.

ISBN: 978-1-64336-574-9 (hardcover)
ISBN: 978-1-64336-575-6 (ebook)

Publication is supported in part by the Wake Forest Legacy Endowed Faculty Fellowship.

In memory of my parents,
Marian M. Parent and
Anthony S. Parent

After we left Albany, we brought our Road a great deal more to the West, that we might comply with your Proposal; but, tho' it was of your own making, your People never observed it, but came and lived on our Side of the Hill, which we don't blame you for, as you live at a great Distance, near the Seas, and cannot be thought to know what your People do in the Back-parts: And on their settling, contrary to your own Proposal, on our new Road, it fell out that our Warriors did some Hurt to your People's Cattle, of which a Complaint was made, and transmitted to us by our Brother Onas [Gov. George Thomas of Pennsylvania]; and we, at his Request, altered the Road again, and brought it to the Foot of the Great Mountain, where it now is; and it is impossible for us to remove it any further to the West, those Parts of the Country being absolutely impassable by either Man or Beast. We had not been long in the Use of this new Road before your People came, like Flocks of Birds, and sat down on both Sides of it.

—Canassatego, an Onondaga sachem, "addressing the
Honourable the Lieutenant-Governor of the Province
[Pennsylvania], and the Honourable the Commissioners
for the Provinces of Virginia and Maryland,"
June 27, 1744

Contents

List of Illustrations

Acknowledgments

Michael McGandy, director of University of South Carolina Press (USCP), initiated this relationship by kindly inviting me and my wife Gigi to dinner on a cold winter night in Minneapolis several years ago. Ehren Foley, acquisitions editor, selected this book for publication and shepherded it through the peer review and editorial process. The staff of USCP provided professional expertise in bringing this book to conclusion.

I never intended to write this book. It grew organically from a longer project on the transformation of Virginia slavery. I was spending so much time in Native country that I thought it could stand on its own. My younger colleagues in the history department at Wake Forest University Miller Wright, now at Old Dominion University, and John [Jake] Ruddiman read an early draft manuscript and assured me it had legs for a book.

Provost Michele Gillespie and chairs of the history department Monique O'Connell and M. Raisur [Rais] Rahman supported my research. The university awarded me a subvention as the inaugural recipient of a Wake Forest Legacy Endowed Faculty Fellowship. The university also a provided me with A Reynolds Senior leave in fall 2022 and Archie and Griffin funds to travel to the New York Public Library; the Huntington Library, San Marino; the John D. Rockefeller Jr. Library, Williamsburg; the Newberry Library, Chicago; and the Lambeth Palace Library, London.

If it takes a village to raise a child, it takes a library to write a book. The Z. Smith Reynolds Library gave me access to a wealth of research both through its fine collection and interlibrary loan section. Kathy Shields, research and instruction librarian; Megan Mulder, special collections librarian; and Kyle Denlinger, digital pedagogy and open education librarian, were particularly helpful.

In spring 2023, I received critical review when I read versions of this work at the annual meetings of the Virginia Forum at Shepherd University, and at Western Society for Eighteenth-Century Studies at California State University, Northridge. Lea Lane, curator, MESDA Collection, reviewed my selection of illustrations and made suggestions on how to procure them. Peter V. Bergstrom, vice president of Literacy InterActives, loaned me his York County Records and abstracts of the Virginia Colonial Records Project.

The launch of *Flocks of Birds* coincides with the fifty-year anniversary of my marriage to Gigi. More than anyone else her love and support has sustained me in my career. Happy Anniversary, Gigi.

Abbreviations

Archives Md. = Archives of Maryland Online
CSPC = Calendar of State Papers Colonial, America and West Indies
DVNCBC = Depositions in the Virginia and North Carolina Boundary Case
EJCCV = *Executive Journals of the Council of Colonial Virginia*
JHB = *Journals of the House of Burgesses of Virginia*
LOC = Library of Congress
LCTP = Lords Commissioners of Trade and Plantations
OED = *Oxford English Dictionary*
OLAS = *The Official Letters of Alexander Spotswood*
SAL = The statutes at large; being a collection of all the laws of Virginia
VCRP = Virginia Colonial Records Project
VMHB = *Virginia Magazine of History and Biography*
VIC = Virginia Indian Company

Introduction

Flocks of Birds explores Virginia colonialism in Native country above the fall line, in the piedmont, and across the southern Appalachians, the continent's spine, and the Indigenous response to it over three generations from 1670 to 1776. This region south of the Ohio and Potomac Rivers encompasses the Appalachian, Allegheny, and Blue Ridge ranges, piedmonts and plateaus, and gaps and valleys, especially the Cumberland Gap and the Shenandoah Valley. In 1685 more than one hundred thousand Indigenous people from dozens of nations lived in the Southern Appalachians. They resided in towns, worked farms, hunted game, fished streams, and traveled trails, particularly the Great Warriors' Path. Their towns and villages were interspersed with fields, dutifully noted in travelers' accounts and maps. Extended families occupied houses in diverse towns, including residents from other nations. Their cyclical calendars integrated hunting, farming, and festivals. Leaving their fields during respite periods in the agricultural cycles, they organized into mixed-gender parties and traveled on well-maintained trails to their territorial hunting grounds.[1]

A Crown colony, Virginia was the largest of the continental colonies, containing proportionately more non-Native people, and the one that expanded most aggressively into Native country. In 1685 Virginia's population of 38,000 whites and 2,600 enslaved Africans dwarfed the 2,900 Native inhabitants, who had been reduced to tributary status. Formerly of Tsenacomoco, or the Powhatan paramount chiefdom, Native people had numbered 15,000 at the point of contact. If for no other reason, Indigenous nations looked askance at the dominion's reach: the Haudenosaunee [Iroquois] and Susquehannock in the north; the Shawnee, the Lenape [Delaware], the Seneca-Cayuga [Mingo], and the Myaamia [Miami] in the northwest; the Monacan, Nottoway, and Saponi in the west; the Tuscarora, and Yamasee in the south; and the Ani'-Yun-wiya [Cherokee], yeh is-WAH h'reh [Catawba], Chahta [Choctaw], Chikashsha' [Chickasaw], and the Muscogee [Creek] in the southwest.[2] Always wary of settler encroachment, Indigenous people nevertheless engaged the Swans, as they referred to the settlers because of their characteristic white identity, or Long Knives, so-called for their penchant to carry cutlasses, for trade goods in exchange for pelts, skins, and furs. They also negotiated with them over boundaries, alliances, and security.

Virginia authorities worried about a triple threat: insurrection, incursion, and invasion. They labeled an action depending on the relationship of the Indigenous people to the colony. They deemed an insurgency by tributaries and enslaved Africans an insurrection, a hostility by a neighboring nation an incursion, and an attack by a "foreign" nation an invasion. Virginia's colonial competitors for Native trade and land included both Carolinas, Maryland, Pennsylvania, and New York. Its international competitors included France and Spain.

For most of the period, Virginia colonialism coincided with the Crown's imperial ambition. Trade and land acquisition informed colonial policy. Colonialists pigeonholed their polities, aped their diplomatic discourse, and brutalized them. Settler colonialism began in earnest as the Seven Year's War wound down. Unspent rage from the wars and promises of bounty lands spurred on settlers to seek land outside of the reach of the slaveholding class. As the continental interests began to diverge from imperial policies, the settlers, some as speculators and others as homesteaders, began to press into Native country despite Crown objections. Virginia's Native policy became more aggressive. Even Virginia governor John Murray, fourth earl of Dunmore, began challenging Pennsylvania's claim to western lands and egging on war with the Native Ohioans, culminating in Dunmore's War of 1775.

The title of this book comes from a 1744 address by Canassatego, an Onondaga sachem who questioned Virginia's inability to abide by agreed-upon boundaries. "We had not been long in the Use of this new Road before your People came, like Flocks of Birds, and sat down on both Sides of it." The bird metaphor has a second meaning for the approach of this book, for it takes a bird's-eye view over the vast expansion, often aspirational, of Virginia colonialism into Native country. This expansive view of a "vast early America" fits within the latest approach to comprehending a more inclusive and mutually connected history. "There is no understanding early Virginia without also understanding" its relationships with enslaved Africans and Native people within a context of transnational imperial histories, writes historian Karin Wulf. "These are not only deeply interrelated histories. They are *mutual* histories."[3] The Indigenous response to Virginia's colonialism demonstrates the centrality of Native history to colonial history. The narrative tracks not only Virginia's interactions with Native nations but also interrelations among Native groups and competition between colonies. It identifies and tracks a multiplicity of Native nations within Virginia's ambition. In a show of respect to indigeneity, it uses the original names of the Native people.

This history is principally drawn from both printed primary and archival sources, often digital, and organized both regionally and chronologically into three parts: "Boundaries," which concerns the period from 1670 until the

1730s; "Hostilities," which chronicles the 1730s to 1755; and "Wars," which concerns the period 1755–76. *Flocks of Birds* employs a methodology of social formation. Unlike the motivations of the European colonizers, Indigenous social formation engendered generational conflicts and aggression over questions of honor more than class antagonisms. Diplomacy, conflict negotiations, and entreaties often invoked familial, gendered, and sexualized tropes. Indigenous gifting likewise eluded European understanding. The economies of gift giving were not payment in kind or a quid pro quo in European terms but expectations and receptions of tribute or honorifics. Historian Gary Y. Okihiro introduced the theory of social formation as a heuristic methodology to uncover "both the social structure and its evolution" of societies dealing with oppression.[4] "Social formation specifies the locations and articulations of power around the axes of race, gender, sexuality, class, and nation. Although power is itself suspected as a discrete category, social formation theory deploys the term without explication except to define power as agency or ability."[5] "Social formation is not solely the intersections or sum of oppressions; it accounts for those meeting points but also their resistances (and accommodations) and the mutually constituting and shifting relations between discourses and the material conditions."[6]

For example, historians Michael Witgen and Kathleen DuVal have both applied a theory of social formation to Native country. "The Anishinaabewaki, the social formation of the Anishinaabe peoples," Witgen argues, "evolved . . . [and] mobilized political power through a variety of social structures formed according to their political economy and ritual calendar."[7] "Every Quapaw belonged to a clan, which had specific rights and responsibilities for rituals and practices," writes DuVal. "Representatives of the clans came together to make political decisions for the whole. . . . While the Quapaw diplomatic chief was male, women wielded considerable economic and political power."[8]

In *Flocks of Birds* I seek to see how these relations develop over a period of one hundred years. Historian Woody Holton's *Forced Founders: Indians, Debtors, Slaves, and the Making of the American Revolution in Virginia* has addressed these concerns by focusing on the relations of overlooked groups, including Native people, but his task, as indicated in his book's title, focused on how these ignored people were drawn into the orbit of the Revolution. Yet *Forced Founders*, like many of the pre–Revolutionary Era studies, takes a teleological path. We can better understand how revolutionary the transformation was by knowing more fully what Virginia colonialism in Native country was like before the great event of the American Revolution.

PART I
Boundaries

They [the Five Nations] were glad the Covenant Chain had been keapt so fast on both sides and that they should allways maintain it on their side. That they and the Govr of Newyork Virginia and Massachusetts Colony were in One Covenant and ye one Covenant and the Chain must allways be kept Clean and Bright. That as Albany was the prefixed place for renewing their Covenants at so they now planted a Great Tree of Peace that it branches may spread as far as the Massachusetts, Virginia, Maryland and all who live under the shade of this Tree.

—"The Maquase Sachims answear [to] Mr Coartland as Agent for the Massachusetts Province," July 30, 1684, Albany, New York

CHAPTER 1

By a Swan, They Signify the English

The Siouan speakers living west of the Virginia and Carolina settlements commonly attributed totemic characteristics to describe physical and mental traits, said John Lederer. "By the figure of a Stag, they imply swiftness; by that of a Serpent, wrath; of a Lion, courage; of a Dog, fidelity; by a Swan, they signifie the English, alluding to their complexion, and flight over the Sea."[1] Their attribution of a white identity and a restive spirit as traits of the English astutely captured Anglo-Virginia's character, priming their motivation for colonialism. They were well aware that Virginia had made tributaries of the Algonquian speakers of the Powhatan chiefdom in the tidewater and wary of the settlers' intentions in their country. When John Lederer showed up, they looked askance at him even though he was German. Even if they were now ready to open trade relations with Virginia, they were still reticent to receive Lederer, suspicious of his motivations. Governor William Berkeley had commissioned Lederer to find a passage through the mountains to the western ocean leading to the Indies. Berkeley was also interested in enhancing trade relations with the Native people, so Lederer paid close attention to their natural resources and their trading acumen.

The Native nations inhabiting the region included "Mahoc [Manohoac], Nuntaneuck, alias Nuntaly, Nahyssan, Sapon [Saponi], Managog, Mangoack, Akenatzy, [Occaneechi] and Monakin [Monacan], etc." These Siouan speakers "differ[ed] in dialects," but they descended from maize-carrying culture bearers who had migrated there from the northwest four hundred years earlier at the invitation of an oracle. Although aware of their husbandry, Lederer undermined their agency by rendering their presence passively: "The parts inhabited here are pleasant and fruitful, because cleared of wood, and laid open to the sun."[2]

Lederer led three expeditions to the mountains of Virginia and Carolina between 1669 and 1670, which offered Virginia its first glimpse of the Native country in the western mountains and valleys. Each expedition began at the fall line of a major river: the York, James, and Rappahannock rivers. The General Assembly had subsidized privately owned forts at the headwaters of its major rivers after winning the third Anglo-Powhatan War of 1644–46. Virginia had erected Fort Charles on the James River, Fort Royal on the York, and Fort James on the Chickahominy for defense against Native incursions and for warehousing trade goods. Licensed Virginia traders and Native vendors exchanged trade goods, captives, and skins at these forts. No doubt they served as staging grounds for Lederer's expeditions. The forts looked outward away from the dominion's tributary nations. Necotowance, *werowance* [chief] of the Pamunkey, authorized the treaty for more than thirty former members of Tsenacomoco, as well as the Accomack and the Chickahominy, which simplified the negotiation for Virginia. Additionally, in exchange for protection from Native adversaries, Necotowance's treaty called for the tributary people to go with Virginia to war against other Native nations and to return all runaways, whether captive Europeans, indentured Indigenous people, or enslaved Africans. In exchange the Pamunkey kept the land "north of the York [upper Pamunkey River] and south of the Blackwater."[3]

In his first expedition, Lederer likely found his three Native guides, Magtakunh, Hopottoguoh, and Naunnughm, at Fort Royal. They began their exploration on March 9, 1669, at the falls of the Pemaeoncock [Pamunkey] River, called by the English the York, and traveled through the marshy peninsula between the Pemaeoncock and the Matapeneugh [Mattaponi] Rivers, which the English called Pamunkey Neck. Following the Powhatans' defeat in the third Anglo-Powhatan War, the English restricted the Pamunkey, the Chickahominy, a former English tributary who had answered Opechancanough's call to arms, and other Algonquian speakers to the Pamunkey Neck.[4] The Pamunkey people called this region Tottopottoma after Totopotomoy, the Pamunkey *werowance* who was killed while leading Pamunkey and Chickahominy warriors into battle in 1656 alongside Col. Edward Hill's Virginia militia, fighting the Ricahecrian and possibly the Monacan and the Nahyssan, at the Battle of Bloody Run, named for the fatalities of one hundred Native warriors and dozens of Virginians. Hill initiated the conflict. Native people had come to the falls of the James River with beaver pelts for trade, but Hill attacked suddenly, killing five of their chiefs, despite orders from the Virginia General Assembly to avoid violence. A contemporary called Hill's behavior "unparalleled hellish treachery and anti-Christian perfidy."[5]

Even though the Pamunkey and Chickahominy people resided at Pamunkey Neck here, Lederer made no mention of their presence, foreshadowing a practice of erasure by later white explorers. In truth, "the Pamunkey Neck provided ready access to the ecosystem that had produced many of the flora Algonquian-speakers had relied upon as a vital component of their subsistence long before the arrival of the English," writes historian Ethan A. Schmidt. "The Pamunkeys had also lived in the general area of Pamunkey Neck . . . for generations and were adept at growing crops there."[6] After reaching the headsprings of the Pemaeoncock, Lederer climbed "an eminent hill," where on March 15, 1669, he saw in the distance what he thought were the Appalachian Mountains. Two days later, when his party reached the Blue Ridge, they could find no passage through it.[7]

Lederer began his second expedition on May 20, 1670, at the falls of the Powhatan [James] River accompanied by a Major William Harris, twenty English horses, and five Native guides, en route to Monacan country. Although he learned of two routes through the mountains from the Monacan, one through Manohoac country and the other through Nahyssan country, Major Harris arrogantly "shaped their course by the compass due west."[8] Traveling like "Land-Crabs," they rigidly kept due west for ten days going up and down "steep and craggy Cliffs," which wore down both men and horse. Accompanied by his Susquehannock guide Jackzetavon, Lederer traveled toward the "unpassable" Akontshuck hills.[9] They parted company with the Virginia expedition and the other Native guides for good on June 5 and travelled southwest by south to avoid the mountains. After a rigorous march of four days, they reached Saponi and Nahyssa country, both on the Roanoke River. Lederer described the Saponi town Sapon as an "advantagious Seat; for though it stands high, and upon a dry land, it enjoyes the benefit of a stately River, and a rich Soyl, capable of producing many Commodities, which may hereafter render the Trade of it considerable." At Pintahae, the seat of Nahyssa, he observed "a great store of Pearl . . . amongst other spoyls from the Indians of Florida."[10]

Following the locals' directions "South and by West," the pair arrived at Occaneechi Island, key entrepôt in the deerskin and slave trades, which Lederer found, even "though small, maintains many inhabitants, who are fix'd here in great security, being naturally fortified with Fastnesses of Mountains, and Water on every side." He met fifty refugees escaping from the Beaver Wars who told him they had traveled a distance of two-months from the northwest, losing most of their party in their trek from an island after crossing a great body of water, which he assumed was "some great arm of the Indian Ocean." Ricahecrian [Erie] survivors, dispersed by the Haudenosaunee, likely crossed near an island in Sandusky Bay, an arm of Lake Erie, and traveled the six-hundred-mile stretch of the Scioto Trail southeasterly through the southern Appalachians, seeking refuge with earlier Erie migrants who first left the Great Lakes region in 1654–56 after battling and losing to the Haudenosaunee. "To confirm my opinion in this point," Lederer said, "I have heard several Indians testifie, that the Nation of Rickohocan [Ricahecrian] who dwell not far to the Westward of the Apalataean [Appalachian] Mountains, are seated upon a Land, as they term it, of great Waves; by which I suppose they mean the Sea-shore."[11]

After their displacement by the Haudenosaunee in the Beaver Wars, the Erie had settled in the piedmont, where they built a fortified town, Ricka-hock, a terminal on the Ricahock path on the Mattaponi River. The Rica-hecrian had traded copper to the Monacan before they were chased out by the Haudenosaunee and moved to the piedmont, where they had access to "Minerals, as Auripigmentum."[12] They located near Virginia partly because of their defensive attitude to the threat of northern Native raiders and partly because of their developing trade relations with Virginia. Following the Bat-tle of Bloody Run in 1656, Virginia traders Abraham Wood and Thomas Stegg negotiated guns for captives with the Ricahecrian, who then supplied the Virginia slavers from the catchment zone from the Savannah River to Florida.[13]

The next day Lederer witnessed the massacre of a Ricahecrian grandee and his retinue of five after being feted at a "ball of their fashion."[14] If what is past is prologue, then this ritualized killing of the embassy signaled the enslavement of the Ricahecrian refugees, perhaps as retribution for their raids on the Occaneechi spurred on by Wood or reprisal for their compe-tition in the slave trade.[15] Afraid for their lives, Lederer and Jackzetavon took a south-by southwest route, "sometimes by a beaten path" that became known as the Great Trading Path or the Occaneechi Path, which ran from Fort Henry, owned by Wood at the falls of the Appomattox River, through Occaneechi Island to yeh is-WAH h'reh [Catawba] country.[16] "The general language here used" in the region, contemporary historian Robert Beverly surmised, "is said to be that of the Occaneeches[Occaneechis], tho they have been but a small Nation," likely because of their location on the Occaneechi-Catawba Path.[17]

Marching a distance of thirty miles in two days, Lederer and Jackzetavon reached Eno [Oenock] country. In his most full-throated description of an Indigenous people, Lederer characterized the Eno as industrious, earning income as porters, and athletic, engaging in a sport "slinging . . . stones." They were also a "democratic" people who respected elderly lawmakers as the recipients of oracles prophecies. "The Country here, by the industry of these Indians, is very open, and clear of wood. . . . They plant abundance of Grain, reap three Crops in a Summer, and out of their Granary supply all the adjacent parts. These and the Mountain-Indians build not their houses of Bark, but of Watling and Plaister. . . . Some houses they have of Reed and Bark; they build them generally round." He found the Shakori people about fourteen miles southwest to be the cultural cousins of the Eno, and the Wa-teree [Keyauwee or Watary], another forty miles away, were "slaves rather than subjects to their King."[18]

FIGURE 1. *A Map of the Whole Territory Traversed by John Lederer in His Three Marches.* Wilson Special Collections Library. Image courtesy of University of North Carolina at Chapel Hill.

Traveling a westerly course from there for thirty miles, Lederer came to Sara (Cheraw) country, where the mountains "lose their height." After learning that continuing either west or north would lead into "inhospitable" Native country and southwest into what he supposed to be Spanish country, Lederer decided on June 20 to return home. Beating a path northeast to avoid Wisacky marsh, he and Jackzetavon bushwhacked across hills and a "barren sandy desert" until arriving at the head of the Eruco River, where they found on July 14 the Tuscarora town "*Katearas,* a place of great Indian Trade and Commerce."[19] What impressed Lederer most about Katearas was the abundance of copper there. Over three days they passed first through the Meherrin [Kauwets'a:ka] town of Kawitziokan upon a branch of the Roanoke River to the Meherrin town of Menchaerinck [Maharineck] and then Nottoway [Cheroenhaka] Town, until on July 19 they reached their destination of Appomattoc [Appomattox] Town [Machodoc] near Fort Henry.[20]

Led by Lederer and Col. John Catlett, the third expedition, with nine English horses and five Native guides, left from the falls of the Rappahannock on August 20, 1670. They passed through the valley, where he noted the plentitude of deer and elk, to the foot of the Appalachians. After finding the path unwieldly for the horses, the party left them at the foot of the mountains. They failed to find a passage through the mountains, however, and agreed to turn back. The Appalachians, which Lederer likened to the Great Wall of China, "deny Virginia passage into the West Continent."[21] If Lederer did not find the western passage, he did discern what opportunities were available to Virginia traders. He distinguished between the neighboring and distant Indigenous communities he encountered. The Virginians wanted "the skins of Deer, Beaver, Otter, Wild-Cat, Fox, Racoon, etc." The Native people "greedily desired . . . Guns, Powder and Shot, etc.," but these items were contraband under Virginia law. Rather, he surmised, for the bordering nations "the best Truck is a sort of coarse Trading Cloth, of which a yard and a half makes a Matchcoat, or Mantle fit for their wear; as also Axes, Hoes, Knives, Sizars [scissors], and all sorts of edge tools." On the other hand, the trade goods best suited for "remoter" people were "other kinds" of supply: "'small Looking-glasses, Pictures, Beads and Bracelets of glass, Knives, Sizars, and all manner of gaudy toys and knacks for children, which are light and portable. For they are apt to admire such trinkets, and will purchase them at any rate, either with their currant Coyn of small shells, which they call *Roanoack* or *Peack*, or perhaps with Pearl, Vermilion, pieces of Christal; and towards *Ushery* [yeh is-WAH h'reh] with some odde pieces of Plate or Bullion, which they sometimes receive in Truck from the *Oustacks* [Westos]."[22]

Clearly spurred by Lederer's expeditions, especially the reconnoitering of the Occaneechi Path, Maj. Gen. Abraham Wood commissioned Thomas Batte, Robert Hallom, and Thomas Woods to find a route to the ocean on the other side of the Appalachians that would lead to the South Sea. If the purported purpose of both Lederer's and Batte and Hallom's expeditions was finding a route through the Appalachians to the ocean, they differed in their secondary objective. Lederer targeted expanding trade prospects in western Native country, while Batte and Hallom sought a new trade corridor directly to the Saponi, sidestepping the Occaneechi Path. They also were keen on claiming land in western Native country. Accompanied by "Perecute, a great Man of the Apomatack Indians," and Jack Neasan, a former servant to Wood, they left on horseback from Appomattoc Town on September 1, 1671. They journeyed forty miles due west from Fort Henry, the northern terminus of the Occaneechi Path at the falls of the Appomattox River, where Wood, William Byrd I, Thomas Stegg, and other licensed Virginia traders had trafficked with Native vendors.[23]

Over the next two days, they zigzagged westwardly along the Roanoke River, averaging about forty miles a day, until they arrived on September 4 first at Saponi Town and then a couple of hours later at Saponi West, or Sapon, where Lederer had visited. Saluted with gunfire and hospitably treated at Saponi West, the party hired a Saponi man to guide them "a nearer way than usual" toward the Totoras. The gunfire salutation gives evidence of the Saponi trade for "arms and ammunition," either with another European supplier or with a contraband supplier, which, Lederer said, "is prohibited in all English Governments." The next morning, they were awakened to gunfire from seven Appomattoc men across the river, who were alerting the party to their presence. Major General Wood had sent them to reinforce the expedition. Slowing their movement, they arrived at the town of Hanathaskies on Long Island on the Staunton River, "about twenty-five miles away northwest," where they were again hospitably treated "like or better" than at Saponi West. Leaving behind Thomas Woods, who was deathly ill from the flux, on September 6, they traveled west by south for twenty miles and the next day another twenty miles westerly. They then hiked over "very hilly and stony Ground," coming in sight of the mountains, while twice crossing the Staunton River. After scaling a second mountain and hiking six miles on September 9, they saw "a lovely descending Valley about six Miles over, with curious small risings: indifferent [in a] good way."[24]

After traveling twenty-five miles that day, they arrived at Totera [Tetera] Town "in a very rich swamp between a branch of the main River of Roanoke" (perhaps New River), where they were "exceedingly civilly entertained."[25] They left Totera Town on September 12 and traveled about twenty-five miles west by north; "the path went over several high mountains and steep Vallies crossing several branches and the River Roanoke, several times, all exceedingly stony ground" to Toteras, a Tutelo [Yesang] settlement, where they quartered. Leaving behind Perecute, who was suffering from a lingering illness, with another Appomattoc man, they hired a local guide. Traveling the path toward the valleys in the west, on September 13 they arrived at the foot of the Great Mountain, a "pleasing tho' dreadfull sight." Near a creek they came across two marked trees, one with the initials MANE etched with coal and the other "cut in with M. T." and several other illegible scribbles, evidence of the earlier presence of a trader, perhaps William Byrd. Byrd lived 250 miles away at the falls of the James River, in a house inherited from his uncle Thomas Stegg. They were competitors of Wood. When Batte and Hallom arrived at Totera, they "immediately had the news of Mr. Byrd and his great company's Discoveries three miles from the Teteras Town."[26]

"We found rich ground but stony curious rising hills and brave meadows with grass above man's height, many Rivers running West north West and several runs from the Southerly Mountains, which we saw as we marched, which run northerly into, the great River. . . . The soil the farther we went, the richer. Stony, full of brave meadows and old fields."[27] The reference to "old fields" meant that the report's author recognized the Indigenous practice of shifting cultivation. As a contemporary noted, "Old fields is a common expression for Land that has been Cultivated by Indians and left fallow, which are generally overrun, with what they call broome grats[broom grass]."[28]

On September 15 the party continued sixteen miles, but the guides had difficulty hunting deer, so they were forced to feed on "some wild geese, berries and exceeding large haw's." The next day the guides, who had heard drums and gunfire northward, brought the party "some exceeding good grapes and killed two turkies" and a deer. They quartered at a place where the Mohican "formerly lived." On September 17, using "a pair of marking Irons," they branded four trees barked by the guides with the names of King Charles II, Gov. William Berkeley, Major General Wood, and Perecute, who said he would become an Englishman. They had not found an arm of the South Sea, but they did locate and claim the Mohican "old fields." The Mohicans were cautious enough to inquire about their purpose. Homeward bound, Batte and Hallom turned back toward Totera Town when they saw the glimmer of what they supposed to be a great bay. When they arrived at Toteras, they "found [that] the Mehetan [Mohican] Indians . . . having intelligence of our coming were afraid it had been to fight them and had sent him [a scout] to the Toteras to inquire. We gave him satisfaction to the contrary and that we came as friends, presented him with three or four shots of powder. He told us by our Interpreter, we had [been] from the mountains halfway to the place they now live at. That the next town beyond them lived on a plain level, from whence came an abundance of salt. That he could inform us no further by reason that there were a great company of Indians that lived upon the great Water."[29]

Mission accomplished, they quickly backtracked first to Toteras, where they were again hospitably treated, and then to Hanakaskies, where they learned Woods had died. They left "with firing of Guns at parting which is more than usual," passed through Saponi Country en route to Appomattoc Town, and finally arrived on October 1 at Fort Henry. If Wood's commission of Thomas Batte and Robert Hallom demonstrated Virginia's cordial relations with the Saponi and the Tutelo, then his commission of James Needham and Gabriel Arthur revealed the colony's discordant relations with the Tamahita [Yuchi] and the Occaneechi. Wood was suspicious of both nations, which were in competition over the slave trade.[30]

Building upon the knowledge gained from Batte and Hallom, Wood reported to his investors that on April 10, 1673, he sent Needham, Arthur, and eight Native men with three months of provisions to discover a course to the "south or west sea."[31] Native people prevented their access at the piedmont.

Adding four horses to the expedition, Wood dispatched Needham and Arthur again on May 17. A Tamahita party traveling from the mountains to Occaneechi country intercepted the Virginia party on June 25. While keeping one of the party hostage at Occaneechi, eleven Tamahita escorted them back to Fort Henry, where Wood could verify their mission with a letter. Once this issue was resolved, the expedition traveled nine days "west by south, past nine rivers and creeks" from Occaneechi to Sitteree, where the road ended at the last Native town before the Tamahita's town, fifteen days away. Arriving at the Tamahita's town, Needham and Arthur and an Appomattoc man accompanying them were honored "even to adoration in their ceremonies of courtesies."[32]

At the feast "two mullato women" likely served them cured stockfish and buffalo, evidenced by the "many horns like bulls' horns [that] lay upon their dunghills," from "the many brass pots and kettles from three gallons to thirty." The bulls' horns suggest that what the report called a dung heap may have been a traditional mound. The report described Tamahita Town as both fortified and stockaded.

> This town is seated on the river side, having the cliffs of the river on the one side being very high for its defense, the other three sides trees of two foot over, pitched on end, twelve feet high, and on the tops, scaffolds placed with parapets to defend the walls and offend their enemies which men stand on to fight. The many nations of Indians inhabit down this river, which runs west upon the salts which they are at war with and to that end keep one hundred and fifty canoes under the command of their fort. The least of them will carry twenty men and made sharp at both ends like a wherry for swiftness. This fort is four square, 300 paces over, and the houses set in streets.[33]

After recuperating a short time and leaving Arthur behind to learn the language, Needham returned in earnest on horseback on September 10 along with the Appomattoc man and a dozen Tamahita, including eight men and four women. Two of the Tamahita had been held captive at a settlement of white and Black people, about eight days' distance downriver from the Tamahita town. Not many years ago, one of the escapees told Needham, the Tamahita sent a score of their people laden with beaver pelts to trade at the settlement of "white people who have long beards and whiskers and wear clothing" and who "have many blacks among them." They raised cattle and "many swine" and trawled for "oysters and many other shellfish." Rather than trade with the Tamahita, they killed ten of them and put another ten in irons. The escapee described a Spanish mission with a brick building where "the white people have a bell which is six foot over which they ring morning and evening, and at that time a great number of people congregate together and talk he knows not what." He did know, however, that "all the white and black people they take they put to death since their twenty men were barbarously handled."[34]

Wood organized a second expedition because of the "good successes of the last journey," even though his solicitation for General Assembly support went unheeded. After a respite of only nine days, Needham set out with the dozen Tamahita. Meanwhile Arthur had passed "in safety" to Eno. Four months later, on January 27, Wood received a "flying report" from Native informants that the Tamahita had killed his people as the British party was 'returning to Fort Henry; afterward "daily came variable reports" of death, but the informants were reluctant to say what they knew, fearing that they would be blamed. Almost a month later, on February 25, Henry Hatcher, an English trader, said to Wood that while trading at Occaneechi he not only learned that Needham was "certainly killed," but he also saw an Occaneechi named John, "a fat thick bluff faced fellow," who had in his possession "Needham's pistols and gun." The Occaneechi, nevertheless, cast blame on the Tamahita. Wood knew John, whose Native name was Hasecoll, because he had been to Fort Henry and had escorted Arthur and Needham during the first journey to Tamahita; he returned with Needham to Wood's house, where he received a reward for his service and promised to go out and protect them again. For this service Wood gave him half of his fee up front and promised the remainder when they returned in the spring.[35]

Wood later learned that Needham had traveled from Eno to Sara with Hasecoll and his party of Tamahita. After going by the Sara River, Hasecoll began needling Needham, who had rebuked a Native man for losing his pack in the river, until they passed Yadkin town and crossed over the Yadkin River. Needham "alighted" and quartered at the "foot of the mountains," where Hasecoll persisted in "wailing and threatening" him. Agitated, Needham picked up an axe and threw it toward Hasecoll's feet, shouting, "What John are you minded [to] kill me?" Hasecoll "cathched" up a gun and, before his fellow expeditioners could act, shot Needham in the head. The Tamahita remonstrated, "What shall we do now you have killed the Englishman? We shall be cut off by the English." Hasecoll retorted by carving out Needham's heart and holding it up; looking "eastward, toward the English plantations . . . [he] said he valued not all the English." The Tamahita vacillated: "How dare you do this, we are *all* afraid of the English." Hasecoll answered that "he had received his reward [for what he had done], and then laid a command upon the Tomahittans that they should dispatch and kill the

Englishman which Needham had left at the Tomahittans." Hasecoll then gathered up Needham's weapons and rode off on his horse.[36]

Acting on Hasecoll's charge, the Tamahita hastened back to Tamahita town to deliver the news of Needham's death and the Occaneechi command to kill Arthur. Their king away, the Occaneechi supporters among the Tamahita held sway, and they

> tied Gabriell Arther to a stake and laid heaps of combustible canes a bout him to burne him, but before ye fire was put too ye King came into ye towne with a gunn upon his shoulder and heareing of ye uprore for some was with it and some a gainst it. ye King ran with great speed to ye place, and said who is that that is goeing to put fire to ye English man. a Weesock borne started up with a fire brand in his hand said that am I. Ye King forthwith cockt his gunn and shot ye wesock dead, and ran to Gabriell and with his knife cutt ye thongs that tide him and had him goe to his house and said lett me see who dares touch him.

The Weesock, Wood wrote, were to the Tamhia what the Janissary were to the Ottoman, tributary children reared to serve militarily. After the rescue, the king reprieved Arthur and "put [him] in arms, gun, tomahawk, and target [shield]" and pressed him into service with fifty warriors "to forage, rob, and spoil other nations . . . [and] the Spaniards, promising him that in the next spring he himself would carry him home to his master."[37]

If Wood heard this account directly from the king, then he learned directly from Arthur what happened to him "while captivated" after the latter arrived at Fort Henry on June 21, 1674. Arthur was unlettered and so did not personally record his journal but rather related his travails to Wood by mouth. After leaving Tamahita town, the war party "traveled eight days west and by south" to an African town in West Florida, "spacious and great, but all wooden buildings." Fearful that they could not stealthily pilfer anything of value and unwilling to engage the Africans directly, they tromped "along by the side of a great cart path [for] about five or six miles" to the Spanish mission, which Needham had detailed earlier, arriving in time to hear the tolling of the evening bell. The party lying in wait in the cart path for "almost seven days to steal for their sustenance," a Tamahita spied, waylaid, and shot a "genteel Spaniard, accoutered with gun, sword, and pistol." He pickpocketed "two pieces of gold and a small gold chain," which he gave to Arthur. They beat a hasty retreat back to the African town, where they encountered a lone African, whom a Tamahita killed with a dart in the back as he ran away. Before fleeing "expeditiously" homeward, they lifted from his body "some toys, which hung in his ears, and bracelets about his neck."[38]

After receiving assurance from the king that the next war party would attack not the English settlement but rather the Native nation nearby, Arthur joined the war party headed toward Port Royal. They marched over the mountain for six days to the Port Royal River, where they built bark piraguas to carry them downriver; as fate would have it, they eavesdropped at an English house and heard a man speak of Christmas, giving Arthur a sense of the time of year. Following the king's directive, they did "no violence" to the English household but continued for six miles to a Native town. Opening a surprise sunrise attack, Gabriel selected the house of another Englishman, whom the party spared and directed to run away, after snatching his "knapsack with beads, knives, and other petty truck in it." Aroused by the commotion of the "slaughter," the English at Port Royal fired their guns, driving off the Tamahita. Two weeks later the war party returned with their spoils to Tamahita town.[39]

The king then ordered Arthur to accompany his war party of sixty to visit his ally the Mohican, their name "signifying" great water, at their populous "great town" on the Big Sandy, which "runs northwest and out of the westerly side of it goes another very great river [the Ohio] about a day's journey lower where the inhabitants are an innumerable company of Indians." The Shawnee inhabited the region. stretching a distance of a twenty day's journey from one end to the other, all these are at war with the Tamahita, the Mohican told Arthur. "When they had taken their leave of the Monetons, they marched three days out of their way to give a clap to some of that great nation, where they fell on with great courage and were as courageously repulsed by their enemy."[40]

After shooting him with two arrows, one in the thigh, the enemy captured Arthur and scrutinized him. His long hair betrayed his nationality, for the Tamahita shaved their hair close to avoid its being grabbed in battle. They "scoured his skin with water and ashes, and when they perceived his skin to be *white*, they made very much of him and admired his knife, gun, and hatchet." Seeing no iron-made materials, Arthur was quick to haggle over the relative cost of his knife and hatchet in pelts. "While he was there, they brought in a fat beaver which they had newly killed and went to swinge it. Gabriel made signs to them that those skins were good amongst the white people toward the rising sun. They would know by signs how many skins they would take for such a knife. He told them four and eight for such a hatchet and made signs that if they would let him return, he would bring many things amongst them."[41]

This exchange closed the deal. So encouraged, they put Arthur on a path to Tamahita with enough rockahominy to carry him there. Upon his return the king organized one last, ostensibly short excursion before Arthur's scheduled return to Virginia. They traveled for five days downriver in their piraguas to the "mouth of the salts," where "they killed many swine, sturgeon, and beavers and barbecued them." Rowing upstream took fifteen days, tripling their time on the return journey home, "but no mountainous land to be seen but all level." True to his word, on or about May 10, 1674, the king "with eighteen more of his people laden with goods"—no doubt the bounty of pelts and skins from their last excursion downriver—"began their journey to come to Fort Henry." Retracing the path to Sara [Cheraw], where the Occaneechi lay in wait for Arthur, they came across the scene of Needham's murder, with the detritus of his belonging strewn about and only four Occaneechi men remaining. Since the four were outnumbered, they roused the sleeping town by yelling that "strange Indians" were attacking, hoping the Cheraw would come to their defense, but the Tamahita escaped into the bushes. In the mayhem, Arthur lost the gold pieces gifted him at the Spanish mission, but he managed to escape with a "Spanish Indian boy" in tow.[42]

Determined to carry out the deed, the Occaneechi pursued Arthur and the boy, who survived in the woods on huckleberries, until the pair reached the sanctuary of Wood's home on June 18. The king and "his two sons and one more" followed, carrying their trade goods "along by Totero under the foot of the mountains, until they met with James river and there made a canoe of bark and came down the river to Manakin. From thence to Powhatan [River] by land, and across the [Pamunkey] neck." On July 20 they arrived at Fort Henry. After hearing how the king had rescued Arthur, Wood rewarded him. The king in turn promised to return "at the fall of the leaf" with a "sufficient" force to "be not intercepted by self-ended traders," determined to block trade to Virginia.[43]

CHAPTER 2

Flights of Pigeons, Their Length No Visible End

Early in the seventeenth century, during the Beaver Wars, the Haudenosaunee dispersed the Erie, the Wyandot [Huron], the Petun, and the Susquehannock, driving them westward into the orbit of the Anishinaabeg. The Haudenosaunee also smashed the coalition of the Erie and the Wyandot, made incursions into Illinois and Myaamia country, and treated for peace with the Wyandot and the Anishinaabeg. After midcentury the tide began to turn against the Haudenosaunee when New France without their permission erected forts and outposts in their territory in the Hudson and St. Lawrence River basins and pressed their authority on the Niagara River, critical to carrying trade. The Anishinaabeg began pushing out the Haudenosaunee from their settlements on the Ontario peninsula and the northern coasts of Lakes Erie and Ontario and pressing the Haudenosaunee for trading access with the English at Albany. The Haudenosaunee also lost their advantage in Ohio country, where the Myaamia began to regroup.[1]

The mourning wars during the Beaver Wars increased a cycle of fighting, dying, and capturing: the more wars fought, the more losses were sustained, and the more captives needed for adoption. The replacement of lost members was part of a larger cultural spectrum that ran the gamut from presents of people from Native nations given in friendship to the Haudenosaunee to captives of traditional enemies taken by mourning war parties.[2]

When the Five Nations make Peace with another Nation, that has taken some of the Five Nations Prisoners, if these Prisoners be dead, or cannot be restored, they usually demand some Indians, in Friendship with the Five Nations, in their stead; who either are adopted in Place of their dead Friends, or restored to their own Nation; and sometimes they desire some of their Enemies to be given to them, and even those frequently are adopted by a Father in Place of a Son, or by a Sister in Place of a Brother, and, most frequently, by a Wife in Place of a Husband lost in the Wars; but if they chance not to be agreeable to the Relations, then they are certainly made Sacrifices to their Revenge.[3]

The mourning wars became a cultural response to any familial death to alleviate psychological anguish when traditional condolent responses became inadequate. Raiding parties related to the aggrieved females targeted captives who were not necessarily responsible for the deaths but who were considered traditional enemies.[4]

Deh-he-wä-mis, herself a captive, explained the motivation for the mourning wars. It is customary "to give to the nearest relative to the dead or absent, a prisoner, if they have chanced to take one, and if not, to give him the scalp of an enemy."[5]

Haudenosaunee mourning wars pressed into the Appalachians and pushed Siouan speakers into the orbit of Virginia. Although isolated and remote from the tidewater plantations between the James and York Rivers, eastern Tsenacomoco still lay open to incursions from northern nations and land pressures from Virginia settlers. When Lederer began his journey in 1670, the Mattaponi, who had resided on the Rappahannock River and now within the bounds of Rappahannock County founded in 1656, were relocated to a reserve on the western shore of the Mattaponi River. They had had to relocate several times in the region partly because of Virginia interlopers patenting their land and partly because of attacks from northern nations.[6] Lawrence Smith petitioned for a four-year extension on the 4,600 acres, which he had patented in 1673, "in New Kent County upon a reedy branch far remote by Mattapony Swamp," partly because of its isolation from other plantations and partly because of his "great feare of ye Indians."[7]

Not unlike the Mattaponi, the Monacan were mobile because of the Haudenosaunee parties making raids on them. The Monacan had coalesced near Occaneechi country, settling on islands in the Roanoke River around 1674. At about the same time and for the same reason, the Saponi relocated north of the Appomattox River close to Fort Henry and the Nahyssan moved from their land on the Canawhay [Kanawha] River (which Abraham Wood called Wood's River after himself in 1654 and Peter Jefferson renamed the New River in 1749) and the Roanoke River basins. The Nahyssan resided there from 1650 until 1674, when they moved again to an area at the intersection of the Occaneechi Path and the Roanoke River.[8]

These events presaged the Haudenosaunee's renewing the Covenant Chain with the English. Originally conceived as a metaphorical rope tethering Dutch ships to the White Pine or Great Tree of Peace, the Haudenosaunee initially offered the Covenant Chain to the English after they had finally seized New Netherlands from the Dutch in 1674. The chain then extended from Haudenosaunee sachems of the Five Nations of the Mohawk, the Oneida, the Onondaga, the Cayuga, and the Seneca to the English governors of the colonies of New York, Maryland, Massachusetts Bay, and Virginia.[9] The Five Nations and the four English colonies affirmed that they together comprised "one Covenant and the Chain must allways be kept Clean and Bright. That as Albany was the prefixed place for renewing their Covenants at so they now planted a Great Tree of Peace that it branches may spread as far as the Massachusetts, Virginia, Maryland and all who live under the shade of this Tree."[10]

Although the Haudenosaunee "had a Desire . . . of making all the Nations round them their Tributaries," their claims to dominion in Ohio country, more a bluff than a reality, were key to this rapprochement. Nevertheless, Albany was receptive to this posturing, because it could negotiate with one entity rather than an assortment of nations.[11] The Haudenosaunee exertions, explains historian Susan Sleeper-Smith, demonstrated their attempts to check the French encroachment disrupting their trade routes ranging from "Powhatan lands in the Chesapeake westward to the eastern Ohio River valley, then north along the Hudson River valley to Lake Champlain and east along the St. Lawrence River to the Atlantic." The Haudenosaunee, in turn were "able to link dispersed communities and created a wide-ranging, flexible notion of themselves as an interconnected Indigenous polity."[12] "Just as the Covenant Chain included the English colonies under the leadership of the governor of New York," historian Daniel Richter writes, "so it encompassed other Indian nations through the mediation of the Iroquois. . . . Yet the Iroquois did claim to speak for other Indian peoples, and they did wield considerable influence over them."[13]

During the Beaver Wars of the 1660s and early 1670s, the Susquehannock were able to battle successfully against the Haudenosaunee, their enemy to their north, partly because of their friendship with the Chesapeake colonies. However, this was not enough to offset their losses, and they felt compelled to shore up relations with the Piscataway and the nations on the southern piedmont. Nevertheless, the Haudenosaunee continued to loom large, conquering the Susquehannock by 1673. Reacting to the greater threat of the Haudenosaunee, Maryland invited the Susquehannock, "newly driven" from their country at the head of the Chesapeake Bay by the Seneca, to settle on the upper Potomac River and the Piscataway Creek, sharing the ground where Gov. Charles Calvert had recently resettled the Piscataway and other Potomac tributaries.[14]

Without the threat of the Haudenosaunee, Virginia acted very differently, attacking rather than aligning with its neighbors. For example, Giles Brent, Gerrard Fowke, John Lord, and George Mason, all Westmoreland planters, had in 1662 accused werowance Wahanganoche of Patawomeck of murdering colonists in an effort to seize land. A committee of the House of Burgesses found this accusation libelous and assessed damages. A year later Wahanganoche was found murdered on the road home from Williamsburg, even though he was wearing the Crown-certified silver badge guaranteeing his safe passage. The General Assembly in 1665 dispossessed the Patawomeck on the southern bank of the Potomac River, claiming eminent domain for constructing a fort. The assembly also claimed authority over the Patawomeck, reserving to themselves the appointment of the werowance. A year later, the Susquehannock, as part of their negotiations with Maryland, released two Patawomeck captives, sons of the late murdered Wahanganoche, to the English.[15] The Council of State called for revenge. They alleged the Nanziattico, the Nansemond, the Protobacco, the Patawomeck, and the Moyumpse [Doeg]had "frequently" murdered settlers over the past four years. Consequently, the councilors ordered "their utter destruction if possible."[16] Militia forces massacred the Patawomeck, killing the men and enslaving the women and children. This campaign served as a dress rehearsal for the Susquehannock War.[17]

The Susquehannock-Anglo War began after a disputed transaction resulted in a skirmish followed by a massacre. Thomas Mathew of Stafford County ignited the conflict. He absolved himself of personal responsibility in his 1705 manuscript, *The Beginning, Progress, and Conclusion of Bacon's Rebellion in Virginia*, alluding to the appearance in 1675 of preternatural phenomenon. A "large comet every evening for a week or more . . . streaming like a horse's taile"; "flights of pigeons, . . . their length there was no visible end"; and "swarms of flyes . . . rising out of spigot holes in the earth" augured "disasters."[18] After Mathew reneged on paying Moyumpse traders, the two sides skirmished, leaving his overseer and several Moyumpse dead. The planters equated Governor Berkeley's hesitancy in dealing with the event as a failure of his patriarchal obligations. It provided speculators in western tracts with the emotive impulse both to protect their constituents and to seize Native lands. In retaliation Mathew, George Mason, George Brent, John Washington, and Isaac Allerton organized the militias. They crossed the Potomac and indiscriminately killed fourteen Susquehannock who had nothing to do with the Moyumpse traders. The Susquehannock measured their response, "killing two Virginians and destroying some crops and livestock." Satisfied that they had avenged their honor, they then sued for peace with Virginia. Virginia chose war, incited by land hunger and bloodlust against "all Indians."[19]

By the fall of 1675, Virginia and Maryland combined to mobilize one thousand men; each colony was accompanied by tributary nations. The English perfidiously murdered four Susquehannock grandees who had approached the Virginians under a flag of truce and "asked the reason of that

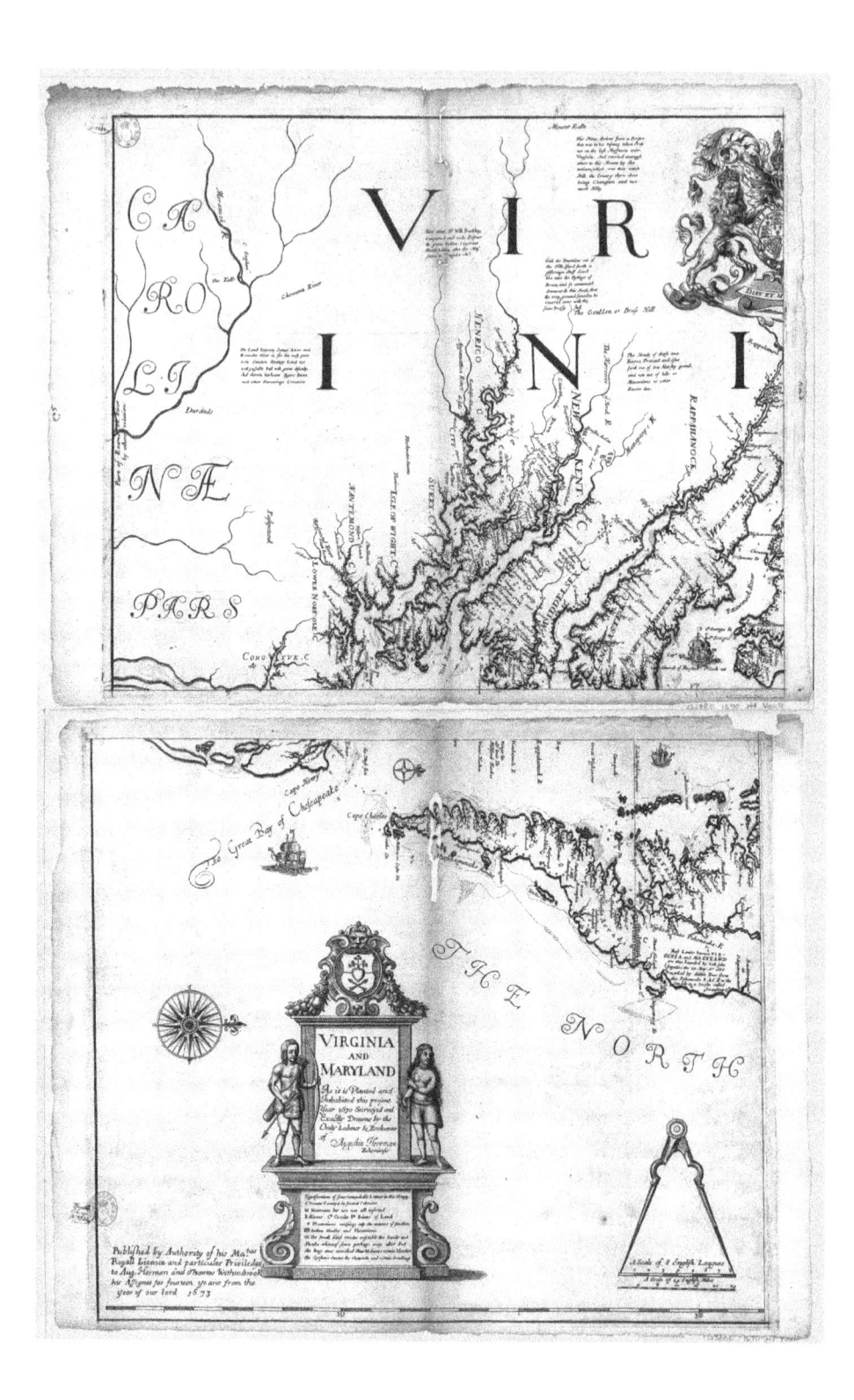

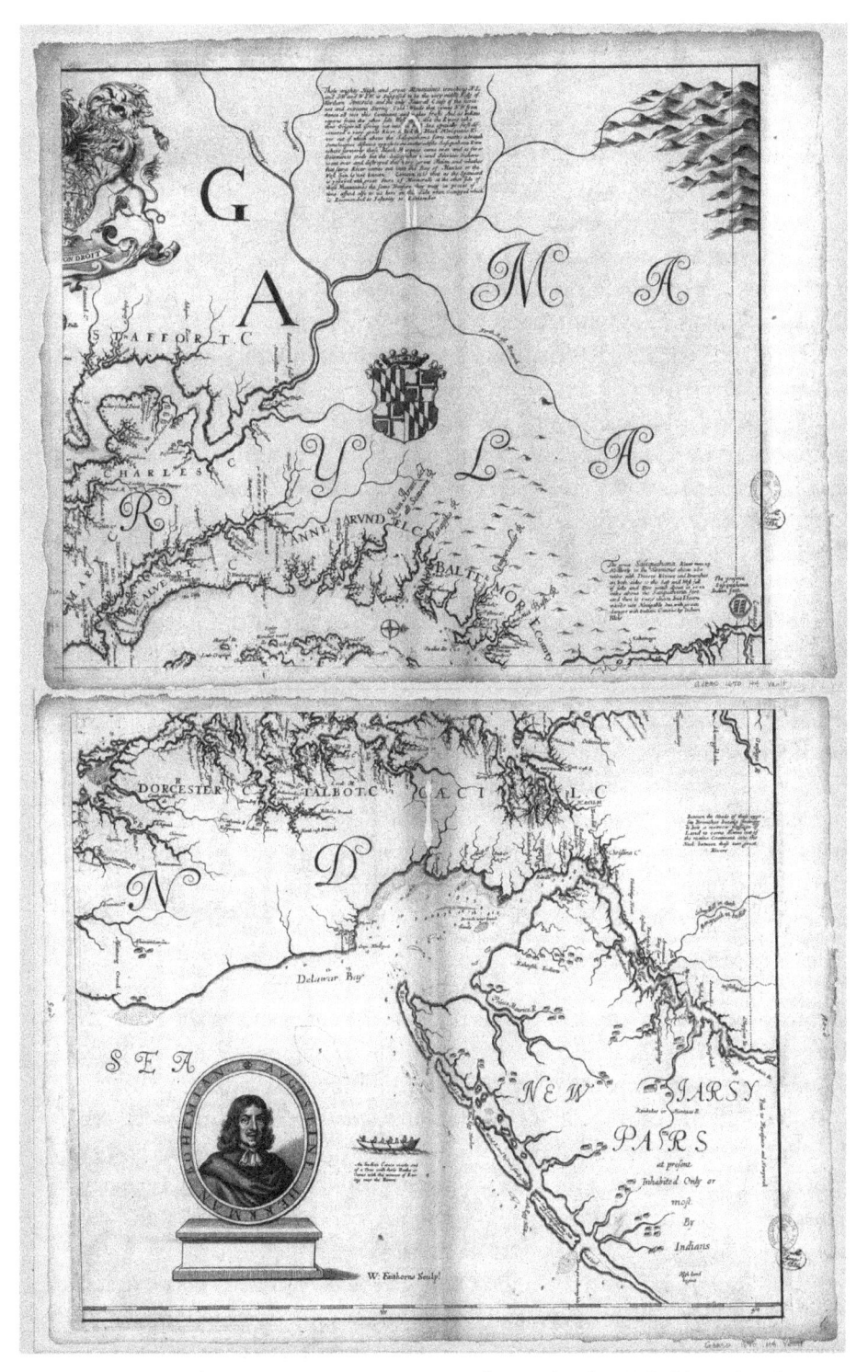

FIGURE 2. Augustine Herrman, *Virginia and Maryland as It Is Planted and Inhabited This Present Year 1670.* Image courtesy of Library of Congress, Geography and Map Division.

hostile appearance." Then the Susquehannock "made an obstinate resistance shooting many of our men, and making frequent, fierce and bloody sallyes," remembered Mathew, "and when they were called to, or offered parley, gave no other answer, than 'where are our four *cockarouses*, i.e., great men?'"[20] The English laid siege to the Piscataway fort for six weeks. Inexplicably, the famished seventy-five Susquehannock staged a breakout. They dispersed, some migrating to the Delaware and the Susquehanna valleys and others crossing the Appalachians into Ohio country.

Those who remained carried the war to Virginia. In addition to the northern front of the Potomac valley, the Susquehannock opened two theaters of war against tributary nations and a southern front on the piedmont. On the northern front, the Susquehannock waged a war of terror, torturing and mutilating English captives. Designed to awe the Virginia countryside, they "took their route over the head of that river [the Potomac], and thence over the heads of Rappahannock and York rivers, killing whom they found of the upmost plantations untill they came to the head of James river."[21] Another Susquehannock band sought unrequited alliances with the Algonquian-speaking tributaries. A major Susquehannock band moved to the southern piedmont and settled on the Roanoke River, where they replenished their losses with mourning campaigns against the Monacan. Responding to earlier raids by the Haudenosaunee, the Monacan had begun to coalesce, settling on islands in the Roanoke River near the Occaneechi. The Occaneechi spurned the Susquehannock offer of an alliance, partly because they were slave trading partners with Virginia and partly because the Susquehannock threatened a new rivalry. Still, the settlers peddled the rumor that the Occaneechi and the Susquehannock had joined together, triggering panic of an "all Indian" coalition.[22]

Some settlers moved toward the more settled tidewater. Those who remained absorbed the shock of the fleeing Susquehannock from the Potomac. Parties of four to six staged reprisals with and visited terror on the James River inhabitants, causing them to shelter behind hastily built palisades. "Neighbours in bodies joined their labours from each plantation to others alternately, taking their arms into the fields, and setting sentinels." The protracted warfare found the English people "often slain," and their anxiety caused them to entertain rumors: "no bullets would pierce beaver skins" and the "rebels' forfeitures would be loyal inheritances."[23]

Reacting to the panic, the militia officers chose Nathaniel Bacon to lead a command of "up to 300 men," and he reached out to Governor Berkeley for a commission. Risking reprisal from the government, Bacon rallied the militia in a counterattack against the Susquehannock at an island on the Roanoke River. His defiance, the opening salvo of Bacon's Rebellion, exploited the panic generated by the James River raids. Bacon gathered together fifty-seven "volunteers" on the upper James River to conduct search-and-destroy raids against the Susquehannock. Quick to assure Virginia of their loyalty, the Occaneechi sold out the Susquehannock by revealing their location on the Roanoke River. Once Bacon's army reached Occaneechi country, they rested at King Posseclay's recommendation. While they slept, the Occaneechi carried out a surprise attack on the Susquehannock, killing 150, including women, children, and their king. They carried away his scalp and seven Susquehannock captives as trophies for Bacon and a store of beaver pelts for themselves as spoils of war.

After ritually torturing their captives at Bacon's request, they refused to give him the pelts. Wrangling carried over into the wee hours of the morning, and the two armies battled until the next afternoon, by which time Posseclay and more than one hundred of his warriors lay dead and their compatriots, fleeing for their lives, had abandoned their fortified settlement. The Occaneechi had overplayed their hand; the reaction of Bacon's volunteers had caught them unawares. They did not comprehend the racialized rage directed at them in this new atmosphere conflating all Indians together. After all, they were in league with the Virginia slave traders and had done Bacon's bidding; why shouldn't they reap the rewards of their assault on the Susquehannock? On the other hand, Bacon's troops not only crippled two powerful nations in one fell swoop but also wiped out the Tutelo and forced the migration of the Saponi and the Monacan, leaving the region open for settlement.[24]

The settlers also coveted the land preserved for the Pamunkey and the Chickahominy. For this reason, the eye of the rebellion centered in Pamunkey country. Two years prior to the outbreak of the rebellion, the council had stayed all sales of reserved land between the settlers and these nations. Now the rebels chased the Pamunkey away from their homes into the Dragon Swamp, where werowansqua Cockacoeske hid for two weeks with her ten-year-old child. After weeks of searching for the Pamunkey, the settlers finally found them and dealt them a severe blow. After Berkeley crushed the rebellion, he restored Cockacoeske to her mantle and the Pamunkey to their land and entered treaty negotiations with the tributary nations.[25]

Bacon's Rebellion concluded with Articles of Peace (1677) between the governor of Virginia and the chiefs of the Pamunkey, the Nottoway, and the Nansemond at the Middle Plantation courthouse. Each nation entered into the treaty as autonomous sovereigns, except for the "several scattered Nations," a remnant of the paramount chiefdom Tsenacomoco, which under Cockacoeske "[did] again own their ancient Subjection and [were] agreed to come in and Plant themselves under her Power and Government." For an annual tribute of three arrows and twenty beaver pelts carried to the governor's residence each March, these Native nations would receive enough land for their subsistence, which they would hold in perpetuity. The English acknowledged that settler encroachment had caused them to seize and slaughter Native livestock. To prevent further breaches, the treaty stipulated "that no English shall Seat or Plant nearer then Three miles of any Indian Town" and that violators would face prosecution. In turn, the tributary nations were to "restore to the respective English Parents and Owners all such Children, Servants and Horses, which they have at any time taken from them."[26]

Placing the tributary nations under Virginia's jurisdiction required them to report any violations against their person or property by an Englishman to a Virginia magistrate. Native people who committed violations against an Englishman were also under the authority of English law. Virginia honored their customary gathering practices, which took them onto byways and streams "Oystering, Fishing, and gathering Tuchahoe, Curtenemons, Wild Oats, Rushes, Puckoone," but they had to secure certificates beforehand from local magistrates. The English could not enslave tributary people, and indentured Indigenous people could serve no longer than an Englishman, nor could they harbor or conceal any Native "Vagrant or Runaway." The governor served as arbitrator if disputes happened between the tributaries "in amity" with the English. The treaty disallowed the presence of "foreign" Native people among the tributaries unless they had secured a certificate from the magistrate. Promised protection from the incursion of a "strange" Native nation, "if necessary, a convenient Party be presently sent out by the next Colonel of the Militia, to Aid, Strengthen and joyn with our friendly Indians against any Foreign Attempt, Incursion or Depredation upon the Indian Towns."[27]

of the Countrey ; upon which Affair the
Governour will confult with the Council
and Affembly, and conclude thereon at their
next meeting.

The Sign of the
Queen of Pamunkey, on
behalf of her felf and the feveral
Indians *under her Subjection.*

The Sign of the
Queen of Waonoke.

The Sign of the King

The Sign of
the King of
the Not-
toways.

of the Nancymond
Indians.

The Sign of Captain John Weft.

Son to the Queen of Pamunkey.

Convenit cum Originali.

Teft. *Tho. Ludwell* Secretary.

Memorandum,

CHAPTER 3

New Incursions Were So Troublesome

Prompted by the custom of mourning wars to replace familial losses with captives, the Haudenosaunee continued their incursions southward, skirting the borderlands of the Chesapeake colonies. Virginia and Maryland found these expeditions "troublesome," partly because they targeted Native nations friendly to them and partly because colonizing settlers got caught up in the web of their raiding parties. For this reason, Maryland dispatched Col. William Coursey to Albany in 1677 to strengthen the southern links of the Covenant Chain. Although the southern colonies and the Haudenosaunee reached an agreement, war parties of the Oneida, Onondaga, and the Seneca, out in the field and unaware of the proceedings, confronted the Susquehannock [Conestoga], a nation in amity with Maryland, killing four and taking six captive. Once they returned home and learned of the treaty, the Seneca immediately freed the five captives they held and returned them with presents to make amends, but the Oneida kept the remaining captive. At the same time, another war party of Oneida and Seneca "went against the Canagesse [Cahnawaas] Indians (Friends of Virginia)," who inhabited the Kanawha River valley, and was subsequently attacked by a Susquehannock troop on horseback, who killed a man and captured a woman. Retaliating, the Haudenosaunee killed and scalped four "inhabitants" and captured six "Christians."[1]

Albany held the Haudenosaunee accountable. In response the Mohawk held themselves blameless, for they had not sent any of their war parties southward. Speaking for the Oneida, Swerise, one of their "chief Sachems," explained at Albany on February 15, 1679, that the Dutch still among them had cast aspersions on the English and portrayed them as the enemy. Yes, they had returned a Christian mother and her child and planned to exchange another Christian mother and her two children for their people captured by Virginia. If they were dead, than the Oneida would accept "some Canastoga [Conestoga] Indians given in their Place." The governor Sir Edmund Andros demanded the immediate release of the six Christians and promised to write to Virginia to begin the process of repatriation. After delivering up six Christians on May 24, 1679, Swerise again brought up the attack on his people by men on horseback. Thirteen of the Oneida war party had headed southwestward to raid "our enemies," when they were attacked by eighteen men. Although they returned fire, killing two men and two horses, they suffered losses for which they demanded replacement from the Cahnawaas [Canagesse], friends of Virginia. He also reminded Andros that "it would be convenient that the Governor tell the People of Virginia, not to send their Men so far from Home; for if they should meet our Parties in their Way against our Enemies, the Cahnawaas, whom the English call Arogisti, we cannot answer for the Consequences."[2]

After the Haudenosaunee continued to raid the Native people neighboring Virginia, the Old Dominion sent two agents, Col. William Kendall and Col. Southley Littleton, to Albany in October 1679. Littleton died waiting for the conference to begin, but Kendall spoke to the Oneida and told them that they had violated the treaty by destroying crops and livestock, killing people of Virginia, and taking them captive without provocation. Speaking separately to the Mohawk and the Seneca, who were not responsible, and then to the Onondaga, who did come until November, and the Oneida, whom he held responsible, he said, "It is certain they did not observe Friendship with Virginia but molested them with reiterated Incursions of their Parties. It is observable, however, that these two Nations, and the Cayuga's, only had French Priests among them at that Time." Not unlike the Dutch who remained among them, these Jesuits spewed mistrust of the English.[3]

Speaking for the Oneida on October 31, 1679, at the house of Albany, Doganitajendachquo answered the propositions made by Kendall the day before. Addressing his "Brethren of ye Virginia," he acknowledged that the Oneida had received not only the message sent in mid-September asking if they planned to meet but also a second message. Their lack of response was not "done out of Contempt or disdain"; they were "hindered by ye Small Pox and other Sicknesse." In response to the accusation of the "dammage that wee have done in Virginia, in destroying your goods and People, and in takeing of your women and Children Captives, etc., wee Confesse to have done soe." But it was done in accordance with the "Covenant made two years ago with Col. Coursey . . . that wee might freely come towards your Plantations, when wee went out a fighting to our Indian Enemyes to Refresh our Selfs if wee were hungry." Although the Oneida came away with nothing but "Indian Corn and Tobacco, . . . the English comeing outt shott some of our People dead, and afterwards wee defended ourselves." Firing upon them, they contended, was unprovoked and occasioned a response. The previous day, Doganitajendachquo reminded, Kendall had said that "what is already Past is forgiven." "Lett all that which is Past not only be forgotten but be Buryed in a Pitt of oblivion," he exhorted; "yea I say in a Bottomlesse Pitt where a Strong Currant of a River Runns throw [through]."

In response to Kendall's assertion that the Oneida must put down their arms and stand down whenever they came into contact with Christians in

Virginia, Doganitajendachquo reminded Kendall that Colonel Coursey said the Natives could enter as friends and be supplied with victuals when fighting their Native enemies. He gave thanks to the Old Dominion for destroying the Oneida's enemy, alluding to the Susquehannock-Anglo War, and for the presents of duffels, rum, and tobacco. He said that they had unconditionally honored Governor Andros's demand for the Christian prisoners and expressed gratitude for the "prudent" attention he had given concerning the liberation of their Native woman now in captivity. On the other hand, they disclaimed responsibility for the Christian girl now in their country. She was carried there by the "dispersed" people called the Conestoga or the Susquehanna, but the sachems pledged to seek her "liberty." After offering the customary wampum, he prayed for their continued friendship with the caveat that the English behave kindly to the Oneida people when they go on incursions against their Native enemies.[4]

About this time (1679), William Byrd I, some scholars believe, effected the destruction of the Monacan and their dispersal from Manakin. "The aborigines, namely the Indians, had reason to choose this place for their settlement," Franz Ludwig Michel wrote.

> Their city, called Manikinton by them, stood there. . . . About thirty years ago they still dwelt there. But when they inflicted some injury upon the Christians, Colonel Bornn [Byrd], who is still alive and who was then living on the frontier, namely at Falensgiig [Falling Creek], as soon as he heard of this ravage, mounted at once his company (he was then captain) and attacked the Indians boldly (who had promised obedience but had not kept it). He soon overcame them after some resistance and put all of them to the sword, without sparing anyone; He also destroyed their settlement and whatever they owned. For this service, the then king of England granted him the whole district between his land and this place, which extends twenty-five miles in length and eighteen miles in width. Those Indians who were not at home or escaped, still camp during the summer not far from their former home.[5]

In the face of continual Virginia encroachment and Haudenosaunee incursions, the Native peoples on the edge of the English settlements negotiated an alliance with Virginia for protection. Responding to both the recent Virginia attacks and northern Native raids, "Indians of Maryland, the Appomattoc, Nanzatico-Portobacco, Manakin [Monacan], Saponi and Meherrin" signed onto the addendum of the Articles of Peace in 1680, which made them Virginia tributaries. Three years later, in September 1683, the Seneca had "reduced and taken ye Mattapony Indian Town, and att present beseiged ye

Chickahominy fort." The council met at Hot Spring to discuss a "speedy" course of action for the "prevention of ye Seneca Indians future Incursions and perpetrations of spoils on ye Stocks and Inhabitants of this Colony." After reading the correspondence from the commanders of the Rappahannock region and other affected counties, they dispatched a messenger to the northern parts of the colony to determine "what posture of defence our Inhabitants are in, what effects are wrought by ye said Indians, what number of them, . . . give directions for constant ranging, against whose returne."[6]

The councilors assigned Byrd, himself a member, to go to either the Chickahominy fort or to the Rappahannock "Indian fort now besieged by ye Seneca Indians, there to treat with them, according to such Instructions." Finding "it absolutely necessary, for ye preservation of our Indians," the councilors proposed that the Rappahannock and the Nanziattico must be "united and incorporated" together. If the Nanziattico are unwilling to confederate, then the Rappahannock accompanied by "a party of horse" must immediately "remove to their new fort" or go to Nanziattico Town. The Rappahannock went to Nanziattico Town, where they joined the Protobacco who resided on the Rappahannock River. After the Seneca forced the dispersal of the Mattaponi again, many sought sanctuary among the Chickahominy and the Pamunkey.[7] In order "to oppose and debar" future incursions, the council ordered the custom collectors at ports to outfit ships entering their jurisdictions with "one thousand weight of shot, bullet, Carbine, pistoll, swan and goose [shot]."[8] For the defense of the western settlements, the council also consigned the mounted militia of Charles City County under Col. Edward Hill's command to report to Colonel Byrd, "alwaies in readinesse," upon his assessment of the "enemies approach or advice of any danger."[9]

Byrd presented an account of Native activity to Lord Howard Effingham, governor of Virginia, given to him by Richard Yarborough. Yarbrough, who resided in the Pamunkey Neck, was an interpreter who spoke several Native languages, including those of the Seneca, Iroquois, Chickahominy, and Pamunkey. On assignment to visit Toteras and return a boy who apparently had been abducted, Yarbrough's party found the Nottoway River impassable, so he sent Pansioela, a Native guide, ahead to alert Toteras that they had the boy in tow. The son of the king of Toteras, a Saponi man, and Nantuccola, the "great man" of the Occaneechi, received them on Friday evening. They were all pleased to receive the boy and "promised" to come to Williamsburg to pay their tribute at the next meeting of the General Court. Although Nantuccola spoke "suspiciously," all three men affirmed that they had not been near the settlements. The Toteras said they had been hunting on the southside of the Meherrin River and could find no evidence that either the Saponi or the Toteras expected to harvest "rare ripe corne." Nevertheless,

Nantuccola's best guess was that the Seneca had been "sculking" around the Appomattoc near the settlements, out of the sight of the rangers.[10]

The persistence of the Haudenosaunee raids despite the Covenant Chain prompted Governor Effingham to visit Albany in 1684, "hopeful [of the] prospect of Setling a firme, and lasting peace, with ye Seneca Indians." He planned to demand that the Haudenosaunee cease and desist raids on Native nations, both tributary and "friends of Virginia."[11] Prompted by "new Incursions [which] were so troublesome" in the Native country near the Virginia and Maryland settlements, where Haudenosaunee war parties had attacked, captured, and killed several settlers, Effingham attended the Albany Covenant meeting in July 1684. Hearing the Dutch interpreter's pronunciation of Effingham's first name, Howard, as *Hower*, the Haudenosaunee translated it to *assarakowa*, "big knife" or "long knife." From this point forward, they addressed Virginia governors with the transliteration *assaragoa*.[12] In *The Proposals Made by the Right Honourable Francis Lord Howard of Effingham, Governor-General of His Majesty's Dominion of Virginia*, he stated that over the past seven years a number of unprovoked incursions led to "several murders and Robberies, carrying away our Christian Women and Children." Despite the earlier diplomatic outreach and a willingness to forgive, promises were "quickly forgot," and the Haudenosaunee engaged in willful violation of the Covenant Chain.[13] "You not only destroyed, and took several of them Prisoners, but you have also killed and burnt our Christian People, destroying Corn and Tobacco, more than you made Use of, killed our Horses, Hogs, and Cattle; not to eat, but to let them lie in the Woods and stink: This you did, when you were not denied any Thing, you said you wanted."[14] He demanded that the Haudenosaunee remove all of their warriors from Virginia and Maryland and not "molest" the Virginians' Native friends "hunting in our mountains . . . their country."[15] Effingham expressed his willingness to let bygones be bygones if the Haudenosaunee would promise "not [to] commit any Incursions on our Christians or Indians living among us, or in Maryland."[16]

After hearing Effingham's charges, Odianne of the Mohawk disclaimed any Mohawk responsibility and chastised his brothers the Oneida, the Onondaga, and the Cayuga for breaking ranks and making incursions into Virginia and Maryland, for "we have always been Obedient and Kept the Covenant Chain." He challenged them to "strictly keep your Covenants."[17] He acknowledged Gov. Thomas Dongan of New York for mediating the dispute, pledged to pay reparations in beaver pelts to Lord Baltimore of Maryland, and finally expressed gratitude to Effingham for willingly forgiving them and not asking for reparations by "throwing the Ax into the pit of oblivion."[18] Arriving on August 5, the Seneca spokesman, after conferring diplomatic niceties, addressed Effingham directly:

> We have heard and understood what Mischief hath been done in Virginia; we have it as perfect as if it were upon our Fingers Ends. . . . We are informed, that the Mohawks, Oneydoes, Onnondagas, and Cayugas, have buried the Axe already; now we that live remotest off, are come to do the same, and to include in this Chain the Cahnawaas, your Friends. . . . You tell us, that the Cahnawaas will come hither, to strengthen the Chain. Let them not make any Excuse, that they are old and feeble, or that their Feet are sore. If the old Sachems cannot, let the young Men come. We shall not fail to come hither, tho' we live farthest off, and then the new Chain will be stronger and brighter. . . . We understand, that because of the Mischief that has been done to the People and Castles of Virginia and Maryland, we must not come near the Heads of your Rivers, nor near your Plantations, but keep at the Foot of the Mountains; for tho' we lay down our Arms, as Friends, we shall not be trusted for the future, but looked on as Robbers. We agree however to this Proposition and shall wholly stay away from Virginia.[19]

He then requested that "the Indians living in Virginia may come soon according to his promise and put their hands into the Covenant Chain here."[20] This request was more than idle curiosity, for the Haudenosaunee were asking Virginia to give one of their allied Native nations to them as a tributary.[21]

A man of his word, Effingham sent Byrd, a member of the council, and his attorney general, Edmund Jennings, with three or four Native sachems in tow. The government had recently tasked Byrd, considered the resident authority on Native people, with checking out a rumor of their activity at the fall line. The General Assembly, sitting in session, sent Byrd home. In April 1684, Easter Monday, within twelve miles of his house at the falls of the James River, Byrd encountered fifty Seneca, who "promised to behave themselves hereafter very peaceable to the English."[22] Now Byrd accused the Haudenosaunee of "taking an Indian Girl from an English Man's House, and four Indian Boys Prisoners. They excused this, by its being done by the Parties that were out when the Peace was concluded, who knew nothing of it, which Accident they had provided against in their Articles. They said, the four Boys were given to the Relations of those Men that were lost; and it would be difficult to obtain their Restoration: But they at last promised to deliver them up."[23] They continued to blame the French priests' influence. Expressing their gratitude for meeting with the nations under Virginia's dominion, the Seneca, the Cayuga, the Oneida, and the Onondaga, each promised never to violate the Virginian tributary nations' hunting grounds nor to attack them on the road. Odianne continued to maintain that the Mohawk were blameless and to admonish for those responsible for the mayhem in Virginia, and he too expressed joy "to see one another face to face in this Covenant house where they always speak of Peace."[24]

On May 7, 1685, the council met to discuss the request in one of the articles of the Five Nations for a delegation of Native nations to visit Albany that summer. A search committee composed of Ralph Wormeley, Col. Richard Lee, Col. William Byrd, John Lear, and Col. Christopher Wormeley was tasked with selecting by July 10 an interpreter, one or two Virginians, and two representatives each from the Appamatuck, the Nanziattico, the Chickahominy, and the Pamunkey to travel to Albany to meet with the Haudenosaunee.[25] On September 15, Popettesammin, king of the Pamunkey; Manahock, sachem of the Chickahominy; and Winteschotan, sachem of the Nanziattico [Nawgiatico] addressed the Five Nations. They said "in obedience to Lord Howard their Govr they were come so far to see and speak with them having never seen them before, that they put them in mind of the Chain of Peace and friendship between them and join hands and Embrace them. They expect they will observe the Articles concluded with Ld Howard and not disturb their Hunting at their Mountains, which is Our Country and not yours. They pray the Sun may Separate all Evil Inclinations that the Covenant Chain may be kept Clear from Rust." Revealing the Mohawk's vulnerability to the French, Odianne deliberately agitated for English protection. The Onondaga and Cayuga joined him in expressing their desire for protection from the French. "If you do not, we shall lose all our Hunting and Beavers, and the French will have all our Beavers, who are angry with us for bringing them to the Brethren," the English. He closed the session by "singing . . . a Song to the *Virginia Indians*."[26]

Demonstrating that this song was a misrepresentation of Haudenosaunee intentions, an Oneida war party two years later in 1687 preyed on the Weyanock, "Friends of Virginia, and killed some of the People of Virginia, who assisted those Indians." The Haudenosaunee, playing their standard refrain, feigned ignorance: "They took six Prisoners, but restored them at Albany, with an Excuse, that they did not know they were Friends of Virginia." Governor Dongan used this event to threaten them with extirpation. Reversing the imagery of a tree as a hospitable place, he warned "that if ever he should hear of the like Complaint, he would dig up the Hatchet, and join with the rest of the English to cut them off Root and Branch."[27]

Around the time of this early reference to the threat of extermination of Native people, the colonial record offers perhaps one of the earliest instances of children dressing up in Indigenous costumes for play. On May 25, 1686, William Byrd I sent Rev. John Clayton, a member of the Royal Society, an "Indian habitt" as a costume for his son's play. "There is a flap or belly clout 1 pair stockings and 1 pair mocosins or Indian shoes also some shells to put about his necke and cap of a wampum. I did not get any dyed hair. . . . These things are put up in an Indian baskett, directed as you desired, there are bow an arrows tyed to itt."[28] When not playing Indian, Clayton also dabbled in natural history. He had come to Virginia as a minister, pastoring for two years in James City Parish. If his occupation was saving souls, his true passion appeared to be science. Habitually collecting flora, fauna, and curiosities, Clayton was a man of the early Enlightenment. An empiricist, he collected more than three hundred Virginia plants not known in England. Observing, experimenting, and testing, he was careful to record herbs and accounts of Indigenous medicinal practices. Clayton's association of Native life and practices so closely with nature provides us an early example of what would become a familiar trope. During his visits to Byrd's plantation at the falls of the James River, he likely learned of Batte and Hallom's 1671 expedition, and likely launched his inquiry into Native life from the staging grounds of Byrd's house. He requested that Byrd send the Indian costume after he returned to England; he also presented Batte and Hallom's 1671 journal to the Royal Society on August 1, 1688, and then published it in *Philosophical Transactions of the Royal Society of London.*

Clayton met and conferred with Native people and others familiar with their medicinal and herbal practices. In 1687 he answered twenty-three queries [oddly, number 13, which for superstitious reasons is sometimes omitted, was entered twice] on Indigenous life in a letter to Nehemiah Grew, a botanist and fellow member of the Royal Society. These observations were primarily about the tributary Native people, for he had little direct knowledge of Native life to draw on outside the journals of Lederer or Batte and Hallom. He observed the *wiochists*, or priests who practiced medicine. They adorned their lodges or temples with relics and sacred herbs. Highly esteemed in their society, they were on par with the war-captains and second in status only to the werowance or chief. Nevertheless, Clayton gendered this occupation by comparing it to English women apothecaries, folk practitioners rather than professional healers. For a remedy or treatment, they bargained for wampum among their own people or, with the English, bartered for a matchcoat, an item not without value, or a gallon or two of rum. For example, one *wiochist* saved the eyesight of a "valued" enslaved man of Colonel Nicholas Spencer using a root remedy. Clayton learned that they had roots or herbs for rattlesnake bites, purges, and even for fishing and deer hunting. He was also an early observer to promulgate the trope that the Indians were vanishing: "The Indian inhabitants in Virginia are now very inconsiderable as to their number; and seems insensibly to decay thigh they live under the English protection and have no violence offered them. They are undoubtedly no great breeders." He tied their extinction to the prophecy of a "famous" *wiochist*, who predicted that "bearded men (for the American Indians have no Beards) should come and take away their Country and that there should be none of the original Indian be left, within a number of years. I think it was an hundred and fifty."[29]

Like his father, William Byrd II aspired to be a natural historian. In 1706 he wrote to Dr. Hans Sloane, secretary of the Royal Society, that his father's death had obliged him to leave England suddenly before he could join that august body. He now hopefully offered his services to demonstrate his desire to become a member. Noting the lack of men capable of scientific endeavor in Virginia, Byrd lamented "that nature has thrown away a large field her great bounty upon us to no purpose." Offering a token of his ambition, he enclosed "a small box of root" that the Native people used "to cure the bite of a rattle-snake." He noted that the traders, who travel "several hundred miles to traffic with the Indians, find it constantly to cure their horses, when they happen to be bit."[30]

The elder William Byrd continued to complain of incursions on the James River in 1688–89. Three times in 1688 his crystal shipments on the James River were returned because of the "fearfulness" of Native raiders, he wrote to his London agents Perry and Lane on June 16, 1688. The crystals, which he had been "informed . . . would be very valuable" when he was last in England, were purchased from Native miners, whom Byrd supplied with tools, because the rock was too hard for their tools to cut the large chunks needed for the English market. Now he had to figure the additional costs of both shipping and production, "considering its above forty miles beyond the Christian inhabitants and what charge must be for cutting of itt."[31] Complaining to Lord Effingham on June 10, 1689, of his inability to traffic from his remote home inherited from Thomas Stegg at the head of the James River, Byrd blamed the "troubles" on "Severall Strange Indians . . . sculking both here and [at] Appomatox anytime these 3 weeks; they have shot Severall Cattell & Hogs." He had twice called up the county militia to no avail. His neighbors were "much terrified" by the rumor that these "northward" intruders were aligned with the French, despite his efforts to mollify them. He beseeched Effingham, along with the governor of New York, "to use their utmost endeavours to keep the five Nations from rambling this way . . . [and] diverting of those Indians from given any disturbance to our frontier plantations."[32]

In July 1690 Byrd wrote separately to his brothers-in-law, Nordest Rand and Daniel Horsmanden, and father-in-law, Warham Horsmanden, about the difficulties at his homeplace. He wrote that he was feeling "indifferent well," because one of his "family," apparently a servant, had been lately murdered and two others abducted by Native people. Given these personal and financial losses, which he attributed to his location at the falls of the James River, he planned to move to a new plantation at Westover, thirty or forty miles downriver, which would be "out of danger." Noting an uptick in Native incursions, Byrd wrote to Rand that if England was still reeling from the recent Glorious Revolution, "our greatest damage hath been here lately caused by the Indians." Nevertheless, he wrote to Daniel Horsmanden, if the French do not join with Native forces, they would be able to withstand "a small incursion now and then."[33]

At the same time in 1690, Byrd planned to meet with the "great men" of the Tuscarora, "a great Nation to the Southward," and the relations of two of their people, one accosted and the other killed by enslaved Native runaways from Virginia masters. Although he had the killer in custody, he did not feel he could meet the families' "demand for satisfaction" and had alerted the president of the council to settle with them or they "might Sett the whole Country in a flame." Byrd also feared the Tuscarora's alliance with the Five Nations might cause them to come "rambling this way . . . if their interest with them now continues with them as great as formerly." This threatened possibility of the French joining the aligned nations "much augment their fears."[34] In late 1690 a Native party surprised in the night and assaulted a hunting party, killing two and wounding several others.[35]

Likely meaning to reduce friction with Native suppliers the Assembly passed "An Act for a Free Trade with Indians" in April 1691. The Assembly prohibited the settlers' participation in fire hunting and required a license from the governor for the settlers hunting remotely away from the settlements. The act also made Native commerce "a free and open trade for all persons at all times and all places."[36] Fire hunting was a ritualized method of controlled burns that forced game into a circle to be killed. Preceding European contact and persisting throughout the colonial era, fire hunting was not uncommon in Indigenous country in Carolina, Virginia, and the Potomac east of the Appalachians. Thousands of miles of burned-out country patched the landscape, and its cleared ground enticed settlers from the Shenandoah Valley northward toward Pennsylvania.[37] "For all the Country is but one continued Forest, with Patches of some hundred Acres here and there cleared either being formerly seated by Indians, or the Trees being burnt in Fire-Hunting," observed travel writer Hugh Jones in 1724; "and old

Fields,. . . . where have been formerly *Indian Towns*, and *poisoned Fields* and *Meadows*, where the Timber has been burnt down in Fire-Hunting."[38]

The ritual of collecting game fit within the Native cultural framework, but meeting the demand of the skin trade corrupted their proprietary sense of conservation. While fire hunting remained technically efficient for collecting game, skinning the animals and leaving the meat was wasteful at best, and burning the saplings and undergrowth of the forest could be ecologically disastrous. Michel called fire hunting the great hunt and credited this custom with the clearance of the forests.

> It takes place in October, in the following manner: From twenty to forty persons and often more gather and make a circle, assigning to each a certain section in the circle. Afterwards each sets fire to the foliage and underbrush, which through the heat is dried up. The flames devour everything before them, until finally the area is much narrowed and the game, fleeing before the fire and the smoke, is driven together to a small space, around which the hunters stand, shooting down everything. Then they take only the skins and as much of the meat as they need. The rest they leave to decay.[39]

Michel also noted that the Native people were "great shots" but held their rifles differently than the English. Contemporary historian Robert Beverley noted similarly that Indigenous Virginia hunters, not having access to guns, expertly hunted with bow and arrow the

> Shores, Marshy Grounds, Swamps, and Savanna's . . . [for] Cranes, Curlews, Herons, Snipes, Woodcocks, Saurers, Ox-eyes, Plover, [and] Larks. . . . But they had a better Way of killing the Elks, Buffaloes, Deer, and greater Game, by a Method which we call Fire-Hunting: That is, a Company of them would go together back into the Woods, any time in the Winter, when the Leaves were fallen, and so dry, that they would burn; and being come to the Place design'd, they wou'd Fire the Woods, in a Circle of Five or Six Miles Compass; and when they had compleated the first Round, they retreated inward, each at his due Distance, and put Fire to the Leaves and Grass afresh, to accelerate the Work, which ought to be finished with the Day. This they repeat, till the Circle be so contracted, that they can see their Game herded all together in the Middle, panting and almost stifled with Heat and Smoak; for the poor Creatures being frighten'd at the Flame, keep running continually round, thinking to run from it, and dare not pass through the Fire; by which Means they are brought at last into a

very narrow Compass. Then the Indians let flie their Arrows at them, and (which is very strange) tho' they stand all round quite clouded in Smoak, yet they rarely shoot each other. By this means they destroy all the Beasts, collected within that Circle. They make all this Slaughter only for the sake of the Skins, leaving the Carcases to perish in the Woods.[40]

Over time, the goal to restrict the settlers from fire hunting came to naught. Answering a query of John Adams in 1813, Thomas Jefferson noted that Native peoples "still remote from the settlements of the whites" and the white settlers within Virginia despite the law engaged in the fire hunt. "They make their circle by firing the leaves fallen on the ground, which gradually forcing the animals to a center, they there slaughter them with arrows, darts and other missiles. this is called firehunting and has been practised in this state within my time by the white inhabitants."[41] Prohibiting the white inhabitants from engaging in fire hunting and hunting remotely unless licensed by the governor was meant to reduce conflict with Native suppliers, while opening trade was meant to meet an expected demand. The act had an immediate effect on the trade. "I had not the quantity of skins and furs as usuall, terade being stopt all last winter," Byrd wrote to his correspondent Perry and Lane on June 4, 1691, "and now its open, a great imposition is laid on all such commodity's as are transported, which I doubt will put a damp on that trade."[42] A year later, on June 2, 1692, he wrote to Daniel Horsmanden that he was only able to send the "skins and furrs" he had in store, since the Native trade had been "prohibited (all last winter." winter); it had reopened, "but with so great an imposition all commoditys of that sort, that I fear itt can never bee worthwhile onely those goods wee have by us must bee sold."[43]

The Assembly remained concerned about Native incursions. In 1693 the council rejected a petition from Henrico prohibiting the Tuscarora "hunting at the heads of their woods and plantations."[44] In the fall of 1695, William Byrd I reported to William Blathwayt: "We had several strange Indians on our frontiers all last summer who did several mischiefs and killed one man, know not wither they are gone of yet, or not."[45]

By the turn of the eighteenth century, the Native tributaries had settled into diplomatic patterns with their English hegemon. During his 1701–2 trip, Michel observed forty deputies from four tributary nations gathered at Manakin [Manikinton] for an annual conference to convey customary gifts to Virginia. Anthropologists have seized upon a sketch he made then as illustrative of Native material culture. Michel drew a longhouse in the distance and depicted the attire of three Native people in a naive style. Claire Brizon asserts that only someone who had personally encountered and interacted

FIGURE 4. Franz Ludwig Michel, *Dreÿ Americans* [Three Americans]. Image courtesy of Burgerbibliothek Bern, Mss.h.h.X.152, f. 64r.

with these people and could be so precise in rendering the colors of their animal skins, pipes, and guns and the fibers and weaves of their garments and baskets. Michel "depicts [them] wearing a combination of animal skins and plant fibers," writes Buck Woodard. "Their hats are described in Beverley's account of 'The History and Present State of Virginia' as being made of bark, round and open on the top and wrought with shell peak to make designs. The baskets are mentioned as being carried on the arms as shown in Michel's account." What Brizon and Woodard called a basket held by the person in the middle of the illustration could be construed as an unfinished sketch of a babe in arms.[46]

By the turn of the century, the Haudenosaunee had restructured their international relationships. When new France shuttered its western markets in 1696 and the fur trade shifted to the Ohio River, Native trappers reoriented to the Ohio Valley. By then the Myaamia not only had secured their territory for ten years but also had taken the fight to the Haudenosaunee on Lake Ontario. After decades of warfare, the Haudenosaunee in 1701 negotiated at Albany with the English the "Deed from the Five Nations to the King, of their Beaver Hunting Ground" or the Nanfan Treaty, which designated as a hunting ground under the protection of the British crown the region of the Great Lakes of Huron, Erie, and Michigan "in length about eight hundred miles and in breadth four hundred miles including the country where the bevers the deers, Elks and such beasts keep."[47]

"The whole country [is tired] having been the most chargeable as ever this poor country knew," surmised the senior Byrd. "The ranging once a fortnight, without exemption of any person whatsoever, is an intolerable burthen. But a mighty war threat'ning us, and securing the country are indisputable arguments" for peace.[48] Understanding that if discretion is the better part of valor, then neutrality is often its handmaid, the Haudenosaunee negotiated peace treaties with the French and the English respectively. This neutrality, which they maintained over the next fifty years, freed the Haudenosaunee to reclaim the fur and skin trades by relocating nations under their dominion to Ohio.[49] "Egged on by the French" and harassed by English encroachers, who were "a constant threat on the borders," editor Marion Tinling concluded, the Haudenosaunee diplomatically bided their time.[50]

CHAPTER 4

Slaves Belonging to Virginia Are amongst the Shawnee

The Shawnee had established towns south of the Ohio River in the seventeenth century, which the French observed and labeled Shawnee Country on their maps. Shawnee Country was in the words of historian Robbie Ethridge, a "shatter zone," a region of instability spawned first by contact with diseased settlers, then by the Beaver Wars from 1642 until 1698, and finally by slavers, all three draining the Middle Ohio basin of people. Virginia traders coordinated slaving expeditions with the Occaneechi and the Tamahita and preyed on the vulnerable Shawnee, enslaving them and spreading disease. These slaving raids from the south combined with the Haudenosaunee mourning raids from the north into a pincer movement in 1669–72, thoroughly overwhelming Shawnee society.[1] "The Six Nations have extended their Territories to the River Illinois," Dr. John Mitchell annotated on his *A Map of the British and French Dominions in North America* (1755), "ever since the year 1672, when they subdued, and were incorporated with, the Antient Chaouanons [Shawnees], the Native Proprietors of these Countries, and the River Ohio."[2]

The Haudenosaunee had ousted several Shawnee clans from Scioto and Ohio River valleys, depopulating the region by the 1680s. Indeed, the Shawnee of the Susquehanna River, where they had three towns, remembered being resettled "out of their own Country [Ohio] which is at a great distance toward the West or Southwest from their homes by their "patrons, . . . after they were almost rooted out and destroyed by their enemies."[3] While surveying Ohio valley lands "as far as to the Great Kanawha," George Washington in the fall of 1770 learned the provenance of the toponym Cut Creek; it was named after "a town or tribe of Indians which, they say, was cut off entirely in a very bloody battle between them and the Six Nations." These people may have been the Cahnawaas [Conoy], whom the Haudenosaunee claimed in the Treaty of Lancaster to have conquered. Not far from here, he found the remains of a "deserted" Lenape town, perhaps also a remnant of Haudenosaunee removal.[4] "It is also quite possible that through the turmoil, dislocation, and depopulation in the Ohio River valley, the formation of some new groups occurred—in particular, the Shawnees," writes historian Susan Sleeper-Smith. "Shawnee history . . . entailed several extraordinarily complex movements between Pennsylvania, the Savannah River, the Great Lakes, and Maryland. Scholars are beginning to explore the idea that the Shawnees formed in response to Iroquois predations and conflicts with Europeans, and that they adjusted to the tumultuous times by adopting a very fluid social structure and becoming highly mobile mercenaries."[5]

The Shawnee still maintained a presence on the Ohio River in 1692 when Shawnee agents traveled to Albany, where they successfully persuaded traders to come to their towns south of the Ohio River in an action that historian Chad Anderson calls the Native discovery of the English.[6] Around 1692 a Pekowitha Shawnee clan migrated from Starved Rock on the Illinois River near where the French established Fort St. Louis and settled along the Youghiogheny River at the invitation the Minisink, the Munsee-dialect-speaking Lenape. Around the turn of the eighteenth century, the Shawnee, the Susquehannock [Conestoga], and the Leni Lenape all coalesced into a cluster of "Mixt Nations" along the Susquehannock, Delaware, and northern Potomac Rivers under Haudenosaunee dominion.[7]

Drawing on his Shawnee informant Annawauneekheek, Rev. John Sergeant wrote that after the Haudenosaunee had "almost rooted out and destroyed" the Shawnee

> the River Indians [the Assateague), whom they [the Shawnee] acknowledge as their patrons, transplanted . . . them some years ago out of their own Country, which is at a great distance toward the West or Southwest . . . and settled them down upon the Susquehanna River. They live in three towns, Mkhauwaumuk, I suppose is the biggest having by all accounts, near five hundred souls in it. The journey on the River *Spunnau weh* [Susquehanna] is about 40 miles, I suppose, is not far distant from Mkauwaumuk. There is frequent intercourse between our Indians [Housatonic], and the Shawanoos [Shawnee]. The River Indians (who are those meant by Grandfather above) live interspersed with them.[8]

A Shawnee whose band had likely migrated from Fort St. Louis to western Maryland provided the information used by Rev. Lawrence Vanden Bosh, an Anglican priest of North Sassafras Parish, to sketch his *Map of the Lower Mississippi River* in 1694. Bosh gave a copy of the map to newly arrived Gov. Francis Nicholson in October 1694. Since the map was generated at Bosh's request, the sketch conforms with European conventions with respect to the natural terrain of rivers and mountains, the locations of towns, and the network of paths connecting them. Annotations on the map denote the Indigenous people in the French sphere to the "left" of the Mississippi. Also depicted are "Lessainy where Monsr. de la Sale was killed," "town of the rich Spaniards," and "mountains of silver and gold mines." The Bosh map deviates from the conventions of Indigenous cartography, which uses circles to indicate nations. Ever curious about the Mississippi River and the Gulf of Mexico, five years later Nicholson himself engaged the Shawnee he met in Savannah Town [not to be confused with Savannah, Georgia, founded by Gen. James Oglethorpe in 1733) to map the path to the Indigenous and French communities to the southwest.[9]

Pressed by Haudenosaunee diplomacy and Pennsylvania encroachment, the Shawnee had settled their towns at the Youghiogheny River, the Susquehanna River, and along the confluence of two branches of the northern Potomac River east of the Alleghenies. Maryland authorities noted in 1697 that "the strange Indians that are at the head of Potomocke neare the mountains do belong to and are part of the nation of Indians at the head of the Bay of the Susquehannahs who are in peace and Amity with us."[10] The following year, at a conference including the Susquehannock, Shawnee, Lenape, and Maryland, the Susquehannock disclaimed any authority over the Native peoples across the mountains. After that conference Maryland and Virginia agreed to send scouts beyond Piscataway country to learn more about these Native peoples across the mountains.[11] Unlike the Susquehannock, the Haudenosaunee claimed dominion over the people on both sides of the Great Mountains. On the western side, they had granted their tributaries a degree of autonomy in exchange for serving as a buffer between them and Maryland and Virginia. Nevertheless, these tributaries overstepped their bounds with the Haudenosaunee when they negotiated and signed a treaty with William Penn in 1701. By ceding lands on both sides of the Susquehanna River to Pennsylvania, they effectively made themselves tributaries of Pennsylvania. In exchange for living "according to the Laws of this Government while they live Near or Amongst the Christian Inhabitants, . . . the Said Indians shall have the full and free privileges and Immunities of all the Said Laws as any other Inhabitants, they Duly Owing and Acknowledging the Authority of the Crown of England and the Government of this Province."[12]

In 1707 a Shawnee party consisting of six men, two women, and three children picked up a twenty-six-year-old captive named Lamhatty at a Shawnee settlement on the upper Savannah River. The presence of women and children suggests that theirs was more a familial trek rather than a hunting expedition, evidence of a Shawnee presence and domesticity in the region. They traversed the piedmont northward for six weeks. They pitched camp at the Rappahannock River headwaters, where "they pierce ye mountains." The opportune terrain enabled Lamhatty's escape down the Rappahannock until he came to branches of the Mattaponi River in the Virginia settlement, where he surrendered himself to the people at Andrew Clark's house. Unable

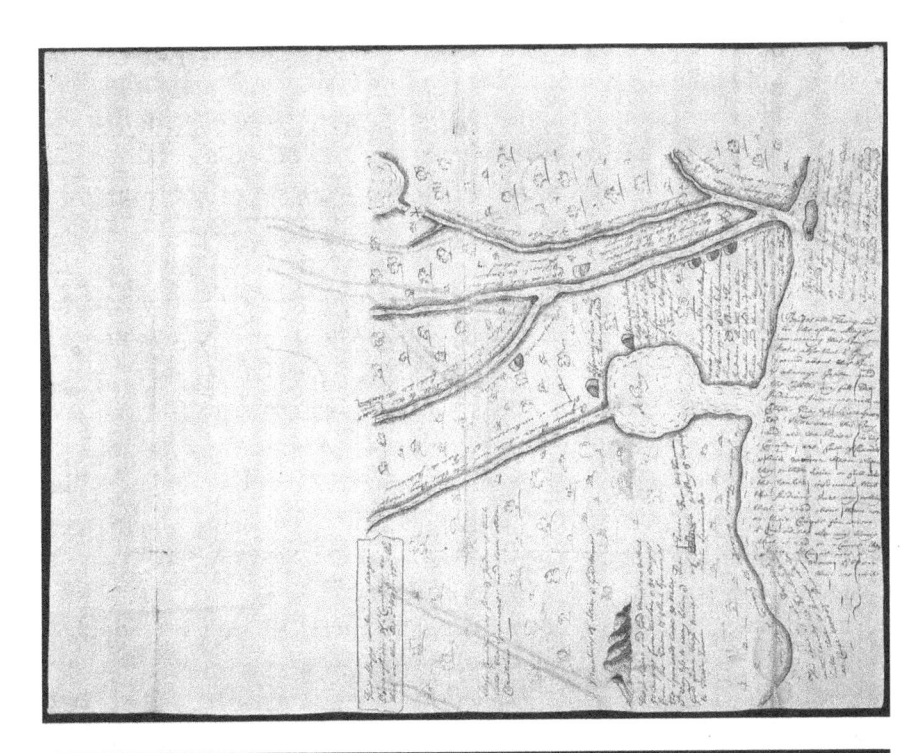

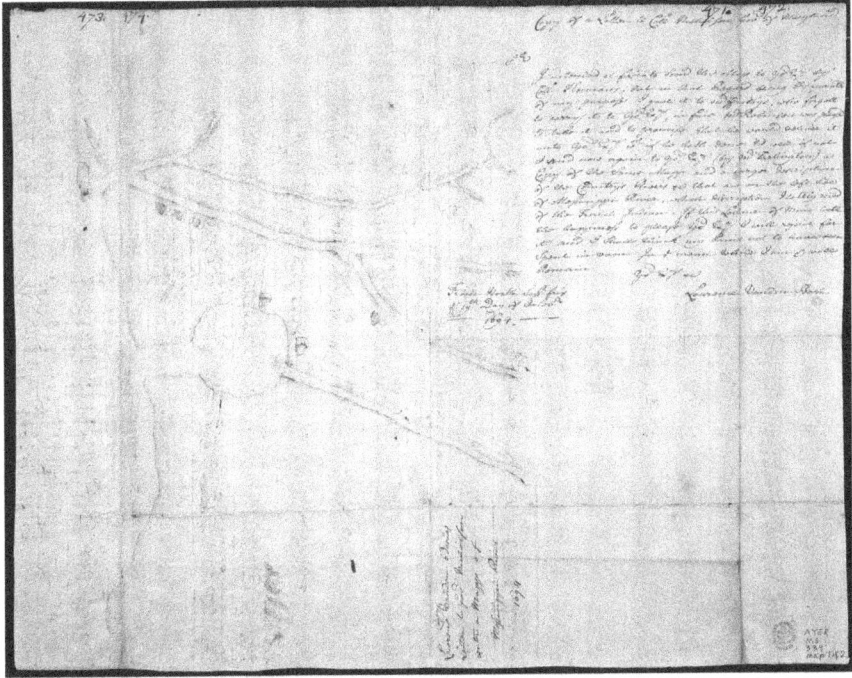

FIGURE 5. *Map of the Lower Mississippi River, Neighboring Coast, and the Country to the Southwest (1694)*, Edward E. Ayer Collection. Image courtesy of the Newberry Library Special Collections.

to understand him, the people took him to Lt. Col. John Walker Sheriff of King and Queen County.[13] Lamhatty gave his narrative of his travels to the historian Robert Beverley, two years after he wrote *The History and Present State of Virginia*. Lamhatty told Beverley that in 1706 the Tuscarora conducted slave raids and destroyed three of ten Tawasa [Tawáha] "nations." They returned the following spring and raided four more; the other two fled, Beverley wrote, "not to be heard from again." He did not mention the other three. A twenty-three-year-old man named Lamhatty was among the captives at the Tawasa town near the Alabama River. During his captivity he moved through several Muscogee [Creek] Towns, first to Apeicah and then to Jäbon for short layovers over a period of six weeks, and then to Tallapoosa, where he "worke in ye ground between three or four months." His captors then carried him on another six-week "easy journey" to Opponys on the Oconee River before crossing the mountains to a Shawnee settlement on the upper Savannah River, "where they sold him."[14]

Beverley attached a map denoting the place-names Lamhatty indicated in his narrative. He added as a postscript that he later learned from some of Lamhatty's indentured countrymen that "he was sometimes ill used by Walker, became very melancholly after fasting and crying several days together sometimes useing little Conjuration and when warme weather came he went away and was never more heard of."[15] Beverley mapped Lamhatty's travels for the same reasons Nicholson teased out maps from the Shawnee. The Tuscarora were the chief trading partner to Virginia in the skin and fur trades. The colony was interested in expanding that trade beyond them to the southwest. At the same time, the Shawnee portion of the journey showed not only their migration from Savannah to the mountains but also a way through them, an interest of the Dominion from the time of Lederer's expedition.

Opessa, who participated in the 1701 treaty negotiations with William Penn, led his band of Pekowitha Shawnee in 1707 from Carolina, where they had been harassed by the yeh is-WAH h'reh, to the Susquehanna River near Conestoga, where he established Pequea as his seat of government. Four years later Opessa became embroiled in a controversy that threatened his chieftaincy, when he was accused of murdering Francis Le Tore [LeTort], an indentured servant who had escaped from John Hans Steelman, a Maryland trader. A Seneca counselor, representing the Haudenosaunee Council at a meeting held at Philadelphia on June 18, 1711, said that Opessa disclaimed any responsibility for the murder and affirmed that he was "entirely innocent." Steelman had come to him and requested that he capture or kill "some of his Slaves and Dogs," alluding to Le Tore and his gang, in exchange for goods, but Opessa declined his bounty. He told Steelman to cease this line of

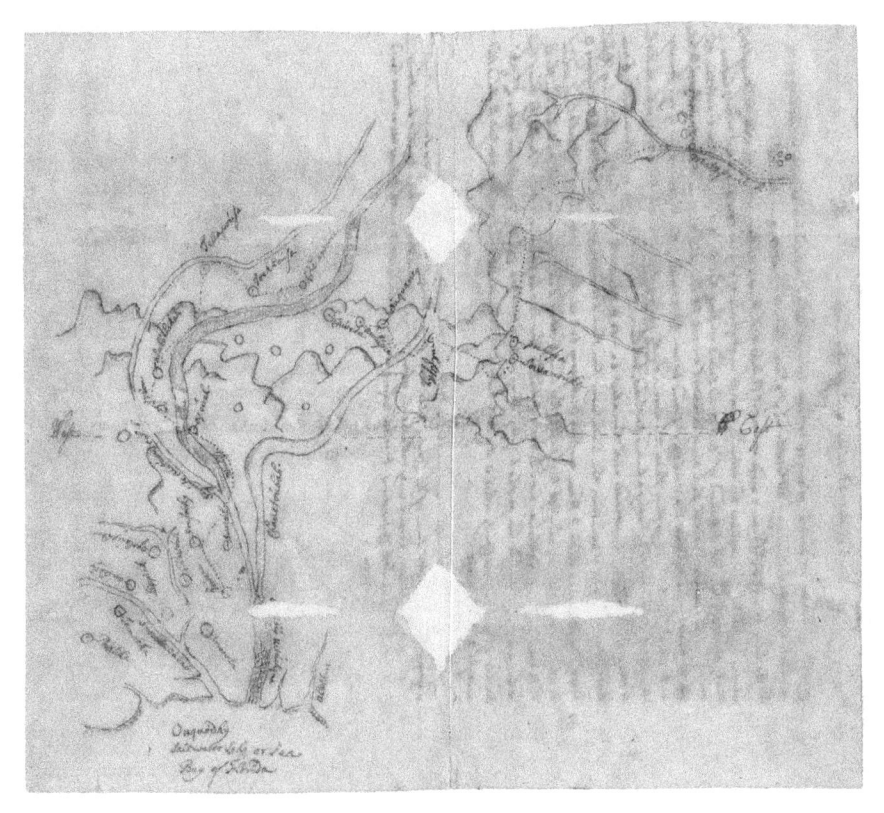

FIGURE 6. Robert Beverley's map of Lamhatty's captivity and escape from the Shawnee to Virginia. Image courtesy of Virginia Museum of History and Culture.

"Discourse," lest some of the young warriors, who were in the woods hunting, take him up on his offer. Apparently, some did, to Opessa's dismay. Blaming the victim, the counselor also accused Le Tore of stealing a boy from them and requested the governor's assistance in securing his return. Seeking to quell the controversy, Opessa abdicated his chieftaincy in 1711, perhaps because his people had lost confidence in him or perhaps because of his fear of English reprisal. Nevertheless, three years later the Haudenosaunee exercised their hegemony over the Shawnee and installed in his place an Oneida sachem, Carondawana.[16]

Opessa later moved his seat of government to the intersection of the headwaters of the Potomac River and the Warrior Path, where he established King Opessa's Town on a site of earlier settlement. The Haudenosaunee's allowance of Opessa's return was hardly an accident. The Haudenosaunee trusted him at this "strategic" location between them and the yeh is-WAH

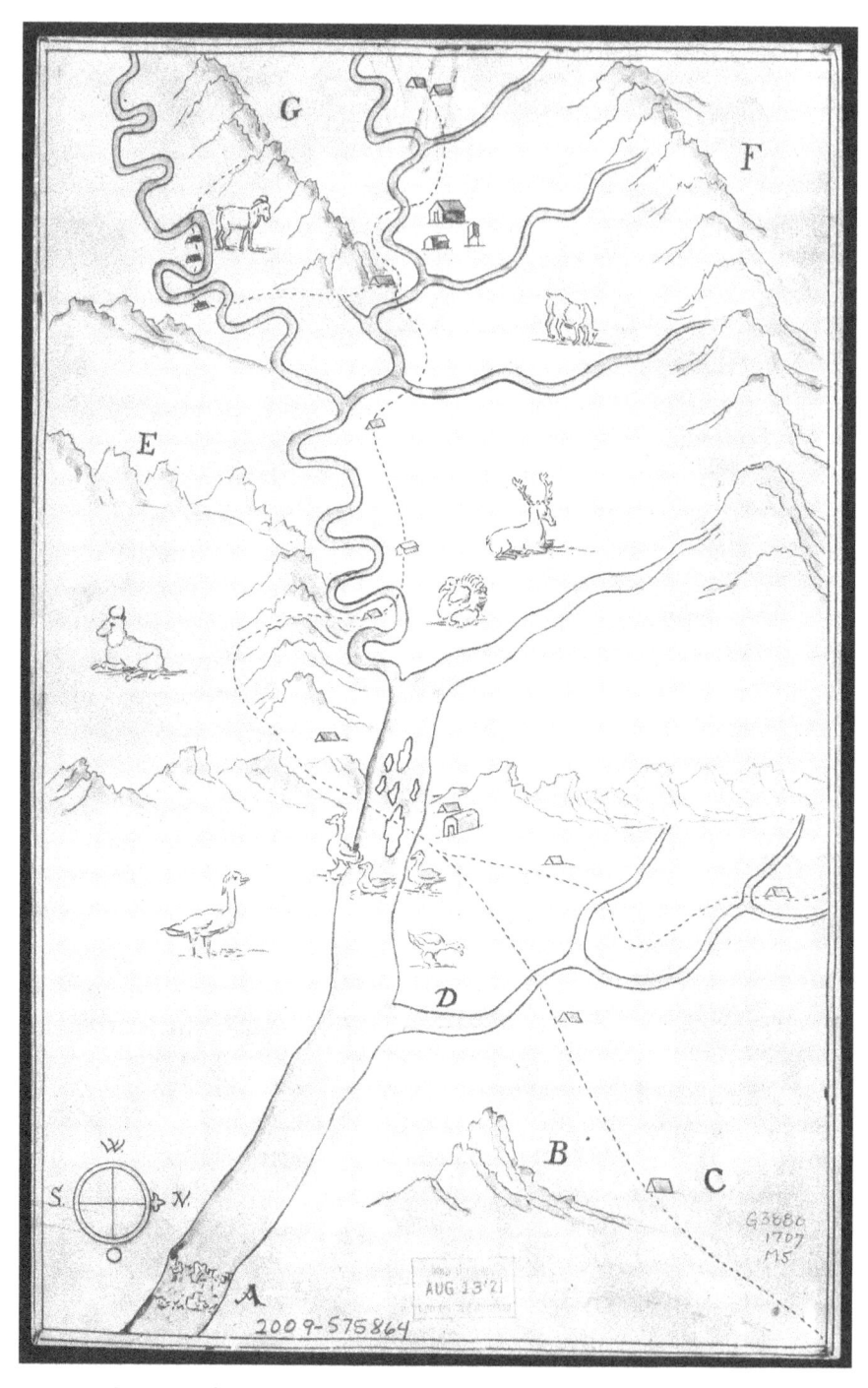

FIGURE 7. Franz Ludwig Michel, *Map of the Shenandoah Valley and Upper Potomac River* ([1702] 1707). Oriented with north to the right. Image courtesy of Library of Congress, Geography and Map Division.

h'reh to the south, Pennsylvania to the north, the Myaamia to the west, and Maryland and Virginia to the east. It offered the vulnerable Shawnee protection and buffered the Haudenosaunee from attack while also checking settler expansion. Although not an ideal entrepôt, it proved the closest Native post to the Chesapeake and Pennsylvania colonies, attracting traders Charles Anderson, Israel Friend, and brothers Edmund and John Cartledge.[17]

The treaty negotiations of 1721–22 put King Opessa's Town in the path of Virginia's expansion because they involved both boundary and fugitive disputes. "The Great Treaty of 1722 between the Five Nations, the Mahicans, and the Colonies of New York, Virginia, and Pennsylvania," negotiated by William Burnet, captain general and governor in chief of the Provinces of New York, New Jersey, and territories, on behalf of governors Alexander Spotswood of Virginia and Sir William Keit, Bart. of the Province of Pennsylvania, and the Counties of New-Castle, Kent and Sussex upon Delaware, spelled out the terms of agreement. The treaty opened up the lands east of the Appalachians to English settlement and enlisted the Haudenosaunee and their tributaries in capturing and returning enslaved runaways.

Governor Spotswood's personal loss in 1721, when enslaved Africans escaped to the mountains from his ironworks in Germanna, the first colonial piedmont settlement established in 1714, prompted the treaty. Spotswood had established Germanna on the Rapidan River, twenty miles above the falls of the Rappahannock, partly to serve as a buffer between the enslaved fugitives and the mountains and partly to check the southern mourning war migration of the Haudenosaunee from entering Virginia. When in 1721 enslaved Africans laboring in Germanna, including his own furnace workers, staged a mass escape to the Blue Ridge, Spotswood enlisted the governors of New York, Pennsylvania, and Maryland to join him in offering bounties to Native hunters and white rangers to capture them dead or alive. New York governor William Burnet responded to this call by working out an accord with the Haudenosaunee. The Haudenosaunee agreed not only to stay west of the Appalachians and north the Potomac River, unless they had obtained a passport from the governor to enter Virginia, but also to return Black fugitives to Virginia. Notice would be sent to the deputies on patrol to notify Native hunting parties of the accord that they should capture fugitives on their return home, promising them that they would be well rewarded.[18]

With the fugitive Africans still at large and the Haudenosaunee making excuses that they were beyond their jurisdiction, Spotswood in August 1722 traveled six hundred miles to Albany to sign the treaty and to remind the sachems of their agreement. Before signing, Spotswood met with them and insisted on a preliminary agreement on two propositions. First, "the great River of Potowmak and the High Ridge of Mountains which extend all along the Frontiers of Virginia to the Westward of the present Settlements of that Colony shall be forever the established Boundaries between the Indians subject to the Dominion of Virginia." The treaty stipulated that the Native nations under the Haudenosaunee would stay on the western side of the "high Mountains" or "Great Mountains" [the Appalachians] and the northern side of the Potomac River unless granted permission by the governor of Virginia. Second, the Haudenosaunee also promised to hunt out and return runaways who had escaped to the Great Mountains. "That if any such Negro or Slave shall hereafter fall into your hands you shall straightway conduct them to Col. George Masons House on Potowmack River and I do in behalf of that Colony engage that you shall there receive immediately upon the delivery of every such Runaway one good Gun and two Blankets, or the value thereof, and in Token of this Proposition and Engagement I lay down 5 Guns and 500 flints."[19]

On his return to Virginia, Spotswood stopped at Conestoga on October 18, 1722, where he addressed the Conestoga, the Leni Lenape, the Ganawese, and the Shawnee. He explained the agreement worked out between the Five Nations of the Haudenosaunee and three colonies of the English: New York, Pennsylvania, and Virginia. If these "Mixt Nations" greeted his presence with "small dread," they received his explanation with great disappointment, for they had hoped for the continued "free liberty to pass and repass" on the Great Indian Warpath [the Seneca Trail]. The Shawnee king, perhaps either Pockaseta or Oneakoopa, wrote to Sir William Keith, governor of the Province of Pennsylvania, on the sanctuary the Shawnee had accorded the runaway Africans, allaying the English fear on the chief point of contention raised by Spotswood.

> These Negroes, Slaves Belonging to Virginia, Are Now at or Amongst the Shawnee [at Opessa's Town]. I will go my own self and take assistance where they are not exceeding the number 10 as directed. And as soon in the Spring as the Bark will run, We will lose no time to perform the taking of them according to Direction, for now they are abroad a hunting, so it can be done no sooner; besides, there will be Hazard in Seizing them, for they are well armed, but we must take them by Guile.[20]

There is no record that the Shawnee king ever seized and returned the fugitives to Virginia. Like Virginia, the Chesapeake colony of Maryland was also vulnerable to the resistance of runaway Africans. Their path to Shawnee country was "the Northwestward of Monocacy River, from the Mouth thereof up the said River, to the fording Place where the Conestoga Path crosses the same, near one Albine's Plantation, and then to the Northwestward of the said Conestoga Path, until it meets with Susquehanna River."[21]

Left out of the Great Treaty of 1722 [also known as Treaty of Albany], Maryland felt compelled to negotiate directly with the Shawnee to return fugitives. As early as 1697, when the Shawnee were considered "strangers" and new to the Potomac, Maryland had negotiated with their Native neighbors for the return of fugitive Africans. The proposal was approved with the addendum that the negotiators come to terms with them for their return because the bounty of "eighty buckskins to the value of the Negroe being thought too little."[22] Recognizing the "evil Consequences" of the Shawnee sanctuary, the Council of Maryland on November 2, 1722, tasked the trader Charles Anderson with carrying presents and terms to sachems Pockaseta and Oneakoop, hoping he would gauge their sincerity with a quid pro quo. On greeting the sachems, he should give each one "a Stroud Match Coat and a pair of Silk Stockings on Behalf of the Lord Baltimore and Charles Calvert Esq." in exchange for them by mid-April "surrendering certain Negro Slaves who for some time past have been entertained at their Towns upon Potomack River." Anderson should also let the Shawnee "know that if they will send down those Negro people [who] have lived among them for the Reward of two Strouds and a Gun . . . we shall look upon the same as a token of their desire to become our Friends and to live as Brethren with us."[23]

At the signing of the Articles of Friendship at Annapolis, the governor pledged a "good Correspondency" between Maryland and the Shawnee and gave more presents to the Shawnee great men. He promised a "Foundation of Trade with them [and] making such a Chain of Friendship between us as shall be kept bright so long as the Sun and Moon shall endure." Evidently the signing never came to pass, for four years later Governor Calvert and the Council of Maryland were still dealing with the "ill Consequences" of the Shawnee's harboring runaway Africans in their towns on the Potomac River. Attempting to resolve the crisis, a magistrate of Prince Georges County extended an invitation to a Shawnee chief to meet at Mononkosey [Monocacy] "to settle a Treaty with them to prevent the loss of any more of Our Slaves, as well as to regain those Already there." Accompanied by a member of the council and "several other Gentlemen," he went as far as the mountains, "but tho we stay'd beyond the appointed time, the Indians for what reason I cannot tell never came."[24]

Once again, the governor and council, on May 20, 1725, invited the great men of King Opessa's Town to meet at Charles Anderson's house at Mononkosey and appointed another trader, John Powell, to act as agent. Powell was instructed to go to King Opessa's Town and acknowledge that Calvert had received their tribute of three skins and would reciprocate with another present. The Marylanders had hoped that around August 5, 1725, the Shawnee would come down to Annapolis, where they would agree to articles of peace and friendship, inducing "their chiefs with a Callico Shirt and a pair of Scarlet Worsted Stockings each and to distribute the four other Shirts" to the principals as they saw fit.[25]

By October 11, 1725, the colony, still hopeful, had yet "to procure Justice from the Shauno [Shawnee] Indians to the Proprietors of those Negroes detained by them and to prevent by treaty the like Inconveniences for the future."[26] To make matters worse, on July 19, 1726, the governor reported to the Upper House of the Assembly that transported Europeans had escaped to the Shawnee, compounding the problem. "Several Convicts have lately attempted (by way of Mononkosey) to make their Escapes and may probably seduce others to follow their Example and also that Sundry negroes have and may by the same way make their Escape to the Shuano town to the great prejudice of the Proprietors."[27] Since the Shawnee were dragging their feet on signing the treaty, Calvert said that "the late Law for taking up negroes is not Comprehensive enough to prevent their Escape." He asked the assembly to write a new law, one "more Effectual to prevent the aforesaid Evills and also give a Suitable reward for the bringing back the Negroes already there and Inflicting severe punishments on such Convicts as shall attempt hereafter to Escape."[28]

The assembly responded on July 23, 1726, by passing "An Act to Encourage the Takers up of Run-away Slaves, That Shall Be Taken up by Any Person and Brought in from the Back Woods." The assembly stated its rationale for the bill: Africans had lately escaped from the plantations into the backwoods, where some have "perished, and others who held it out (as to their Lives) have been entertained and encouraged to live and inhabit with the Shewan-Indians, And forasmuch as many Negroes (upon hearing the Success some of their Fellow-Slaves have met with) are daily making Attempts to go the same Way."[29] Seeking to stanch this activity, the proprietorship offered a bounty of £5 current money and an allowance of fees to the sheriff for the expense of jailing and delivering of each fugitive. To discourage recidivist behavior, the fugitive "for the first Offence shall have One of his Ears cut off, by such Person as such Commissioner as aforesaid, shall for that Purpose authorize and if afterwards he shall be guilty of a Second Offence in the same kind, that then he shall have the other Ear cut off, and be branded on the Chin with the Letter R."[30]

The Shawnee's refusal to stop offering a refuge for runaways both incurred the wrath of Virginia and Maryland and raised the hackles of the Haudenosaunee. The removal of the Lenape from Kittatinny [Kittochtinny] Hills to the western banks of the Susquehanna and Ohio Rivers was part of a larger strategy of the Haudenosaunee to create a buffer between the French and the English in Ohio country and secure for themselves the deer and beaver reserves. After the Shawnee ignored entreaties by the Haudenosaunee to join with the Lenape in attacking Pennsylvania, the Haudenosaunee directed the Shawnee: "Look back towards Ohio, the place from whence you Came, and Return, . . . for now, wee Shall Take pity on the English and Lett them have all this Land."[31]

Pushed out by the Haudenosaunee, the Shawnee also began migrating back to their ancestral homelands from the Susquehanna and Potomac Rivers in 1726. They abandoned King Opessa's Town and other towns on the Potomac River and resettled in the Ohio and Scioto valleys, establishing their towns on both sides of the Ohio River. William Byrd II and the commissioners surveying the Northern Neck proprietary in 1736 and 1737 documented two abandoned towns from the northern shore of the Potomac: "Shawno Old Fields Deserted" on Benjamin Winslow's map. Other mapmakers dutifully followed suit. William Mayo's *Map of the Northern Neck in Virginia Situate betwixt the Rivers Patomack & Rappahanock According to a Late Survey Drawn in the Year 1737* and Peter Jefferson, who had also surveyed the region in making the *Map of the Northern Neck* in 1747, both depicted the "deserted" fields.[32]

In 1736 a Shawnee party "lately returned from their country" from the winter meeting at Kittanning on the Allegheny River, to Housatonic, Connecticut, where a reservation of 2,500 acres was recently established on the Housatonic River. One member of the party, Annawauneekheek, brought with him three belts of wampum. He explained that each belt carried a "particular message" of Shawnee resettlement in Pennsylvania. Rev. John Sergeant provided this epistle with a "literal translation," except perhaps as he admitted in the margin, when referring to his wishful translation of Lord God. Annawauneekheek offered the first belt to our older brother Netoh Kun [Nanticoke] and said: "Don't think your Khesum (younger brother) is run away to hide himself in the woods: I propose to abide where I am as long as our Lord God shall spare my life. As often as you look here, you will find your brother residing at M Khau wau muk [Cuyahoga?] at the great island and at the river Spunnau weh [Susquehanna]." Then he handed the second belt and said: "Brother when I arise in the morning, I will plant my corn, at noon it will be ripe, so that I shall have enough to eat till night, the next morning I will do the same again, and so from time to time as long as our Lord God shall give me life and strength." This meant, Sergeant wrote, that "they design from year to year to plant and till their ground at those places where they are settled." Then he handed the third belt signifying caution: "Brother, hide no good thing from me. . . . Brother, when we both in the

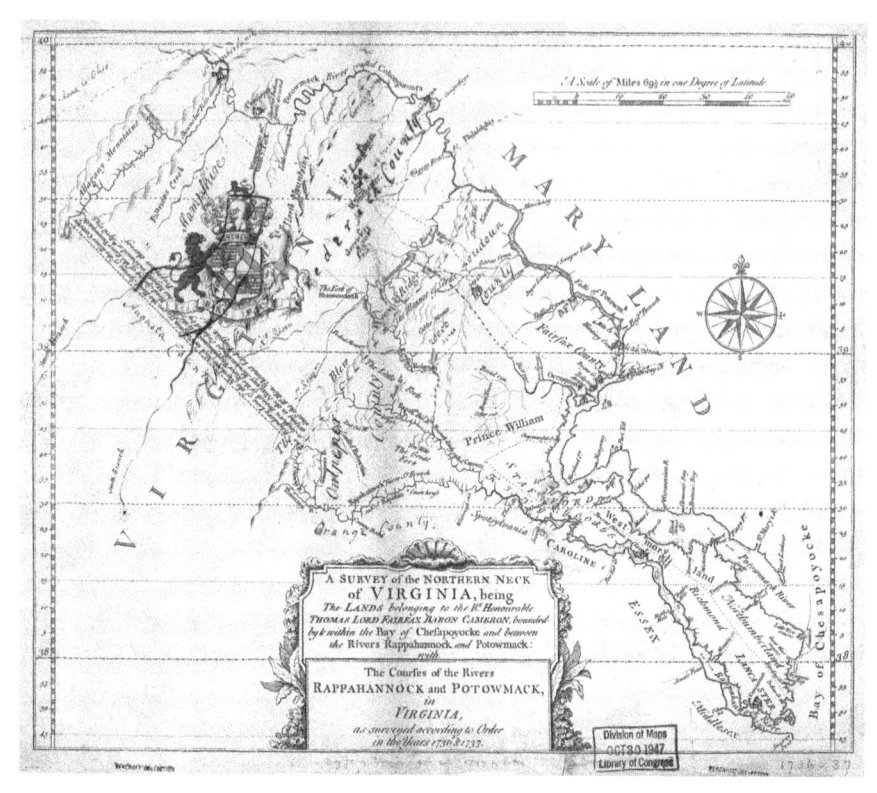

FIGURE 8. John Warner, *Survey of the Northern Neck of Virginia.* Image courtesy of Museum of Early Southern Decorative Arts.

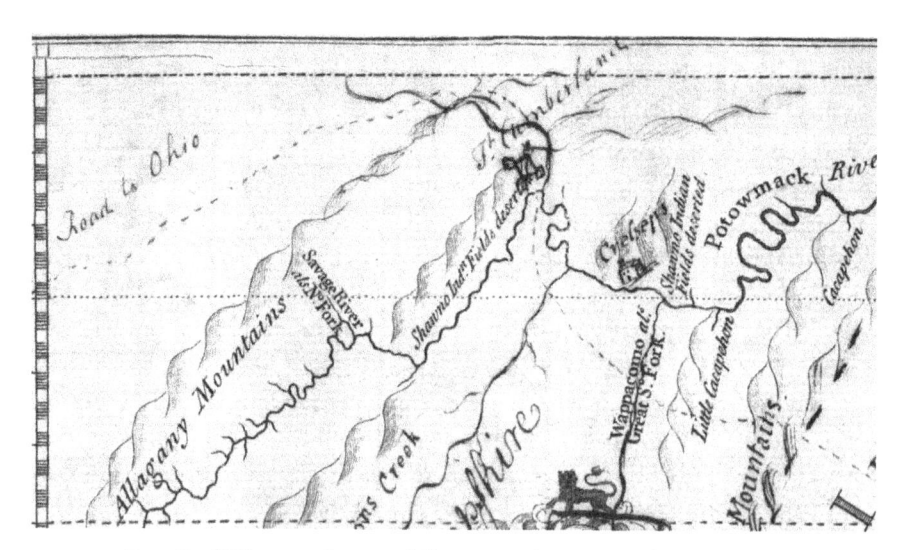

FIGURE 9. Detail of Warner, *Survey*, "Showing Shawno Ind[ian] Field deserted." Image courtesy of Museum of Early Southern Decorative Arts.

Indian language, 'tis the Dual number, have found out any good thing with consolation and advice, let us hold it fast as long as God shall spare our lives, let us teach our children only that which is good as long as we live."[33]

The returning Shawnee found in Ohio the seemingly primeval lands cultivated by their ancestors. The forests of ash, cottonwood, elm, hickory, oak, maple, sycamore, and walnut trees teemed with game. The few grassy clearings in the Great Black Swamp served as habitats to flocks of magpies, egrets, and spoonbills; herds of deer, elk, and lynx; packs of wolves; cougars; and domains of bears, badgers, beavers, and muskrats. Yet what they found was neither primeval nor wilderness nor new, for its use was imprinted on its landscape by their ancestors. Shawnee men steadily cleared forests and opened meadows for hunters of elk, deer, and bear. They also hunted the vast prairie, teeming with not only deer and elk but also bison, south of the Ohio River, which backed into the Virginia and Carolinas settlements. They navigated rivers and traversed roads that webbed their commercial zones. Shawnee women cultivated these fields, especially in the plains of western Ohio, where they carefully seeded nutritionally balanced maize, beans, and squash—the "Three Sisters"—which provided growth in a time-tested sequence, each plant drawing on and benefiting the other. The women skinned and finished the furs and pelts in the Shawnee towns along the Scioto and Ohio Rivers.[34]

By the 1730s, the fur trade sustained more than two hundred families populating these towns in Ohio country, often combining a mix of nations. Serpentine columns of rough-and-ready housing, homes to matrilineal clans, hugged the riverbanks, marking a makeshift appearance on the landscape. These Shawnee families found a wholesome environment, free of disease, to build their communities. Since the only gateway to their territory traversed the Cumberland Gap, the Shawnee towns hugging the Ohio River tributaries avoided smallpox epidemics skirting the Ohio Valley and ravaging Haudenosaunee and Illinois communities. About 1738 the Shawnee established Lower Shawnee Town at the mouth of the Scioto River, an entrepôt servicing the Great Indian Road, which cut across the Ohio River and over the Appalachians into the Great Valley Road into the Carolina piedmont.[35]

CHAPTER 5

Securing the Peace of the Country against the Indians

As early as the 1680s, Virginia settlers began encroaching upon land at the headwaters of the James, Appomattox, and Blackwater Rivers, a region inhabited by tributaries—the Nottoway, the Meherrin, the Weyanock, and the Nansemond—and contested by North Carolina, Virginia, and Tuscarora. The Dominion had to perform a balancing act to keep all these parties in check. Virginia had resettled their tributaries there partly to open piedmont land to settlers, partly as a foil to squatters, and partly as a result of the border dispute with North Carolina. By 1690 the council worried that the settlers' swindles in the surveys and other unscrupulous practices had so exasperated the tributaries that they might retaliate. They could attack a settler family in a false flag strategy, deceptively blaming another party, which could escalate into war. Anxious about this possibility, the council voided the patents south of the Blackwater Swamp.[1]

On February 22, 1699, the great men representing the tributary nations Nottoway, Meherrin, Nansemond, Pamunkey, Chickahominy, and Nanziattico "confessed" to the council that they proposed treating for peace with the Myaamia and "other foreign Indians." Each nation had prepared a peake or wampum belt, an entreaty of alliance, which the Nanziattico, the most western nation among them, planned to carry to the Myaamia. Treaty making was subversive partly because the tributaries had conducted it secretly, partly because they asserted their sovereignty, and partly because they presented a united front.[2]

Four great men of the Nottoway reported to the council that in 1703 they petitioned to the council for a pass to go northward in August 1704 to negotiate with strange Native people they supposed to be Susquehannock, whom they accused of kidnapping "their king and two children" during their hunt last summer. They are now held captive by the Tamahita, and a woman by the Susquehannock. They asked for the governor and council to request that the governor of Maryland look into their condition, intercede on their behalf, and secure their return.[3] The council deflected the request, fearing "a very dangerous consequence" if the Nottoway were allowed to proceed on their own, but did offer to engage in efforts to redeem their king. The council dispatched an interpreter to ascertain the facts of the king's location to aid

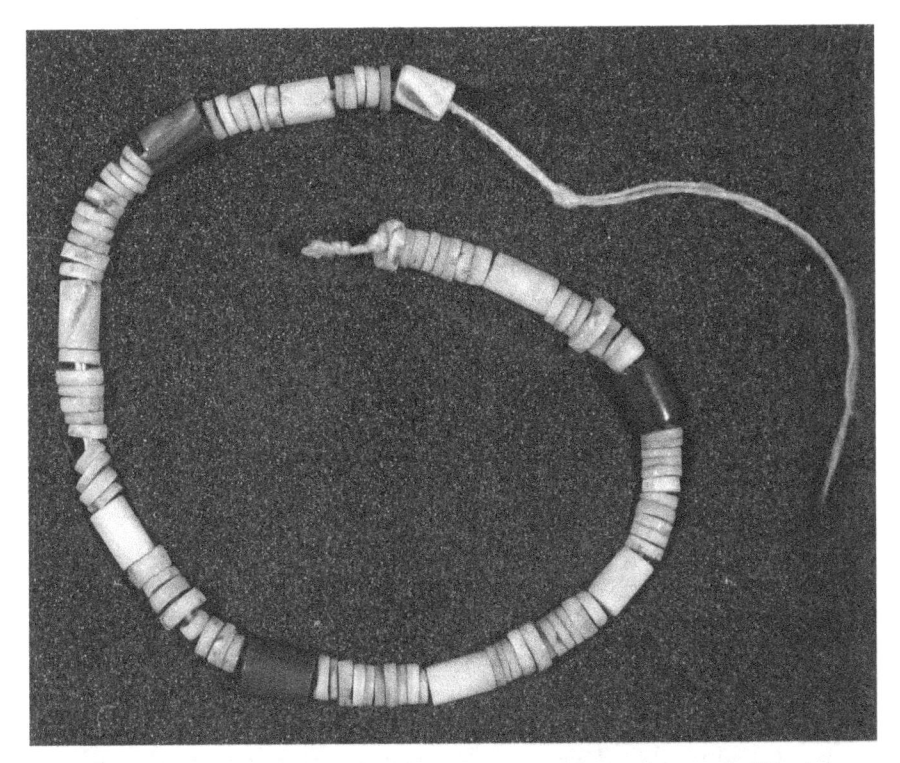

FIGURE 10. Wampum string made by a Moratico or Rappahannock, Virginia. Image courtesy of Canterbury Cathedral Archives and Library.

its efforts to return him.[4] Seeking strength in numbers, in August 1704 the Nottoway, Meherrin, Nansemond, Pamunkey, Chickahominy, and Nanziattico again petitioned the council regarding their desire to leave the Dominion with two representatives from each nation to negotiate with a foreign nation. This time they spelled out their intentions to go northward to negotiate the return of the Nottoway king from the Seneca. To this end they also requested a Tuscarora accompaniment of two representatives. Again their request was denied. The council permitted them to travel only to the limits of Virginia on the condition they be accompanied by at least one or two of the selected interpreters; Capt. Joshua Wynne, Capt. Thomas Wynne, or James Adams were to be present at all negotiations. With this caveat the Nottoway were not permitted to enter into any agreement that would be prejudicial against the colony. If they were willing to abide by these restrictions, then the government would prepare passes for two representatives from each tributary nation to go to the "northern bounds" of Virginia.[5]

In May 1704 the Nanziattico complained to the council because Thomas Kendall of Essex County had torn down their fences and forced them from their land. Rather than a return of their land, they sought redress in a newly carved-out preserve consistent with their population. After hearing the Committee of Propositions and Grievances' report, the burgesses agreed that if the review found Kendall liable, the Nanziattico "ought to have Justice done them according as the Equity of their pretentions." The council took their case under consideration and referred it to the attorney general for advisement of an equitable recompense.[6] Their petition for redress was never dealt with, because Nanziattico youth attacked a settler family in September 1704. Ritually painted for war or the hunt, likely the red-pigmented vermilion popular among men in the Eastern woodland, a party of ten surprised the Rowley family in Richmond County near the Rappahannock River, killing John Rowley and his wife, son, and mother-in-law. Somehow a daughter escaped.[7]

Given the diplomatic efforts of the Nanziattico great men working to unite with the other tributary nations to negotiate with Virginia to the east, the Myaamia to the west, the Seneca to the north, and the Tuscarora to the south, the attack seems ill timed. At best it was a restoration movement, and at worst it was revolutionary suicide.[8] Either the youth believed their action might initiate a millenarian movement to restore their country, or they believed their action risked their lives so they might realize life anew. Perhaps the youth had tired of their dependent status with respect to the Dominion. The Tuscarora youth were checked by their elders from attacking North Carolina seven years later, while, on the other hand, Opessa was unable to deter his Shawnee youth, who attacked Le Tore that same year. Perhaps the youth were impatient with their elders and looked to restore a culture vanishing before their eyes. The ceremonial characteristic of painting themselves before the attack suggests that they were calling upon restorative spiritual powers. Rather than an isolated event, perhaps they believed an attack on the Rowley family portended a fundamental transformation in society. Perhaps their war paint was a false flag operation, a tatical effort to cast blame on another nation, a reaction to unscrupulous settler behavior. The council had earlier conceived a tributary nation could "Cutt off a Family and pretend it to be done by Strange Indians."[9]

Nevertheless, the Nanziattico men were immediately suspected, because they reputedly had "often threatened" the family. Letters from Col. Tayloe, Col. Robert Carter, and Col. Corbin all gave accounts of the murders, accusing the Nanziattico. Captain Robinson moved swiftly to arrest "diverse" Nanziattico who allegedly "confessed" to the crime. Fearful the witnesses among them might be pressured to retract their testimony, the council ordered them into protective custody. The authorities placed the accused in custody of the Richmond militia and ordered them brought to the

Williamsburg jail. Fearful that the "Piscataway or some other Foreign Indians may be in Confederacy with them," the council ordered the militias to the frontiers and the Pamunkey, the Chickahominy, the Nottoway, and the Meherrin to remain in their towns. They were to alert the militia commanders if either the Nanziattico or any foreign nations come into their towns; if they disobeyed either directive, they would be branded as accomplices.[10]

After taking into consideration the expense of gathering the evidence and moving the trial of the suspected Nanziattico men to the capitol, the council issued a commission of oyer and terminer for the trial to be held in Richmond County instead. The reason for the change of venue was partly because the Nanziattico were tributary to Virginia and partly because it aligned their status with enslaved Africans, whose oyer and terminer hearings were held in the county where the crime was alleged. Holding the trial locally demonstrated settler's' authority, asserts historian Gwenda Morgan, through the "majesty" of the law and the mechanisms of control: the courtroom, the whipping post, and the gallows.[11]

Setting the trial date for October 5, the council assigned four of its own as members of the jury: John Lightfoot, Robert Carter, Philip Ludwell, and John Smith. Of the four only Carter and Smith presided, along with Speaker Peter Beverley of the House of Burgesses. Local jurists included the chief commissioners of peace from Richmond, Westmoreland, Stafford, and Essex Counties and all the justices of peace from Richmond County. The council ordered "two or three of the Great men" from each of the tributary nations of the Meherrin, the Nottoway, the Nansemond, the Pamunkey, and the Chickahominy to attend the trial with their interpreters to be "witnesses of the equity of the Proceeding . . . and that they may be able to informe the rest of their Nations at their return." The court was not only to determine the guilt of the accused but also to advise how best "the acquitted together with the women and children may be disposed."[12]

The one-day show trial took place as scheduled. Historian Rebecca Goetz sums up the scanty trial testimony recorded without attribution to witnesses: "A Nanziattico man the English called Jack the Fiddler allegedly stabbed William Rowley with a knife, this 'one mortal wound' under Rowley's right ear 'to a depth of six Inches.' Another Nanziattico man the English called Bearded Jack apparently struck Mary Webb in the head ten times with a tomahawk. A Nanziattico man the English called Frank was accused of striking John Rowley in 'the hinder part of the head,' causing a mortal wound four inches deep."

Since the court record is silent on witness testimony, we cannot determine how this sequence of events was prosecuted. Perhaps the jury had learned of the attack from the forced interrogation of the accused. Perhaps Rowley's daughter witnessed the assault. Perhaps Frank turned state's evidence, which explains his acquittal. Following the reading of the guilty verdicts, the authorities rushed Old Master Thomas, Bearded Jack, Jack the Fiddler, Tom Anthony, and George outside to the gallows and hanged them.[13] After hearing the report of the commissioners of the oyer and terminer court, the council queried about what to do with the acquitted, Frank, and recommended to the assembly commutation of the death sentence for two of the condemned, Long Tom and Young Toby, scheduled for execution in December. They had confessed, pleaded guilty, and given testimony, which in the opinion of the commissioners made them worthy of transportation or banishment for life. Nevertheless, they too were apparently hanged.[14]

The council ordered an inventory of "all the Wampum, Peake, Skins and all other the goods and Chattels . . . found at [the Nanziattico] town" and convoyed the remaining Nanziattico men, women, and children to Williamsburg. After hearing "The Report of Ye Conferrees with the Council Concerning the Most Proper Method for Securing the Peace of the Country against the Indians," the General Assembly debated their fate.[15] The assembly passed "An act Concerning the Nanziattico and Other Indians," which Governor Nicholson signed on the final day of the session. Here the assembly spelled out the terms of what they euphemistically termed the "Nanziattico Affair." In truth it was a genocide.[16] The assembly drew on "An Act Concerning Indians" (1665), which blamed people of an adjacent Native town for the murder of a settler. Although the act ambiguously called for "their lives or liberties to the use of the publique," it did not specify transportation, indentureship, or the disposition of children.[17] Nevertheless, in the Nanziattico case, people older than twelve years old were to be transported by sea, sold as indentured servants for a seven year-term, and prohibited from returning to the colony under the pain of death. The children remaining in the colony would be brought up as Christians and serve as indentured laborers until the age of twenty-four. The children born during their mothers' indenture would serve twenty-four years. Once their term of service was completed, the Nanziattico were forbidden to live in a Native town, emphasizing that the point was ethnic cleansing. The House refused the council's amendment to free and exempt Mattox Will, an elderly man, and Betty, a woman, from transportation, underscoring the totality of the retribution. Why the council chose to lobby for these two and no one else is unknown.[18]

The Nanziattico, in prison while awaiting transportation to Antigua, petitioned that their clothes and other chattels be returned to them along with any debts owed to them. The council voted to honor their request on May 31, 1705.[19] A month later the council directed William Tayloe of Richmond County to seize the goods belonging to the Nanziattico looted by the settlers, sell off any perishables, and retain an accounting.[20] The lion's share of what Tayloe collected went for the expenses of guarding, jailing, and convoying the Nanziattico to Williamsburg.[21] John Martin shipped the Nanziattico to Antigua and sold them for an indentureship of seven years, which he had certified by the governor of Antigua to redeem his bond guaranteeing he would not sell them as slaves.[22]

On May 12, 1705, the council adjudged thirteen Nanziattico children to be under twelve years old, divvied them up among the council members, and indentured them. The council had adapted a 1680 law titled "An Act Ascertaining the Time When Negroe Children Shall Be Tithable." Virginia slaveholders were required to bring African children to the county courthouse, "their ages adjudged by the justices and recorded within three months of their arrival," because they would be taxable at twelve years old.[23] The length of service of a child born of an indentrued Nanziattico mother was seven years shorter than that mandated by the law of interracial bastardy. The child of "any woman servant" or "free Christian white woman . . . by a negro, or mulatto" shall serve for thirty-one years.[24] After council president John Lightfoot took for himself Simon (ten years old), Little Jack (six), Betty (ten), and Little Betty (nine), the councilors drew lots for the remaining nine. John Smith acquired Jack (six); John Lewis, Charles (five); John Lightfoot, Nanny (ten); William Basset, Moll (eleven); Henry Duke, Little Nanny (three); John Custis, Kate (one); Robert Carter, Ben (eighteen months); Benjamin Harrison, Lizy (one); and Philip Ludwell, Janie (nine months).[25] Goetz searched exhaustively for these children in the probate records of their owners and was not been able to locate any of them. She questions whether they were ever freed. If freed at twenty-four, they likely melted into the free Black population. Nor was she able to find the forty Nanziattico transported to Antigua. Did Antigua honor their indentures, or enslave them and work them to death?[26]

The Nanziattico genocide triggered the council's realignment of other tributary nations. Concerned about the burgeoning relations among them in April 1705, Governor Nicholson presented "several letters," including one from Col. Benjamin Harrison dated April 6, containing "a Report of some secret practices" of the Nottoway and Tuscarora, to the General Assembly. Allegedly two hundred Tuscarora convened at Nottoway Town with an "intention to fall on the English." Still reeling from the Nanziattico uprising and its suggestions of a united Native front, Speaker Robertson of the House of Burgesses "ordered the great Men" of the Nottoway, the Nansemond, and the Meherrin to Williamsburg. The council elicited confirmation of the report from Mr. Henry Harrison, Col. Bassett, and Capt. Teate. After visiting Nottoway Town and finding only ten Tuscarora there, Henry

Harrison said the report was "groundless, . . . and that they had no design on the English."[27]

Suspicion of the Nottoway persisted. On June 10, 1706, the council reported that the Nottoway "have lately behaved themselves very insolently toward the English by several Speeches and discourses of some of the said Indians [which] give great suspicion of some ill design Speedily to be executed on ye English inhabitants living near them." The council ordered Benjamin Harrison to investigate the report, examine the people, and determine what security measures needed to be put in place. If necessary, he should apprehend suspicious parties and send them to Williamsburg for further inquiry.[28] By then the Nottoway had absorbed both the remnants of the Weyanock and the Nansemond, writes historian Helen Rountree, and were "beginning to emerge as a force with which the English had to contend."[29]

Following the recommendation laid out in an "Act Concerning the Nansiatico and Other Indians" the council "directed with all convenient speed" the county surveyors of Prince George, Surry, and Nansemond to "lay out and Survey the several tracts of Land appropriated" for the Meherrin and the Nottoway. The burgesses also ordered a census of both the Nottoway and the Meherrin. Acting on the "Report of the Conference with the Council Concerning the Most Proper Method for Securing the Peace," on April 28, 1705, the Burgesses set the new boundaries of the Nottoway and Meherrin. The Nottoway were allotted "a Circle Three Miles Round Their Fort where they now Live, and another parcel of Land on The South Side Nottoway River Six Miles Square [and] . . . an Island upon The South Side of Nottoway River between The Two Mouths of Racoon Swamp." The Meherrin were allotted the land running "up The Middle of The Neck between Meherrin River and Nottoway River from The Mouths of ye Said Rivers . . . Equal in Quantity to a Circle of Three Miles Round Their Town."[30]

The four Nottoway great men asked the council on October 26, 1705, to "reserve" for them unincorporated lands that they had "cleared and tended." The council commissioned Harrison to investigate and report if any settlers had encroached on the land and determine "to the end that when Patents shall be granted to such Persons, the possession of the said Indians may be reserved to them for such time as shall be thought reasonable."[31] The Nottoway made a special plea on May 23, 1706, that the council grant them land adjacent to the land already reserved on the southside of the Nottoway River and their *quioccasin* or ossuary. The council deemed their request reasonable and ordered that they had "free liberty to pass and repass between their own land and the said Quiocosin house by water without interruption of any of the proprietors of the Land adjoining on ye River or Creeks between the said places."[32]

Once the Dominion had removed the Nottoway from their land negotiated in the 1677 Middle Plantations treaty, Virginia moved to open for settlement "the Lands in Pamunkey Neck and on The South Side of The Blackwater Swamp and Nottoway River."[33] This pursuit of Nottoway land dovetailed with the surveyor of North Carolina's recent activity measuring and mapping plats on the south side of the James River. The council not only found this conduct "specious" but also lacking the "least Shadow of Right" to this land for the proprietary. For this reason, the council challenged North Carolina's claim "for any Lands on the Nottoway or Meherin Rivers or to the Northward of the said Weyanock Creek."[34]

In order to make this claim, the Dominion had to demonstrate that its tributary nations resided on these lands prior to Carolina's charter. Accordingly, Virginia's relations to its tributaries informed the questions of the "Commissioners appointed for settling the boundary betwixt Virginia and Carolina," who met from 1707 until 1711. Philip Ludwell and Nathaniel Harrison led the commission, surveyed the North Carolina–Virginia boundary, and scheduled the witnesses. The commissioners had the authority to summon and depose anyone they deemed knowledgeable about landholdings, especially of the tributaries, and about their memories of Weyanock Creek. The questions centered around the Weyanock migrations, settlements, and place-names in relation to the Nansemond, Nottoway, Meherrin, and Tuscarora. The commission deposed men who were Virginia and Carolina traders, settlers, and soldiers, who testified to their experiences, observations, and inquiries of Indigenous informants. The commissioners queried these white witnesses about their memory of place-names when they first arrived in the region. Henry Briggs, Benjamin Harrison, and Francis Tomes were principals among the white informants. They were "interrogated on oath."[35]

The commissioners also examined Native informants directly. They were keenly interested in Native memories about who had claims to the land. They primarily gleaned their most significant information from the answers of the Native witnesses. Native testimony was based on both memory and oral history passed down by elders and ancestors. Signpost events included wars, migrations, and settlement. They measured their land tenure at a place by the "acknowledgment" they paid for its use and reckoned time by the number of times they planted corn there. They detailed the terrain surrounding their towns. Especially significant to them were the rivers—Weyanock, Nottoway, Meherrin—and the creeks: Cotchawesco, Wycocoms Quauraurawke, and especially Weyanock. Swamps, although recollected, perhaps even as "great," nevertheless remained nameless. The Tuscarora, who had a strong claim to the land, were noticeably absent. A prime example of the commissioners' method of inquiry was the memorials of Great Peter, the Nansemond

werowance. Great Peter memorialized the reasons for Weyanock migrations and their places of settlement. Briggs, the interpreter, interspersed his
testimony with answers recollected from what Great Peter told him. Great
Peter's testimony was supported by three elderly Weyanock women who
lived at Nottoway Town and several elderly Meherrin and Nottoway men
who lived at Nansemond Town. Native deponents were "charged not to tell
any untruth for fear of displeasing or in hopes of pleasing anybody and being
charged to tell the whole truth."

After arriving at Nottoway Town on September 22, 1710, Ludwell and
Harrison interviewed three elderly Weyanock women but not the Nottoway
"old men," who had gone out to forage Chinquapin.[36] The commissioners
gave the women "strict Charge to tell nothing but the truth." They got a piece
of good fortune, for the women's full-throated testimony provided a blue-
print for their questions to others. Jenny, the daughter of Captain Pearce;
Mary, like Jenny about sixty years old; and Betty, the oldest of the three, all
recalled the oral history, which they had learned from their "fathers and the
old people." After their people were "removed" from their ancestral home on
the James River, they "first planted corn . . . at a place named to-Way-Wink"
[Towaywink]. The Tuscarora sold them this farmland and hunting grounds
"to the mouth of Roanoke River, up Chowan River to the mouth of Meherin
River, together with all ye Beasts upon ye Land and fish on the Said River."
They built their "chief town and fort" at the fork, which they named Wicocons [Wicoconne], "little River or Creek."

From there they moved to Warrecake, where the resided "for some considerable time" until the Pochaick [Pochick-Nansemond] attacked them and
killed their king and a half-dozen others. After sending a delegation to meet
with Virginia, "they very well remember that the English came out and
guarded them in amongst them near James River where they stayed but a
very short time before they returned to Warrecake." Upon their return they
revenged themselves on the Pochaick by killing their king and war captains.[37]
They went to Cotchawesk, "where they stayed almost a whole winter, and
from thence the[y] went to the Chowan and there stayed one Summer and
made corne and then they went ye no. side Ma: R: Unoonteh they Planted
corne."[38] After the Tuscarora attacked them, killing four, the Weyanock sent
a runner to inform the English, who sent several men "to fetch them." They
"stayed with the English remaining part of Summer and the winter following and were by the English at the Spring appointed to go to the South Side
of ye Blackwater Swamp. "They have been told by their old people that the
Chowans had corne fields on ye north side Blackwater opposite to Nottoway
River. . . . Their nation have ever since they can remember called Nottoway

River by that name at the mouth and they never heard it called of any other name—the same of Meherin River."[39]

Armed with the testimony of the three women, Ludwell and Harrison interviewed Great Peter the next day. In the main his testimony corroborated the three women's deposition, but he made no mention of the Weyanock's retribution against the Pochaick. Great Peter said he had "heard from the old men of his Nation" that the Weyanock "removed from the James River for fear of the English" after Opechancanough's "Great Assault" in 1644 and settled at Towaywink on the Roanoke River. The Tuscarora, who possessed the land, demanded to know their reason for being there. After the Weyanock responded that they were looking for a place to settle, the Tuscarora "sold them" the land from "the mouth of the Morattuck and up Chowan to Meherrin River," including all hunting and fishing rights. From there they moved to grounds surrounded by swamps and pocosins. The organic soil of the mucky wetlands proved hospitable to growing both corn and tuckahoes, bountifully enough to supply the town while the young men were away on the hunt. So situated, they built a fort at the head of the creek, which drained into the Meherrin River, about three miles from their town of Wycocons [Wicoconne]. Great Peter related that the Nottoway and the Meherrin Rivers had "always borne these names." Other than their residence on the Nottoway River, this place, he "always heard from all ye Indians, was called Weyanock ever since he can remember." He had responded to the best of his knowledge refreshed from "Patop and James, two very old Wyanoke Indians which lived at the Nansemond Indians town, both dyed last Spring."[40]

After his interview Great Peter told them that the North Carolina authorities Governor Edward Hyde; Col. Thomas Pollock, president of the council; and Surveyor General John Lawson examined him about the Weyanock people and Weyanoak Creek. He said to Ludwell and Harrison that he had given them the same history that he had just divulged, which angered the Carolinians. They said that "such storys would do the Proprietors a mischief; he answered that he did not come of himself to tell any storys, but was sent for, and if he desired to hear it, he would tell him the truth, but if that would not please him he would not tell him a lye."[41]

Great Peter's testimony prompted the commission to interview Henry Briggs, interpreter to the southern nations, on October 3, 1710. Briggs recalled that around 1695 that he had a "verry serious discourse with Great Peter," who he called "the greatest man of the Wyanoke." Earlier Great Peter had been identified as a werowance of the Nansemond; Briggs documented that the Weyanock had ceased to be a polity and had coalesced along with the Nansemond under the Nottoway. Great Peter told him that when he was a "lusty young man" the Weyanock "fled" after Opechancanough's "Great Assault" on the Virginia settlement in 1644. Breaking with the Paramount Chiefdom, they abandoned their ancestral home on the James River to the Roanoke River and "halted for a while" in a great swamp, likely the Dismal Swamp, above the Tuscarora Path with both the English and the Powhatan in hot pursuit. Opechancanough sent eighty men after them, but the Weyanock killed them. They then fled to Towaywink, which the Tuscarora called Chanoh, on the lower Roanoke River, "the first place they planted corne after they left the James River. After they had bene there a while the Tuscarooras demanded the Reason of their comeing there upon theyr Land; the Weyanocks answered they were driven off by the English and were willing to buy the Land of them." They then "purchased land upon a great Creek which Run into Blackwater, where it is a great River below Meherrin River, and att betwixt it and Roanoke River."[42]

Apprehending danger from another Indigenous people with whom they had quarreled, the Weyanock then moved to the Nottoway country where they purchased land, which they paid for with Indian money [rawrenoc] for the "privilege of living there." After the Pochaick killed the Weyanock's King Geoffrey about eighteen years later (ca. 1662), the English returned them to the James River. Later they went to Cotchawesk and then to the Chowan, where they planted corn one summer, and finally to Unoonteh, where they again planted corn. After the Tuscarora attacked them, they again found refuge with the English. They moved out and settled at Musketank, but when Bacon's rebels began attacking Indigenous people, they returned to their "old fort at Cotchawesk near their old town at Wicocons [Wicoconne]."[43]

Briggs also noted the diplomatic role the queens played in interethnic relations. He recalled a conversation with the queen of Weyanock, who told him that during Bacon's Rebellion the Weyanock returned to Towaywink and Wesco, which belonged to the Tuscarora, on the "same creek they lived on before." Finally, Briggs recalled that he was present at the Weyanock Town about 1694 when the queen of Tuscarora "brought a present of Deerskins (which I saw) to ye Weyanock Queen, and that she perswaded the Weyanock Queen to Remove from Blackwater to the Land they had bought from Tuscarooras." The Weyanock, including their queen, said they paid "a great deal of Roanoke [rawrenoc] for the privilege of living" on the Nottoway River.[44]

On May 22, 1711, the commission examined Nick Major and an old man of the Meherrin, aged about sixty years. They said that they have been "informed by their ancestors" that the Weyanock left their ancestral home on the James River shortly after Opechancanough's capture, fearing retribution of the English for their role in the uprising of 1644. They settled at Warrecake and "planted Corne" until the English came and drove them to a place on the

Roanoke River, which they called Towaywink, where "they planted corne and lived about two years." They then migrated to a creek southward of the Meherrin River and settled at a fork surrounded by swamp and bogs, which the Weyanock called Wicoconne. They lived there and "at a place about two miles from it called "Cotchawesco for about seven years and planted corn on both sides the creek."[45]

They had "heard their old men say" that two kings and a queen of the Tuscarora had sold the Weyanock "all the land to ye Southward of Cotchawesco Creek and upon Wycocons [Wicoconne] Creek and on ye North side of Roanoke River from the heads of those creeks downward to Chowan." Nick Major said he "knew very well" the kings Nicotaw Warr and Corrowhaughcoheh and the queen Ervetsahekeh. They said they had "heard both from their ancestors and the Tuscarooras that these Lands did Really belong to these Kings." They also said that the Weyanocks went from Wycocon to Cotchawesco to Wareekeck upon Nottoway River "where they lived a long time." When he was "a likely boy," Major said, the Nottoway king settled them at a site then "called Ro no tough" [Rowanty, Rowontee?], in the town "Wyanohkinke, but the Wyanoke called the place where the Towne stood Wareekeck" [Warrecake]. He also remembered that when the Weyanock lived on the Blackwater, "their Towne was called Weyanockkink, and Wareekeck was noe more called Wyanohkink after they left it."[46]

Thomas Wynn's knowledge of the Weyanock derived from his "Discourse with the old Meherin." They told him that around 1680 that Weyanock Creek was about eight to ten miles south of the "present Meherin town." They also had seated "a great while ago, in a Forke between two Swamps at the head of that creeke." The Meherrin also told Wynn that Weyanock who "lived at Wariecake on Nottaway River . . . paid an acknowledgment to the Nottaways for the liberty of Living there." Wynn further testified that the Nottoway towns dotted the Nottoway River until about 1679, when "they removed and settled their great Town upon Atsamonsock Swamp, at the place now called the old Town." About 1676 the Meherrin "lived parte at Cowonchahawkon and parte at Unote; and about two and twenty years [1688] ago they settled their chief Town at the mouth of the River where they now live."[47]

Benjamin Harrison, Esq., about sixty-three years old, was deposed in 1707. A Virginia trader to the Native people for the past thirty-five years, Harrison testified that in September 1663 the Weyanock reported to Governor Berkeley that the Pochaick had killed their king. Berkeley sent out a guard to bring in the queen and several other Weyanock. After a few days, Harrison accompanied another guard Berkeley sent to take the queen and her retinue back; they found the Weyanock "by the side of a great Swamp to the Westward of Nottoway River sheltered with a peace [piece] of a puncheon fort; about five or six miles from their Town; which was then called Wariecoke, standing near the banke along the South side of Nottoway River."[48] The militia took them to live among the English, with whom they stayed for two years. With the English becoming "uneasy" with their presence, the Weyanock moved "Southward" of the Meherrin River, where after a couple of years (about 1682) came into "some difference" with the Tuscarora. They then moved to the Meherrin River, "where (as they said) the Tuscarora fell upon the Waynoaks, at their last settlement upon Blackwater Swamp." The Nottoway joined the Tuscarora to the chagrin of the queen of the Weyanock, who complained to Harrison that the Nottoway "did them wrong." They had "paid them a yearly acknowledgement for their liberty of living at Warueake [upon Nottoway River] as long as they lived there, and afterwards they paid them for the liberty of living upon the Blackwater." Yes, the Nottoway "confirmed," the Weyanock had paid them an acknowledgment for their residences but took umbrage when they violated their covenant by making the 1677 Articles of Peace with the English; "then they looked upon themselves to have no further right to any land than those articles do." The Weyanock again took refuge among the Virginians and settled on the south side of the Blackwater Swamp, staying there about seven or eight years until they moved four miles downstream.[49]

Francis Tomes, deposed in North Carolina on September 27, 1710, and aged seventy-seven years, remembered when the Nansemond murdered the Weyanoke king around 1661. He "was sent out under the Command of Capt. Potter to bring the Weyanoak Indians in among the English Inhabitants." During that march he recalled passing through three great swamps before his troop arrived at Nottoway Town. He learned from one of the interpreters that "the water flowing into the swamp was a branch of Wyanoak River." His troop then marched another six or seven miles southwesterly to Wyanoak Town on the southside of the Wyanoak River. Tomes had not heard the river called by any other name than Wyanoke. He saw an apple orchard and an "an English built house," where the king had been shot. "From thence they went about two or three miles to the Westward where in an elbow of a swamp stood a Fort near which in the Swamp the murdered King was laid on a scaffold and covered with Skins and matts, which I saw."[50]

Tomes moved to North Carolina around 1664 from Ware Neck, between the North and Ware Rivers, Gloucester County. En route he "passed over a Swamp" into Coppahaunk, a Nottoway town, before arriving at the Nansemond Town, where "the Indians on a large Cyprus tree" told him that "the Coppahaunk Town was called Coppahaunk Swamp, but lower down at their Second crossing it, before they came to Nansemond Indian Town it was called Blackwater." The first time he heard the name Nottoway River was about 1669.[51] Robert Bolling, Thomas Wynn, and James Thweat, all of Prince George County, Virginia, and deposed in 1707, testified that they knew the Nottoway as Indigenous to the Nottoway River region and knew of no other name for the river. They all recalled that the Nottoway had towns on both the south and north banks of the river. Tonnatorah and Rowontee, about four miles above the mouth of Monksneck Creek, were both on the northern shore.[52]

Harrison and Ludwell concluded that the settler evidence and the Native accounts together corroborated that the place presently called Weycoconim is the Weyanoak Creek in the Carolina charter and derived its name from the Weyanock people who paid for and lived "very near it for several years." The witnesses were also unanimous in their agreement that the Weyanock paid an acknowledgment to the Nottoway people and that the Nottoway River derived its name from the Nottoway on it. If they located the latitude of Weyanock Creek near the bounds granted Carolina, as established by their survey, then the Nottoway River appeared to be thirty degrees north of the Carolina boundary.[53]

The Nottoway not only had absorbed the Wyanoke, but they also continued to contest their tributary status. In the early spring of 1711, they convened with several northern nations. According to tributaries who reported this conference to William Byrd II on March 26, 1711, they planned "to cut them off." Byrd reported this news to Governor Spotswood, who in turn sent a message to Nottoway to stand down. He then sent Colonel Harrison to demand that representatives of the northern nations come to Williamsburg "to declare their business."[54]

CHAPTER 6

Without Making the Tuscarora Acquainted

The Tuscarora's relations with their tributaries roiled Virginia, principally because the relationships threatened the colony's dominion over them. Adding to the Dominion's apprehension, the tributaries often acted as intermediaries between the Tuscarora and Virginia.[1] The Tuscarora–North Carolina War in 1711 opened a new southern front of Native incursions. Virginia-Tuscarora relations had soured over allegations of murder, instigations of attacks, and questions of sovereignty. Allegations against free Black Virginia traders to stir up warfare between Native and white people foreshadowed the Tuscarora War. North Carolina governor Robert Daniel of complained to Virginia on November 2, 1703, that "two free Negro Men," both Virginia traders, had engaged in "some Pernicious Practices" of encouraging the Winyaw to go to war with the Wiapie, both nations under South Carolina's dominion. The council assigned Col. William Byrd and Col. Benjamin Harrison to investigate the allegation. The council advised that the two men, John Fontain [Fountain] and Hubert, not engage in such practices in the future under the threat of being "severely punished."[2]

A year later, on September 18, 1704, Governor Daniel again accused Fontain and two other "free Negro Men," John Davis and Daniel, also Virginia traders, of encouraging the Tuscarora "to cutt off" Pamplico and Neuse settlements. The council again ordered Byrd to make an inquiry with the other Virginia traders regarding this behavior and summoned the formerly accused Fontain, Davis, and Hubert to appear. The council also asked the governor to produce any evidence he might have of their behavior.[3] Fontain, Hubert, and Davis appeared before Gov. Francis Nicholson and the council on October 26 to answer Governor Daniel's allegations, supported by an affidavit made against them by William Duckenfeild of St. Paul's Parish, Chowan County. Not only did they deny the charges, "but on the contrary [they] had endeavoured to promote Peace amongst all the Indians where they have traded." Finding "no Proof against them at present," the council dismissed the charges and gave permission to Fontain to return to Tuscarora country "to sell several trading goods left by him."[4]

After the Tuscarora made a complaint to the Virginia authorities against Simon Kilcrease for "killing one of their nation" in King William County, on August 26, 1707, the council ordered Kilcrease's arrest and confinement in the county jail until he could post bail pursuant to his appearance at the next general court in Williamsburg. On October 22 the grand jury heard the evidence against Kilcrease and his version of the events, after which the colonial board dismissed the complaint, determining that the Tuscarora was the aggressor. A week earlier, on October 14, six Tuscarora, "Charles, Tom Jumper, Stephen, George, Jack Mason and Will Mason," allegedly murdered Jeremiah Pate at the head of the Pamunkey River in New Kent County. Implicated by one of their party, they were arrested and confined at Cornet Winston's house. They broke out with five other compatriots. Two weeks later, on October 25, the council called out the militias in New Kent, King William, Henrico, Prince George, and Surry Counties "to range on the frontiers" and recapture the escapees. The council further ordered that the accused be committed to the jail in New Kent County and that their "arms, ammunition, and skins" serve as security.[5]

Maj. Nathaniel Harrison volunteered to command the expedition to recapture the fugitives, and the council placed under his command Maj. Joshua Wynne of Prince George's County, who was well acquainted with the Tuscarora. They were to take the Surry County militia to Nottoway Town to search for the accused. The council placed blame on settlers "who for their own private interest harbour and furnish them with Guns Powder and Shott and sell them rum and other strong Liquors which gives rise to many quarrels." Consequently, the council prohibited trafficking "Gunns, Powder or Shott" with the Tuscarora or any "foreign Indian under the "utmost Severity of the law." On October 29 the council issued a proclamation stating that they had recaptured two of the six accused and two of their companions in New Kent County.

The council also ordered the indicted Tuscarora be sent "with all convenient speed" to Williamsburg, where they would stand trial before an oyer and terminer court on November 19, 1707. The council summoned six freeholders who lived in the vicinity of the murder to give material evidence to the court. Likewise the council ordered the other Tuscarora remanded to serve as witnesses. The order for the Tuscarora's appearance at the capitol, even though the crime was committed in New Kent County, differed from the treatment of enslaved Africans and Native tributaries whose oyer and terminer hearings were tried in the county where the crime was alleged. The reason likely was that the Tuscarora were not tributary to Virginia. Whites were also tried at the capitol for capital offenses after 1710, when the government extended regular courts of oyer and terminer jurisdiction to them.[6]

President of the council Edmund Jenings tasked Henry Briggs to be "interpreter to ye Southern Indians," to go to the king of the Tuscarora and alert him of the proceeding, and to dispense other interpreters to the Nottoway, Meherrin, Nansemond, Pamunkey, and Chickahominy, all tributaries to the Crown, to encourage them "to bring with them two of the Great men of the respective nations" to the trial. The attorney general chose Rev. John Clayton to assist him at the trial. The council then queried Harrison, because he was "best acquainted with the temper of the Indians," whether he should send his traders or the tributaries to give notice to the Tuscarora of the impending trial. The council received word from Harrison on November 21 that the message had been sent to the Tuscarora and they had replied that they were sending two of their great men and one of the accused in a couple of days. The other three were not in their towns. The council postponed the trial until January 1708 and demanded that the Tuscarora surrender the fugitives.[7]

After the trial of Jack Mason, an inquiry into his whereabouts during the killing fleshed out an alibi: he was at Colonel Hill's, "at the place he usually slept," the night Pate was killed. Since he had already been convicted of murder and sentenced to death, the board, unanimously concurring that Jack Mason was the "proper object of mercy" and lacking the power to overturn the verdict, petitioned the Crown for a reprieve on March 18, 1708. The council then ordered Harrison to task two or three traders by conveying the message that the colony was still seeking the extradition of the suspected murderers. Rather than stand trial, George and Thom Jumper purportedly poisoned themselves. The council learned from "their own Indians" that Charles, Stephen, and Will Mason were being secreted in the Tuscarora towns. It warned the Tuscarora that if they did not surrender these accused, then "they must expect this Government will fetch them."[8]

In addition, the government demanded the return of Will, Lotto, Jamice, and Roger, who served as witnesses at Mason's trial. The traders were ordered not only to keep "an exact Journal" of their conferences with the Tuscarora but also to surreptitiously "inform themselves as well as they can (without making the Tuscaruros acquainted) of the number and strength of each particular town."[9]

The council recorded on April 20, 1708, that Harrison had learned from the traders to the Tuscarora towns that some were willing to turn over those suspected of Pate's murder, but others said they would "rather hazard their lives" before they extradited Charles. The traders had given the Tuscarora the council's demand that they had twenty days to surrender Charles, Stephen, and Will Mason or to explain their noncompliance. The council ordered the sheriffs of Henrico, Prince George, Surry, Isle of Wight, and Nansemond Counties "to signify to every one of the Indian Traders within their respective Countys . . . that they do not furnish or sell to the s^d Tuscaruro Indians or any other for their use any Arms powder or Shott untill further order, Which they may expect as soon as Satisfaction is made to this Government concerning ye three Indians suspected of the aforesaid Murder." Since that deadline was fast approaching, on June 10, 1708, the council affirmed its belief that the withdrawal of commerce was the most expedient means to force the extradition of the suspects and ordered the drawing up of a proclamation to that effect. On July 29, 1708, President Jenings sought council's consideration on the continuing impasse with the Tuscarora. The council ordered the restraint of trade continued and sent a letter to the governor of North Carolina asking that the colony also "prohibit the supplying the said Indians with powder and Shott."[10]

A complaint and warrant against George Fountain, a free Black man likely related to John Fountain, brought to the council's attention on October 26, 1708, that Virginia traders were continuing to trade with the Tuscarora even after the issuance of the proclamation. A year after the alleged murder of Jeremiah Pate, the council on October 28, 1708, ordered the sheriff of Prince George County to arrest Fountain for violating the proclamation and to hold him in custody until he was able to post bail. They had to admit that the proclamation had not had its desired effect, because traders had covertly continued that commerce under the pretense that they were trading to the tributaries Nottoway and Meherrin. In light of this discovery, the council ordered a new proclamation restricting trade not only to the Tuscarora but also to any Native people "living to the Southward of James River."[11]

Even the Nottoway, who associated themselves with the Tuscarora, on October 30, 1708, accused them of a nighttime attack that left two Nottoway and a white man dead. The council gave them leave not only to pursue the perpetrators but also to align themselves with any other tributary willing to accompany them.[12] In turn, as Col. Randolph reported in February 1709, the Tuscarora sent two Nansemond and two Meherrin to investigate whether the white man lived. If so they would send in those accused of attacking the Nottoway. By April they had yet to deliver up the offenders. Nevertheless, Harrison reversed course on trade. Now he believed "the trade should be open, contrary to what he thought before."[13] A year later, on June 21, 1709, Benjamin Harrison reported that the Nottoway and the Tuscarora were complicit in the murder of two Saponi, tributaries to Virginia. The council ordered that he provide "what Satisfaction the Saponies can have in this particular according to [their] Custome."[14]

In addition to the Pate murder, both Spotswood and the author of a report titled "Memorial from the Virginia Indian Company" alleged that before the Tuscarora War, Native-on-English murders were frequent. The memorialist alleged that the Tuscarora had "committed divers murders on the inhabitants of Virginia," which led to government to prohibit trade with them, but the "prohibition proved ineffectual to restrain divers loose and disorderly people . . . who supplied them with arms and ammunition." Spotswood explained that the "abundance of loose people employing themselves in that trade and having no stock of their own were obliged to purchase goods at a dear rate, and thereby either become losers by the bargain, or to use such frauds in their dealings with the Indians, as have too frequently incited them to revenge the injustice by private murders."[15] They were trying to shift the blame, but not a bit of it was true. Spotswood had not reported "divers murders" occurring until after the war. He wrote on September 14, 1713: "The Alarms on the Frontiers of this Colony have been very much increas'd since the So. Carolina Indians [were] dispers'd by the Tuscaruros; these having settled themselves on the heads of our Rivers, and being, (as is Generally believ'd,) joyn'd by some of the Northern Nations, make frequent incursions, and have committed divers murders on our Inhab'ts."[16]

If Virginia gathered intelligence of the Tuscarora towns and put them on notice by not supplying them with arms and ammunition, the Tuscarora never capitulated to Virginia's demand to surrender Charles, Stephen, and Will Mason. Virginia's effort to show a united front with North Carolina against the Tuscarora coincided with the arrival of Palatine, Swiss, and German refugees in the two colonies. In 1709 Georg Ritter and Company, the leaders of the twenty thousand Palatine, Swiss, and German refugees who had dispersed to the three kingdoms in Great Britain, received funding from the Crown for their transportation to America because of British hostility to the immigrants. Francis Ludwig Michel and Christoph von Graffenried legally joined the company in 1710. Highly influenced by Michel's descriptions of the Potomac River region, Graffenried even had a map made of the area. They received a great deal of encouragement from Gov. Spotswood and contracted "above the falls of the Potomac, which [they] . . . paid 175£."[17] Spotswood welcomed eight hundred refugees on the Potomac River who "restored themselves a little in Virginia."[18]

Not to be outdone, the Lords Proprietors of Carolina offered Graffenried more than a little encouragement. As an enticement the Lords Proprietors even bestowed him with the status of baron, keeping up the feudalistic pretenses of John Locke's *Fundamental Constitutions of Carolina*. Graffenried in 1710 sent another 650 immigrants to a "tongue of land [between the Neuse and the Trent rivers] called Chattawka," which to Native speakers meant "where the fish were taken out" but to the settlers meant the "very hottest and most unhealthy place." He arrived with 150 more later that year. The "dishonest" Surveyor General John Larson, who showed him the tract, assured him it was both "unencumbered" and uninhabited by Native people.[19]

After surveying the land and parceling out tracts to heads of households, the Swiss refugees "within 18 months, managed to build homes and make themselves so comfortable, that they made more progress in that length of time, than the English inhabitants in several years."[20]

Although their progress induced jealousy among their Carolina neighbors, their difficulties came from the plots of the Native people "reacting to the rebel adherents of Col. Cary." Spotswood had intelligence that Cary had hesitated in his planned coup d'état against the government of Governor Hyde and his council, retreating westward where he recruited both rebels and the Tuscarora. After landing a party of his supporters and firing on Hyde's delegation with cannon, Cary, "his Mobb not being so great in action as in imagination," retreated to the backcountry, where he sought to gather a "greater Force" and threatens "to bring down the Tuscaruro Indians to his Assistance." Spotswood dispatched marines spare from his home defense to assist in putting down the insurrection, which he likened to Bacon's "fatal Rebellion."[21]

Spotswood later learned that Cary had promised the Tuscarora "great Rewards to engage them to cut off all the Inhabitants of that part of Carolina that adhered to Mr. Hyde." His offer was embraced by the young warriors, but "their old men who have the greatest Sway in their Counsels being of their own Nature suspicious that there was some trick intended them, or else directed by a Superior providence, refused to be concerned in that barbarous design."[22] Eventually, with Governor Spotswood's assistance, Cary was arrested and sent back to London to stand trial. Luckily for him, his case was returned to Carolina for judgment. This turmoil, which slandered both Hyde and Graffenried, fueled anti-English sentiment among the Native people. They believed that Graffenried "had come to expel them from their lands, and that they would be compelled to settle much further, towards, or even in, the mountains." "I convinced them that such was not my intention, and they could ascertain it by the gentleness and civility of my behaviour towards them," said Graffenried, "and by the payment which I made to them of the lands where I had settled at first, and where I had founded the small town of Newbern, although I had already paid double their worth to the Surveyor Lawson, who sold them to me as free of whole incumbrance, not telling me that there were Indians. Again, I had made peace and alliance with the King and his Indian dependents, which were well satisfied with me."[23]

Some "turbulent Carolinians" rode roughshod over the Native inhabitants, cheating them in trade, restricting their hunting near their plantations, and seizing "their game, arms, and ammunition," ostensibly for their trespass. Fed up with this abuse, the Native people "began to think of their

safety and of vengeance, what they did very secretly," which caught Graffenried unawares. On a pleasure excursion exploring the region, Graffenried
became lost and wandered into the community that had been removed from
Chattawka. Although he had good relations with them, he was nevertheless
apprehensive: "They would have had a good occasion to revenge themselves
on me, if I had done them any harm." To his relief he was well received by the
community and feted by the king.

> The King made me a present of a large piece of venison, they had bon-
> fires through all the night, and danced and sung during I was alone
> with my footman in the small tent which I got pitched to lie down, but
> I could not sleep on account of that noise. The next morning, the King
> gave me an escort of two Indians who saw me home; after having given
> them plenty to eat, I made them a small present and sent to the King
> in return of his cider two bottles of rum, a kind of brandy made out of
> sugar-dregs, which were gladly received.

This present-giving gesture likely saved his life: later this same king inter-
ceded on Graffenried's behalf when he was "made a prisoner and sentenced
by the Indians of the Upper-River."[24]

Later that year, in September 1711, Surveyor General Lawson had persuaded Graffenried to accompany him up the Neuse River to pick wild grapes
and to scope out how high up the river could be navigated and where a "a new
road to Virginia might be laid out." Graffenried certainly would not take
exception to these reasons. After all, Lawson had written in his *New Voyage to Carolina* that a "great Advantage comes from its being near Virginia,
where we come often to a good Market, at the Return of the Guinea-Ships
for Negro's, and the Remnant of their Stores, which is very commodious for
the Indian-Trade."[25] If Graffenried was interested in extending his colony
into the Old Dominion, he was also curious about the distance from Chattawka to the mountains. Lawson assured him that there was no threat from
Native people living along that branch of the river, for as he had written, the
"one great Advantage of North-Carolina is, That we are not a Frontier, and
near the Enemy." He had mortally miscalculated, for the Tuscarora were in
fact nearby, and a worthy adversary.

Still skeptical of Lawson, for security Graffenried brought with him two
close Native "neighbors, which we knew well, . . . and we thought that . . . we
had nothing to fear from the others." He also added two enslaved Africans
to the expedition to row their boat. They set out with provisions enough
for a two-week excursion. While searching for a place for the Virginia road,
Lawson borrowed one of Graffenried's horses and rode to the "great village

of Catechna." The Tuscarora wanted to know what he was doing there with a horse, an unusual sight in the area. He answered that he was returning the horse to Graffenried and that they were exploring upriver. This news "immediately alarmed" the Tuscarora, who kept the horse and warned the party "not to advance further in their country, that they would not allow it, and that we had to turn back, by the orders of the King who resided there."[26]

Upon hearing this news, Graffenried said they should "turn back at once," but Lawson laughed at him. Soon afterward Native people surrounded the party, captured them, and led them over two days to the town of Coerntha, where the river shallowed to less than three feet. At their request they were taken to Catechna, where they hoped to "justify" themselves to King Hancock [Hencock]. When they arrived at the fortified town, they were surprised to see Hancock sitting "in state, with his Council, on a kind of scaffold." At first they were free to walk about the town and were fed "'dumplins,' and some venison." That evening people from neighboring towns crowded the capital for the convening of the "Assembly of the Great, 40 elders sitting on the ground around a fire according to their custom, . . . to discuss two matters: (1) How they would avenge themselves for the rough dealings of a few wicked English Carolinians who lived near the Pamptego, News, & Trent Rivers; (2) to feel their way as to the help which they could expect from their Indian neighbors."[27]

Before these matters could be decided, the king questioned Graffenried and Lawson. They were provided with a counsel "who knew English very well"; the "youngest of the Assembly" was tasked "to represent and defend the interest of the Council." Satisfied that their purpose was not staking out a settlement but rather an excursion to forage for wild grapes and to explore the river's navigation "in order that goods could be brought to them by water and trade carried on with them," the council queried them about the point of the convention: what role did they play in the recent routing of the Native people by Carolinians living along the Pantego, Neuse, and Trent Rivers? Although named among the offenders, Lawson acquitted himself well enough and the council voted to free the men.[28]

The next day before they could get to their canoe, some of the councilors and two "foreign Kings" waylaid Graffenried and Lawson, curious to know more about their "reasons of justification" for the slaughter. They were taken about two miles away from Catechna to the town of Core, where the king reproached Lawson and provoked a quarrel with him. Although Graffenried tried to calm Lawson down, he persisted in quarreling. After their "examination," when they were free to walk about, Graffenried upbraided Lawson for his insolence. Then "three or four of the 'Great' pounced" on them, took them to a Council of War meeting, and sentenced them to death.

Graffenried's suspicion for the turnabout was soon confirmed by a Native "dressed like a Christian who spoke English well." He asked, "Why Lawson had quarreled with Cor Tom? That we had threatened that we would avenge ourselves on the Indians."[29] Hearing this interpretation, Graffenried pleaded for his life. He maintained that he was blameless, pointing out that he had repeatedly remonstrated against Lawson's menacing bombast. Taken to the execution grounds and forced to endure the ritual that preceded carrying out the sentence, Graffenried made one last plea professing his innocence. Knowing someone among them could translate his words, he said that he had come to North Carolina as an emissary of the queen of England to "live on good terms with them" and that she would "avenge my blood." He also made his intentions known that he could be of service to them. He noted a grandee among them, a relative to King Taylor, who had sold him the land Chattawka, who could vouch for him. Clearly moved by his plea, the war council decided to seek King Tom Blunt's referral and recommended Hancock should "liberate" Graffenried, but they still executed Lawson.[30]

The day after Lawson's execution, the town notables alerted Graffenried of their intention to make war on North Carolina, singling out for their vitriol the settlers on the rivers of Pantego, Neuse, and Trent and on Core Sound. For this reason they would delay his release for six weeks, lest he warn the colony of their planned attack. They promised not to attack his Chattawka, which could serve as a refuge. He observed that after the war began a force of five hundred warriors arrived from "different places," including the lower "part" of the Tuscarora, but not from "the most important villages." They converged with the Mattamuskeet, the Coree, and others from the "Bory, Wetock, Pamptego, News, [and] Trent" Rivers.[31] On his own accord, Graffenried sounded out a peace between his German colony and the Tuscarora and "their neighbors from Core, Wilkinson's Point, King Taylor, those of Pamptego and others from that country."[32]

The treaty consisted of six parts. First, the two parties pledged future friendship and to "let bygones be bygones." Second, the German colony would remain neutral in the continuing war with the English. Third, Graffenried pledged not to expand his colony any further into Native country "without due warning to the King and his nation." Fourth, he promised a fifteen-day truce to secure the peace. Fifth, the Native people had free access to hunt, except on the plantations, least they frighten the cattle or start fires. Sixth, the German colony would sell trade goods at a "reasonable price," and the Native signatories would not molest any home where the door bore the letter N, "the mark of News [Neuse]."[33]

Reacting both to the war waged by "some of the Towns of the Tuscarora and other Indians on the Frontiers" in North Carolina and to Graffenried's

FIGURE 11. Baron Christoph von Graffenried, Surveyor General John Lawson, and an enslaved African at Core. Image courtesy of Burgerbibliothek Bern, Mss.Mül.466.

detention, the council, meeting at Maj. Nathaniel Harrison's house, extended its ban on trading from weapons to "any Sort of Commodity" to the Tuscarora and "any other Indians." They also sent Peter Poythress [Pothres), a trader, interpreter, and militia officer in Prince George County, to invite the Tuscarora towns that had not participated in the late raids on the North Carolina river settlements to a conference at the Nottoway town on October 17. The council offered to lift the trade embargo and assured the Saponi safe passage to and from the meeting by sending a guard to Saponi Town to escort them. They also enclosed a letter to the town where Graffenried was being held, threatening the "whole town or Nation" if he suffered "any violence." Understanding that a demonstration of "the Strength and force of this Colony may be very necessary to awe the said Tuscarora Indians not only to continue in peace with us but also to joine in the Destruction of those Assassines It is Ordered that the whole Militia of the Countys of Isle of Wight Surry and Prince George be drawn together under arms at the Nottoway town with six day's provisions against the time the said Tuscarora are expected there."[34] "As they stand in Awe of this Government," Spotswood wrote to the council, "both from the opinion they have of our Strength and their apprehensions of the loss of our Trade upon a Rupture, I hope at this Conference to work so far on their Fears and interest as at least to preserve their Friendship."[35]

The reasons the upper Tuscarora towns did not participate in the 1711 attack and remained neutral, historian Thomas Parramore explains, were partly commercial and partly racial.[36] King Tom Blunt, his name bearing out the creolization among the upper Tuscarora, took a wait-and-see attitude, conscious of their entrenched relations with the English. The original meaning of the term, which originated with the Portuguese *Crioulo*, the Spanish *Criollo* meant American-born Africans and later applied to the American born regardless of nationality. Atlantic Creoles were people, Indigenous or not, who participated in commercial networks forged in the Atlantic world, according to historian Ira Berlin.[37] They spoke the trade language, often a combination of their language and the language of the chief commercial partner, sometimes called pidgin but often called Creole. They were certainly conscious of Christianity, if not Christian themselves, and could have intermarried with Europeans. Their names often reflected their personal relations to colonizers and traders. Not only had the upper Tuscarora traded extensively with both Virginia and North Carolina, but they also intermarried with the English more so than the lower Tuscarora. The splintering between the two regions became evident with the reaction to turning over suspects in the Pate murder in 1707. Not unlike Blunt, the four witnesses and six accused, all Tuscarora, all had English names.

Intergenerational conflict also reared its head, Governor Spotswood indicated, when in June 1711 Cary tried to incite the Tuscarora to attack Governor Hyde. The elders held in check the young warriors ready to wage war.[38]

A week later, on October 15, the council convened again and came up with the following contingencies. First, Virginia's best course of action would be to persuade the neutral Tuscarora "to carry on a War by themselves" against the Native belligerents. For this consideration they proposed paying a bounty of "suitable rewards . . . for the head of each man of the Indian Enemy which they shall kill and bring in, and also for each Woman or Child taken prisoners and delivered here." Second, if the neutral Tuscarora decided to remain on the sidelines, then the Dominion would ally with Carolina to wage war and then hostages would have to be taken to ensure "their fidelity." Third, the council put the frontier counties on alert by ordering a militia unit of ten under an officer to patrol at least three days a week to prevent incursions.

Finally, in order to distinguish the friendlies from the hostiles, the government required Native tributaries to wear copper badges and Native people "in Amity" with Virginia to wear pewter badges when hunting or interacting with settlers within the Dominion.[39]

Wearing badges when abroad was not a new thing. Robert Beverley, the colony's historian, had noted an earlier law that required Native people to paint their bodies to "distinguish themselves" from one another because they are "often much embroiled in War one with another." Over time it came to pass "that the Virginia Assembly took up the humour, of making Badges of Silver, Copper or Brass, of which they gave a sufficient number, to each Nation in amity with the English, and then made a Law, that the Indians should not travel among the English Plantations, without one of these Badges in their Company to show that they are Friends."[40]

Before word of the treaty could be delivered to New Bern by Graffenried's enslaved man, "some strange Indians with a horse" arrived with the injunction dated October 8, 1711. Governor Spotswood demanded Graffenried's release, warning that "we intimate and command you in the name of the Queen of Great Britain, whose subject he is, that at sight of this order you liberate him and send him to our Government. And we let you know by these presents that if you kill him or do him any violence or harm whatever, We shall avenge his blood, and spare neither men, nor women or children." To demonstrate his resolve, Spotswood led a "strong escort" to the Native town of Ratoway, where he commanded the "neighboring militia" to stand ready. Since no one could translate the letter, the cautious Native warders allowed Graffenried to go to the Tuscarora town Tasqui, where a Virginia trader who could corroborate his reading of the letter resided. He then went on his horse with four "notables of Catechna" to the "most important" town of Paski, "fortified with palisades, and the houses or cabins were neatly made out of tree bark, they stood in a circle, and in the midst of them was a beautiful round place, in its centre a big fire, and around it the Council sitting on the ground, that is the leaders of the Tuscoruros' nation." Graffenried met them accompanied by the four notables and the Virginia trader, who sojourned there. Although the trader spoke for Graffenried "the best he could" and the four Native emissaries who accompanied him attested to his innocence and the need to be liberate him, especially in light of Spotswood's threat, the "seven delegates from Catechna would not yield to this."

On November 17, 1711, Spotswood reported to the Lords Commissioners on his efforts to defend the southern borders by engaging the deputies of the Tuscarora of the upper towns.[41] He had already assembled at a militia of six hundred men from three neighboring counties, which "very much surprised" their five great men when they arrived at Nottoway Town. The deputies distanced themselves from the war in North Carolina and resolved to remain at peace with Virginia. However, Spotswood wanted more. Putting into play the plan worked out the month before with the council at Major Harrison's house, he demanded that they "carry the war against . . . those Assassins" and deliver two children of the great men of each town to act as hostages and to be educated at white schools: "The delivering their Children as Hostages will not only prove the most effectual Security for their fidelity," he reasoned, "but may be a good step towards the Conversion of that whole Nation to the Christian faith."[42]

Having offered a ransom for Graffenried and a threat if he was not liberated, Spotswood "made three proposals to the Tuscaroras: that they would join with the English to cut off those Indians that had killed the people of Carolina, that they should have 40 shillings for every head they brought in of those guilty Indians and be paid the price of a slave for all they brought in alive, and that they should send one of the chief men's sons out of every town to the College."[43] On October 24 Spotswood said that "pursuant" to the resolution passed nine days earlier, on October 15, he met with the Tuscarora emissaries, who were "very desirous" for peace with both Virginia and Carolina, at the Nottoway town conference, where they agreed to terms. These upper Tuscarora towns were motivated enough to align themselves with the English against the Native people responsible for the "late Massacre, upon promise of a reward of six blankets for the head of each man of the said Indians killed by the Tuscaruros, and the usual price of slaves for each woman and Child delivered [as] captives." They asked that Virginia wait until November 25 for them to return to Williamsburg with their final answer because they had to consult with their "respective towns . . . before "entering into the said War and their delivering Hostages for their Fidelity."[44]

Taking advantage of this "favorable conjuncture," Spotswood proposed to the tributary nations that they too send their children to college, offering to remit their "whole tribute of skins as long as they kept their Children at the College." The tributary nations had shied away from sending their children to college, because "instead of their Children receiving the promised education they were transported (as they say) to other Countrys and sold as Slaves." Spotswood pleaded for more funding, because the backing of Boyle Charity, an endowment from the estate of the scientist Robert Boyle for the room, board, and education of Native youth at the Brafferton Indian School in Williamsburg, was insufficient to his goal for the "the Conversion of that whole Nation." He had some success in persuading them otherwise, he wrote to Lord Dartmouth: "The King of the Nansemonds has already sent his son and Cousin, the Nottoways and Meherrins have sent each two of their Chief men's Sons to be brought up to Learning and Christianity, and the Queen of Pamunkey, upon seeing how well these Indian Children are treated, has engaged to send her son and the Son of one of the Chief men upon the same foot, and I also expect another boy from the Chickahominys."[45]

By December Spotswood could claim that he had in custody at the college "hostages from all the Towns of our Tributary Indians." Part of the conversion process meant clothing them "after the English manner," a process that Spotswood contended they cherished. Although the Tuscarora had agreed in their treaty with Virginia to surrender hostages from eight towns to ensure their fidelity, their status was in jeopardy, because the burgesses had such loathing for them that they were for "extirpating all the Indians, without distinction of Friends or Enemys." Rather than supporting Spotswood's hostage plan, the burgesses joined with South Carolina in condemning all the Tuscarora and offering twenty thousand pounds in support of the war against those "concerned in the late Massacre." After the delegation of the upper towns arrived and explained their lateness and "expressed their readiness to assist us against the Indians concerned in ye late Massacre, and their desire to continue in a strict Friendship with all her Maj'ty's Subjects, and more especially by their interposing for the delivery of the Baron de Graffenried out of the hands of the Enemy, upon my desire, having given proofs of their good disposition to peace."[46]

Although Graffenried's Native advocates were wary of Spotswood's military threat, they appeared more concerned about losing the promised presents. They allowed that they would liberate him once the king and his council assented, yet despite the Virginia trader's offer of surety for the presents, "they insisted upon keeping my negro as a security, until the ransom would be paid." Despite assurances, Graffenried feared he would "be burnt on that inflamed wood-pile, or to be secretly slaughtered in that terrible desert." On his return to Catechna, which he described as being "in the midst of a dreadful desert, surrounded with thickets, thorns, and swamps, there was a fine wheat-field, with an Indian cabin, and the place was surrounded with a deep river, which made a small island of the whole, so that nature had built there a small fort well-nigh impregnable[47]."

Nevertheless, the absence of any warriors and the presence of only women, children, and old people added to his anxiety, which redoubled with the Native advance against the Carolinians. Three hundred "rogue" Indians had convened at Catechna before raiding nearby Christian settlements, including the Palatines, and returning "with some horses, victuals, hats, boots, and a few jerkins." After their next expedition, they returned "in triumph with the booty and christian prisoners." Graffenried observed that in celebration

> they burnt bonfires in the night,—especially, they built a big one in the great place of executions, where they raised three wolf's hides, figuring as many Protectors or Gods, and the women brought offerings, consisting in their jewels, for instance necklaces of wampon, which are a kind of coral, made out of white, violet, and golden colored shells, previously burnt. There was, in the midst of that circle, the Conjuror, I mean their priest, who made all kind of contortions, conjurations, and

threatenings, and all the remaining populace danced in a circle around the hides. A couple of days after the festival, Graffenried once again pleaded his case to the king. Assured because of their victories, the king and council consented to his "entire liberation" but would not offer him an escort back to Chattawka.[48]

After his liberation he bushwhacked through the Catechna forest to find his way home. Arriving "half dead," he was pleased to find the town of New Bern "fortified . . . since I knew only too much about the cruel raid of the Indians along the rivers Pamptego [Pantego], News [Neuse], and Trent, where, resolved to lay waste the whole country, they burnt, killed, and plundered whomsoever and whatever they found in their way."[49] After his recovery he learned that sixty to seventy of his colony had been "slaughtered, the others, who ran away, were robbed and plundered," leaving only about forty men capable of bearing arms. For these reasons he requested that the governor "supply us with the necessary provisions and ammunition, and with well-armed troops" to repel the Tuscarora. He registered his disgust that the Albemarle region residents looked with "scandalous" indifference on the people nearest the danger.[50]

After his ordeal Graffenried began to rethink the causes of the war. In addition to the abuses by the Carolinians, he now concluded the "negligence and carelessness" of the proprietary government in dealing with the Native people had contributed to the war. Trusting them "too much," the administration had neither built forts nor filled granaries. Nor had they organized an army to defend the colony but had pieced together one or two militia companies, where "everyone pretended to keep and defend his own house," giving the Native warriors the "good opportunity" to pick off one plantation at a time. Since he now believed the Native people would not abide by their treaties, he advised that Carolina "mislead them with my truce, as has already been said so as to gain time to gather men in sufficient number, and necessary stores as well in ammunitions as in victuals, in order, not only to be on a good foot of defense, but even to drive them away from the territory, far more, to render them powerless for harm in the future, so as to have nothing more to fear from them."[51]

After his release Graffenried was the target of invective by the North Carolinians who felt that his conduct was complicit in the Native attack. His appearance was compelled before the General Assembly, which consisted of the upper house of the Lord Proprietors and the lower Delegates of Commons. He had to defend himself against the secret accusations, which led to as many as twenty-three articles being drawn up against him by "false accusers and slanderers" who feared revealing themselves because they had "some inkling" of how he had acquitted himself to governors Hyde and Spotswood. Nevertheless, without reassurance from Hyde, he began to entertain future prospects for his Palatines in Virginia and Maryland. His present concerns, however, had to do with the security of the settlers, for they were woefully unprepared to defend themselves. In addition to their inadequate supply of provisions, they lacked guns, ammunition, and gunpowder. He began to look to Virginia to see if Spotswood would give them a lift. Noting that they could not field even three hundred able-bodied soldiers, and these "neither well clothed nor well-armed, had no ammunition, and felt not at all inclined to go to battle," Graffenried received a commission to negotiate with Governor Spotswood for "men and sufficient provisions." In response Spotswood, offering his services "in the name of the Queen of Great Britain, provided a settled salary would be paid to the soldiers and the eatables and war provisions returned."[52]

Even though the House of Burgesses had endorsed the treaty with the Tuscarora "concluded" at the Nottoway Town conference, it did not, when meeting in February 1712, provide the funding necessary to carry the treaty out. Nevertheless, drawing on the credit of individual councilors, Spotswood determined his best course of action to keep the Dominion safe was to carry out the treaty obligations to keep the upper Tuscarora towns "in our interest." He still had concerns about the French inciting their Native trading partners to the west and the Seneca, "a numerous people," who had lately stirred up "scattered bodies" of the Native peoples bordering Virginia to revenge themselves "on us on account of one of their Kings being killed some time ago by an Inhabitant of this Colony as he was hunting." To guard against this threat, Spotswood proposed outfitting a troop of three hundred soldiers to guard the frontier. Admittedly the greater danger continued to be in North Carolina, "where the Indians daily gather strength and have already besieged a party of the Inhabitants in a small Fort they had built for their protection."[53]

Baron de Graffenried's treaty, which he had negotiated under duress, safeguarded his Palatine colony with a promise of neutrality and offered North Carolina a diplomatic approach to the war. No good deed goes unpunished, however: Graffenried was suspected by North Carolina even though he pledged his loyalty to the proprietary. Yet he had the "very great advantage" of his experience, which made him uniquely qualified to share his knowledge of Tuscarora's strength and plans. Nevertheless, the combined threats of retaliation if the Tuscarora learned of his duplicity and of prosecution if North Carolina brought him to trial had caused him to reconsider settlement in Virginia. Not only would the removal to Virginia avail both his colony and new immigrants from Germany and Switzerland, Spotswood opined, but it also offered a "great advantage to this Country and [would] prove a strong Barrier against the incursions of the Indians if they were properly disposed above our Inhabitants."[54]

If he believed that defending the frontiers to the south was incumbent, he also noted that Graffenried, now out of Hyde's clutches, searched the Potomac region for silver mines and settlement sites. He had "come hither with a design to settle himself and sev'll Swiss familys in the fforks of Potomack, but . . . he now finds Claims made to it both by the Proprietors of Maryland and the Northern Neck." For this reason he began to look to the frontier reaches, where his colony could serve as a barrier to western and northern Native nations. In the end he chose a site just below the fall of the Potomac River and an island upriver, which he named Canavest, where his colony would christen their settlement, partly because "it was very well situated to carry on trade in Virginia, Maryland and Pennsylvania" and partly because the Native people "had planted some fine Indian corn."[55]

Col. John Barnwell, dispatched by South Carolina as commander of the Tuscarora expedition, organized a force of Native peoples at a fraction of the cost Spotswood demanded. Barnwell's letters documented his campaign against the Tuscarora from the banks of the Neuse River Fort, beginning on February 4, 1712, to the treaty following the siege of Hancock's fort, which he renamed Fort Barnwell, signed on April 20, 1712. Barnwell recorded that he had ordered Captain Bull to recruit Native men, collecting 200 during the march from the Pee Dee River to the Cape Fear River. By the time he crossed the Neuse River on February 4, two-thirds had deserted. Only sixty-seven remained when they entered Fort Narhantes, where his gathered forces numbered 495 Native warriors and 33 white ones, including Captain Bull, Major Mackay, and himself. Barnwell deployed them in four units: (1) Captain Steel's Troop, comprising 30 white men including Palatines, 158 Yamasee, and 155 Essaw; (2) Yamasee Company, with 87 Yamasee, 10 Hog Logees, 56 Apalatchees, and 5 Corsaboy; (3) Essaw Captain Jack's Company, comprising 28 Watterees, 20 Sagarees, 40 yeh is-WAH h'reh, 27 Suterees, 27 Waxaws, and 13 Congrees and Sattee; (4) Captain Bull's Company, consisting of 28 Watterees, 18 Pedees, 24 Weneaws, 11 Cape Feare, 11 Hoopengs, 9 Wareperes, 42 Saraws, and 22 Saxapahaws.[56]

On February 5, 1712, Barnwell's army marched through six Native towns and several "ruined" plantations with 178 Native and 25 white troops, suffered a casualty rate of about ten percent, and achieved victory.

Early in February a force of 700 South Carolina Indigenous warriors under Barnwell's command destroyed six Tuscarora towns, captured an "abundance of prisoners, and found among them a considerable Booty of English goods." He prayed that this victory would prevent the Tuscarora

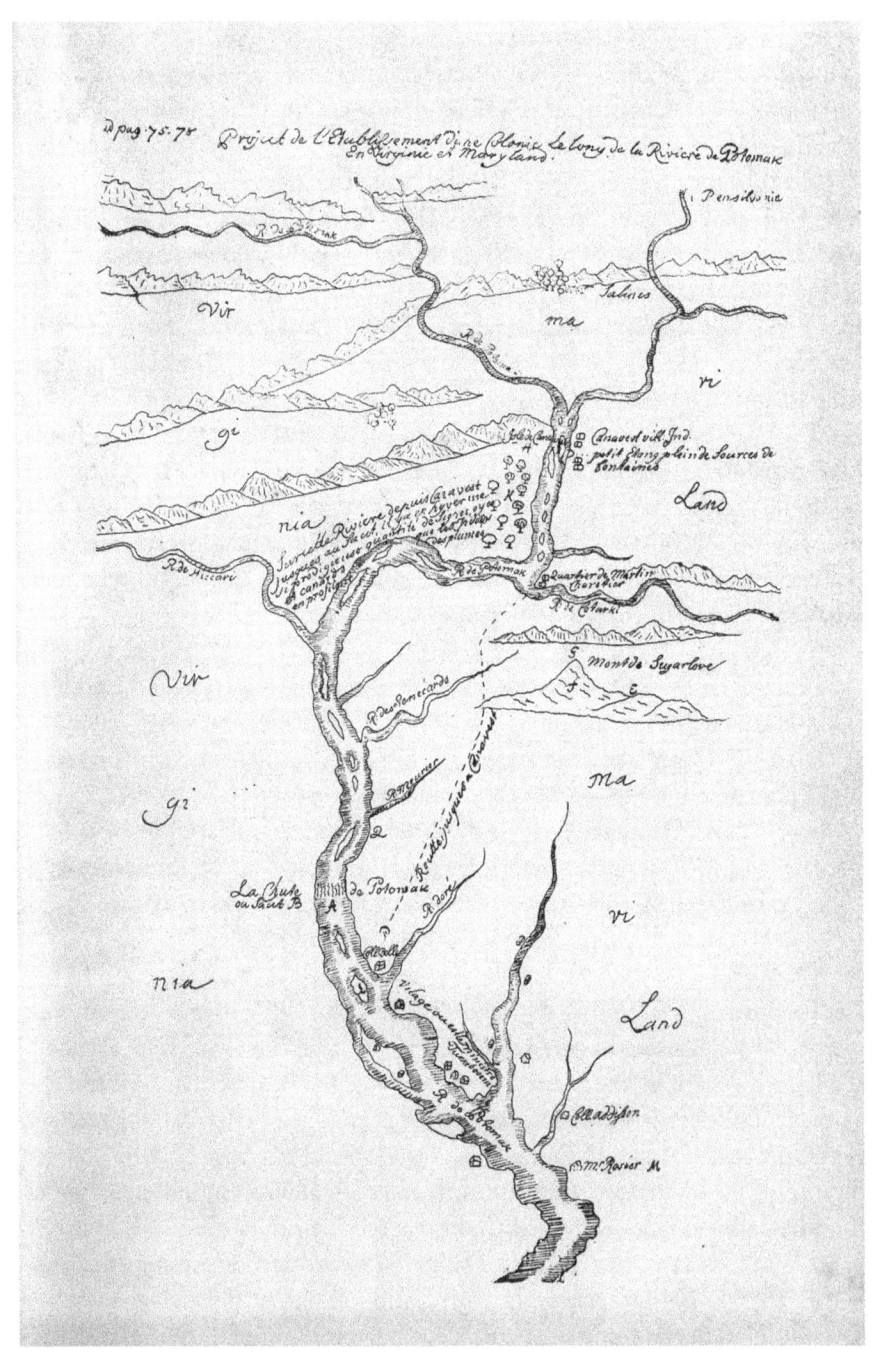

FIGURE 12. *Map of the Potomac River, 1711*, in Baron Christophe von Graffenried, *Relation du Voyage d'Amérique* (1716), reprinted by A. B. Faust. Wilson Special Collections Library. Image courtesy of University of North Carolina at Chapel Hill.

strategy of aligning with the Seneca in a "formal war" against North Carolina and Virginia. The Seneca had about thirty advisers among them, promising supplies of English arms and ammunition and "the Assistance of the whole Strength of that Nation."[57]

On February 5, 1712, Barnwell called upon the Yamasee to stay the course even though they were "in the heart of the Enemy's Country." They replied absolutely with the exclamation—"Wough!"—with no one dissenting. The prisoners told Barnwell that "most of the young men were gone down to Hancock, where they would compose a force of less than 500 armed men," but not under one command. "The rest were fled towards Virginia as old men women and children, that they were obliged to disperse into small parcells because they had no provisions but must gather hickory nutts."[58] A month later, on March 5, Barnwell's army had finally arrived at King Hancock's fort, which he learned later had been designed by Harry, a fugitive African who had fled from Virginia to the Tuscarora. Dove Williamson, an assemblyman representing Berkeley County, South Carolina, where the enslaved laborers grew rice, had him "sold into Virginia for roguery."

> I immediately viewed the Fort with a prospective glass and found it strong as well by situation on the river's bank as Workmanship, having a large Earthen Trench thrown up against the puncheons with 2 teer of port holes; the lower teer they could stop at pleasure with plugs, and large limbs of trees lay confusedly about it to make the approach intricate, and all about much with large reeds and canes to run into people's leg. The Earthen work was so high that it signified nothing to burn the puncheons, and it had 4 round Bastions or Flankers.[59]

Their stronghold proved impenetrable; Barnwell's troops were unable to breach it despite two attempts. After the siege Barnwell was "amazed" at Harry's design of the fort: "I never saw such subtill contrivance for Defence. . . . I might see by the strength of the place a good many would be killed before it could be forced." Perhaps Barnwell would not have been so amazed if he took into consideration the skill set of enslaved engineers in South Carolina's forced labor camps who constructed the colony's levees, floodgates, dams, and dikes for its rice fields. Historian David La Vere argues that, unlike customary Native tactics, the fortification design meant that the warfare took place "underground." After the siege Barnwell complained that the Tuscarora's supply of "forty buckskins worth of ammunition" purchased from Virginia traders—paid for with gold plundered from the plantations, which he learned about from correspondence with Governor Hyde and "relations of redeemed captives"—proved decisive. At the same time, North Carolina's inability to supply Barnwell with "but four days of provisions more" limited any siege opportunity. At the end of the day, after six white men killed and thirty-five wounded and one Native man each killed and wounded, and all at risk of starvation, Barnwell moved in the same way as Virginia, which he had a month earlier criticized: "the surrendering thereof upon articles, which leaves above 100 murderers unpunished besides the women and children of those villains killed and executed."[60]

Under the agreed-upon articles, the Tuscarora released twenty-four white captives and two enslaved Africans. Identified as a rogue, Harry, the fort's architect, was "cut to pieces immediately," the quickness and the ghastliness of the act indicative of the fury the English felt over his design. The Natives surrendered King Hancock, whom Barnwell sent to Virginia, three others deemed responsible for the initial attack, two sons of the Tuscarora king, and a brother of the Cove king as hostages. They "immediately" surrendered the fort, as well as "all the horses, skins, and plunder," and corn for the departing Native allies. To Barnwell's chagrin, he "got as much [corn] as furnished 40 Indians Essaws and Palatchees and sent them away, but to my great loss one of my slaves ran away with them." To Barnwell's connivance, he got the Tuscarora "entirely agreed" to surrender their allies, the disgruntled Coves, to him as slaves. The Tuscarora also entirely agreed to become tributary to North Carolina and pay an annual tribute to its governor in March. As tributaries they promised to present any grievances with the white colonials to the magistrates regularly. The final terms spelled out the limits of their country and their hunting grounds. They were now restricted to farm only on the creek where their fort was located on the Neuse River and to fish only on the Bear River between the Neuse and Pamplico Rivers. They were "to quit all pretentions" to hunt, forage, or fish on the lands between the Neuse and Cape Fear Rivers, now rewarded to the Carolina Native people who had aligned with the English. Any incursion into this region would be treated as an act of war. Finally, not only did the British demolish the Tuscarora flanks and forts, but they also demanded "the English have Liberty to march through the same with all Ensigns of honor."[61]

President Thomas Pollock and the General Assembly of North Carolina resolved not to agree to any "treaty of peace, neutrality or commerce" with the upper Tuscarora towns until they surrendered anyone "either alive or dead" who had participated with King Hancock in the attack and deliver "the great quantity of English goods and clothes with the scalps of white people found there." Conscious of Virginia's comity with the upper Tuscarora towns, North Carolina also wanted this announcement sent to Governor Spotswood to apprise him of these developments. North Carolina refused any renewal of relationships with nations that had aligned with

Hancock in the attack but would follow South Carolina's "laudable" policy "entirely to extirpate them."[62]

Barnwell contrasted this achievement to Virginia's failure to secure a complete victory. This realization "has struck the Dominion of Virginia into amazement and wonder, who a month before with 1,500 men in arms believed (to their great shame) they had obtained a glorious victory, when by the dreadful terror of their troops they begged a most ignominious neutrality of those cowardly miscreants, which they were so gracious to grant upon Condition to have goods at a cheaper rate and their children brought up at the College."[63]

Spotswood concurred on February 27, 1712, with Barnwell's assessment and lamented that Virginia had missed its "expected . . . share in cutting off those Indians." He blamed the shortfall on the General Assembly. "Our Assembly having voted twenty thousand pounds for that service; but after consulting the means how to raise it they found it too large for their purses, and instead of going on as they began thought of nothing more than how to get off that hasty Resolution." He did credit Barnwell for his victory over the Tuscarora and their Seneca advisers.

Unable to secure collateral for their military assistance, Spotswood continued his diplomatic schemes to co-opt the northern Tuscarora towns. On March 1, 1712, William Byrd II recorded in his diary that Peter Poythress had brought fourteen Tuscarora to negotiate with Governor Spotswood.

> They told us the Carolina men had killed no more than about 20 old men and women of their people and had taken about 30 children prisoners when all the young men were not at home, that the Tuscaroras could [cut] them all off but that they saw some English among them which hindered them and their business with the Governor was to give the reason why they could not perform their articles and to inquire whether they might defend themselves in case they're attacked.

Yet on March 16, 1712, Byrd learned from Peter Poythress that Spotswood had "received the Tuscaroras very coldly and ordered them to go and help the people of Carolina cut off Hancock town, which they all said they would."[64]

Little did they know that Barnwell had already sued for peace at Hancock Town.

By May Spotswood felt Barnwell had missed his opportunity to score an unconditional surrender. He acknowledged the "tolerable success" of his end of January march through the Tuscarora towns with a force of seven hundred Native warriors until he suffered the desertion of at least five hundred. His continued march and siege without waiting for either his supply line or reinforcement at the siege of Hancock's fort left him "so weak as to clap up a peace with the Indians upon very unaccountable conditions, and suffered about 160 of them to escape after he had reduced them to the last extremity, and could not have missed taking their Fort in a few hours, nor of breaking (in all humane probability) the power of those Indians, had he but waited for the arrival of the succours designed him."[65]

Barnwell examined several prisoners about what provoked the initial attack on the English. He found that they "all agree in one story." While they were treating with a mission of a dozen Seneca, the English unduly punished an inebriated Native man over a "small fault," not unlike the earlier affronts to Tuscarora sensibility. The Seneca said to them, "The Whites had imposed upon them and that when the whites had used them so, they knocked them on the head, they advised them that they were fools to slave and hunt to furnish themselves with the white people's food, it was but killing of them and become possessed of their substance, that they did not fear the want of ammunition for that, they would come twice a year and furnish them with it." After the consultation two Seneca remained with them, apparently guarantors of Haudenosaunee support. The prisoners were also in concert with their respective responses to the inquiry of whether any white people had "incited" them. "They unanimously answered no," but they did allow that the Virginia traders told them afterward that "the people Massacred were outlandish men and not English, and so they doubted not but soon to make peace with the English and that they were then about it."[66]

Barnwell had "clapt up a peace with the Indians upon very odd and unaccountable conditions," Spotswood wrote. He himself broke the peace he had made and apparently never intended to keep by seizing "a great many Captives of those who looked upon themselves as secure under the Treaty he had made with them." Spotswood credited this action and Barnwell's "treachery" as the cause of two new "massacres," forcing the inhabitants of the Neuse and Pamlico Rivers to abandon their homes. Closer to home, a Tuscarora attack on a tributary Nottoway hunting party near the settlements left two wounded and three dead, which, Spotswood presaged, "seems only prelude to what we may expect after their conjunction with the Senecas."[67]

Of his hostages at the college, which Barnwell had ridiculed, Spotswood wrote to the bishop of London that he now had fourteen Native children and expected the arrival of six more from "our Neighbouring Nations." The neighboring nations, he clarified, were the tributary people: the Pamunkey, Chickahominy, Nansemond, Nottoway, Meherrin, Saponi, Stuckanox, Occaneechis, and Tutelo, "for there are no other foreign Nations near this Colony." He also solicited from the Society for Propagating the Gospel "one or two missionaries to reside at the principal towns of the neighboring nations."[68] Their population numbered 700, including about 250 warriors. Their principal commerce was with Virginia, where they exchange skins and furs for "clothing, powder and shot, and other European manufactures."[69] They were incentivized by Spotswood's offer to permanently quit the collection of tribute as long as the hostages remained at the college. "By this method of Civilizing and instructing their Youth in the principles of Christianity, there may be great hopes in time, of Converting the whole Nations to which they belong."[70] Two years later he reported of "several that can read and write tolerably well, can repeat the Church Catechism, and know how to make their responses in ye Church[;] both the parents, and the boys themselves, have shewn a great desire they should be admitted to Baptizm."[71]

Virginia had "no other Nations that frequent our frontiers besides the Tuscarora." Even as late as 1712, the Tuscarora boasted two thousand warriors. North Carolina considered Tuscarora, although independent, to be within its dominion. Before the outbreak of war, the Tuscarora had engaged in "a constant Trade" with Virginia for goods, as had the tributary nations. With the outbreak of hostilities, Spotswood, in support of North Carolina, embargoed "all Commerce with them till they give satisfaction for the murders committed in Carolina."[72]

Although he had concluded a "solemn treaty" with the upper-town Tuscarora to join the English the war against the lower towns, the governments of North Carolina and Virgina reneged on their promise to provide "wholly for their succor and the Relief of the Captives." Rather North Carolina refused to recognize the distinction between the Tuscarora towns, condemning all of them "in general" and not giving the upper towns the opportunity to demonstrate their fidelity.[73] For this reason, Spotswood lamented to Colonel Nehemiah Blakiston, "the Indians that committed the Massacre in Carolina are become very insolent upon their success and the faint attempts that have been made on them by the people of that Country, so that we daily expect, when it will be our turn, to be attacked by them."[74]

Drawing on a New York report addressed to North Carolina, Spotswood learned that the French had been "very active" in recruiting the Seneca to fully enter the war.[75] Spotswood considered Tuscarora War costly:

> We are now in very great apprehension of an Indian War; the Indians who committed the Massacre in Carolina being so elated with their Success and the weak efforts made against them by the people of that province, that they are become unaccountably insolent and daring, and we daily expect they will begin the like Tragedy here as they acted there, and upon such an Event, I'm sure there was never greater Occasion since Bacon's Rebellion.[76]

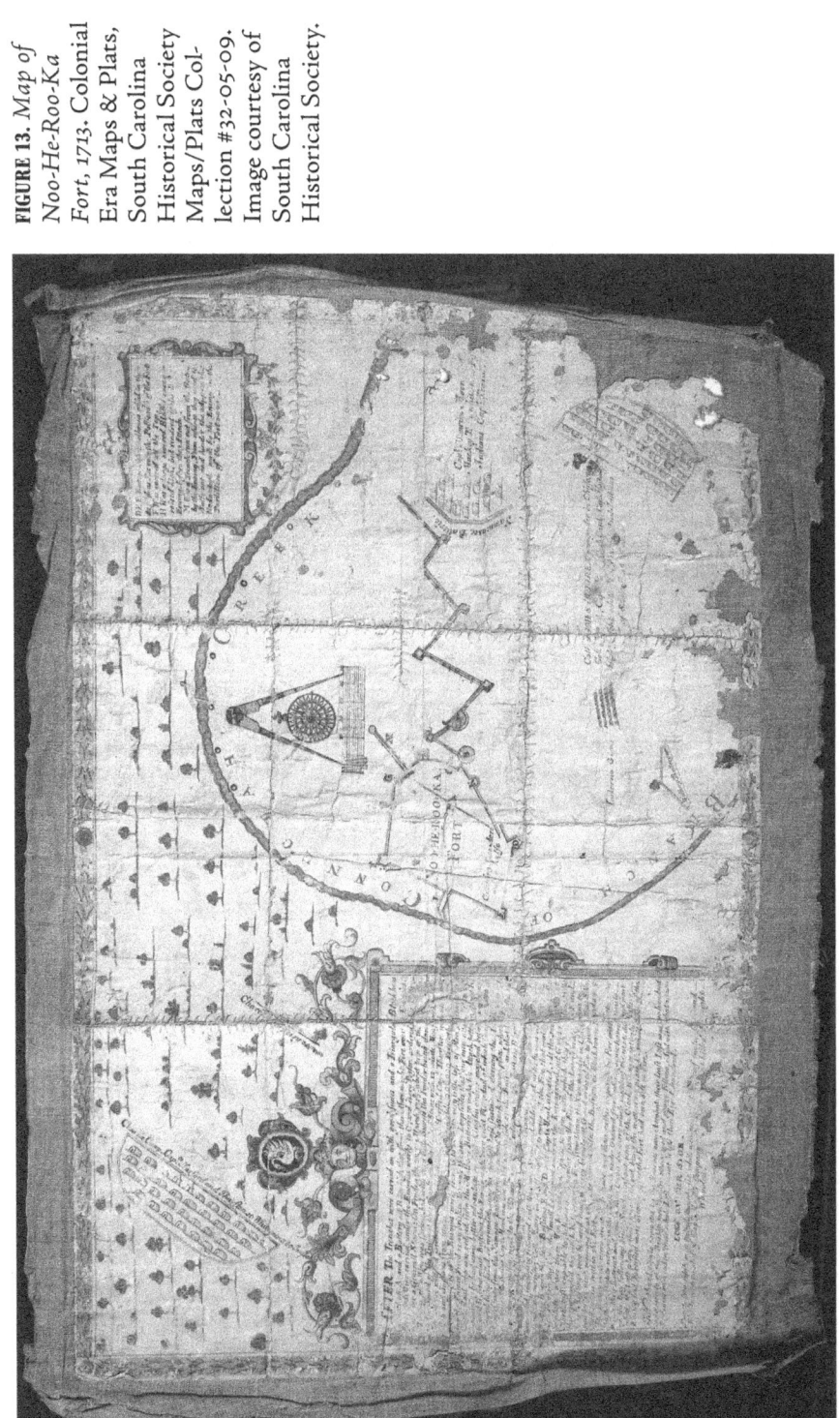

FIGURE 13. *Map of Noo-He-Roo-Ka Fort, 1713.* Colonial Era Maps & Plats, South Carolina Historical Society Maps/Plats Collection #32-05-09. Image courtesy of South Carolina Historical Society.

Peace still elusive, North Carolina chose Col. James Moore to lead the second expedition against the Tuscarora. He was victorious in battles fought to the Virginia border.[77] Drawing on the lessons of Harry's design at Hancock's fort at Catechna, the Tuscaroa built a "semi-subterranean" fort at Noo-He-Roo-Ka [Neoheroka] fronted on three sides by the Contentnea Creek. On April 16, 1713, Spotswood presented to the council a letter from President Thomas Pollock, acting governor of North Carolina. It detailed Col. James Moore's victory over the Tuscarora at the battle of Noo-He-Roo-Ka on March 20–23, 1713, when his army captured and killed as many as eight hundred Native combatants and took their fort. The timing could not be more fortuitous for North Carolina. Moore's success coincided with the withdrawal of the "greatest part" of his Native mercenaries from South Carolina. At the same time, North Carolina had exhausted its armed forces in the assault on the fort. Given this paucity of people and the "poverty" of the colony, the North Carolina Assembly would unlikely be willing to finance the war effort. With their inability to continue prosecuting the war, their prospects were "much bettered by the destruction of so great a number of their Enemy."[78] Spotswood counseled Pollock to negotiate a treaty with the Tuscarora at that point, "while their late Defeat was fresh in their memory." Undoubtedly, the Tuscarora were ready "to embrace any terms of peace . . . offered them." In order to maintain a lasting peace and the fidelity of King Tom Blunt, the sole adherent of the upper Tuscarora to the English side, Spotswood advised, recognize him as the chief of the Native people in North Carolina under the state's dominion and protection.[79]

CHAPTER 7

The White Men Would Come and Fetch the Yamasees in One Night

The "rumors" of Fontain and the other free Black Virginia traders promoting incursions, together with the embargo on Tuscarora trade in 1708, may have inspired the South Carolina Assembly to seize the merchandise of Virginia traders and to restrict their access in the western Native trade. These restrictions meant that Virginia traders had to go far afield for Native skins and furs. David Crawley, a Virginia trader, had qualms with the proprietary of South Carolina over the Native trade. Together with Robert Hix, a fellow Virginia trader, Crawley made a complaint to the Virginia council against the proprietary of South Carolina. In September 1707 they were "out trading" with "western" Native nations for a "considerable quantity of Skins and furrs," which they stored in "a certain nation of Indians called the Usherees [Euchees, Yuchi]." The government of South Carolina not only had seized and carried away their supply but also had issued an order to strip the partners of their goods on their return and send them back to Virginia. Hix went to Charles Town to find out why the governor seized their goods and to seek restitution for their losses. After several weeks of waiting for an audience at considerable expense, the governor "detained [him] without any redress" and obliged him to post £500 sterling bond, stipulating that he was "never to cross the Santee River again" without good cause.[1]

The difficulties Hix and Crawley experienced in 1708 were compounded by the "indisputable truth" of the Virginia-Native trade. The "Memorial from the Virginia Indian Company" (1717) blamed inflated prices relative to the "value of the commodity" for the "decay of commerce." Since the trade was "managed solely by persons of mean and rank circumstances" who were unable to purchase the goods from England, the traders were obliged to purchase the merchandise on credit from the merchant stores in country. Consequently, they passed on the higher cost of the goods to the Native buyers. Seeing the "great difference" in both the price and quality of the goods and feeling "too fatally the ill-usage," the Native traders judged that new traders would treat them better. So around 1708 Hix and Crawley mustered all the credit they had to make a trip to the Western nations, where they "disposed parts of their goods for skins and furrs." They were "sett upon by South Carolina traders who took both their skins and British trade goods from them under the pretense of laying a duty on skins and furrs and requiring them to and the exporters the same duty at the Port of Charlestown." The Virginia president and council appealed their treatment to the Privy Council, finding their traders unable to struggle with the South Carolina traders supported by their government.[2]

The LCTP took up its case, because South Carolina had "no authority to monopolize all the Indian trade exclusive of her Maj[t]y Subjects of her other plantations." The Lords Commissioners found this action "so strange and surprising," because they could not find any precedent. Indeed Virginians had engaged in the Native trade "without restraint" and wondered "whether there be any new authority granted them [South Carolina] or other cause happened for intercepting our Trade." The LCTP now insisted that "the bond so extorted may be cancelled and the restriction removed till such pretensions be adjusted."[3] On November 2, 1708, the Lords Commissioners ordered Hix and Crawley to inventory their loss.[4] In June 1709 the council learned that Virginia's trade with the Carolina nations had been "adjusted" by the Crown.[5] The council announced that the Crown had on September 26, 1709, supported its position and directed the government of South Carolina not to "for the future interrupt or molest the Indian Traders of this Colony passing through that Government"; a proclamation of this policy was issued and posted in the "several Countys where the Indian Traders dwell."[6] By December, Spotswood complained to the Lords Commissoners that he had "lately received Complaints of fresh interruptions given to our Indian Traders," which prompted "an Express to be sent to South Carolina."[7] Nevertheless, a year later, on September 5, 1711, Spotswood reported to the LCTP that contrary to the Crown's "positive Orders," South Carolina continued to exact a tax on Virginia traders passing through the province en route to trade with "western" Native people. The South Carolina Assembly had passed an act in June "in contradiction to her Majesty's Order" that proved an imposition to the Virginia traders.[8]

By 1710 Virginia began coveting tramontane Native country for settlement, security, and trade. In the fall Spotswood commissioned the Company of Adventurers, who explored the "highest" peak of the Great Mountains, about one hundred miles above the Virginia's "upper" settlement, finding the mountains easily traversable on horseback both upslope and downslope. New intelligence from Indigenous informants located the James River's source as a lake on the western side of the Great Mountains, which passes through their country. Securing permits from the Native inhabitants there would lead to settlements. Settling on the James westward of the Great Mountains would thwart the French designs from the Mississippi, enabling Virginia "to cutt off that communication and fix themselves so strongly there that it would not be in the power of the French to dislodge them." Settling there also meant "that a very profitable Trade might be established with foreign Nations of Indians, and our Indian Traders would find convenient places of Refreshment without being obliged (as they are now) to travell some hundreds of miles through Desarts before they can vend their Commoditys."[9] Because several unidentified Native people had been seen at the "head of the Rappahannock River, Col. Carter had ordered the militia to patrol to protect the inhabitants in the region."[10]

The Tuscarora War combined with South Carolina's duty had a substantial effect on Virginia's commerce with the western nations. Virginia suspended its trade with the outbreak of war in October 1711 in support of North Carolina until the Tuscarora give "satisfaction for the murders committed in Carolina." South Carolina, on the other hand, continued their trade. Since these nations had no congress with the Tuscarora, Spotswood said, under the "advice of the Council" he reopened that commerce in 1712, "lest it should be lost to us, and the Indians obliged to sue to the French for those Supplys which South Carolina can't furnish them." The route skirting the mountains to the southwestern Native trade markets required access through South Carolina, which the proprietary had prohibitively taxed. Spotswood once again raised his grievance: "It is still more unreasonable that the Carolina men should impose dutys and seize the goods of her Majesty's Subjects for barely passing through their Country." On the other hand, "our Traders assured me, they must travell at least 1,500 miles to come at the most considerable of them who live on the back of the Mountains in the Latitude of Virginia."[11]

The yeh is-WAH h'reh and the other piedmont nations had had a long history of trade with Virginia, dating back to before the John Lederer expedition. The yeh is-WAH h'reh had even positioned themselves as brokers between Virginia and the Ani'-Yun-wiya [Cherokee]. "Our Traders have ye Chiefest Traffique for Skins live some 4 or 500 miles to the So. West of us," Spotswood admitted in 1712, "and their names scarce known to any but the Traders."[12]

"The Ocheese Creek, Euchee, Savannah, Apalachee, and Yamasee villages," writes historian William L. Ramsey, had "formed a coherent zone of settlement along Carolina's oldest and most lucrative trade route, extending south and southwest from Charles Town into central Georgia."[13] For this reason Carolina had thwarted the Virginia traders' access to both the Carolina piedmont and western nations by exacting a duty on them. South Carolina was also late to trade with the Ani'-Yun-wiya, not engaging directly with them until 1713, and did not trade with the Chahta until 1714; Carolina traders Thomas Nairne and Pryce Hughes had promoted both of these relationships. The Welsh-born Hughes frequented the towns of the Natchez, Chahta, Chikashsha', and Ani'-Yun-wiya. He was an associate of Nairne, South Carolina's Indian agent, and together they promoted not only trade relations with the western Nations but also an alliance with the English against French Louisiana. Hughes's bond with the Natchez and the Chahta was particularly troubling to the French because both nations were formally aligned with Louisiana.

Although Spotswood had heard Hughes "was killed by some French Traders last war at one of the Chickasaw Indian Towns," the record of his death is muddled. Nevertheless, his "rambling" among "those Nations . . . more contiguous to the French Settlements than the English" had contributed mightily to a motive for his death. At the same time, both the Ani'-Yun-wiya and the Chahta continued to have access to the Louisiana French traders, who like the Virginia traders were willing to buy the usual arrangement of beaver pelts rather than insisting on the recent demand of deerskins now in vogue. Consequently, Carolina traders had to offer better terms to compete, and Carolina officials worked to limit the competition with both Louisiana and Virginia. These relationships with both Virginia and Carolina traders served as a disincentive to the western Nations' joining the Yamasee in their war against South Carolina.[14]

The Yamasee burned Nairne alive, an opening salvo in the war with South Carolina. On May 23, 1715, Gov. Charles Craven of South Carolina reported to Lord Townshend about the outbreak of a "most bloody war" two months earlier. He asserted that at the instigation of the French in Mobile and the Spaniards in St. Augustine, "our" Yamasee had allied with "neighboring" nations against them, "about 8,000 of them . . . [who] till now [were] entirely in our interest, and with whom we had a constant trade and commerce."[15] By using the possessive *our* in identifying the Yamasee, Craven revealed the sense of proprietorship with which Carolina viewed the Yamasee and the rationale for calling the war an insurrection rather than an invasion. The Carolina authorities had that learned an uprising was afoot in mid-April when a Yamasee let slip to a couple of traders living among them that the Yamasee had been "contriving to cutt off all the English and become sole masters of their fine and flourishing plantations." This plot frightened the "poor people" settled on the frontier so much that they requested time for the traders to beat a path to Charles Town, promising "that anything would be done to give them satisfaction." After "rideing night and day," the traders met with the council and apprised them of the situation. The council in turn dispatched the two Indian agents to offer convening a conference where "our chief men [could] hear and redress their complaints and grievances." Within a dozen hours of meeting with the Yamasee, the two agents "were knock'd on the head by the Indians, with several more white people who were barbarously tortured and murthered by them."[16]

The Yamasee had in the preceding half-century, argues historian John E. Worth, organized as a confederacy rather than a chiefdom. "While it seems likely that most or all of the Yamassee chiefs were indeed descendants of chiefly matrilineages . . . and that the individual towns they each ruled represented the human remnants of depopulated chiefdoms, the administration of the multi-community unit known as Yamassee appears to have been neither centralized nor hereditary"; rather, Worth argues, it is "a purely contingent social formation that united refugee towns from a number of collapsed chiefdoms into a social entity that eventually became a de facto ethnic group."[17]

In giving Craven, the "King at Charles Town," their justification for going to war with Carolina, the mico [chief] Huspah quoted the Indian agent: "Mr. Wright said that the white men would come and fetch [illegible] the Yamasees in one night and that they would hang four of the head men and take all the rest of them for slaves, and that he would send them all off the country, for he said that the men of the Yamasees were like women, and shew'd his hands one to the other, and what he said vex'd the great warrier's, and this made them begin the war."[18] It is thus no wonder that the Yamasee killed Wright and the other Indian agent, Nairne, at Pocotaligo Town to begin the war. Why they also tortured Nairne, who offered conciliation, is another question.[19] Mico Huspah said to Craven that the Yamasee considered him a brother, worthy of their love and of their compassion, and "may goe off himself." He also promised to spare the white men who chose not to fight but would kill those that did and make captives of their women and children. He continued that "the Indians have kill'd forty or fifty white persons, and the Indians are all comeing to take all the Country. They are three hundd. that are goeing to watch to take the Fort at Capt. Woodwards and that at Well Town for in short all the Indians upon the main are comeing and they say that the white People will not be a handful for them for they say they will fight Six year's but they will take the Country."[20]

The Yamasee immediately destroyed the nearby settlements, though "most of the people escaped" the assault. Hearing of "several massacres," Governor Craven mustered a "mount of men" and Native people "who live among us" and marched to cut off the Yamasee before they were reenforced by other nations. The Carolinians caught up with them and killed eleven Yamasee, while a score of Carolinians were wounded. Losing "several of their chief warriors and abundance of them being wounded, they flew from their towns and settlements and left their provisions and good plunder for our men," taking refuge in the swamp. The immediate threat gone, Carolina began the process of strengthening their defenses and buffering the

Lowcountry plantations. Recognizing their "sorry" number of only 1,500 white men, and these scattered throughout the colony, Craven moved to shore up their armed force by enlisting "200 stout Negro men. . . . These with a party of white men and Indians are marching towards the enemy." Although this mass mobilization meant fewer hands producing crops of corn and rice, which would be acutely realized at the next harvest, his "greatest discouragement . . . [was] the want of arms and ammunition."[21]

When William Byrd II, receiver general of Virginia, met with the Lords Commissioners on July 14, 1715, he placed the blame for the Native insurrection squarely on Carolina. When asked about the strength of Native forces, he said that the Yamasee and the Ani'-Yun-wiya were the "two most powerful nations" in the region. He estimated sixteen to seventeen thousand warriors among Native peoples bordering the "back of our plantations" from Carolina to New England. "If they should jointly attack Carolina, it would be impossible to prevent their destroying that province, Charles Town being the only place fortified, the rest of that province being all open country, and the settlements dispersed at great distances." He was not at all apprehensive about an uprising against Virginia. Not only did the Dominion have good relations with the Native nations, having "always well treated them," he said, but also Virginia was prepared to defend itself. Its ten-thousand-man militia measured ten percent of the Dominion's white population. The colony had also received "arms and ammunition for 300 men" from the Crown two years previously. He could not say the same for Carolina. The present hostility was "in a great measure owing to the Carolinians themselves, for their traders have so abused and so imposed upon the Indians in selling them goods at exorbitant prices, and receiving their peltry at very low rates, that they have been thereby very much disgusted." The Carolinians' greed extended to their trade policy, restricting Virginia's access to the Native market, ostensibly because these Native people resided within the boundaries of the proprietary's charter. Additionally, the Carolinians encouraged neighboring nations to wage war against other Native people to make captives for the slave trade. Some managed to escape and returned to tell what had happened to them. "This with the impositions upon them in trade, has so alienated them, that he thought it would be very difficult to make a peace with them, but especially to get them re-united in friendship with us."[22]

Ten days later Byrd returned to the Lords Commisioners with David Crawley, "lately arrived from Virginia," to answer questions about the Native insurrection in Carolina. Crawley, a Virginia trader, had had qualms with Carolina over the Native trade. Because of this experience and knowledge with South Carolina in the western Native trade, Byrd asked Crawley to address the LCTP on July 26, 1715.

Mr. Crawley said that he believed the Yameses who consist of about three hundred men, were the occasion of the said insurrection, for that the Indian traders had very much misused them; that he had seen the said traders frequently take from them their hogs, poultry, corn and other provisions, as they wanted it, and had only paid the Indians for it, what they thought fit, and if they offered to scruple at that, they would beat and abuse them. That he has heard they have frequently debauched the Indians wives and daughters, and that when they would not consent, they have proceeded so far as to force them. That they have made the said Indians carry their burthens, thro' the woods for little or nothing, and beat and abused them when they scrupled it. He added that he believed the Indians now combined against Carolina, might be in number about 15,000.[23]

Crawley wrote to William Byrd on July 30, 1715, in response to a request of the Lords Commissioners to shed additional light on what he had said about the Native insurrection within Carolina. He reported that "their defection" was in reaction to their treatment by the Carolina traders: "Of these abuses I have seen many." He had traveled "throughout their whole trade at almost every town of Indians except the Yamasees." He had "seen their traders when they have had occasion for anything the Indians had as sumtimes killing their hoggs, Fowles, etc., go to their plantations and take what they pleased without leave, into their watermillion ground and take them, and when they came to demand satisfaction give them a small mater not half the value, and if the Indians grumbled or deemed discontented threaten to beat and very often did beat them very cruelly."

They also exploited Native porters who carried skins into Carolina or trade goods out, demanding but "so many men as was able to do it" and no more. If they refused," the Carolinians would treat them in the same abusive manner. The porters were forced to carry loads as much as seventy to eighty pounds for as far as five hundred miles. Crawley knew some of these traders sent their Native servants two hundred to three hundred miles just to deliver a letter of insult to their fellow traders. Not only did they "pay them very little" for their labor, but while the men were away either on the traders' "business" or hunting, the traders bragged of "debauching their wives, sumtime force them," which Crawley himself had witnessed on one occasion. John Wright, the Indian agent in South Carolina, "when out amongst the Indians," had them lug around his "luggage and packs of skins from one town to another purely out of ostentation saying in my hearing he would make them honour him as their governour. . . . These things I believe may bee the occasion of their present sufrings from the Indians."[24]

Although the Virginians had an axe to grind against South Carolina, their reasoning for the causes of the war anticipates scholars' best historical interpretation. Wright's statement to the Yamasee as reported by mico Huspah is consistent with his character as described by Crawley. Byrd and Crawley had identified the slave trade as a grievance, noting that some captives had escaped and returned home to tell their story. They also characterized the war as an insurrection rather than an invasion since the nations most engaged in the war were within South Carolina's sphere. Not only were they proximate to the proprietary colony, but they were also lined up in its commercial zone. For its part Carolina considered them tributary even though the Yamasee had never been conquered by Carolina nor agreed to submit to such a status. Hemmed in by the Carolinians, their reasoning for going to war was existential. They had participated in the fighting with and enslaving of the Tuscarora and knew a similar fate was in store for them.

The Yamasee's three hundred warriors had no chance against a South Carolina force five times as large unless they aligned themselves with neighboring nations. This alliance included the nations of the Savannah and the Lower Muscogee, also within South Carolina's commercial zone. These core combatants were reluctantly reinforced by the Upper Muscogee, Chahta, Ani'-Yun-wiya, and yeh is-WAH h'reh. Their reluctance can be partly explained by their having alternative trading relationships with South Carolina. The proprietary had yet to make inroads into Ani'-Yun-wiya country. The Muscogee and Chahta had access to both the Spanish and French markets. The yeh is-WAH h'reh and the piedmont nations traded with Virginia.[25]

If this demographic connection trumped all other considerations, other grievances identified by the Virginians still held sway in the Yamasee's decision to go to war with Carolina. Byrd duly noted the abusive practices of the Carolina traders. Selling trade goods at exorbitant prices and buying their peltry at very low rates raised the ire of the Yamasee. Restricting access to Virginia traders by claiming these nations within its dominion only exacerbated these market conditions. In addition, Byrd and Crawley listed the practice of seizing personal property or repossession for defaulting on debt. The abuse of the Carolina traders extended to their cruel exploitation of their servants, especially the porters who transported both their imports and exports hundreds of miles. Likewise Byrd and Crawley pointed to the sensitive issue of sexual abuse perpetrated by the Carolina traders while Native women's porter husbands were away.[26]

Interestingly, the Crown anticipated a pan-Native response, querying Byrd on the number of warriors a Native alliance could present. Although Byrd indicated an overall strength on the colonial borders, he did anticipate the thrust of the attack to be against South Carolina, contending that

Virginia had maintained good relations with the Native people. In August 1715 the LCTP recorded that Virginia had no problems with their tributary people and would assist South Carolina by supplying a militia of 1,000 soldiers at the cost of thirty shillings per month each. The colony had already dispatched 130.[27]

Francis Kennedy had been commissioned by Spotswood and the council to recoup the cost of the aid and assistance given to save South Carolina from the the "formidable power" and insurrection of the Native people and to visit the Spanish governor in Saint Augustine. But the Dominion had given him "no consideration" for ten months, and he sought redress for expenses "upwards of £200" incurred during his travels to South Carolina and Saint Augustine on behalf of Virginia. He asked the Crown to intervene by sharing with him Virginia's quitrents in lieu of his loss.[28]

Pryce Hughes had mapped the geography of the region, which Spotswood enclosed in a letter to the Board of Trade. Spotswood wrote that even though "most of those Nations are more contiguous to the French Settlements than the English," the English have usurped the trade that the French were not able to supply. Nevertheless, he feared that the recent French trade with the Coosa people, who inhabited a region on the river bearing their name, would bring them into Ani'-Yun-wiya country. At the same time, South Carolina traders

> had already abandoned y't Trade, and our Virginia Traders like to do so too because of the low price of Skins and furrs in England and ye high Duty thereon, especially on furrs, so, that unless those Dutys be lessened, whereby Encouragement may be given to prosecute the Indian Trade, the Great Nation of the Cherokees will soon fall into the French Interest, and as these are the nearest and most considerable Body of Indians on our Southern ffrontiers, and consist of upwards of four thousand fighting Men, so they have generally been very friendly and Affectionate to the English, and are the only Indians we ought to depend on to balla[nce] the North'n Nations if they should attempt to be troublesome to these Plantacons.[29]

Spotswood wrote that "methods most practicable" for settling and taking possession of the "lakes on the back parts of Virginia" were based on his travels and his research, which he garnered from the "most Credible and Intelligent persons," including Native informants and traders' accounts. These methods were too complicated to communicate in correspondence, however, and would require an in-person presentation. "I have also informed myself of the Nature of the Country where the Designs are to be executed, the

Temper and Inclinations of the Indians, and how to gain their friendship," Spotswood asserted. Did he envision the Great Lakes? Spotswood had no more knowledge of the backcountry he planned to colonize than Lederer had fifty years earlier.[30]

Following the Yamasee War, the southern nations found the Native slave trade drying up and turned their attention to the trade in deerskins. The Ani'-Yun-wiya and the Chikashsha' pushed to supply Virginia and bypass the yeh is-WAH h'reh. Despite Spotswood's best efforts, the demise of the Virginia Indian Company weakened the Dominion's reach. South Carolina was better positioned geographically to take advantage of the shift in the market. Recognizing this turn of events, the great men of the Ani'-Yun-wiya and of the Chikashsha' journeyed to Williamsburg in October 1721. Together they entered the council chamber "singing, according to their Custom." A great man of the Ani'-Yun-wiya informed the governor "that their Nation observing ye Factors of the late Indian Comp had totally withdrawn their Effects out of their Country, by which they were apprehensive they shou'd have no further Trade with this Colony; their Nation had thereupon sent them hither to desire ye continuance of the Trade with Virg."[31]

A great man of the Chikashsha', "a Nation inhabiting near the mouth of the River Mississippi," presented acting Governor Jenings with a deerskin and a calumet of peace. After offering blandishments of friendship, he said that the Chikashsha' were at war with France and needed weapons. He then offered to trade with the Dominion for arms and ammunition, since South Carolina lacked the horse carriages necessary to supply them.[32] After consulting with the council, Jenings returned two days later with a response. Williamsburg must "always be ready to treat the Chickasaws as Friends" but hesitated to supply them with arms. The traders had not found "sufficient Encouragement for continuing that Commerce," but also "the frequent Wars between them and the Neighbouring Indians renders it dangerous for our Traders to go among them. . . . because it is uncertain when any of the said Traders will go that way, If the Chickasaws think it worth their while, they may be supplyed with Arms and Ammunition at Christanna provided they come thither in such manner as may give no uneasiness to the Inhabitants."[33]

Former Virginia governor Francis Nicholson, who had received in 1694 during his installation as governor of Maryland *The Map of the Lower Mississippi River*, a generation later after becoming governor of South Carolina received two deerskin maps bearing the same name: *A Map Describing the Situation of the Several Nations of Indians between South Carolina and the Massisipi River*. They were both "Copyed from a Draught Drawn & Painted upon a Deer Skin by an Indian Cacique" The first was likely a gift from his installation in 1721 and the second a gift from the Chikashsha' in 1723.

Nicholson might have accepted these gifts as curios, but the caciques grasped its import.

Instead of a conventional northward orientation, the stylized 1721 map disorients Western viewers even as the reproduction specifies that the several nations depicted were northwesterly of South Carolina. The cacique represented the eleven nations depicted as circles: the Ani'-Yun-wiya, the Chikashsha', and nine yeh is-WAH h'reh nations. After the Yamasee War, the yeh is-WAH h'reh organized into a confederation of nine towns. Trading paths connected Native entrepôts to Charles Town, which is depicted on the left-hand border by a town grid and harbor with a pictograph of a ship. Since South Carolina had harassed and placed duties on the skin and fur trade to Virginia, limiting its access, the yeh is-WAH h'reh turned their attention to Charles Town, positioning the "English Path to Nasaw," a yeh is-WAH h'reh dominion, leading to Charles Town and from Nasaw another path leading to Virginia. Demonstrating a direct trade route with South Carolina, the serpentine road snakes around yeh is-WAH h'reh country from Ani'-Yun-wiya to Charles Town. On the other hand, no paths lead from Ani'-Yun-wiya to Virginia, which is pictured as square and blocked. If the map decenters the English colonies by placing Virginia and Charles Town at its peripheries, it illuminates a pictograph of a menacing warrior above Virginia, likely depicting the Haudenosaunee threat.

Drawing on both documentary evidence and ethnographic insight, historian Ian Chambers traces the provenance of the map in Ani'-Yun-wiya rather than in yeh is-WAH h'reh, as conventional wisdom has it. He argues that the map depicts three pictograms symbolic of the Ani'-Yun-wiya creation myth: Kana'tï the hunter father, Selu the corn mother, and a deer. The corn mother looms large near Ani'-Yun-wiya country, emphasizing her responsibility as cultivator and custodian; the hunter is dwarfed in the distance away from Ani'-Yun-wiya, the deer signifies his role as provider and envoy.[34]

At Savannah Town on September 14, 1723, Fani Minko'', the squirrel king of the Chikashsha', presented a deerskin map to Governor Nicholson in gratitude for his providing refuge to the Chikashsha' from the French. Like the 1721 map, it represented the Indigenous nations in circles, centering the Chikashsha'. The other Native nations featured are the Ani'-Yun-wiya, the Muscogee, and the Chahta. Unlike the 1721 map, the English settlement, clearly South Carolina, also appears as a circle. Like spokes from a wheel, paths connect Chikashsha' with its commercial and diplomatic partners. Smaller circles appear, mapping people less significant; some in Louisiana and Alabama regions mark with the letter "F" indicate French aligned nations. The yeh is-WAH h'reh are noticeably absent from the map. They had brokered the Chikashsha' trade to Virginia prior to the Yamasee War,

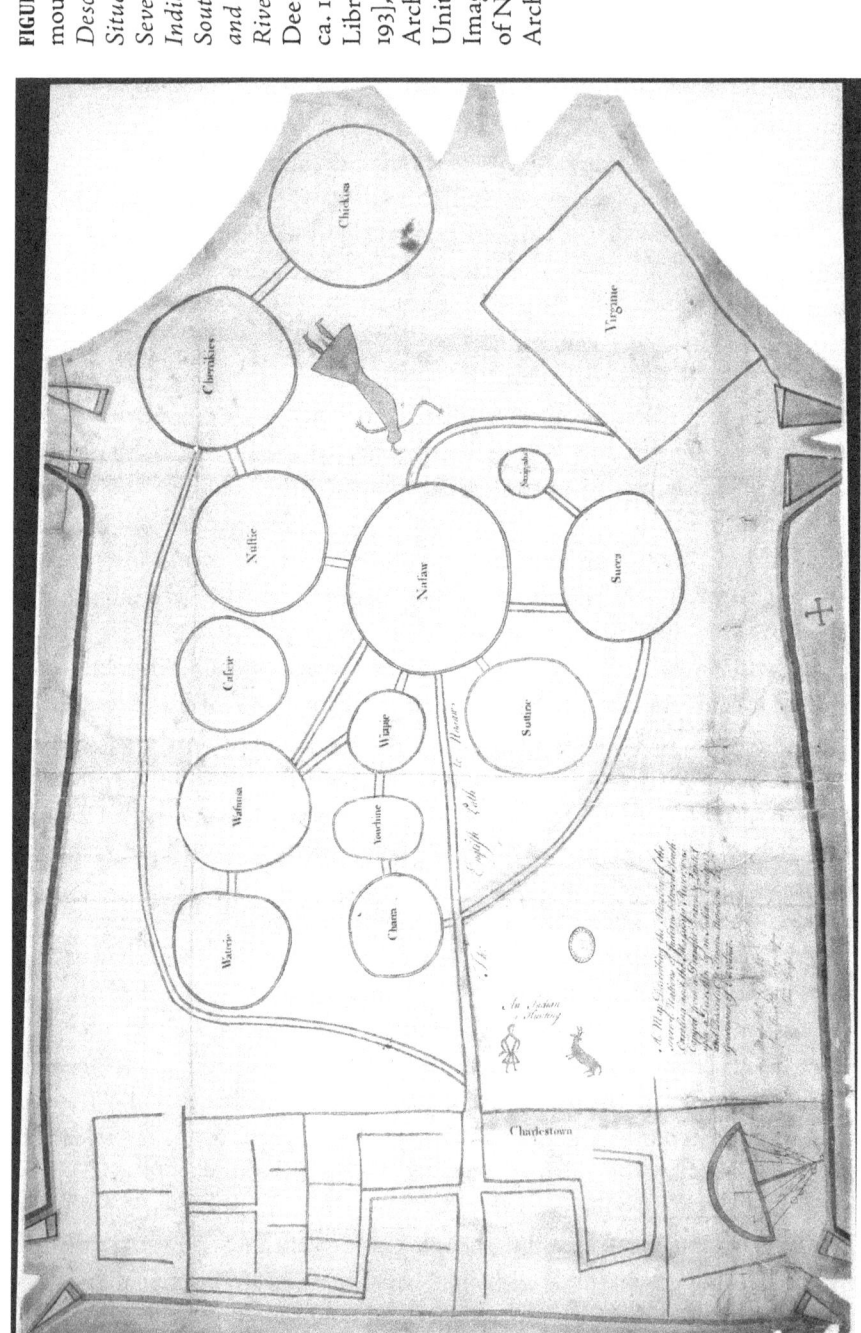

FIGURE 14. Anonymous, *A Map Describing the Situation of the Several Nations of Indians between South Carolina and the Massisipi River* (Catawba Deerskin Map), ca. 1721. Image Library [SEM 193], National Archives of the United Kingdom. Image courtesy of National Archives.

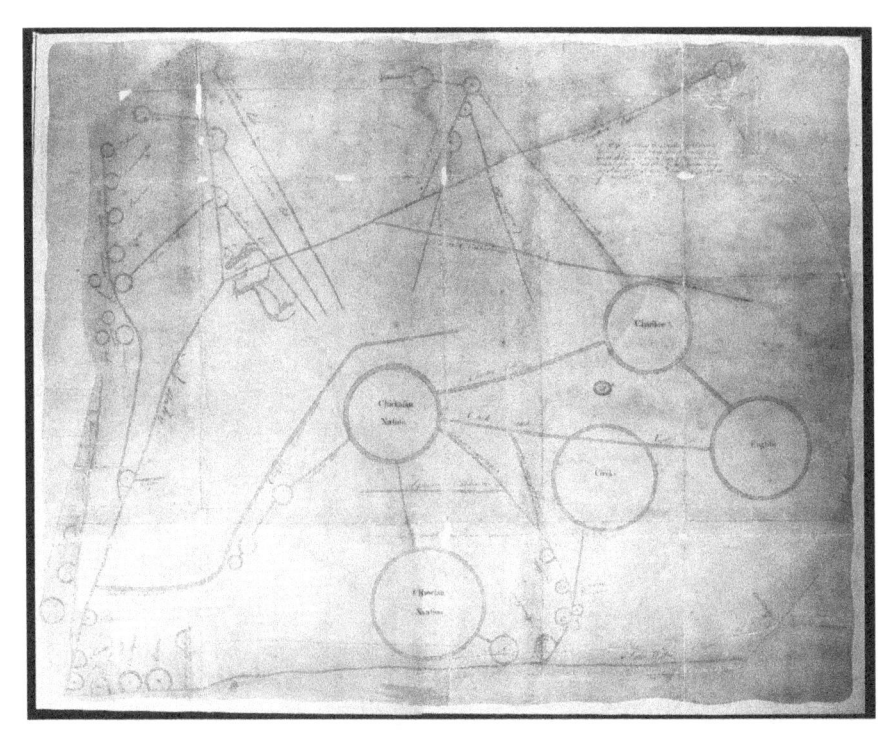

FIGURE 15. Anonymous, *A Map Describing the Situation of the Several Nations of Indians between South Carolina and the Massisipi River* (Chickasaw Deerskin Map), ca. 1723. Image Library [SEM 192], National Archives of the United Kingdom. Image courtesy of National Archives.

but Virginia's unwillingness to commence commerce is why the Dominion and yeh is-WAH h'reh do not appear. The Mississippi, Yazoo, Tennessee, Tombigbee, and the Ohio Rivers are depicted. Trails, the lines of travel and transit, are delineated. The pictograph in the upper left corner features a bowman holding a horse by its rein, evidence of the burgeoning horse culture in the region.[35]

The indicated Cherokee Path on the 1721 deerskin map was likely the Keowee Path. Keowee Town in the northwest piedmont of present-day South Carolina was not only the most prominent of the Ani'-Yun-wiya Lower Towns but also was once a major hub of activity. George Hunter, a surveyor, annotated Col. John Herbert's map of the Ani'-Yun-wiya country on May 21, 1730. His project likely got him promoted to surveyor general of South Carolina. Hunter was engaged by traders to the Ani'-Yun-wiya to append his "own Observations" on the face of the map along with the names of the rivers and creeks. Herbert's map showed the Cherokee path from Keowee Town to Charles Town. This well-traveled road, likely used by "the Cherokee,

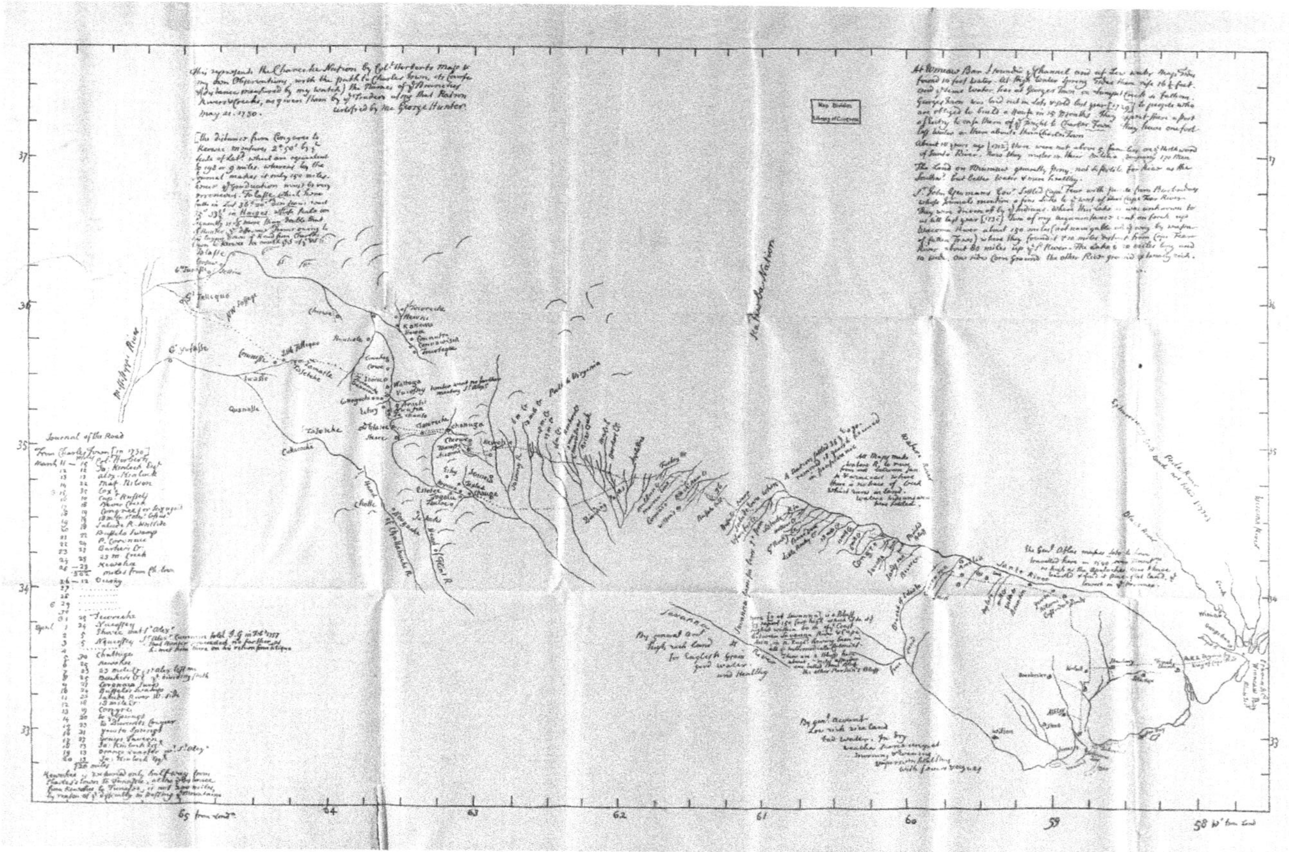

FIGURE 16. George Hunter, *Map of the Cherokee Country and the Path thereto in 1730.* South Caroliniana Library. Image courtesy of University of South Carolina, Columbia.

Catawba, Cusabo, Cheraw, Saluda, Etiwan, Santee, Yemassee, Waxhaw, Pee Dee, Congaree," among others, became the main corridor of the skin and fur trade to Charles Town. The Keowee Path connected Charles Town to the Ani'-Yun-wiya towns and was the major thoroughfare through the piedmont linking all of the Ani'-Yun-wiya towns.[36]

In the mid-seventeenth century, the Ani'-Yun-wiya population numbered 22,000, giving them a tenfold majority over the incipient settler population; the population rose to 32,000 in 1685, when the forced arrival of 500 Africans foreshadowed the emergence of a slave society. Their number was "halved by the Great Epidemic of 1696–9" but rebounded to about 20,000 during the 1720s. The Ani'-Yun-wiya population declined in 1738 when a smallpox epidemic again halved their population to about 10,000. Meanwhile, the white population had grown from 12,000 in 1720 to 15,000 in 1740. Africans had become the majority, their number growing from 8,600 in 1715 to 40,600 in 1745. Following the epidemic and the discovery of the path to the northwest, settlers pressed Ani'-Yun-wiya autonomy and began moving into the region. The British used the occasion of the Creek War in 1752 to build Prince George Fort on their land. By midcentury the 25,000 white settlers worried more about the 39,000 enslaved Africans, who might again rise up as they had in the 1739 Stono Rebellion, than with an invasion from the Ani'-Yun-wiya.[37] Conversely, Virginia began to woo the Ani'-Yun-wiya, the most formidable Native nation to its south. Governor Dinwiddie of Virginia said that they were a "much more numerous and more extensive" nation than the yeh is-WAH h'reh, reportedly outnumbering them ten to one.[38]

CHAPTER 8

A New Method for Bringing the Indians under a Regulation

The forest bordering Virginia and North Carolina proved vulnerable both to Black maroonage and to northern nation attacks on western tributaries. Fugitive Africans could join receptive nations, especially the Shawnee, or establish permanent settlements in the region. Native people warded off raiding mourning parties tacking south, especially the Seneca. The piedmont settlements were most susceptible to Native attack. Still reeling from the Tuscarora incursion and ever more concerned about foreign invasion and Black insurrection, Virginia over time developed methods to deal with these threats. Virginia increased military preparedness in this most vulnerable region, enlisted Native people in hunting maroons in the woods and mountains, and promoted both tributary relocation and colonial settlement in the areas between the mountains and tidewater plantations. The manipulation of the tributary nations was key to this strategy, first in opening up plantation settlement and protecting the land from attack; then in capturing and securing enslaved fugitives, holding tributary children hostage either at the Brafferton Indian School at the College of William and Mary or at Fort Christanna; and finally in Christianizing them at the school or fort and in their towns. Providing the children with a Christian education and English clothing was intended to acculturate them.[1]

These methods, however, required funding. As early as October 15, 1712, Spotswood addressed the triple threat of incursion, invasion, and insurrection in a missive to the LCTP. If the threats of a foreign invasion by sea "are now happily removed by peace," he still worried about the French instigating the Seneca into a proxy invasion by land to join the Tuscarora incursion. The Seneca, however, remained in the role of advisers to the Tuscarora rather than join them in war. "The Insurrections of our own Negroes, or the Invasions of the Indians," Spotswood thought, "are no less to be dreaded" than the continued Native "incursions in North Carolina." Yet he found the General Assembly "stupidly averse" to raising the funds necessary to guard "against either of these events."[2] Spotswood also wanted to relocate the tributary nations to intimidate both the Black maroons escaping to the mountains and the Five Nations, who were using the eastern side of the Blue Ridge Mountains as a road for their fur-hunting and mourning-captive expeditions.

Also, to guard against enslaved fugitives, the commissioners of the Indian trade "seated" the Winyaw on the Santee River for the express purpose of "keeping the Negroes there in Awe."[3]

By mid-May 1713, following Moore's siege of the Tuscarora fort and the South Carolina Native allies' withdrawal, Spotswood sued for peace with Tom Blunt, chief of the upper Tuscarora towns that remained neutral during the conflict. The terms included Blunt's assuring the Tuscarora's continuing fidelity by surrendering twenty of the masterminds of the attack identified by North Carolina and hostages. Spotswood was still concerned about the role that the Seneca in particular and the Haudenosaunee in general might continue to play in their relations.

> Blunt confesses that during the Siege of the aforementioned fort, one of their Sachems commanding a body of 200 men, after having robb'd our Traders as they were going to the Western Indians, came to his Town and endeavour'd to perswade him and the other Neutral Towns, to joyn in attacking the So. Carolina Indians and raising the Siege. Soon after a Party of our Tributary Indians happening to meet with these Northern Indians, kill'd some of them, which brought 19 [of] them down on our Frontiers; whereupon I sent out a party of 140 Men in search of them, but it seems they took another road and so escap'd with their booty, and some murders committed this winter on our Frontiers are suspect'd to have been done by those Northern Indians in their march to the Tuscaruro Country.[4]

Six months later, on December 20, 1713, "several of the Great men of the Tuscaruro Nation" met with Governor Spotswood in Williamsburg to sue for peace. They desired both to become tributary to Virginia and to settle on the Roanoke River. While Spotswood was open to their bid to become tributary, he rebuffed their entreaty to settle on the Roanoke, because their presence there could provoke the Native nations of South Carolina, which would necessitate Virginia coming to their assistance. Rather, conscious of the void left by the genocide of the Nanziattico, he countered that they should relocate within the Dominion at the headwaters between the James and the Rappahannock Rivers. Not only would this location shield the settlements from southern Native incursions, but it also would "cutt off their communication with North Carolina." The emissaries received these terms warmly but, uneasy with the place of resettlement, said they had "to consult with the rest of their Nation promising to return with full power to conclude upon every particular by the middle of February." In addition they represented that "their people were in extreme want of Corne for their subsistence" and requested permission for a score of their men to come into the Dominion "to purchase as much as they could at once conveniently carry."[5]

If Tuscarora expected tributary status with a degree of autonomy, Spotswood's scheme projected tutelage. He recognized that this treaty negotiation occasioned an opportunity for Virginia to realign relations with the Native nations. Becoming tributary to Virginia now involved a series of steps: resettlement, incorporation with other nations, surveillance by a militia presence, and Christian education. Living among the English, Spotswood reasoned, offered them "the advantages they would receive by this Settlement, such as their having a large tract of land to hunt in, a body of the English to live among them, and to instruct their Children in Literature and the principles of Christianity, to bring them to a more civilized and plentiful manner of living, and to establish a constant intercourse of Trade between them and the Inhabitants of this Colony."[6]

On January 27, 1714, Spotswood presented the "scheme he had framed for the Settlement of the Indians and the Security of the Frontiers" to the council. What he had omitted in his earlier negotiation with the Tuscarora was his plan to police their presence within Virginia. As he had negotiated with the Tuscarora, Spotswood proposed that their settlement and their hunting grounds would be between the James and the Rappahannock Rivers. While this location at first glance appears to have been intended as a barrier to Virginia's westward expansion, Spotswood was more concerned about the Shawnee settlements in the Shenandoah Valley. Situating a tributary Tuscarora there would also serve as a foil both to northern and western Native attacks on backcountry residents and to African escapes to the mountains. He also proposed in his scheme that they would be supervised by a dozen militiamen. The patrols "ranging along the Frontiers" would prevent "the Incursion of all straggling Parties of foreign Indians" and discourage the Tuscarora from future designs against the English. To give satisfaction to North Carolina, he proposed that the intended treaty with the Tuscarora include their surrendering "such of that nation as shall be discovered to have been concerned in the Massacre."[7]

Blunt did deliver Hancock to Williamsburg. On July 26, 1712, Spotswood noted that a report from Albany to North Carolina corroborated the confession of a Tuscarora chief delivered shortly before his execution. He "declared at his death that the Senequas had promised to joine the Tuscaruros with a strong Body of their people by the latter end of next month [August]."[8]

Spotswood's proposal for Virginia's neighboring nations was just as intrusive. He proposed "incorporating" the Meherrin and the Nottoway and resettling them on the Roanoke River on the land that the Tuscarora wanted. The Meherrin and the Nottoway had sought guarantees from Spotswood to the land they claimed was reserved for them in 1677. Spotswood had reported in 1710 that "some nations of our Tributary Indians who live in the contested bounds between this Colony and Carolina" had sent him "a petition desiring . . . the Land reserved to them in this region" by the 1677 Middle Plantations Treaty. More so than the request, Spotswood felt the letter furnished him with greater leverage in his negotiations with Carolina, for it recognized Virginia's suzerainty over both the people and the region, underscored by the annual tribute to the government for their land of three Indian arrowheads in "token of their subjection."[9]

That Spotswood was less concerned with tributary rights to the land than dominion "within the controverted bounds" with Carolina can be seen in his response to Governor Hyde's complaint of injury to Carolina settlers by the Meherrin. "I think they [settlers] have as little reason to complain as they have right to be there. I'm sure none of them have had any Liberty from this Government to take up Land in those parts, and I hope the Government of Carolina have had the same Regard to their own publick engagements not to suffer any encroachments to be made by the Inhab'ts of that Province, which We have had the more reason to expect from them out of respect to her Majesty, in whose behalf all along that land has been claimed."[10] After assuring Hyde that Virginia law offered redress to any white settlers injured by Native tributaries, Spotswood reiterated that the Meherrin were the rightful possessors of the land. "As to their [the Meherrin] disturbing the possessors of Land within three miles of their Town, I don't know by what Right anyone came to settle there, it being contrary to the articles of Peace concluded with those Indians, which have the Regal approbation." Sensitive to the difficulties of restraining settlers from encroaching into Native country, "but I am credibly informed the Indians have more reason to complain of injustice from the people of Carolina, who are daily trespassing upon them, and if they do sometimes retaliate it is more excusable because your people have been the first aggressors, by seating without Right on the Lands of which the Indians had the first possession."[11]

Not unlike with his proposal for the Tuscarora, Spotswood anticipated "a party of twelve English men to reside among them, who shall observe all their motions and some of them to go out constantly with their hunting Parties and that the grounds for their hunting be assigned them between Roanoke River and Appomattox." Their presence "consisting of a considerable body of Indians would serve as a good Barrier to the Inhabitants against the Southern Indians, whose incursions are now most to be dreaded." As a barrier to incursion of northern nations, he grouped the Saponi, the Stuckanox [Stukanox], the Occaneechis, and the Toteras together, where they would "have a Fort built for them above the Fork of James River. That fifteen men and an Officer be appointed in like manner to reside among them, and that two pieces of Cannon be carryed up to their Fort. That this Settlement being in the Center of the others will be a proper place to settle a Missionary for the Instruction of the Indians, if the Society for propagating the Gospel shall think fit to send one for that purpose."[12]

After hearing the report of terms given to the great men attending the December meeting, three Tuscarora emissaries, representing the "late Tuscaruro Towns of Raroucaithee, Kentha, Jounonitz and Taughoagkkee," returned to Williamsburg. On February 26, 1714, they appeared before the council "humbly to beg that a peace may be granted them, that they may be admitted Tributaries under the Protection of this Government and have land assigned them for their Settlement as the other Tributaries have." They not only agreed to resettle in their new territory between the James and the Rappahannock Rivers by October but also "as soon as a Minister and Schoolmaster shall be settled among them, all their Children shall be put to learn the English Language and be instructed in the principles of the Christian Religion according to the Governor's proposal." They agreed to sign a treaty once the other terms introduced by the governor and the council "were communicated and fully explained by the Interpreters . . . agreed unto by the S^d Deputys." Wasting no time, Spotswood ordered the treaty replete with the stated articles ready for signing in the morning.[13]

Spotswood's plans to build a fort on the Rapidan River, where it flowed into the Rappahannock River near the falls, to garrison a dozen militia troops overseeing the Tuscarora resettlement fell through when the Tuscarora reneged on their promise and returned to North Carolina. Capt. Robert Hix, "Commander of the Rangers in Surry County," reported that the Tuscarora had "refused to deliver their Hostages according to the late Treaty, giving out that they intend to return into Carolina, having made a peace with Coll. Pollock and Coll. Moore." The Nottoway teerheer [chief] sent a message to the board that several of the Tuscarora were "desirous to incorporate" with them. The teerheer asked to come to Williamsburg with the Tuscarora chief and "that leave be granted them in the meantime to continue among the Nottoway." Williamsburg endorsed the Saponi on the Roanoke River supervised by fifteen rangers and the Nottoway between the Roanoke and the James Rivers with a dozen militia in their town, and maintained that "none of the Tuscaruros be permitted to cross Roanoke River or come upon the Frontiers of this Colony untill the Government shall receive better assurance of their future peaceable behaviour towards her Majesties Subjects."[14]

For this reason Governor Spotswood and the council altered their Native resettlement and their backcountry security plans. Instead of the Tuscarora resettlement, Spotswood proposed a German settlement there. Toward this end the assembly passed "The Act for Exempting Certain German Protestants from the Payment of Levys." These immigrants had been earlier recruited by Baron Christoph von de Graffenried "to find out mines" in Virginia. Graffenried had with Spotswood's "own charge, and the contributions of some gentlemen," settled them on the upper Rappahannock.[15] In addition to the ironworks, Germanna, the first white settlement in the piedmont, established in 1714 with forty Germans on the Rapidan River twenty miles above the falls of the Rappahannock, could block the southern migration of the Haudenosaunee in search of furs and captives.[16] Spotswood summed up the event:

> The Tuscaruros, induced . . . by the people of Carolina, have departed from their agreements with this Governm't, and gon[e] to settle once more upon that Province, I continue, all resolv'd, to settle out our Tributary Indians as a guard to ye Frontiers, and in order to supply that part, w'ch was to have been covered by the Tuscaruros, I have placed here a number of Protestant Germans, built them a Fort, and finish'd it with 2 pieces of Cannon and some Ammunition, which will awe the Stragling partys of Northern Indians, and be a good Barrier for all that part of the Country.[17]

The Germanna settlement became an essential element in Spotswood's "new Method . . . for guarding our Frontiers and bringing the Indians under a Regulation for the better Security." On March 28, 1715, he boasted that this new design had contributed to eighteen months of peace from northern incursions. Seeking a "perfect design," he set off on another expedition to meet with the deputies of three or four remote nations.[18] After exploring for six weeks the Meherrin River near the North Carolina border, Spotswood settled on a six-mile tract, where he garrisoned a dozen rangers and an officer. He also began construction of Fort Christanna where the "the land . . . is well timbered and very good."[19]

The Nottoway had resisted moving there partly because of the nearness to the Saponi and partly because of the character of the land proposed. They then agreed to be incorporated with Meherrin on the north side of the river. On the south side, the Nansemond "confederated together" with the Saponi, Occaneechi, Stuckanox, and Tutelo, "being a people speaking much the same language, . . . tho" still preserving their different Rules." Both the resettlements and the incorporations, the council reasoned, would "strengthen those Settlements as well as to remove them to places where they may be less lyable to differences with the English Inhabitants and for the greater conveniency of instructing their Children in Christianity by the Missionarys intended at those two Settlements."[20] The governor and the council assigned "Nathaniel Harrison to discourse the Great men of those Nations concerning their Removal and make Report of their Resolutions therein to the Governor with the first Conveniency."[21]

The Crown enjoined North Carolina with the Lords Proprietors of Carolina in concert with Virginia to resolve the contentious border issue on March 30, 1714. As a remedy the council proposed that the two governments coordinate in removing those settlers "illegally seated there" and surveying the dividing line. The colonies' haggling over the boundary line left open the region of the Roanoke River to unscrupulous settlers willing to trade guns and ammunition to the Tuscarora, leading to Virginia's proposal to remove these scoundrels and preclude settlement in the disputed territory until the bounds could be properly surveyed. The council ascertained that North Carolina "did still suffer their Surveyors to lay out, and people to settle on the Lands in those parts," however this scheme proved prejudicial to both colonies since "this liberty" has led to the "abundance of disorderly people going out to settle on Roanoke River [who] have held a constant Trade and Correspondence with the Tuscaruros and made them less inclined an accommodation with the English while they cannot without it be Supplyed with ammunition." The council even ordered the attorney general to prosecute Robert Poythress, brother of the interpreter, "accused of Supplying the Tuscaruros with Ammunition during the prohibition of Trade . . . at the next General Court for his contempt of the orders of the Government in a matter of such consequence to the Safety of her Majesties Subjects."[22] Nevertheless, this "direct correspondence carried on by the old Indian traders" went unpunished, because the laws were defective in not providing a punishment for that crime.[23]

Prompted by these trade irregularities, Spotswood in the winter of 1714 proposed chartering a company with exclusive rights to the Native trade to the assembly, which passed "An Act for the Better Regulation of the Indian Trade." The governor and the council added a carrot to encourage tributary relocation by restricting trade of the tributaries living on the south side of the James River be conducted at Fort Christanna. As chief beneficiary of that legislation, the Virginia Indian Company (VIC) had a twenty-year responsibility to build and maintain a schoolhouse for the children.[24] He explained in a letter on January 27, 1715, to the LCTP that the poorer traders operating in the market where they had to pay high were prone to fraudulent practices, which they blamed on the Native people, leading them to kill in retribution. As a consequence the relations had degenerated into "frequent quarrels" between the Native suppliers and the English traders, to the point of the "entire loss of that Commerce."[25]

The act awarded a monopoly to the VIC for twenty years at Fort Christanna on the Meherrin River. Restricting traffic "to one place and that too in open market . . . will engage all our tributaries to fix there for the great conveniency of their trading; whereby that place will become a sufficient barrier against the incursions of any foreign enemy." Mindful of the recent war and of safety precautions, the act empowered the governor with the authority to totally shutoff all supplies of ammunition, the "surest way to bring them to reason." For the privilege of solely conducting this commerce, the company was responsible for erecting a munitions magazine at Williamsburg as well as the schoolhouse for the Native children at Christanna. In addition, after two years the VIC would take on full responsibility for garrisoning a dozen men and an officer and maintaining the fortifications at Christanna. He asserted that this "regulation" would not only render the Native people "useful, instead of being . . . a burden to the country," but also lay a foundation of civility that would "prove an encouragement to bring them over to Christianity."[26]

When Rev. John Fontaine traveled from Williamsburg through tributary reserves near the Mattaponi River in 1715 and 1716, he documented Virginia-occupied Native country, the six-mile reserve of Nottoway land on the Nottoway River, and Saponi Town near Fort Christanna. Fontaine was hosted by three great planters in Caroline County: John Baylor at his plantation Mantua on the north side of Mattaponi River, Baylor's brother-in-law Augustine Moore, and finally, thirty miles away, Robert Beverly at his Chase plantation. On his way to Chase on November 12, 1715, he observed a Native house "built with posts put into the ground, the one by the other, as close as they could lay and about seven feet high all of an equal length. It was built four square and a sort of roof upon it covered with the bark of trees. They say it keeps out the rain very well. . . . Their beds were mats made of bullrushes. They lie upon them and had one blanket to cover them. All the household goods they had was a pot."[27] Fontaine was most taken aback by the scanty dress of the Native women in the region. They wore "only a girdle they had tied about their waist, and they had about a yard of blanketing which they passed one end under the fore part of the girdle, and they pull this cloth so fastened before between their thighs and fasten the other end under the girdle behind, which covers their nakedness."[28]

The confederated nations, "who go under the general name of Saponies,"[29] then numbered three hundred, including seventy children, whom Spotswood had assigned to an Englishman, Charles Griffin, "at the salary of fifty pounds per annum," paid for out of his own pocket. Spotswood credited the "good disposition" of the Saponi toward the education of their children, which "encouraged" him to establish the school.[30] "These children and their

Parents seem much delighted with the hopes of their being made Christians and taught to read. Among those under the care of this School M'r was the Queen of that Nation, a Girl of about ten years of age and of a very promising disposition, who dyed some days ago. I had promised to be her God-father when she should be Christened, and at her death she seem'd to express herself with much concern that she could not see us."[31] By the time Fontaine arrived at Fort Christanna, Griffin had one hundred children under his care. Fontaine observed Griffin at work at Fort Christanna: "He remains in this place and teaches them to read the Bible and Common Prayers, as also to write, and the English tongue. He hath had good success amongst them. He hath now been a year amongst them. He told the Governor that the Indian Chiefs or Great Men, as they style themselves, were coming to the Fort to compliment him." Fontaine related on April 19, 1716, that "after breakfast we assembled ourselves and read the Common Prayer. There was with us eight of the Indian boys who answered very well to the prayers and understand what is read."[32]

The arrival of the other confederated nations had been delayed, bearing on the Seneca, "haunting near their habitations, (and with whom they are on no good Terms)." The Nottoway, despite their misgivings about the Saponi and the land proffered by Virginia, promised to send a dozen of their children to the schoolhouse, newly built by the VIC, until one could be built for them. However, they reneged on that promise, refused to deliver hostages to Williamsburg, and went back to their "old land." A critic even accused the governor of putting their teerheer "and Six of his Chief Men in Irons for Petitioning the Assembly for relief from Starving." The teerheer died while in custody. Accused of murder, Spotswood protested too much. First, he diminished the status of their king by deprecating his authority: "There is not so great distinction between their Kings and their People." Then he responded that the point of contention was not relief, as stated, but their "Clamorous Grievance" rested on "their obstinate Refusal to deliver Hostages for their fidelity, as by their Treaty they were obliged to do." For this "insolent behaviour," he, with the consent of the council, put the teerheer and his emissaries in "a light iron Shackle put upon each of them for two or three days, without confining them, but letting them walk with the same about the Town. . . . The same Methods have frequently taken by the Governours here when the Indians have misbehaved themselves and have been found the best means of bring'g those Savages to Reason."[33]

The Meherrin continued to reside in their homeland and participated in the commerce regulated by the VIC. For example, Reverend Fontaine observed the arrival of Meherrin vendors at Fort Christanna "laden with beaver, deer and bear skins" to trade with the VIC for goods. In order to enter the fort, however, they had to deposit their arms and skins with the white soldiers there. They were not permitted to reside overnight within the fort but stayed in the woods until they finished their business.[34]

Only the Saponi had "changed their Seat of habitation." "Much pleas'd with their present settlement," Spotswood said in 1716, the Saponi are the "most considerable Nation . . . settled on our Frontiers at a fort I have lately built, and w'ch is to be maintain'd by the Gentlemen of the Indian Company. These tributary nations were under the Dominion's "entire subjection," which by the method employed should "rather prove [them] useful friends than dangerous Enemys to us." That method included their resettlement on the frontier at Fort Christanna "lately built and maintained" by the VIC.

> The Land they are seated on is extraordinary Good. All the Indian trade of this Colony is carryed on at their fort, and the Company have, out of regard to their Permitting their children to be educated in the Christian religion, agreed to furnish them with goods at a Cheaper rate than any other forreign Indians. So that they are well pleas'd with their Circumstances, and as they are an increasing Nation, I doubt not they will both prove a good Barrier on that Quarter against the Incursions of any forreign Indians, and also keep in awe our other Tributarys, (who already stand in fear of them).[35]

That same year, on April 17, 1716, Fontaine described the Saponi town, "which is about a musket shot from Fort Christanna."

> This town lieth in a plain by the river side. I walked round the town to view it. The houses join all the one to the other and altogether make a circle. The walls of their houses are large pieces of timber, which are squared and being sharpened at the lower end, they are put above two feet in the ground and about seven feet above the ground. They laid them as close as they could the one to the other, and when these posts are all fixed after this manner then they make a sort of a roof with rafters and cover the house with oak or hickory bark, which they strip off in great flakes, and lay it so closely that no rain can come in. Some of their houses are covered in a circular manner which they do by getting long saplings and stick each end in the ground and so cover them with bark, but there is none of the houses in this town so covered. There is three ways of coming into this town or circle of houses which are passages of about 6 feet wide between two of the houses. All the doors of the houses are on the inside of the ring and it is very level withinside which is in common with all the people to divert themselves. There is

also in the centre of the inside circle a great stump of a tree. I asked the reason they left that stand, and they informed me it was for one of their head men to stand on when he had anything of consequence to relate to them, that being raised, he may the better be heard.[36]

The Native women at Saponi town "bind their children to a board that is cut after the shape of the child. There is two pieces at the bottom of this board to tye the child's legs to, and a piece cut out behind so that all that the child doth."[37]

When on April 27, 1716, Spotswood's entourage departed Christanna, a Saponi honor guard accompanied them. At daybreak, when they arrived at Saponi Town, a dozen armed young men on foot headed by an old man joined them. The governor provided the chief with a horse, an experience that demonstrated the absence of horses in Saponi culture. When the Englishmen swam with their horses across the Meherrin River, he stripped down to his belt, unsaddled the horse, and led it across the river. Later that afternoon, after the horse threw him, he gamely remounted. Finally, after another mile he relinquished the horse, saying he "could not imagine what good they were for, if it was not to cripple the Indians." The escort accompanied them fifteen miles farther to the Nottoway River, where the governor gave each one a gratuity of pound of shot and a proportionate amount of power.[38]

Virginia's relations with the yeh is-WAH h'reh took a turn for the better with the treaty negotiations ending their participation in the Yamasee War. Spotswood gave the example of their consideration for the Dominion when they sparred some Virginia residents "who fell into their hands amongst the Carolina people, and by applying to this Government to beg a peace."[39] Spotswood convinced them that once they had made peace with South Carolina they could participate in the exclusive trade and access of the market at Fort Christanna with the VIC. The price of the ticket was sending children to Christanna as hostages. "The Chief man of the Cattawba Nation, with sundry other Chiefs of the Nations in that Confederacy," arrived at Fort Christanna early in April 1717 with their child hostages in tow. They pitched their camp fifty yards outside of the fort and convened with Spotswood on April 9. At the meeting they pledged their fealty to the English. Animus for the yeh is-WAH h'reh prompted a party of Seneca and Tuscarora to attack them at dawn the following morning, "discharging their firearms all of a sudden," killing five, wounding two, and abducting a dozen. After affecting curative statements to quell their anxiety of English duplicity,

Spotswood regained the Natives' fealty, which they demonstrated by leaving behind eleven children with the other tributary hostages at the Christanna school. The Tuscarora had refused to give up their children as hostages and returned to North Carolina, but "this unexpected Event" soured relations with Virginia.[40]

On May 10, 1717, Micajah Perry and William Byrd II, representing merchants trading with Virginia, complained about the act, which created the VIC, to the Board of Trade. Arguing from the vantage point of British merchants rather than Virginia planters, Perry and Byrd said that in addition to violating Crown policy and parliamentary law, the act had hurt the trade. "The quantity of skins imported from Virginia is less than formerly and the price from 1s. 6d. to 3s. 6d. for which he had sold them, is now advanced to 7s. and 10s., tho' this might indeed be partly occasioned by Indian War. That the Indian Company in Virginia employ factors of their own, . . . and will not buy the goods of any other British merchant, whereby the latter is excluded the benefit of that trade, which Mr. Perry said, himself had enjoyed for thirty years."[41]

The VIC responded that the reasons for the company's founding had to do with recovering a trade that was "apparently lost" to Virginia. Spotswood and the General Assembly had responded to the avarice of South Carolina, which had "entirely engrossed" the Native trade they had once shared with Virginia. This exclusion opened the door for the Native people to look to the French if they felt South Carolina overcharged or failed to supply them. Sensitive to the recent Yamasee War, Native nations creating a disturbance could find unscrupulous traders willing to sell arms and ammunition for "private gain." On the other hand, a "regulated company" could reclaim Virginia's market share, offset "loose traders," and hinder the French.

The assembly concluded that the "whole consumption" of commodities in the Native trade had not exceeded three hundred pounds per annum. Although the petitioners said they spoke for merchants and inhabitants trading to and residing in the Chesapeake colonies, only three or four of the nine signers were Virginia traders. The others were either shipmasters to Maryland or "so far from being Virginia merchants or inhabitants we are . . . unacquainted with their present characters." With the exception of Henry Offley, who about "two or three years ago" sent in a cargo of eighty to one hundred pounds of trade goods consigned to Robert Bolling, "we are well informed from both the ancient traders themselves and from the entries and courthouse's accounts that not one appears ever purchased one hogshead of skins of the Indians" or "invest one penny of their own risque [risk] in that Trade." The VIC also noted that since one could not distinguish between Native and English trade goods, "except vermilion, Tinsey Lace and Beads," which could be covered by fifty pounds a year, the company has access to "great quantities of goods" going into Virginia for trade.[42]

What might appear to be a monopoly was rather a joint stock company, the VIC memorialists said, which anyone had the liberty to subscribe to. Also, in return for their incorporation they had spent "considerable sums of money" for the public good; they had built and supplied powder for the public magazine at Williamsburg, maintained the garrison at Fort Christanna for defense of the southern frontier, and also built a fort for the public school for "no less than 70" Native children.[43] They had also been at a "considerable charge of sending out men to discover a passage over the great mountains," which had been found to be "impracticable." Efforts to open a trade with the Native people on the other side of the mountains have "proved abortive" after sickness broke out among the men sent to make the discovery. Without finding a passage through the mountains, it was impossible to expand their share because of South Carolina, so that the expenses would outrun the profits and eventually "eat out the principal stock."[44] Undeterred, the VIC proposed a forty-man expedition with two hundred horses packed with merchandise, for "recovering that beneficial Trade at such an expense no private trader can support."[45]

"The Chief Aim of my Expedition over the great Mountains in 1716," Spotswood memorialized, "was to satisfy my Self whether it was practicable to come at the Lakes." Not unlike Lederer's expedition a half-century earlier, he sought a route to the reputed Great Water on the other side of the mountains, his aims profiling the slow pace of colonial expansion. He found an "easy passage" over the Blue Ridge with the direction of Native people, "who frequent those parts, . . . but three Days" March to a great Nation of Indians living on a River [the Shawnee on the Ohio River?] w'ch discharges itself in the Lake Erie," clearly a mistake. From that vantage point on the "western side of one of the small Mountains," he spied a lake and encountered three French traders, who accessed it on their voyage from Montreal down the St. Lawrence to the Mississippi and "Maville [Mobile], their Chief Town in their New Settlement of Louisiana." He acknowledged "by this Communication and the forts they have already built, the British Plantations are in a manner Surrounded by their Commerce w'th the numerous Nations of Indians seated on both sides of the Lakes; they may not only Engross the whole Skin Trade, but may, when they please, Send out such Bodys of Indians on the back of these Plantations as may greatly distress his Maj'ty's Subjects here."[46]

In 1718 the Saponi felt so menaced by the Haudenosaunee in general or the Seneca in particular that they messaged the commanding officer at Fort Christanna "to demand that Nation of Indians to be delivered up to them." They had no recourse for the "obstinacy" of the assembly in refusing to fund the guard at the fort and abandoning them once the Crown dissolved the VIC's charter on May 24. Despite the Crown's recommendation that the government take up the slack, the assembly no longer intended to honor the treaty and revoked the terms, which kept hostages, ordering that the children matriculating at the college should be sent back to their people and grinding to a halt Native Christianization.[47] Spotswood said that the policy was inexcusable and inhumane: to desert "a people that had voluntarily submitted to the orders of the Government, desired to be Ruled according to such Methods as We should direct and agreed to have all their children brought up Christians at the school w'ch I have established there." Consequently, he removed the Saponi from their town to the fort, which he fortified sufficiently to repulse "any Indian Enemy"—enough so, he believed, that the Five Nations, "being sensible that it was impracticable to attack them there, have since offered them peace."[48]

Virginia's relations with its tributary nations took a turn for the worse when the Crown vetoed the 1714 act regulating of the Native trade and the assembly refused to fund either the school or garrison at Christanna. Adding insult to injury, neither the Crown nor the assembly was willing to compensate the VIC for their investment in Fort Christanna. The assembly sent hostages of the tributary nations enrolled in the school back to their respective nations. It then asserted that since the frontier defense was now "slighted," then the tributary nations who had moved to the fort "to serve as a Barrier to the Inhabitants are voted to be entitled to no other protection than the other Tributarys, (who refused to perform their Engagements.)"[49]

Not only would the Saponi continue in their role as a barrier against the Seneca, the Tuscarora, and other nations, but the English also intended a Christian education for their children paid out of Spotswood's own pocket, as a buffer against their elders. All that came to naught in 1729 after a fifteen-year residence, when the Saponi relinquished their allegiance to Virginia after two incidents involving inebriated Saponi. In the first case in 1724, the justices in Spotsylvania County "examined" a Saponi man named Sawnie, "lately returned from Canada," after his "insolently threatening" the settlers with an imminent invasion of "French Indians." Sawnie had been made captive and "carried into Canada" by a Northern Nation, likely the Seneca, two years earlier. He had participated in an incursion with his captors in New England and had visited Albany with them, where the English officials there arranged for his return to Virginia. Allegedly, he made his threatening comments in Germanna while he was "in drink." After further examination, he denied that he had conveyed to the Saponi or any of the other Virginia tributaries any message of incursion or expressed any intention to return to the

French Indians. The justices sentenced him to prison "unless the Great Men of his Nation shall engage for his good behavior, and that he shall not depart out of this Government or hold correspondence with any Foreign Indians."[50]

The disassociation of the Saponi from Virginia five years later involved competing jurisdictions and capital punishment, not unlike what first soured Tuscarora-Virginia relations. In the second case, the colony tried and hanged a Saponi man who while drunk with rum had committed homicide. William Byrd II, a member of the council in Virginia, recollected that Virginia had hanged a Native notable after he killed an Englishman in a drunken brawl. Byrd wrote:

> In earnest they [the Saponi] would have served well enough for that purpose [a barrier to other Indians], if the white people in the neighbourhood had not debauched their morals, and ruined their health with rum, which was the cause of many disorders, and ended at last in a barbarous murder committed by one of these Indians when he was drunk, for which the poor wretch was executed when he was sober. It was matter of great concern to them, however, that one of their grandees should be put to so ignominious a death. . . . The Saponies took this execution so much to heart, that they soon after quitted their settlement and removed in a body to the Catawba.[51]

Byrd summed up the Native history in the area. He placed the Meherrin and the Nansemond in northeastern North Carolina outside the boundaries of Virginia. Iroquoian-speaking, they could put a brake on the yeh is-WAH h'reh and Ani'-Yun-wiya movement into the region. On the other hand, unable to withstand their "implacable enemies," the Seneca from the north and the Tuscarora, "most of those to the south," the Saponi had sought "refuge in Virginia." "Disturbed" by the Tuscarora, the Saponi, were now retired into the protection of yeh is-WAH h'reh. The Saponi, who had aligned with Monacan and signed the Middle Plantations Treaty in 1680, were driven away from their ancestral land in the piedmont of the Blue Ridge near the Yadkin River in 1703 by the Haudenosaunee. They were relocated in 1715 following the Tuscarora War by Virginia. The Saponi then comprised "the remnants of several other nations, . . . speaking the same language, and using the same customs," including the Occaneechis and Stoukenhock, who had joined them for self-protection. "They dwelt formerly not far below the mountains, upon Yadkin river, about two hundred miles west and by south from the falls of Roanoke."[52]

Disaffected after two years, the Saponi left yeh is-WAH h'reh and returned to Virginia on May 5, 1732, beseeching the governor for a renewal of their tributary status. Governor Sir William Gooch accepted the allegiance of several Saponi, together with the Cheraw [Saraw or Saura] willing to co-habit with them, and permitted them "to seat themselves on any Lands they shall chuse not being granted to any of his Majesties' Subjects either on the River Roanoke or Appamatox [Appomattox] . . . equal to that they formerly held at Christanna." This incorporation was short-lived, for the Saponi in 1740 migrated from here to Shamokin, where they were adopted by the Cayuga, an alignment that the council guarded against twenty years earlier.[53]

By the time Byrd's expedition arrived at Cattashowrock, Nottoway Town, in 1728, they were the most consequential tributary nation remaining in Virginia, numbering about two hundred men, women, and children. They traded exclusively with the English, exchanging skins for guns, powder, and shot. Byrd described their palisaded town:

> This fort was a square piece of ground, inclosed with substantial puncheons, or strong palisades, about ten feet high, and leaning a little outwards, to make a scalade more difficult. Each side of the square might be about a hundred yards long, with loop-holes at proper distances, through which they may fire upon the enemy. Within this inclosure we found bark cabins sufficient to lodge all their people, in case they should be obliged to retire thither. These cabins are no other but close arbours made of saplings, arched at the top, and covered so well with bark as to be proof against all weather. The fire is made in the middle, according to the Hibernian fashion, the smoke whereof finds no other vent but at the door, and so keeps the whole family warm, at the expense both of their eyes and complexion. The Indians have no standing furniture in their cabins but hurdles to repose their persons upon, which they cover with mats and deer-skins.

Byrd also described a ceremonial dance. The men, "painted" for war, danced and sang to the beat of drums made from large gourds, their feet keeping exact time, their arms and head gesticulating wildly. The women, wrapped in red and blue matchcoats, watched stoically, their hair beaded, their necks and wrists adorned with blue conch shells. The color blue was prized in Nottoway society, and blue shells were also used as currency.[54]

Attentive to the settlers' encroachment, some Monacan dispersed locally sixty miles south of their ancestral homeland; others converged on Bear Mountain (in present-day Amherst County), "now considered the sacred home of the Monacan people," where they adopted log cabin habitation, masking their regional persistence. Long-distance migrants relocated north to Pennsylvania and Ontario and south to the yeh is-WAH h'reh.

Still other Monacan people joined the Saponi at Christanna. "There remain only the Pamunkey on the York River and they reduced to a very inconsiderable Number and the Nottoway on the south side of the James River whose Strength settlements and exceeds not fifty fighting men," said James Logan in 1736. These nations lived in "peace and amity" within the bounds of Virginia.[55]

PART II
Hostilities

Fathers Both you and the English are White. We live in a Country between, therefore the Land does not belong either to one or the other; but the Great Being above allow'd it to be a Place of residence for us; so Fathers, I desire you to withdraw, as I have done our Brothers the English, for I will keep you at Arm's length. I lay this down as a Tryal for both, to see which will have the greatest regard to it, and that Side we will stand by, and make equal Sharers with us.

—Tanaghrisson, Seneca-Cayuga sachem, to the French commandant Paul Marin de la Malgue, September 3, 1753

CHAPTER 9

Remembrance of These Things Is Faithfully Preserved

Scores of spectators jammed into the halls and galleries of the Great Meeting House in Philadelphia on October 2, 1736, to witness the negotiations between the British officials and the Haudenosaunee sachems. Onondaga served as the capital where the Haudenosaunee kindled the council fire, deliberated among themselves, and arrived at consensus. The Haudenosaunee had returned to Philadelphia to give their responses to articles raised at the August 1732 treaty meeting. If they met at the Great Meeting House rather than at the Grand Council in the Long House, which symbolized the unity of the Six Nations, Haudenosaunee house rules nevertheless applied. Exchanging both gifts and merchandise, presenting wampum strategically, and deliberating unhurriedly were the Haudenosaunee practices of diplomacy.[1]

The Haudenosaunee long tradition of diplomacy peppered negotiations with rhetorical flourishes of the Covenant Chain. Kanickhungo, a Seneca, spoke for the Six Nations. Characterized by the Haudenosaunee as "a true good Man" who "spoke their Words, and our Words, and not his own," Johann Conrad Weiser translated for Kanickhungo. Opening with the fire and iron keynotes in the custom of their culture, Kanickhungo said that they Haudenosaunee were grateful for the warmth of their host's fire, which they wished would burn eternally. They were also appreciative of the road, which Onas, George Thomas, lieutenant governor and commander in chief of the Province of Pennsylvania and the Counties of New Castle, Kent, and Sussex upon Delaware, had made, and desired that it should remain clear of debris and open for mutual convenience. Onas was an appellation first given to William Penn, meaning in Haudenosaunee a quill, evidently a personification signifying his ability to sign treaties. They reaffirmed their alliance made in 1732—"the brightening of the Chain of Friendship between us, and the preserving it free from all Rust and Spots." They also extended it to the Lenape, Piscataway, and other tributaries under the Haudenosaunee's dominion living on the Susquehanna and the Ohio Rivers, all under the "strictest charge to behave themselves" when abroad.[2] Following the British advice of the 1732 treaty meeting, the Haudenosaunee had made alliances with "the Onichkaryagoes, Sissaghees, Tioumitihagas, Attawantenis, Twechtwese [Myaamia], and Oachtamughs" and sought the return and reconnection of remnants of the Haudenosaunee now in Canada."The French were formerly our cruel Enemies, and we are taking Such Measures as we hope will be effectual to bring back our People, if any new Breach Should happen."[3]

When the two delegations returned to the Meeting House on October 13, James Logan, president of the Pennsylvania Provincial Council, addressed the issues raised by the Haudenosaunee. Affecting Haudenosaunee diplomatic formalities recommended by Weiser, and using metaphors of light, a "brightened chain" uniting the English and the Haudenosaunee, and a "kindled fire" blazing a path between both peoples, making them one, Logan dealt with the demand for the surrender of a white man who had killed a Native man. During a drunken brawl in the Alleghenies, when the Native man slashed the other with a knife, the white man bashed his head several times and killed him, then escaped "Southward of Virginia."[4]

The Haudenosaunee demanded not only his surrender but also the removal of English traders from the Ohio Valley, the Alleghenies, and the banks of the Susquehanna. The torturous punishment reserved for white offenders extradited to the Haudenosaunee and its consequent demoralizing effect on the settlers were reasons for pause. Logan said to the Haudenosaunee that the English would apprehend and try him under British law. If the court determined that he was guilty of murder, they would hang him, a shameful but far less painful way to die than mutilation, dismemberment, and immolation, but they would free him if the court found he had acted in self-defense. With respect to the removal of all English traders, Logan supposed rum was the key to the disorder; but discouraged the removal remedy, reminding the Haudenosaunee that their people had become dependent on English trade goods, especially gunpowder for their rifles and clothes for their bodies. Logan agreed that the sale of rum should be suppressed, but he reminded them that Native people were "universally fond" of it despite English efforts to discourage its consumption.[5]

Perhaps *universally* was too inclusive a term. Logan was surely aware of the role rum had played in the disassociation of the Saponi from Virginia ten years earlier, a case likewise involving competing jurisdictions and capital punishment. Logan soon learned of another example. Among a Shawnee party "lately returned from their country" in the south to Housatonic, Connecticut, Annawauneekheek related a "remarkable" account to missionary John Sergeant. Some time previously, the Shawnee, deciding to trade no more in rum because of its demoralizing effects, had "broken some caggs [kegs] which traders have brought them."[6] Logan came to know all too well of this event. Both he and William Penn received a letter, dated March 20, 1738, depicting the destruction of the rum kegs, signed by three Shawnee chiefs—"Loyparcowah (Opessa's Son), Newcheconner (Deputy King), and Coycacolenne, or Coracolenne (Chief Counselor)"—enclosed with a petition calling for a ban on alcohol in the Shawnee towns for four years, signed by ninety-eight Shawnee and two traders, Peter Chartier and George Miranda.

> The proposal of stopping the rum and all strong liquors was made to the rest [remaining at the council meeting] in the winter, and they were all willing. As soon as it was concluded of, all the rum that was in the Towns was all staved and spilled, belonging both to Indians and white people, which in quantity consisted of about forty gallons, that was thrown in the street; and we have appointed four men to stave all the rum, or strong liquors that is brought to the Towns hereafter, either by Indians or white men, during the four years.[7]

In this atmosphere of distrust, Logan promised to discourage the rum trade but feigned an inability to prevent traders from hawking their goods where they chose. Logan also questioned how the Haudenosaunee's claims on lands in Virginia and Maryland, including their assertions in Ohio country, were "supported." The lands on the Susquehanna River, "we believe belong to the Six Nations, by the conquest of the Indians of that River; but how their Pretensions are made good to the Lands to the Southward, we know not." Noting the treaty of 1732, on the other hand, Logan asserted that the British had "desired . . . all our Indians, the Delaware, Shawnee, and others should be recalled from Ohio." Fearing both a war with the French and suspicious of the affinity that the Shawnee had shown them, Logan proposed, rather than leaving the Native Ohioans "scattered" and exposed, consolidating them into "one body."[8]

Yet rather than tackle the most important land issue, Logan punted. The British concluded the treaty with "Articles, to be kept in perpetual Remembrance by them and us, and by our Children and their Children to all Generations," with the caveat on the Haudenosaunee's land claims on Virginia and Maryland: "We ought to be better informed before we can write on this Head."[9]

The Haudenosaunee had not forgotten, drawing on their historical memory through their spoken practice from "father to son . . . an Account of all these Things. . . . You will find the Remembrance of them is faithfully preserved, and our succeeding Generations are made acquainted with what has passed, that it may not be forgot as long as the Earth remains."[10] Since the Haudenosaunee had fully answered the articles of the fire, the road, and the chain of friendship, the proprietors promised them two hundred pounds in merchandise and Weiser a commission of twenty pounds for his interpretative services. The Haudenosaunee accepted the proffered presents with gratitude.[11]

Although the English had "found means to avoid" dealing with the disputed boundaries of the Chesapeake colonies, the Haudenosaunee, after traveling one hundred miles "homewards," delivered a "parting" shot. They compelled Weiser, who had accompanied them, to send a letter on their behalf "exceedingly pressing" their claims on the boundaries of the Chesapeake colonies, for "we expect some Consideration for Our Land now in their Occupation and if so be that they are willing to make some Consideration."[12] In turn, Logan enclosed their dispatch with a cover letter to both Gov. Samuel Ogle of Maryland and Gov. William Gooch of Virginia, conveying their demand "to make them Satisfaction for the Lands those Governments are possessed of lower on Susquehanna and Chesapeake, Shenandoah and the Parts adjacent, belonging as they say, to them the said Indians, for which they have never been paid."[13]

Concerned about French incursions into the south, the British at Albany sought an end to the Haudenosaunee raids against the yeh is-WAH h'reh. The British were also concerned that the Haudenosaunee might switch their allegiance to the French. Trying to dodge this drift, they invited the Haudenosaunee to convene at Albany. Responding to the "earnest request" of the southern nations of the yeh is-WAH h'reh and the Ani'-Yun-wiya to end the "continual incursions" of the Haudenosaunee, colonial authorities tentatively arranged a treaty meeting set in Albany. Governor Gooch was certainly aware that the French had sent an expedition against the southern nations bordering Georgia and South Carolina when he began parleys with the Ani'-Yun-wiya and the yeh is-WAH h'reh. Even though they were not "immediate dependents" of Virginia, he deemed it both too expensive and too dangerous to include them, enemies of the Haudenosaunee, in the negotiations in New York or Pennsylvania.[14] Not only were the southern nations hesitant to travel to Albany for the meetings, but Gooch also thought its cost "unreasonable since Virginia had no other interest in the negotiation."[15]

A letter written in Dutch to Laurens Claese Van der Volgen [Lawrence Claessen], interpreter between the Six Nations and the governors of New York, Pennsylvania, and Virginia, reported the resolutions of the Commissioners of Indian Affairs on March 6, 1738. Supporting documents enclosed with the letter included copies of letters from the Ani'-Yun-wiya and the yeh is-WAH h'reh to Governor Gooch of Virginia. The Ani'-Yun-wiya and the yeh is-WAH h'reh were resolved "to come early in the Spring directly here to Albany, to conclude a peace with the Six Nations, which has been under discussion for such a long time."[16] The commissioners dispatched Captain

Verplank along with two Mohawks to alert the Six Nations by delivering this message first to Seneca country and then immediately to Onondaga. The correspondent asked that Van der Volgen do his "best so that the Six Nations do no harm" to them.

> We have learned from the Maquasse Indians [Mohawk] that the Indian that who set Aaron [a Mohawk sachem] free when he was a prisoner is now a prisoner at Onondage (Onondaga). So we ask you to do your best to prevent any harm coming to him, and that you tell the Onondages that we expect them to bring him with them when they come here to conclude the peace, so that we can deliver him over to the ambassadors who are coming here to conclude the aforesaid peace.[17]

Negotiations ended in August 1738 when the Haudenosaunee made a "treacherous attack" on the yeh is-WAH h'reh, "which so exasperated that nation that they pursued their northern enemies as far as the River Cahongarooton [Cohongoruton, upper Potomac] and gave them a notable defeat." After the yeh is-WAH h'reh withdrew, Gooch accused the Haudenosaunee of taking out their frustration on three settler families, alleging that they had "barbarously massacred" eleven of the settlers. Gooch "immediately sent to the nearest Six Nations towns to demand they hand over the perpetrators, but they pretend to know nothing of the matter and endeavor to charge it on the French-aligned Native peoples from Lake Erie. But if it was the French, as I am very sure it was not, the Six Nations ought to be accountable since it must be them that taught the French the way to our frontier."[18] The Council of Trade and Plantations deemed the deed a "folly not pardonable even to savages."[19] Because both the Ani'-Yun-wiya and the yeh is-WAH h'reh were reputedly under British dominion, the Haudenosaunee were "effectually doing the work of our common enemy." The council reasoned it an imperative to reign in the Haudenosaunee, the Ani'-Yun-wiya, and the yeh is-WAH h'reh into their "proper bounds," hammered out by Spotswood in the Treaty of 1722.[20]

When the Haudenosaunee and the Shawnee chiefs again convened with the British delegates at the Meeting House in Philadelphia on July 6, 1742, Governor Thomas wasted no time on diplomatic niceties. As soon as the crowded hall quieted down, he got right to the point of contention from six years earlier. The Haudenosaunee were to relinquish their claims to the lands on both the north and south banks of the Susquehanna River extending to Pennsylvania's southern boundary and to the lands in the Kittatinny Hills (from the Lenape *Kitahtëne*, meaning "Endless Mountains"), the ridge ranging in its northeastern corner between the Delaware and the Susquehanna

Rivers.[21] In return the British conveyed a duplicate list of deferred goods to the Haudenosaunee and their tributaries, the first installment having been paid six years earlier. Only then, quick to seal the deal, did Thomas brandish the diplomatic fustian, kindling the fire and brightening the chain, before laying down a belt of wampum.[22]

Unlike Thomas, Canassatego, an Onondaga sachem, waded slowly into the particulars of the proceedings, reminding his audience of the long friendship his nation had had with the British, fondly invoking the memory of William Penn, the first *onas*. Over two days he elaborated on the significance of renewing the friendship chain and throwing fuel on the fire to brighten their relations. After acknowledging the receipt of the promised presents, Canassatego made clear he understood the English intent too well. He said, "We know our Lands are now become more valuable. The white People think we do not know their Value; but we are sensible that the Land is everlasting, and the few Goods we receive for it are soon worn out and gone." Governor Thomas immediately volleyed, "It is very true, that Lands are of late become more valuable, but what raises their Value? Is it not entirely owing to the Industry and Labor used by the white People in their Cultivation and Improvement? . . . Had not they come amongst you, these Lands would have been of no Use to you, any further than to maintain you."[23]

Canassatego said, "If you have not done anything, we now renew our Request, and desire you will inform the Person whose People are seated on our Lands, that that Country belongs to us in Right of Conquest. We having bought it with our Blood and taken it from our Enemies in fair War; and we expect, as Owners of that Land, to receive such a Consideration for it as the Land is worth."[24] Thomas had paid attention to Canassatego's complaint of settlers illicitly settling westward of the Kittatinny Hills. True to his word given at the July treaty meeting, Thomas issued a proclamation on October 5, 1742, "strictly requiring" all squatters to vacate the lands west of the Kittatinny Hills, "appropriated to the use of the Indians on this side of those Hills," or "they will answer the contrary at their highest Peril."[25]

Governor Thomas, on the other hand, caught Canassatego unawares with a complaint of the Lenape's refusal to remove themselves from land that Pennsylvania claimed from a deed of sale fifty years earlier, first signed by nine Lenape chiefs and then reiterated about fifteen years previously. After reviewing the deeds of sale, Canassatego had to concede. He turned his vitriol on the Lenape, emasculating them by calling them women, "the highest affront that can be offered," wrote French Jesuit Pierre-Francois-Xavier Charlevoix in 1744. Charlevoix noted that the "effeminacy and lubricity" of men who "wear the dress of women . . . are held in the most sovereign contempt."[26] "We conquered you; we made Women of you," Canassatego said. "You know you are Women and can no more sell Land than Women."

He also ordered the Lenape not to engage in any more land transactions with the English. The treaty meeting ended abruptly after Canassatego reiterated: "You act a dishonest Part, not only in this but in other Matters: Your Ears are ever open to slanderous Reports about our Brethren; you receive them with as much Greediness as lewd Women receive the Embraces of bad Men. . . . You are Women. Take the Advice of a wife Man and remove immediately . . . either to Wyoming (on the Susquehanna River) or Shamokin."[27] The Lenape left the council and soon after relocated themselves from the Delaware Forks to Wyoming, Shamokin, and Ohio. The 1742 agreement also stipulated that the Ani'-Yun-wiya and the yeh is-WAH h'reh would send emissaries to Albany to confirm the peace and to establish trade, but they reneged. The Ani'-Yun-wiya later did follow through and ratified the peace, but the yeh is-WAH h'reh "refused to come" and added a slur: "We [the Haudenosaunee] were but Women, that they were Men, and double Men, for they had two P[enise]s; that they could make Women of us and would be always at War with us."[28]

After taking account of the negotiations, Governor Gooch anticipated that it was "absolutely necessary" for the Chesapeake colonies of Virginia and Maryland to come to "fair and just terms" and establish peace with their Native neighbors. The commissioners cautioned that they should proceed from a posture of strength, "justice, and honor" and not project weakness, "fear, or apprehension of injury."[29] Concerned about British encroachment to their south, the Haudenosaunee claimed the land as an ancestral right either from time immemorial or by right of conquest over "ancient possessors." They averred that the settlers had entered their territory without permission and demanded compensation. The Haudenosaunee again agreed to meet with the British colonial representatives in Lancaster, Pennsylvania, in June 1744 to arrange a treaty when the sachems sent a letter to Logan complaining that the Virginians had settled in their country without their permission and demanding consideration, a complaint lodged at the 1736 meeting but still unresolved. The colonial Chesapeake governors demonstrated a "truly equitable Disposition" to negotiate with the Haudenosaunee and desired to convene a site for the treaty, but before they could move forward, a "skirmish happened in the back Parts of Virginia between some of the Militia there, and a Party of the Indian Warriors of the Six Nations, with some Loss on both Sides."[30]

CHAPTER 10

Exposing Ourselves to All Manner of Hardships

Deviating from the general practice for great planter engrossment, which had characterized Virginia history, for a brief interlude between 1730 and 1732, the nine grant recipients of 385,000 acres in the Shenandoah Valley, with the notable exception of William Beverley, were neither members of the slaveholding elite nor even Virginians but European agents promising to settle Protestants across the Blue Ridge. This singularity of purpose resulted from a consolidation of imperial interests. Fears of French continental expansion, Native contestation of colonial boundaries, and African maroonage in the mountains, along with the Crown's protection of the Fairfax proprietary, all combined to alter the distribution of land grants. The Crown instructed Governor Gooch to bypass the council's business-as-usual land office practices for a scheme to buffer the settlements with Protestant immigrants. If Thomas, sixth Lord Fairfax, frowned on foreign immigration, Gooch encouraged German Palatine, Ulster Irish, Scotch Irish, and Swiss immigrants to populate the Shenandoah Valley. If these foreign freeholders preempted great planters' designs to populate the Shenandoah Valley with enslaved laborers, who by the 1750s numbered only 4 percent there, the Crown succeeded in its exigencies to create a buffer zone there.[1]

Beverley's desire to settle the Shenandoah Valley with Protestants from Pennsylvania if he could procure a grant from the council aligned with imperial interests, but it also explains his exceptionality. His proposal dovetailed with the Crown's current tramontane policy. He wrote in April 1732 to an unnamed authority in Williamsburg, likely Gooch, "I am persuaded that I can get a number of people from Pennsylvania to settle on Shenandoah, if I can obtain an order of Council for some Land there." Beverley sought fifteen thousand acres on both sides of the river, including Massanutten Town at the foot of the Blue Ridge. "Northern men are fond of buying land there, because they can buy it, for six or seven pounds per hundred acres, cheaper than they can take up land in Pennsylvania and they don't care to go as far as Williamsburg." In a pilot case, Beverley had surveyed and sold valley land to a Pennsylvania man for three pounds Pennsylvania currency per one hundred acres. "But I hope he will be balkt [steadfast], and not take our money and labor from us; we have so dearly earned it by exposing ourselves to all manner of hardships for ye discovery of the frontiers."[2] "Soon that part of Virginia on the other side of the great Mountains may be Peopled, if proper Encouragements for that Purpose were given," wrote Gooch, by "Germans lately come into Pennsylvania, where being disappointed of the qu[ality] of Land . . . have chosen to fix their habitations in this uninhabited part of Virginia. . . . By this means a strong Barrier will be Settled between us and the French."[3]

Partly because of his efforts in the Shenandoah Valley and partly because of his service on the Northern Neck survey in 1736, Beverley, a burgess of Orange County, received a grant of almost 120,000 acres in what became Augusta County. He also received in 1737 an order-in-council for 30,000 acres, which he offered to share a quarter of (along with its charges) with Capt. James Patton of Kirkcudbright, Scotland, for "doing your utmost endeavor to procure families to come in and settle it." He envisioned they would "make money on the Land" by holding it "undivided" until sold, unless we decide to settle it ourselves. At the same time, on a more realistic note, Beverley negotiated the sale of either 1,000 or 1,500 acres of his own land to Patton or his relatives. He refused goods at 60 percent, since he could secure them on better terms in country. Rather, "I expect to have money for ye Land here unless you should have any tradesmen or gardeners to dispose of, and then perhaps I can be your chap, and for ye bolting mill or machine [for shifting flour]. . . . If your relation come, he may have the land."[4]

Beverley nevertheless still referred to the western region in Virginia as a "wilderness." He had to contend with squatters who presently inhabited the region. "We have had very scarce times in this river [Rappahannock]," he wrote to John Fairchild of Barbados on August 25, 1738. "Several poor people having lived on herbs growing in the fields without either bread or meat."[5] John Bartram, a botanist, came to a similar conclusion that same year when he visited Opequon, where he found the "mountains very thinly inhabited with [English people] that is lately settled there and lives a lazy life and subsists by hunting." Historian Stephen Warren Hofstra explains that theirs was a "fusion of European and Indian practices," combining the Indigenous art of tracking and the European access to guns, including the long rifle, their weapon of choice.[6] Governor Gooch cast aspersions of laziness, reminiscent of European revilement of Native hunters: "The Common people and some of the Better Sort," weaving cloth on looms for themselves and their enslaved Africans, both new dwellers on western side of the mountains, "make tolerable Linen with their own Flax."[7]

Beverley also petitioned in 1738 for an easement for Lord Fairfax's lands from the headspring of the southern branch of the Rappahannock and the headspring of the Potomac. He prayed that the council would recognize the "plain meaning" of the proprietary, "though I doubt not but our Great Men here have done your Lordship all the injury in their power."[8] He was spot on. They carried their opposition to the Treasury, with a report containing "dark passages" stirring "all prejudices imaginable." Nevertheless, Beverley remained hopeful that Fairfax would overcome "stumbling blocks" and obtain an order for Beverley to run his "boundary line." Beverley felt Fairfax had an "undoubted right" to his proprietary lands so that he could settle freeholders in the fork of the Rappahannock.[9] Partitioning Prince William into two counties evidenced their success, with the "part above Occoquan" becoming Fairfax County in 1742.[10]

Conscious of the value of office holding for attaining elite status in Virginia, Beverley closely eyed Secretary John Carter's health. On March 10, 1741, he informed his correspondent Charles Smyth not only of Carter's being deathly ill with "dropsy in the belly" but also of his interest in procuring Carter's post, which the dying man had purchased for 1,500 guineas or about £1,575 sterling. Even though he had heard that "several gentlemen" had expressed their desire to purchase this position for life for £2,000 or 27 percent more than Carter had paid, Beverley offered to pay even more rather than miss this opportunity. He also asked that Smyth procure for him a letter of appointment to the council in Carter's place. "I beg you will do the best you can for me; and although I have not much ready cash, yet I have a very considerable Estate in Lands and Negroes and this shall oblige me to repay you what money you shall advance for me in this affair together with Interest."[11] After Carter died on July 31, 1742, Beverley asked Smyth to carry out his previous instructions for the commission if it was still available. He reiterated his desire for credit: "I have so little money in your hands it is a strange presumption in me to desire you to advance about £2000 Sterling for me who am a stranger to you."[12] (After Commissary John Blair's death the following year, he once again was unsuccessful seeking Blair's place on the council.)[13]

At least one of Beverley's neighbors was restless and pressed the council for a land grant further west. The council had approved John Howard's petition on October 17, 1737, to explore together with several of his neighbors at their own expense "the Lakes and Rivers of the Mississippi" with the caveat that he neither "offer any Hostility to any Indians or others he may happen to meet with, nor go to any effort or Garrison possessed by the French on the said Lakes or River." He had petitioned the council because the Virginia settlements had experienced "more than a hundred" attacks by "unknown savages." He decided the best way of dealing with this crisis was to visit and make treaties with the Native nations. After meeting with Gooch, he petitioned the council for a commission authorizing him "to enlist a small company of volunteers to go into the back parts of Virginia, as far as the River

Mississippi, there to visit the Indians who lived in those parts to make peace with them and so establish a durable treaty." "This enterprise having been abandoned for reasons which it would be tiresome to relate, I returned to my home." In an affidavit given to the French after his capture, Howard gave self-defense as the rationale for his intrusion into la Louisiane. He said the predatory attacks had continued, resulting in the deaths of half of his neighbors at a meetinghouse. Following this incident Howard again consulted with Gooch, who gave him a "new commission" to go after the perpetrators in the upper Mississippi River region. Visiting several Native nations, he saw the scalps of his neighbors and learned that the offenders, "fearing we would take vengeance," had escaped toward the Great Lakes. "Some of them," he learned, "were taken and punished." Even though this event gave Howard pause, he began to reconsider his original plan. Since Gooch was called away from Williamsburg because of the war with Spain, Howard assumed that his "original commission . . . was still in force and set out on March 8, 1742."[14]

He went to visit John Peter Salley, a German immigrant from Pennsylvania, who had in 1740 settled in at a "fork of James River close under the Blue Ridge of Mountains on the West Side." In his narrative of the journey, Salley said Howard came to his house with an offer of equal shares of the ten-thousand-acre grant promised in the council's commission to explore the western lands as far as the Mississippi River.[15] On March 16, 1742, the party of five—John Howard and his son Josias, John Patteet, Charles Cinekler, and Salley—set off from Salley's house to go five miles to Cedar Creek, where Salley described the Natural Bridge: "It is a solid Rock and is two hundred and three feet high, having a very large Spacious arch, where the Water runs through." Then they proceeded eighty-five miles to the Mondongachate [New] River, where they slaughtered and skinned five buffaloes, casing a coracle with their hides, perhaps a use of an Irish and Welsh technique, betraying Howard's ethnic origins. After traveling 250 miles down the Mondongachate River, he found "it very Rocky, having a great many Falls therein, one of which we computed to be thirty feet perpendicular and all along surrounded with inaccessible Mountains, high precipices, which obliged us to leave said River."[16]

They then traveled southwest by land another eighty-five miles before coming to another river running through mountainous terrain, where "farther down the plainer in those Mountains, we found great plenty of Coals, for which we named it Coal River." They continued on Coal River to its confluence at the Great Kanawha, where they entered the Ohio River and floated down to the Falls (now at Louisville), which were "three miles long in which is a small Island, the body of the Stream running on the North side, through which is no passing by reason of great Rocks and large Whirlpools, by which

FIGURE 17. William Roberts, *The Natural Bridge, Virginia*, 1808 (aquatint by Joseph Constantine Stadler). Image courtesy of Museum of Early Southern Decorative Arts.

we went down on the south side of said Island without much Danger or Difficulty and in time of a Fresh in the River." From there they traveled to the Mississippi River, entering it in June, and continued their passage until July 2, 1742, when they were suddenly surprised by "a Company of Men, Viz. to the Number of Ninety, Consisting of Frenchmen, Negroes, and Indians, who took us prisoners." Not one Native nation was named in their journey westward in either Howard's affidavit or in Salley's narrative. That Salley and Howard never mentioned Native nations would not have surprised Louisiana governor Jean-Baptiste Le Moyne de Bienville. Despite their protestations, Bienville believed not only that they were spies but also that they were from Carolina. "If they had been from Carolina, I would agree with" [Howard], said Bienville, "but the Virginians have no such knowledge of the country or of the tribes which dwell here as to have made such a rendezvous."[17]

CHAPTER 11

Invasions, Incursions, and Insurrections

In September 1730 Africans began massing throughout the tidewater region, prompted by the rumor that Governor Spotswood was returning to the Dominion to emancipate Christians. Why Spotswood would be the focus of the rumor is a puzzlement. After all, he had negotiated with the Haudenosaunee and the Shawnee to return African fugitives to the colony. He himself had become a great landholder and enslaver. The rumor may have emanated from his efforts with the attorney general to hold a woman responsible for beating her enslaved woman servant to death. Nevertheless, the rumor resonated with the increased number of both enslaved converts in the colony and the recent captives from Christian Kingdom of Kongo. Happening during the harvest gave the gatherings the rudimentary elements of a work stoppage. The militia broke up the assemblies and forced the Africans to return to harvesting the tobacco crop. Six weeks later, what the colonial authorities feared in September came to fruition when two hundred Africans massed in Norfolk and Princess Anne Counties and chose "'Officers to command them" in their "intended Insurrection." More than three hundred rebels staged a mass breakout into the Dismal Swamp. They established maroon settlements there for some time, until they were "discovered or hunted out by the Indians." The authorities summarily hanged at least two dozen rebels whom Native bounty hunters had found in the woods.[1]

In September 1730 the seven chiefs of the Ani'-Yun-wiya nation in negotiation with Virginia had resigned themselves to the presence of English settlers on both sides of the Great Mountains. They also agreed to capture and return enslaved runaways to the plantations for a bounty of a gun and a matchcoat for each one returned. Native people bound by these treaties of 1722 and 1730 routinely searched for fugitives, but only after the search was deemed futile by white bounty hunters. John Brickell explained how invaluable Native people were in finding Africans who "frequently run away from their Masters into the Woods, . . . as it happened in Virginia not long since [in 1730]." Native slave catchers, who knew the headwaters of rivers six or seven hundred miles away from their homes, could find a fugitive in one-tenth the time that it took white men. Moreover, they were relentless in their pursuit, continuing to search for the runaways until "they destroy[ed] or hunt[ed] them out of the Woods."[2]

FIGURE 18. *Cherokee Delegations to England*, 1730. Engraved by Isaac Basire (1704–68) after a painting by Markham 1740–60. Image courtesy of British Museum.

Perhaps because of the Ani'-Yun-wiya negotiations with Virginia in 1730, the Haudenosaunee felt the need to extend their hunting grounds across the Cumberland Gap into Kentucky. Deh-he-wä-mis recalled that her second husband, Hiokatoo, a Seneca renowned for valor, reveled in recounting his war exploits. As a young man in 1731, he was a "runner," responsible for recruiting warriors for warfare "against Cotawpes [Quapaws], Cherokee, and other southern Indians. A large army was collected, and after a long and fatiguing march, met its enemies in what was then called the 'low, dark and bloody lands,' near the mouth of Red River (and the Cumberland) in what is now called the state of Kentucky." The Cotawpes may have been the Quapaws. In 1729 the French were preoccupied with the Natchez, and the war allowed the Quapaw to develop new relations. The Ani'-Yun-wiya may have aligned with the Quapaw to assist them against the Haudenosaunee. The Haudenosaunee probably had forced them out of their ancestral lands in the Ohio basin and downriver to Arkansas. The Cotawpes became aware of their advance and laid in wait for them, but the Haudenosaunee scoped out

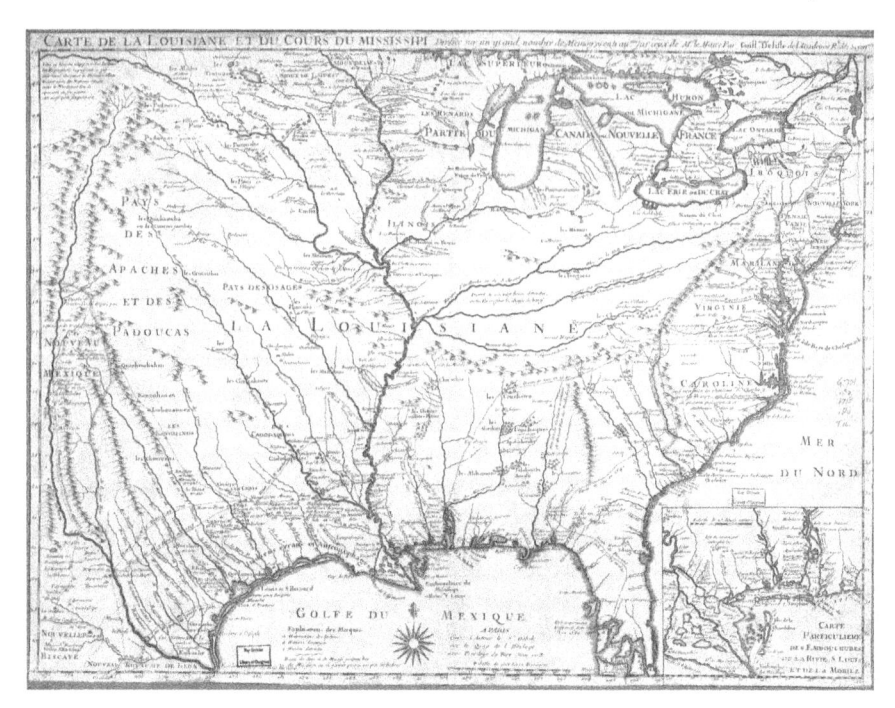

FIGURE 19. Guillaume de L'Isle, *Carte de la Louisiane et du Cours du Missisipi . . .* (Paris, France, June 1718). Image courtesy of Colonial Williamsburg Foundation Museum Purchase.

their ambuscade and, during two days of battle, killed twelve hundred of them. The Cotawpes suffered greater casualties among the southern nations. The Haudenosaunee also lost many dead "but gained the hunting ground, which was their grand object, though the Cherokee would not give it up in a treaty, or consent to make peace."³ The necessity of the Ani'-Yun-wiya asking permission to hunt can be explained by the Haudenosaunee victory over the Ani'-Yun-wiya and other southern nations at the battle near the mouth of Red River in 1731, in what is now called Kentucky, when the Haudenosaunee gained the hunting grounds, even though the Ani'-Yun-wiya never conceded the terrain by treaty.

Ever attentive to French intentions, on May 24, 1739, Gov. George Clarke of New York sent to the Committee of Trade and Plantations an intercepted French map. *A Map of the Countery of the Five Nations belonging to the Province of New York and of the Lakes near Which the Nations of Far Indians Live within Part of Canada & River St. Lawrence.* "Drawn in red ink," this map was apparently adapted from Guillaume Delisle's *Carte de la Louisiane et du cours du Missisipi [Mississippi]: Dressée sur un grand nombre de mémoires entrautres sur ceux de Mr. le Maire* (1718). Deeming their boundaries incorrect, Clark said it still served English purposes, because one could situate

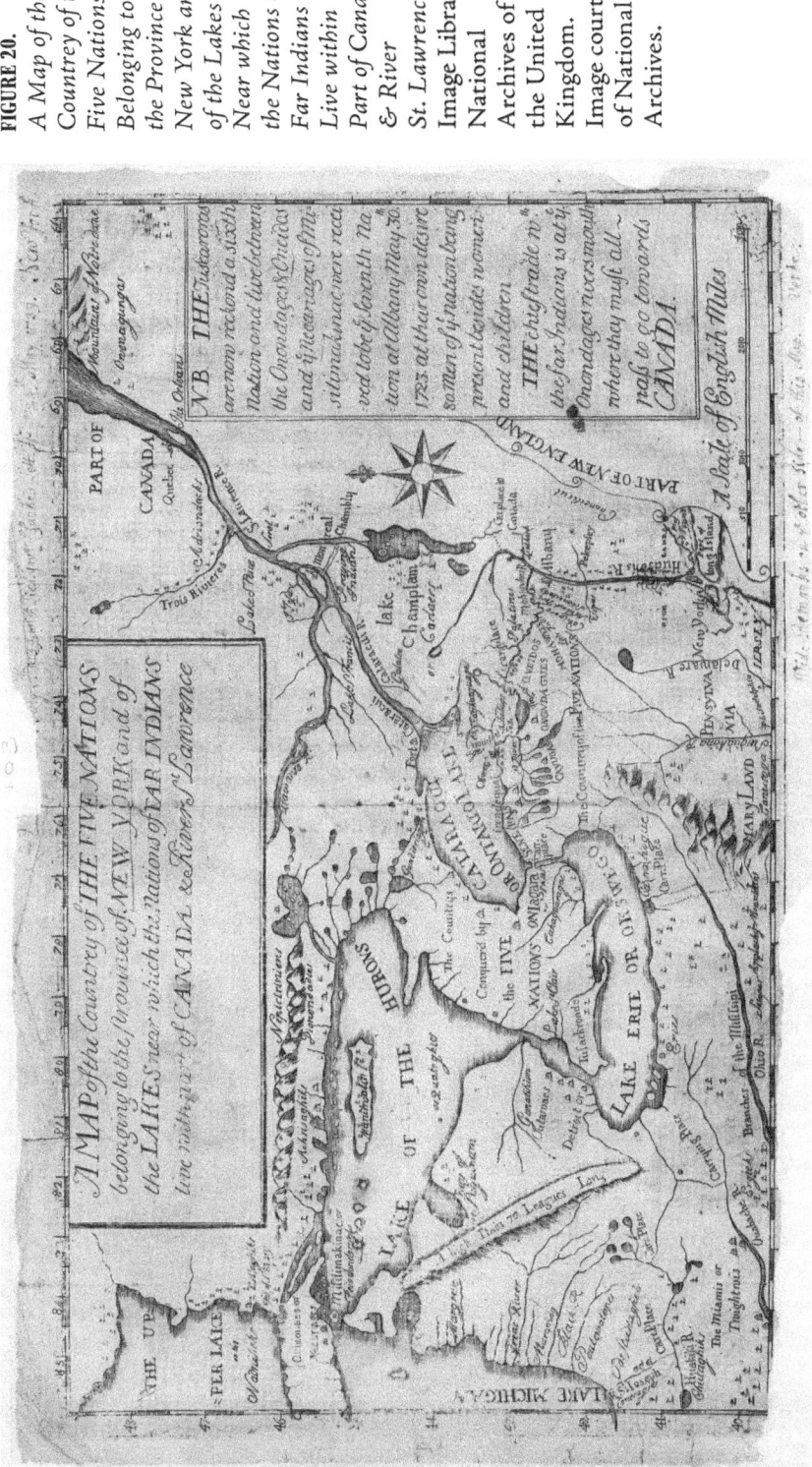

FIGURE 20.
A Map of the Country of the Five Nations Belonging to the Province of New York and of the Lakes Near which the Nations of Far Indians Live within Part of Canada & River St. Lawrence. Image Library, National Archives of the United Kingdom. Image courtesy of National Archives.

"those places on your own maps." He then challenged the convention of map-ping rivers and lakes as the "most natural and proper boundary," privileg-ing Louisiana and curbing the Haudenosaunee's buffer between New France and British America. For example, he pointed to the Seneca's "claim [to] a large country on the opposite shore of the Lake Cadracqui [Cataraqui] which they conquered long ago from the nations of Indians then inhabiting it." The French, on the other hand, "pretend to claim all the land so farr as the spring heads of any rivers or waters that empty themselves into any of the Lakes that disembogue into the River of St Lawrence." "If these pretensions had any foundation the greatest part of the Six Nations coming close to Virginia and other colonies . . . confine the English dominions to the limits of our present settlements."[4]

The British had good reason to cultivate relations with the Haudeno-saunee. Situated on colonial boundaries, they could act as friend, foe, or neutral, respectively offering protection to their allies, devastation to their enemies, and intelligence to their neutrals. One had to make "some allow-ance for their Prejudices and Passions," and some "presents" for their needs. Key to this relationship were conceptions of land and territorial integrity. For their part, the Haudenosaunee reaffirmed their allegiance to the Crown despite governor of New France Charles de la Boische's efforts to further French interests. "We assure you, the Governor of Canada pays our Nations great Court at this Time, well knowing of what Consequence we are to the French Interest. He has already told us, he was uncovering the Hatchet and sharpening it, and hoped, if he should be obliged to lift it up against the Eng-lish, their Nations would remain neuter and assist neither Side."[5]

Yet security had to contend not only with the Spanish and French inva-sion from without but also with threats of servile insurrection and native insurgency from within. After the king of Spain had issued a proclamation offering refuge and freedom to runaways from English plantations, fugitives from Captain Davis's plantation escaped to Florida. Governor Oglethorpe, the likely author of "An Account of the Negroe Insurrection in South Caro-lina," sent an emissary to Florida to retrieve the runaways, but the Span-ish governor refused the entreaty. The matter was out of his hands, he said, because he was under royal edict. Enslaved Africans quickly grasped the significance of this event, apparently learning about it from "Spanish emis-saries." Others followed. Four or five cattlemen, aided by their knowledge of the terrain and their autonomy chasing strays, stole horses, killed one man, and wounded another. While in Georgia, where they passed near the Prot-estant Ebenezer Salzburger settlement, rangers and Native people pursued them, killing one and wounding another, the casualties now balanced out on both sides. Once they arrived at Saint Augustine, the Spaniards draped the leader with a velvet cord and honored him with a commission. The English were fearful of an Iberian alliance with the Africans. They were certainly cognizant of the ethnic origins of their enslaved people in West Central Africa, where the Portuguese aligned with the king of Kongo, who had received the Jesuits and spoke Portuguese. They were suspicious of "strolling" Spanish spies. Even an official envoy, Don Pedro, disembarking at Charles Town to give a message to Oglethorpe had caused the English to cringe. Several had responded to the Spanish call; at least one went to the gallows for his reply.[6]

Twenty Congolese led by Jemmy, probably a recent captive from the Kingdom of Kongo, where he had learned military tactics, massed together on a Sunday, September 9, 1739, when they were able to work for themselves. The rebels first seized the warehouse at the Stono River, killing the two occupants and arming themselves with "many small arms and powder." Beckoning others to join their ranks, rallying them with cries of liberty, the insurgents marched to the beat of drums and under colors on the road southward toward Georgia. They went from house to house, killing the English indiscriminately, "Man Woman and Child." They spared the life of a man who had been good to his enslaved people and missed another hidden by them. Swelling their ranks from sixty to one hundred, the rebels cut a ten-mile swath of destruction. Reveling in their success, the Africans assembled in a field, where they drank and danced to the beat of drummers.[7]

Governor William Bull accidentally discovered the danger when he spied the rebels on the road and sounded the alarm. A vigilant militia quickly confronted the rebels at the field later called Battleground for the event. By then they had seized arms, burned houses, and killed twenty-one white people. Despite the Africans' "behaving boldly," the militia responding to Bull's alarm with "much expedition and bravery" and routed the rebels by 4:00 P.M., killing them "on the Spot." Others retreated to their plantations, hoping no one had noticed their absence. Vigilantes summarily executed them. Torture was not part of this reaction; in this case the business of death was quick. Bull also called out Native bounty hunters, some already engaged in tracking down fugitives, and sent notices to the chiefs of the Chikashsha' and the yeh is-WAH h'reh.[8]

Trying "to pursue and seize all Negroes" fleeing to Florida, Governor Oglethorpe proclaimed a state of emergency, dispatched troops, put Georgia on alert, and garrisoned both Port Royal and the "abandoned" Palichocolas fortification on the Savannah River, where the insurgents had "formerly passed." The government pardoned those not directly involved. About thirty had escaped, one-third of them to the south. These ten "fought stoutly" when the militia caught up with them; the other twenty were still at large. All told, twenty-one settlers and forty Africans died.[9]

The *Virginia Gazette* published an October 22, 1739 dispatch from a ship at Cape Fear, reporting that the Spanish governor at Saint Augustine had issued a proclamation offering refuge to enslaved and indentured runaways who escaped to Florida. The article stated that even before hearing of the proclamation, a "great number" of slaveholders had moved their plantations to South Carolina from Georgia "to avoid danger they appended from the Spanish."[10] Later in 1739, the British learned that "some of our Six Nations joined the French although several had given their promises not to engage with them."[11] Governor Clarke sent a report from the Commissioners for Indian Affairs at Albany to Gooch. The report warned that the British had obtained intelligence that the French had deployed "an army from Montreal of about 200 French and 500 Indians" marching southward from Montreal to attack the Chikashsha' and the Chahta, nations friendly to Virginia and Georgia, "situated on some of the southwest branches of Mississippi River." In addition, the British army employed a Frenchman, ransomed from the Indians by Governor Oglethorpe of Georgia, as a guide, who directed soldiers to "the habitations of those Indians." The commissioners concluded with grave import for the British interest, for if these people are "surprised, subdued, and extirpated by the French, it would strike a terror in all the nations on the continent and in process of time induce them to join the French against H[is] M[ajesty]'s subjects."[12]

Governor Bull of South Carolina characterized this strategy as part of a "grand design" of New France to confine the British to its existing boundaries.

> I have been informed that the French have a Design to cut off the Chickasaw's entirely, and to reduce and subdue the Choctaws, if they should succeed in these attempts, it would discourage the Indians in Amity with us from withstanding or opposing them in any attempt of the like nature. The French have for a long time wanted an opportunity to get an Interest among the Cherokee and build a Fort there. As this army which the French now have on its March from Montreal will come down a branch of the Mississippi River which runs near the Cherokee, they will probably endeavor to get the consent of those People to build a Fort there which may enable them to have a Considerable Influence in that Nation as they have already among the Upper Creeks by their Fort at the Alabama's. Such a Considerable step towards their grand design of Surrounding the British Colonies.[13]

Getting ready for the Spanish menace troubled the Virginia General Assembly. Seeking "security" for borrowed money at 6 percent, Gooch found the duties on spirits and enslaved immigrants the best methods of raising revenue since the burgesses were paid wages by their counties. "Seeking a militia with . . . stricter Discipline, more frequently trained and Exercised; and . . . better armed," Gooch authorized two thousand pounds for arms, especially for the poor. Cognizant of the "incapacity" of the "poorer sort of people" to arm themselves, the militia had ceased annual meetings, avoiding fines. Because of this concern, Gooch had in 1736 proposed that the General Assembly raise a fund for purchasing arms for those lacking the "wherewithal to purchase them themselves." Yet the only methods to raise the funds, either a poll tax or a levy on tobacco, were not only "too burthensome" but also would "fall heavy upon the Poor." Since African captives were sold for "ready Money or Bills of Exchange," applying a duty was the best way to raise the revenue. The poorer sort not having the capacity to purchase with cash or credit could not afford enslaved people. The remedy for alleviating the affliction was levying an ad valorem duty paid by the buyer. Applying an additional 5 percent duty on both liquor and enslaved captives was the easiest custom, the least onerous to slavers, and the best method for providing security for borrowed money at 6 percent because the burgesses were paid in cash by their counties. The new act provided that the militia be "completely armed, which will be the best security for this Colony."[14]

Modeled on the 1732 "Act for laying a Duty upon Slaves to be paid by the Buyers," Gooch explained, "An Act, for Laying an Additional Duty on Slaves, to Be Paid by the Buyer, for Encouraging Persons to Enlist in His Majesty's Service: And for Preventing Desertion" (1740) provided security on both the military and the loan. The reason for the new tax was to arm the poor and remedy the problem with the poll tax by taxing newly imported captives paid by the buyer, a 5 percent value-added tax in addition to the previous duty. Gooch called this the "most Easy Expedient," which would be in "no ways burthensome to the Traders in Slaves." Gooch began enlisting men for an intended expedition against Spain, sending circulars to county commanding officers, offering a pistole per month for each recruit. The bounty was increased by proclamation from two guineas to three pistoles in addition to a half-crown enlistment bonus, not payable until the recruit was aboard ship. "I can't as yet tell . . . with any certainty what number of men I shall be able to raise, for "tho[ugh] the Encouragement offered is very Extraordinary. I have not in a moneth [month] gott above fifty. The number of White People, compared with the slaves is inconsiderable, and those who have [slaves] are all Planters and such as have their Plantations under their own management." In other words, the white men in supervisory positions were not available.[15] Anticipating a Spanish invasion of one thousand troops from Havana, Gooch in July 1742 assessed his internal defense; he was especially concerned with the inhabitants west of the Great Mountains "who live dispersed" and need militia support.[16]

CHAPTER 12
Several Nations of Our Indians

By 1742 the colonial governors gauged their security on both internal and external fronts. For example, Gooch received an "express by sea" on July 12, 1742, from William Bull, the governor of South Carolina, requesting aid for an imminent Spanish invasion in southern Georgia. Anticipating a landing of one thousand troops from Havana, Gooch assessed his internal defense. On July 14, 1742, Ogle sent an "express" dispatch to Gooch, writing he had been "much alarmed for some time past," both with the discovery of a conspiracy of the tributary nations with the nations northward and with intelligence from the governor of Pennsylvania that "Indians instigated by the French have Extraordinary Designs in Cogitation." He enclosed interrogations of the chiefs in custody, which compelled him to characterize it as a "Real Conspiracy."[1]

After interrogating Jemmy Smalhommoney, an Atchawamp of Great Choptank, and Jemmy Pasimmons, a Choptank, respectively, on June 25, 1742, the English learned an uprising was afoot in Maryland. Smalhommoney and Pasimmons both said that twenty-three Shawnee had met with tributary people the Nanticoke, the Choptank, the Assateague [meaning "Swiftly Moving Water"], and the Pocomoke from Somerset and Dorset Counties in mid-May at Chicacoan Town on Nanticoke River, where they agreed to attack the English, killing all in their path. Following this discovery, John Ross, deputy agent for Lord Baltimore, ordered the interrogation of Sam Panquash (Nanticoke) and other chiefs now in the custody of the sheriff of Arundel County. He issued a summons for the people at the logged storehouse in the Pocomoke Swamp to deliver up their arms or face an attack without quarter. He also issued an arrest warrant for any "strange Indians" present among the tributaries, all in an effort "to make the most exact Enquiry into the real Designs of the Indians." Threatening a stick of enmity, they would hunt them out if recalcitrant; offering a carrot of friendship, they would treat them with respect if "innocent." For defensive purposes the proprietary would also be on guard to stop any effort of the people in the Pocomoke Swamp from breaking out and escaping north to alert their allies.[2]

Fully armed with the particulars of the case after a round of interrogation, the council on July 10 recalled several detainees two days later, with "an Interpreter sworn to explain to the best of his Knowledge the Meaning in English, of what the Indians declare in their own Language."[3] The board wanted clarification of the roles played by the two envoys Pattasahook and Joshua and the Indian river doctor and the imports of the logged storehouse in the swamp and the convening at Winnasoccum.

Giving specificity to earlier testimony, Joshua broke down the profile of the twenty-three in the party he saw at Chicacoan Town: eighteen Shawnee men, three Piscataway [Conoy] men, one Native woman, and Messowan, the Shawnee war captain. They had come ostensibly to inquire into the health of the great men at Chicacoan Town but actually to treat for peace [alliance]. Joshua was present for three days at Conoy Town, where he heard both the Seneca and the Shawnee agitating for war with the English. When he returned home, he "found Panquash and Our Indians in the Swamp and no strange Indians with them." Although he sojourned there for a week, he said he did not know why the people had "left their Towns," because he was away during that time for sixteen days, visiting Conoy Town, where Panquash had sent him to find out what had happened to the Shawnee at Bohemia and if the "Peace . . . was lost." Pattasahook, who accompanied Joshua, said Panquash ordered him to go to Conoy Town, both to convey news from Panquash and to learn whether the Shawnee had found peace. While at Conoy Town, he heard the plans to destroy the English. Pattasahook said he later "overtook" a party of twenty warriors under war captain Messowan at Bohemia, where he gave the news that the plan "was knocked on the head for that Season." After eighteen days he returned to Maryland, finding "Panquash and the rest of the Indians in the Swamp." He "stayed three Days after his Return, and then all the Indians left the Swamp."[4]

James (Jemmey) Cohonk, in his first examination on July 1, said he "often observed" over the course of two nights Panquash and Dixon Coursey conferring privately with the Shawnee war captain at Winnasoccum. A few days later after the Shawnee left, Cohonk said he had heard from several people that Coursey and Panquash had met at Winnasoccum, where they told the assembled "Nations of Our Indians" of the planned attack with the Shawnee on the English. The invasion of five hundred Shawnee and other nations attacking Pennsylvania and Maryland from the north and the French and their allied Native nations attacking from the west were to dovetail with the tributary nations rising in Somerset and Dorset Counties to cut off the English "at several places in one and the same night."[5]

Questioned a second time ten days later about what Patasahook had said to him, Cohonk hemmed and hawed. "About a month earlier, Pattasahook said to Cohonk that he was at Conoy Town, where the Piscataway of Chicacoan Town (Dorchester County) told him what the Tutelo had said to them: "The Indians of the five Nations would come down to the Governor of Pennsylvania under Pretense of selling their Lands, and that in Exchange they would take from him nothing but Arms, Ammunition, and other Weapons, and that the Indians would make the Governor a Present of two Deer Skins apiece."[6] Pattasahook also said to him that he had heard two hundred to four hundred Native people were coming to attack Maryland once they had secured arms and ammunition from the governor of Pennsylvania to destroy both the English and their allies. In preparation for the offensive, Cohonk said, several nations had built a fifteen-by-twenty-foot log house in the Pocomoke Swamp to store guns, ammunition, and a "large quantity" of brass-pointed arrows.[7] Captain John, supporting one of Panqauash's assertions, said he had not seen the Shawnee at Chicacoan Town but had heard they had "come down to sell Skins, Matchcoats, and Guns."[8]

Questioned about the meeting at Winnasoccum, Cohonk said the people had left their towns, responding to a call to hunt for three hundred skins and to choose an emperor. Everyone came to the swamp expecting food from the kill, but they left when "they heard the English knew of their being there."[9] In his second testimony (July 12), Sam Isaac also placed Panquash, George Rokahomp, John Wittonka, Teague Wogg, George Terrakell, and Jeremy Peake together at Winnasoccum, where he witnessed both Mulberry and Oliver each buying a gun and Chinehopper buying two from the Shawnee.[10]

Offering additional details, Anthony said that early in June Panquash had directed him to Winnasoccum, where the people were gathering for a weeklong hunt. The hunting party, which included more than twenty Shawnee under a war captain, gave way to a war party, which "continued dancing for Six Nights together with Drums beating, firing of Guns and Tomahawks in their hands, . . . often saying the English Men were like Children and knew not how to fight." During the gathering, the tributary nations and the Shawnee planned the annihilation of the English in Maryland and Pennsylvania. Assisted by a massive French landing on the eastern shore of Somerset County, the Shawnee would enter Chicacoan Town under the cover of night either "this Moon, or in Apple time." Before leaving Winnasoccum, Anthony observed an Indian river doctor "boiling" batches of poison, likely stockpiling it with "Guns, Powder, Shot, and poisoned Arrow" at the logged house in the swamp, which he had also heard about from "several Indians." Panquash warned him and "all the other Indians" that he would kill anyone who betrayed their plot.[11]

Yes, Panquash said, he had issued the call for all the tributary nations to leave their towns, including women, children, and the elderly, "and go to Winnasoccum to choose an emperor because they had not Provision to give them in their Towns." However, they had returned home without choosing an emperor "because they had not Money nor Skins enough to bear their Expenses." While at Winnasoccum, Panquash said, "he drank of the Liquor prepared by the Indian River Doctor to cure him of a Cough."[12] In Winnasoccum, as Bastobello, Panquash's emissary for the deer hunt to make an emperor, said, neither Panquash nor anyone else had ever solicited him to kill the English. At the end of the day, "they had not skins enough" for a coronation. Suffering stomach pangs during his three-day stay in the swamp, Bastobello drank the potion prepared by the river doctor to fight "off a fever and ague."[13] The river doctor had also formulated a special potion, which Dixon Coursey said he drank for nourishment and flexibility. He had no idea why the assembled had not chosen an emperor but knew the reason why they abandoned the swamp: "their powder was gone."[14]

Jemmy Ashquash, a resident of Chicacoan, was at Winnasoccum, where the people gathered painted for war; where George Terraquett (Pocomoke) told him and Uncle Abraham Ashquash of their plan to destroy the English; and where Mulberry, Panquash, Chinehopper, and Oliver each bought a gun from the Shawnee. He also believed the people had gathered in the swamp "because they were sent for by Panquash and they left the Swamp because the English heard of their being there."[15] Knowing nothing of the planned uprising, nor of a logged storehouse in the swamp, Robert Nandum of Somerset County said he had accompanied Tallouid to Winnasoccum to hunt deer and choose an emperor, but they had not chosen an emperor because they had not raised enough money. He said he "drank a Spoonful of the Liquor prepared by the Indian River Doctor to make all well."[16]

After the testimonies cast suspicion on several of the detainees, the council retained Panquash, Coursey, Pattasahook, Joshua, Simon [Alsechqueck], Captain John, Robin Hood, Bastobello, Robert Nandum, Chinehopper, and Hopping Sam but released and forgave those who "have been drawn in by your Chiefs." "Fully convinced of your having entered into a Conspiracy to destroy all the white People of this Province," Governor Ogle said to them, "we have it in Our Power to take all Your Lands from you and use you as your ill Designs against Us have deserved."[17]

The Maryland Assembly capped the episode by making it illegal for the tributary chiefs to declare war or make peace with other Native nations without the governor's consent "for the time being." The assembly also issued an order of protection for those who confessed to the conspiracy: "If they or any of their Subjects shall kill or hurt Jamy Small hominy [Jemmy Smalhommoney] or any Indian who hath lately confessed a Conspiracy against the English, the Guilty person or persons shall be delivered up to be punished with death."[18]

Governor Ogle then sent Governor Gooch an express letter on July 14 informing him of "a Conspiracy between the Indians of the Eastern Shore of Maryland, and the Northern Indians, to Attack the Inhabitants of

Pennsylvania and Maryland" with an enclosure of the investigation imploring militia assistance. Since it was illegal to send the militia outside of Virginia, the council thought it unlikely that they could persuade volunteers to cross the Potomac. On the other hand, if Maryland could provide "a Premium or Encouragement . . . there would be no reason to doubt, but a good Number of Men might be raised in Virginia for that Service." On July 23, 1742, Ogle presented a letter from James Logan dated December 20, 1736, to the Maryland Council, documenting the reason for the planned continent-wide war directed at the Chesapeake colonies: the Crown had not properly compensated the Haudenosaunee for the boundary lands "now possessed by the people of Maryland and Virginia."[19]

CHAPTER 13

Skirmish in the Back Parts of Virginia

After receiving the report of the conspiracy of the Maryland tributary nations, organized by the Shawnee, promoted by the Haudenosaunee, and "stirred up it seems by the French," Governor Gooch and the council took this communiqué under advisement. Later in 1742, anticipating a Spanish invasion of one thousand troops from Havana, Gooch assessed his internal defense. Concerned with the inhabitants "who live dispersed" west of the Great Mountains, he offered militia support and sought aid from Maryland. By the Treaty of 1722 but still in dispute after the Treaty of 1736, the Haudenosaunee were not to come eastward of the Great Mountains, nor were the Native people to go westward, "but by a Perversion of that text they now maintain the English were not to pass that Boundary."[1] Gooch offered militia support but received no assistance from Maryland. Well aware of the recent events of the Nanticoke in Maryland and of the Haudenosaunee in Virginia, Ogle balked at providing aid to his Chesapeake neighbor, fearing the triple threats of the insurrection of enslaved Africans, the insurgency of Native peoples, and the invasion by the Spanish, French, and allied Indigenous nations.[2] On July 19, 1742, Gooch advised shoring up the western settlements. Thinking the Native people "too artful" not to begin their attack "westward of the Great Mountains," where the clusters were "thinly seated, more exposed, and an easier Conquest," Gooch "sent power and ball" to the western settlements and directed families at "first alarm" to seek refuge, where the militia under county commanders patrol and rangers were at the ready.[3]

In October 1742 Gooch's anxiety heightened about Virginia's and Maryland's western boundaries, when "warriors of the Six Nations" and "some of the militia there" engaged in a skirmish in the "back parts of Virginia . . . with some Loss on both Sides" threatened to scuttle the scheduled meeting in Philadelphia. James Patton, militia commander, had reported to Gooch that thirty-six Haudenosaunee "equipp'd for War" had entered Augusta County, presenting a letter dated September 10, signed by James Silver near Harris's Ferry in Pennsylvania, and addressed to William Hogg, a justice of the peace, requesting a pass to travel through Virginia, ostensibly to visit the yeh is-WAH h'reh, their internecine enemy. The letter had served as a passport because Silver's signature was "well known," but instead of traveling directly on the road, they "visited most of our Plantations, killing our Stock and taking Provisions by force."[4]

Seeking Patton's consul, Capt. John McDowell reported both the warriors' "insolent Behaviour" and the settlers' "uneasiness." Even though "the Law of Nature and Nations" required them to use force to repel the intrusion, Patton advised him and Captain Buchanan to supply them with provisions instead, paid for by the government, and to shadow them until they had left the county. Undeterred, on September 16–17 the Haudenosaunee killed "several valuable horses" and seized "many [others] for their Luggage." The militia was so undone by this event that it "upbraided" McDowell and Buchanan for behaving "with cowardice." On October 18 the captains sent two men under the cover of a white flag, seeking "Peace and Friendship"; the Haudenosaunee answered, "O Friends are you there, have we found you?" and then "fir'd on our Flag," instantly killing McDowell and six others. Buchanan, flanked by "a very few men, . . . stood his ground," leaving eight, including two captains, "dead on the spot" after a forty-five-minute skirmish. Buchanan and eight men pursued the Haudenosaunee to the thicket before returning to the field, but the men, agitated, refused to follow him.

Departing the night before, marching with twenty-three men, Patton met Buchanan about fourteen miles away from the site of the skirmish, retreating with the wounded. The next day Patton went to the scene of the carnage and recovered the bodies of their eight dead. Following Gooch's earlier directive, Patton then ordered patrollers on all the boundaries, drafted a "certain number of young men from each company" as rangers on the ready where needed, directed captains to guard their own precincts, and appointed a place of rendezvous for the "straggling Families that lived at a distance." The skirmish boded invasion. He also warned Gooch that he had intelligence that 150 Haudenosaunee rendezvoused only seventy miles away and about the same number had "lately cross Potowmack on their way here."[5]

Reporting the skirmish to the Board of Trade, Gooch added a wrinkle: "some white men supposed to be French" accompanied the Haudenosaunee in committing their outrages on the settlers on the west side of the Great Mountains. Here was the rub, as Gooch understood it: The Treaty of Albany in 1722 negotiated by Governor Spotswood with the Haudenosaunee stipulated the Great Mountains as the dividing line between Virginia's tributary nations on the west and the Haudenosaunee's tributaries on the east. "But these same Indians having taken into their Heads, now we have many Families settled to the Westward of those Mountains, that the English as well as the Indians are under the Restriction, and why? Because the Land on the west side they say belongs to them." For this reason, they felt it their right to pillage the English homesteads illicitly placed on the west side of the Great Mountains. "As these Savages have no better Title to the Lands in dispute than they have to any other Part of Virginia," Gooch retorted, "their Behaviour is both Barbarous and Absurd." Noting that this skirmish happened when Maryland, Virginia, and the Haudenosaunee were deliberating over a place where they could meet, Gooch recommended ending the controversy by "paying them for the Lands, since nothing less than Blood or Money will satiate them."[6]

The Haudenosaunee version of the skirmish, given in depositions at the Harrisburg, Pennsylvania, courthouse, differed significantly from the Virginians. In the "Narrative of One Who Calls Shikellimo [Shikellamy] His Grandfather . . . Present in the Engagement in Virginia," the deponent said Jonhaty led a party of seven Oneida and twenty-two Onondaga, who crossed the Potomac and trekked toward Jonontore (Shenandoah Valley). Along the way they could find neither a justice to certify their visit nor any deer to restore their vigor, nor anyone to refresh their victuals. At the risk of starvation after they entered Jonontore, they slaughtered a hog. Crossing over the hills, they then sent out a three-man search party to find the road, when they were confronted by three white men. The white men not only interrogated them but also tried to seize their guns. They resisted and escaped after one of them backed them down with his knife. They reported what had happened when they returned to their party. Captain Onodagoc said to them that "it was some foolish People only, not worthwhile to be taken notice of." Two days later they were accosted by ten white men, including one brandishing a pitchfork, who followed as they "stopped every now and then." When one of them stopped "to make Water," the white men hustled them along until they came to a "big house," where a "great Number of People" gathered. The white men invited them inside, but the main party, wary of their intentions, "staid out some Distance from the House." The oldest among them went inside and thought it prudent to show them their Pennsylvania pass. The white men responded that they should turn back. As more gathered outside, their "friends" called for them to leave. The white men restrained the elders and "sent out a Captain, with a Sword on his side, to bring the others in." Seeing his "naked sword they made a field Cry and took up their Arms in order to defend themselves," but their captain "commanded [them] to be quiet till they were hurt, and to let the white People begin Violence."[7]

Ignoring the captain with the sword, the Haudenosaunee "took up their Bundles and travelled all night." They encamped for two nights, where they discussed their situation, "hunted for deer," and decided to continue their journey south. Breaking camp in the morning, they traveled "peaceably" toward the hills, where they encamped that night. A white man greeted them at daybreak and took stock of them. Suspicious of his motives, they questioned what he was doing here. "He said a hunting." When he left, they sent a spy after him, who observed him climbing over the hills, reversing his course, and running the other way. The Haudenosaunee again made haste on the road south, when two boys bringing up the rear "heard . . . and saw a Great number of white Men on horseback." The mounted men "order'd them to come up," but they ran away instead. The white men fired at them and missed, and the boys carried the alarm to the captain. Seeing that they were unhurt and the white combatants were flying a white flag, he ordered his warriors to "be quiet for that a white Colour was all ways a token of Peace with the white Men." They soon realized that it was a false flag, for "the white Men alighted from their Horses just by and fired the second Time and Killed two upon the Spott," including Shikellamy's cousin. "Commanded by their Captain to fight for Life," they rallied with "a field Cry" as they rushed the militia. After the captain "had fired off his Gun, took to his Hatchett, and exhorted the Stoutest to follow him, . . . they ran in amongst the white People and did Execution with their Hatchetts, which put the white Men to flight immediately." The captain did not order a pursuit, because "they had not come to fight the white Men, but the Cawtabaws."

The Haudenosaunee collected their casualties and corpses, marched about two miles away, and treated their five wounded, losing one. Only one of the four remained in critical condition. They found another missing warrior, wounded in the foot, who had chased the white soldiers. He had witnessed two white men felled by arrows and shot as they ran away. The following morning, the captain sent his men back to the scene of the skirmish, near the Galudoghson [James] River, where they scavenged the eight dead white men and grazing horse for provisions, "for which they stood in great Want." The captain then dispatched ten men to Onondaga and led the remainder up the river toward the mountains en route home. "These ten Men mett the two Men of McKee in the Woods, asked them for a Share of their Provisions, which the Men gave them, but they told nothing of what had happened."[8]

Thomas McKee, a trader with a store on the Susquehanna River, near Bigg Island, Shawnee country, did eventually hear the Haudenosaunee's version of the event. On January 12 or 13, around noon, he heard a "Dead Hollow," a cry signaling a meeting. He went to the Shawnee gathering, where a speaker representing the Haudenosaunee related recent events. In the narrative given in "Mingo" and translated to McKee, the narrator, one of ten warriors dispatched from Virginia to relay recent events to the Shawnee, said "White Men" had killed ten people belonging to the Haudenosaunee. He said that some time last fall a party of thirty of the Haudenosaunee had come down from Susquehanna in their canoes to John Harris's and then trekked through Pennsylvania and the back parts of Virginia for a raid "against some Southern Indians."[9]

They had applied to John Hogg, magistrates of Lancaster County, for safe passage through Pennsylvania, which he granted with the caveat that it was not applicable in Virginia, where they might run into trouble. They passed through Pennsylvania, "behaving Civilly" and meeting "no Interruption" from white people until they arrived at the Shenandoah River in Virginia, where they camped overnight.[10] Seeking provisions, the next morning three of them approached a house where two were seized by three or four white men who tried to bind them, but they were rescued by the third yielding a French knife. Beating a hasty retreat, the Haudenosaunee marched to another plantation, where a "number of men" welcomed them inside once they disarmed. Some complied, but others did not, suspicious and "uneasy" until their compatriots came back outside. The white men not only pursued them but also sent one of their number to the "thicker settlements," the Haudenosaunee believed, to raise reinforcements to pursue them.[11]

Hurrying along for the rest of the day, they finally set up camp and rested. The next morning, while readying themselves for the next leg of their journey, they "heard a great Noise of Horses in the Woods" coming toward them, and then they saw "a great number of White men on Horseback with firearms and Colors flying." The Haudenosaunee's captain had ordered them to hold their fire until they knew the white men's intentions, but the latter fired a gunshot, killing a boy in the rear. The captain ordered them to return fire; they dropped "some" of the Whites including the flag bearer. They then engaged them in close combat; the Haudenosaunee, using their tomahawks, "worsted the white men," who then retreated. The Haudenosaunee also withdrew, carrying away ten dead and four wounded, to whom they administered a physic after making camp. They returned the next day to the scene of the skirmish, where they found the dead white men still there, their provisions scattered about and their horses grazing nearby. They gathered up the provisions and horses, "stripped the dead bodies, and left them." After the engagement, the captain dispatched ten warriors to Onondaga to report what had happened and to receive direction on how to respond, "with orders that as there were different Sorts of white People," they should avoid them on the road lest they "mistakenly kill . . . those in friendship with them." The Virginians pursued them to the Potomac River, where they "narrowly escaped them."[12]

Picking up this refrain of white heterogeneity, McKee spoke up, saying that the Pennsylvanians, mindful of their treaties made with the Haudenosaunee, were not responsible for the actions of the Virginians. Not waiting for McKee to respond, a Shawnee man retorted, "The white people are all of one Color and as one Body, and in this case of War would Assist one another." Then McKee asked the warriors if they had met his men on the road, whom he had sent "out to Chiniotta for Skins." The narrator said the Haudenosaunee had avoided fresh tracks on the Allegany Path, but before he could finish his answer, another Shawnee man preempted him: they could not have so because the white man would have "cut them off." McKee later called an elderly Shawnee to his store, giving him twists of tobacco and asking him to deliver it to the council in hopes they reconsider their treaty ties. Yet after a white woman captive from the Carolina wars presaged his fate, he quit Shawnee country, abandoning a "considerable Quantity of Goods," lock, stock, and barrel.[13]

Outraged after hearing the testimony presented to the Provincial Council of Pennsylvania, the Shawnee wanted to exact retribution, yet their Oneida overseer Shikellamy [aka Swatana] dissuaded them.[14] Cloaking himself in the mantle of the Haudenosaunee, he admonished both the Lenape and the Shawnee and prohibited them from attacking the English. "You shall not pretend to Revenge our People that have been killed in Virginia. We are the Chiefs of all the Indians."[15] Rebuking the settlers as susceptible to lies, he warned them to give up their rumor mongering, for it is "dangerous to the Chain of friendship." Since the Virginians had struck first, leaving "a Hatchet Struck in their Head, the Governor of Virginia must wash off the Blood first." Then he must "take the Hatchet out of their Head and Dress the Wound (according to Custom he that Struck first must do it), and the Council of the Six Nations will speak to him and be reconciled to him and bury that affair in the ground."[16]

On June 26, 1743, John Bartram, a naturalist, wrote to Cadwallader Colden, historian of the Five Nations, that he was preparing a "journey up the Susquehanna with our interpreter to introduce 'A peaceable understanding between the Virginians and the five nations.'" Believing the venue would be Onondaga, he solicited Colden for a letter from the British commander in the region for safe passage through Mohawk country.[17] Bartram and mapmaker Lewis Evans accompanied Johann Conrad Weiser on the diplomatic mission from the government of Pennsylvania to Onondaga to resolve the conflict between the Haudenosaunee and Virginia, but they did not participate in the negotiations. Their exploration resulted in Bartram's *Observations on the Inhabitants, Climate, Soil, Rivers, Productions, Animals, and Other Matters Worthy of Note* (1751) and contributed to Evans's *General Map of the Middle British Colonies in America* (1755). If Bartram's book is silent on Native American life and culture, Evans's map is replete with Indigenous place-names. Weiser, who negotiated with Shikellamy representing the Six Nations, kept a journal titled "Conrad Weiser's Report of His Journey to Onondago on the Affairs of Virginia."[18]

After arriving at Onondaga, Weiser met with Shikellamy and Canassatego on September 23 and discussed the terms of negotiation and engagement. Haudenosaunee house rules applied. After reviewing the recommendations of Onas and Assaragoa, Governors Thompson and Gooch, respectively, and the Philadelphia depositions, they then "acquainted them [the council] with the whole Message in advance." The following day the Onondaga Council sent for Jonhaty, captain of the Haudenosaunee party engaged in the skirmish, and asked him "to tell the story from the beginning how everything happened." Appearing with two companions, he gave his version of the event. "He seemed to be a very thoughtful and honest Man," said Weiser, "and took a deal of Time in telling the Story." The council summoned Weiser and Shikellamy on September 29 to a "private" meeting, where "everything was discoursed over again." Weiser at first stood in for Assaragoa, but after this meeting "we agreed that Canassatego should speak on behalf of the Government of Virginia, . . . because they knew it required some Ceremonies with which I was not acquainted." Observing the protocol of the condolence ceremony, the Haudenosaunee divvied up the Virginia presents to the grieving families of Oneida and Onondaga and to the councilors representing the united nations. "My People are charged with having begun Hostilities; I will not Dispute with you about it," Canassatego said, speaking as Assaragoa on September 31. "I and the Old and wise People of my Country [Virginia] highly Disapproved the Action. I therefore came here to your fire to fetch home the Hatchet, from an Apprehension that it might have been unadvisedly made Use of by my People, and I assure You, by this Belt of Wampum, that there shall be no more use made of it for the future, but it shall be buried."[19]

Governor Gooch had lubricated the Covenant Chain without admitting striking the first blow and, from Shikellamy's point of view, dressed the wound. He had gifted goods valued at £100 sterling to the Haudenosaunee, neither as a payment for the disputed land nor as a compensation for any wrongdoing but "in Token of the Continuance of their Friendship." The two parties agreed to "bury" the event into "oblivion," opening a path to negotiations between the Haudenosaunee and Virginia and Maryland.[20] Attempting "to mend this breach," the governor of Pennsylvania mediated an agreement between Onondaga and Williamsburg and Annapolis to continue negotiations at Lancaster in 1744. Thomas convened the meeting in June. The Onondaga, Seneca, Cayuga, Oneida, and Tuscarora each sent representatives. The Chesapeake colonies each sent commissioners: Virginia sent Thomas Lee, called Assaragoa, president of the Virginia Council, and Col. William Beverley; Maryland sent Edmund Jennings, Philip Thomas, Robert King, and Thomas Colville. Using the conventional diplomatic tropes of fire and light, Thomas said the meeting had convened "to enlarge the Fire, which was almost gone out, and to make it burn clearer; to brighten the Chain which had contracted some Rust, and to renew their Friendship with you."[21]

Speaking for the Haudenosaunee, Canassatego responded to Thomas's call to fasten again the Covenant Chain with the Chesapeake colonies. The Haudenosaunee wanted "to brighten the Chain of Friendship with them, . . . but since there are some Disputes between respecting the Lands possessed by them, which formerly belonged to us, we, according to our Custom, propose to have those Differences first adjusted." They asserted that the Great Mountains were the agreed-upon boundaries separating them in the Great Treaty of 1722, with a dividing line down the middle and both sides having jurisdiction on their side, to the point of requiring passports and hanging trespassers. As a result the Haudenosaunee moved their southern road westerly, and moved it a second time to the foot of the Great Mountains after receiving complaints of warriors injuring some of the settlers' cattle. Nevertheless, the white colonials settled on both sides of the road like "Flocks of Birds."[22]

Sweetening the pot, Logan offered them £300 in presents, which after the Haudenosaunee questioned their worth was later reckoned at £220, 15 shillings, Pennsylvania currency. After review the Virginians concluded that the Haudenosaunee had earlier relinquished any claim on the Shenandoah Valley to the Crown. Lee, representing Virginia, said that even if the Haudenosaunee had conquered nations west of the Great Mountains after the Treaty of 1736, they not only "deserted" but also "never possessed" the land, leaving it "free for any People to enter upon, as [have] the People of Virginia." "If the Six Nations have made any Conquest over Indians that may at any Time have lived on the West-side of the Great Mountains of Virginia, yet they never possessed any Lands there that we have ever heard of. That Part was altogether deserted, and free for any People to enter upon, as the People of Virginia have done, by Order of the Great King, very justly, as well by an ancient Right; as by its being freed from the Possession of any other, and from any Claim even of you the Six Nations, our Brethren, until within these eight Years."[23]

Believing that there must still be a misunderstanding, Lee asked the Haudenosaunee to recollect their memory of the treaties and to relate what possessors of land they had conquered in Virginia. Tachanoontia, an Onondaga sachem, in a speech heralded by poet and politician alike, said the Haudenosaunee had never relinquished their right to the land, "a Right too dearly purchased, and which cost us too much Blood, to give up without any Reason at all. . . . All the World knows we conquered the several Nations living on Sasquahanna [Susquehanna], Cohongoronta, [upper Potomac], and on the Back of the Great Mountains in *Virginia*; Conoy-uch-fuch-roona [Piscataway], Coch-now-was-roonan [of the Kanawha River], Toboa-irough-roonan [Tutelo/Nahyssan], and Connutſkin-ough-roonaw, feel the Effects of our Conquests, being now a Part of our Nations, and their Lands at our Disposal." On the other hand, Virginia had not conquered "anyone who lived there," despite their claims to the contrary. Granted, "they have conquered the *Sachdagughroonaw* [Sachdagughroonaw] and drove back the *Tuscarroraws* [Tuscarora] . . . ; but as to what lies beyond the Mountains, we conquered the Nations residing there, and that Land, if the *Virginians* ever get a good Right to it, it, it must be by us."[24]

Responding to the British for the Haudenosaunee, Gachradodow waxed poetic on their differences of skin color, custom, and religious belief. "The World at the first was made on the other Side of the Great Water different from what it is on this Side, as may be known from the different Colours of our Skin, and of our Flesh, and that which you call Justice may not be so amongst us; you have your Laws and Customs, and so have we. The Great King might send you over to conquer the Indians, but it looks to us that God did not approve of it; if he had, he would not have placed the Sea where it is, as the Limits between us and you."[25]

For the Virginia lands in dispute, the Crown agreed to give the Haudenosaunee goods in kind at the cost of two hundred pounds Pennsylvania currency and two hundred pounds in gold, "upon Condition that you immediately make a Deed recognizing the King's Right to all the Lands that are, or shall be, by his Majesty's Appointment in the Colony of Virginia." Accepting these terms, the Haudenosaunee asked for future consideration with settlement, requesting that the governors manage resources by limiting the number of cows and sheep in the region, which ate the grass, leaving not enough for the deer, and they made their case to the king for future compensation "when the Settlement increased much further back." As to the Great Indian Road, running from Cohongaronto north of the Potomac River southward through Jonontore [Shenandoah Valley] to the Carolinas, a trail trod by the Haudenosaunee during their raids on the yeh is-WAH h'reh, the Haudenosaunee accepted acknowledgement that the road should be shared and insisted that "we are to have reasonable Victuals when we are in want." Both sides agreed the road would be "clear and open."[26]

Charles Thomson, leader of the Young Junto, a group founded in 1750 in homage to Benjamin Franklin's junto, summed up the Lancaster Treaty negotiation. The Haudenosaunee presented the "grounds for their Claim to some Lands in Virginia and Maryland." They complained that the Pennsylvania, Maryland, and Virginia governors had divvied up the lands among themselves and, "left to their honor and justice," paid them accordingly. The Maryland commissioners readily agreed to compensate the Haudenosaunee three hundred pounds currency. The claim against Virginia "lay to the south of the Potomack, and westward of a high Ridge of Mountains that extended along the Frontier-Settlements of Virginia." Unwilling to recognize their claim, the Virginia commission nevertheless offered the Haudenosaunee two hundred pounds Pennsylvania currency and two hundred pounds in gold upon the "condition they immediately . . . Deed" this land to Virginia. The Haudenosaunee agreed with the caveat that a further consideration be allowed with settler expansion. The Virginia commissioners not only accepted these terms but underscored their affirmation of the Crown's support with a "promised . . . writing under their Hands and Seals." That said, they signed the deed.[27]

Gooch could not count on Governor Ogle of Maryland, who was reluctant to provide aid to Virginia against Native attacks, fearing an insurrection of the enslaved people at home.[28] At the same time, the western counties had difficulty impressing on the General Assembly the security significance of patrolling the mountain passes. Highly sensitive to the possibility of both insurrection and invasion, William Beverley, again a burgess now from Essex County and a member of the Committee of Claims, on September 14, 1744, pressed for the payment of patrollers charged with "scouring" the mountains for runaways. Although the General Assembly, dominated by the tidewater planters, was quick to collect taxes from western settlers, it was slow to use those funds for western security. The Committee on Claims not only disallowed the payment for the patrollers but also demanded regulation for the cost of the wagons used to carry arms up the mountains, because "it appears exorbitant."[29]

If the eastern planters needed prompting of the dangers in a slave society, an "extract of a letter" published from Kingston in the *Virginia Gazette* on August 22, 1745, of an insurrection in Jamaica reminded them of the lurking dangers. The "wild" rebels, armed with knives and cutlasses, had killed two white people and five Black people and burned down a planter's house. Not only was it dangerous for white people to be out at night, but the rebels also had the "audacity to be out and about in town during the day." The authorities even discovered one insurrectionist disguised as a woman, armed with "several knives."[30]

Closer to home early in September 1745, *Virginia Gazette* readers learned of discord between the Haudenosaunee and the Shawnee. Drawing on intelligence from Shamokin, an entrepôt, where the west and north tributaries of the Susquehanna River mingled, the Lenape king Allumapees [Sasoonan] resided, and the Piscataway [Conoy] and the Nanticoke lived, the gazette reported a scouting team of the Haudenosaunee had found the Shawnee who had robbed English traders. The Shawnee fearfully "entrenched and fortified themselves" on the Ohio River, in advance of four hundred warriors on their way to attack them. The Haudenosaunee believed that the Shawnee "intended to revolt to the Catawba, their Enemies." Nevertheless, Pennsylvania continued to assuage the Haudenosaunee, offering them £150 in goods at a scheduled treaty meeting to be held for October 4, 1745, in Albany.[31]

By June 1746 Gooch again placed the colonies on war footing, a necessary check to the danger of French invasion with troops and funds proportionately raised from each colony, and began seeking the assistance of the Haudenosaunee. Governor Clinton of New York gave a speech to the General Assembly in which he was pleased to report that the Crown had ordered an expedition to check the French settlements in Canada. As commander, he could raise troops with the other colonial governors to be "employed with Regular Forces on this important service." Since the necessity of preparing for an anticipated French invasion across the English Channel limited the British deployment, Clinton recommended raising five hundred able-bodied men from the westward colonies, one hundred men each from New York, New Jersey, Pennsylvania, Maryland, and Virginia "formed into one Corps to be commanded" by Gooch, who was promoted for this event to rank of brigadier general. Clinton also wrote the governors of Massachusetts Bay and Connecticut, requesting that they share their proportion for "engaging the Indians, . . . necessary for both assurance of success and . . . to the security of our Northern Frontiers."[32]

On June 9, 1746, the New York General Assembly responded by allotting six pounds per volunteer and six thousand pounds for purchasing provisions for the armed forces. On June 18, Governor Clinton advised the General Assembly that the Haudenosaunee and their dependents "should be engaged with us in the War" and ordered the head commissioner of Indian Affairs to invite them to Albany next month, requisitioning for the meeting the "proper" presents and recommending the other colonies should likewise have additional presents to offer. He advised that it was better sooner than later to let them know what bounties and provisions they could count on for their service. He reported that the Crown would support tents and other particulars "except Arms and clothing." The assembly offered an additional forty shillings and a blanket to the first thousand volunteers and requested each colony proportionately bear the burden of supplying the Haudenosaunee and the king's troops but should not expect to bear the burden of supplying blankets, tents, and "other necessaries required."[33] John Bartram wrote to Jan Frederik Gronovius on December 15, 1746: "I have not travelled much abroad this year by reason of ye wars and troubles both in europ and on our back inhabitants ye French Indians hath been very troublesome which hath made travailing very dangerous beyond our inhabitants."[34]

Mindful of the continuing threats, the Virginia General Assembly enacted "An Act for Making Provision against Invasions and Insurrections" in October 1748. Since militias were the best defense against these threats, the public should fund them. During a crisis, the governor had the full authority of martial law to use whatever means necessary to lead and deploy troops wherever needed until the crisis was dissipated. At the site of the event, every militia officer must first act to thwart the danger, by deploying forces to the point of the menace, then pressing into service men, boats, and horses, then notifying up the chain of command to the governor the danger, and finally staying on guard until orders arrive back. Failure to do so would result retrogressively in loss of pay for "every lieutenant of a county, the sum of fifty pounds, every colonel, lieutenant colonel, or major, thirty pounds, and every captain, lieutenant, cornet, or ensign, twenty pounds; and every soldier who shall be summoned to appear, upon any such occasion, and shall fail so to do, or shall fail to bring with him his arms and accoutrements, together with one pound of powder, and four pounds of ball, shall forfeit and pay the sum of ten pounds." Making militias the first line of defense dealt with the three I's, invasion, incursion, and insurrection—"invasions of foreign enemies by sea, and incursions of Indians at land, and great dangers . . . by the insurrections of Negroes, and others," the Native tributaries.[35]

CHAPTER 14

The Rich Back Lands

If the peace of 1743 with the Haudenosaunee negotiated on behalf of Virginia by Johann Conrad Weiser reduced tension in the backcountry, two separate events in 1743 bridged the old and the new land grabs. William Byrd II, the patriarch of Westover, during his penultimate year of life, patented more than 100,000 acres near the Dan River. This venture and his earlier grant from the council of 100,000 acres on the Roanoke River in 1735 for "the Settlement of a Number of Swiss Protestants . . . on the like Terms as have been allowed to other Strangers coming in to Settle the Frontiers," belonged to Old Dominion land schemes.[1] Also in 1743 James Patton and John Tayloe I presented a petition to the council for a two-hundred-thousand-acre grant where the Kanawha and the Ohio Rivers mingled. Their plan intrigued the councilors, who knew a good thing when they saw it. Their ancestors, like Byrd's, had, after all, become wealthy by grabbing the "rich back lands" of Virginia.[2]

Before attending to the petition, the councilors served themselves first, awarding the 100,000-acre Greenbrier grant in the Kanawha basin to John Robinson, speaker of the House of Burgesses and treasurer, who also maintained an interest in the Dismal Swamp. The council granted Patton and Tayloe 100,000 acres, promising the remainder once they had developed the first grant. Shortly afterward the council granted Commissary John Blair, a member, acres in the upper Potomac. William Beverley informed Lord Fairfax in April 1743 that Blair had died before asking permission to settle his proprietary lands west of the Blue Ridge and patent "up to 10,000 acres" south of the Potomac River, where there were "some very rich low grounds." He also sought another 10,000 acres adjacent to Robert Carter's 1729 grant of a 50,212-acre tract on the Shenandoah River. "This I suppose may contain as much bad land as good which if your Lordship is pleased to grant me, I purpose to preserve in my family and to fill ye good Land with tenants when I can get them."[3]

After reviewing the proposal, the councilors capaciously looked westward. The Lancaster Treaty with the Haudenosaunee in 1744 presumably cleared the way, but the French still had designs on the Ohio Valley. In 1747 the council also awarded sixty thousand acres adjoining the Blair's land grant west of the Potomac River and northwest of Lord Fairfax's proprietary on the branches of Youghiogheny and Monongahela Rivers to John Neal,

Lewis Neal, William Neal, and fourteen other investors. (Twenty years later George Washington instructed William Crawford to survey this tract.) The council provided that the grantees had five years to survey, patent, and record their acreage, known as Neal's Grant. Not to be outdone, Thomas Lee of Stratford had cut his teeth working the Fairfax proprietary in the Northern Neck, acquiring sixteen thousand acres on the Potomac River and parleying with the Haudenosaunee over the Treaty of Lancaster. A founding member of the Ohio Company, Lee petitioned the Council in 1747 for two hundred thousand acres along the Allegheny River. The following year Lee became president of the Ohio Company, partly to trade with the Indigenous people and partly to settle their land with foreign Protestants.[4]

The new land activity likely prompted Lord Thomas Fairfax's return to Virginia in 1747 after a twenty-year hiatus in England. At the Belvoir estate of his cousin William Fairfax in the newly incorporated Fairfax County, he met Lawrence Washington, a founding member of the Ohio Company and William's son-in-law. Later in 1748 Fairfax met Lawrence's younger brother, George, whom he commissioned to survey his lands west of the Blue Ridge.

Governor Gooch had perfunctorily approved the earlier activity but now worried that Lee's grant might perturb French interests in the region. Despite his concern the Crown approved not only the two hundred thousand acres, but also half-million-acre request. So sanctioned, the Council then issued a one-hundred-thousand-acre grant to Robinson's brother-in-law and a four-hundred-thousand-acre grant to his friends. The council then awarded the Loyal Land Company, headed by John Lewis and Dr. Thomas Walker, the biggest prize of all: eight hundred thousand acres across the Alleghenies. John Hanbury and the incorporators of the Ohio Company petitioned the Lords of Trade, seeking two hundred thousand of five hundred thousand acres between Monongahela and the Kanawha for immediate settlement of the Ohio Valley in 1748, free of quitrents for ten years, conditional on their erecting a fort and settling one hundred families within seven years. Once meeting these conditions, they would receive the other three hundred thousand acres. The company pointed to the strategic significance of the location of the land, bearing "one small Ridge of Mountains, easily passable" to the Mississippi and the Potomac Rivers, opening trade opportunities of British manufactures to Indigenous inhabitants and settlement possibilities to Protestant immigrants.[5]

The Haudenosaunee said they had "extirpated" the Native Ohioans and claimed "all the lands west of Virginia and to and on the Waters of the Mississippi and the Lake" by right of conquest.[6] For example George Croghan remembered that about 1744 or 1745 a party of Shawnee headed by One Charlie had received permission from Monacatootha, an Oneida warrior chief, and

Tanaghrisson the Half King, acting under their authority endowed by the Haudenosaunee, "took possession of and formed a settlement on a large river which falls into the Ohio, between the mouths of Oubache [Ouabache, Wabash] on the West, and the Tennessee or Cherokee River on the East Side of the Ohio, which river was afterwards called and known by the name of the Shawanese River, and that the Distance from Fort Pitt, to the mouth of the Shawanese River is computed to be upwards of one thousand miles."[7]

By the treaty of Lancaster and by a deed dated July 2, 1744, they now "yield up and make over and forever quit claim to your Majesty and your successors all their said lands west of Virginia."[8] Gooch said to the General Assembly that the conclusion of the Treaty of Peace and Friendship with the Haudenosaunee had secured for settlers west of the Appalachians "a quiet Possession of all the Lands to which those Nations claimed a Right."[9]

During the twenty-year period between 1730 and 1749, the Myaamia [Twightwee], Wyandot [Huron], and Odawa [Ottawa], partly prompted by New France and partly by the opportunity to traffic with expanding English traders; the Seneca-Cayuga [Mingo], relocated by the Haudenosaunee; and the Shawnee, acting on their own accord, began to return in earnest, coalescing in Ohio. Around 1740 the Lenape, feeling land pressure from Pennsylvania, began moving into the Tuscarawas and Muskingum River valleys, against the wishes of the Haudenosaunee. Then in 1742 the Haudenosaunee upbraided them at the treaty meeting in Philadelphia for selling land on their own accord fifty years earlier to the English and dispatched them either to Wyoming Valley or Shamokin. Some also migrated to Ohio. Prompted by New France, the Odawa, who had occupied Ohio in the 1650s, returned in 1741 to northwestern Ohio, settling on the Cuyahoga and the Maumee Rivers. The Lenape welcomed their uncles the fur-trapping Wyandot who began migrating around 1745 from Montreal and Detroit into northern Ohio, where they and English traders jointly constructed a blockhouse at Fort Sandoské.[10]

The French had curtailed gifting during the mid-1740s, causing the Myaamia to leave and seek new relations with the Haudenosaunee and their access to Pennsylvania and Virginia traders. Around 1747 the Myaamia, who once resided in the Maumee Valley, broke their alliance with their French "family" and moved from the Great Lakes to the Great Miami River basin, establishing Myaamia. They had a major town, Pinkwaawilenionki [Pickawillany], where the Great Miami River mingled with Loramie Creek, fast becoming an entrepôt for the western people fleeing the French alliance and swelling to four hundred households of at least sixteen hundred residents. The Myaamia began trading with the Pekuwe Shawnee, "one of the five septs or divisions of Shawnee"; the Tacon; the Piankashaw [Piankeshaw]; the

Lenape; the Wyandot; the Pennsylvanians; and the Virginians. In 1748 the Myaamia aligned with the Haudenosaunee, the Shawnee, and the Lenape. Troubled by this turn of events, about 250 Odawa and Ojibwe burned Pink-waawilenionki in 1752 on behalf of the French alliance.[11]

The Great Miami River reached back from Myaamia into the Wabash River basin. The Ohio River stretched from its forks near the Monongahela, a prime site of contention during this era, to Logstown in the Appalachian foothills. The eighty-mile stretch of Piqua Road connected Pinkwaawile-nionk to Kiihkayonki. Towns settled by a diversity of nations, strategically situated on these routes of the fur trade, opened an exchange for traders. Longhouses dotted the landscape, some planked, others barked, still others logged, their roofs vaulted with saplings and matted with cattail, reflecting the region's heterogeneity. The Seneca-Cayuga [Mingo], the most western of the Six Nations, to shore up Haudenosaunee hegemony in Ohio first settled the Sandusky and Cayuga River regions of northeastern Ohio in the 1740s and 1750s. They finally settled the basin at the juncture of the Olentangy and Scioto Rivers during the 1750s and 1760s and established an entrepôt on the Ohio River about two miles below Logstown, called Mingo Town by the English, which by 1770 housed about seventy inhabitants in twenty cabins.[12] Maj. Edward Ward remembered that in 1752 "a small Village Inhabited by the Delawares, on the South East side of the Allegheny River, in the neighborhood of that place, and that old Kittanning on the same side of the said River, was then Inhabited by the Delawares, that about one third of the Shawanese Inhabited Loggo Town, on the West Side of the Ohio, and tended Corn on the East Side of the River—and the other part of the Nation lived on the Scioto River."[13]

Deh-he-wä-mis remembered her life with the Seneca at the town of She-nan-jee situated at the conjunction of the Shenanjee, Scioto, and Ohio Rivers, where she was held captive in the late 1750s.

> The town where they lived was pleasantly situated on the Ohio, at the mouth of the Shenanjee:[14] The land produced good corn; the woods furnished a plenty of game, and the waters abounded with fish. Another river emptied itself into the Ohio, directly opposite the mouth of the Shenanjee. We spent the summer at that place, where we planted, hoed, and harvested a large crop of corn, of an excellent quality. . . . The corn being harvested, the Indians took it on horses and in canoes, and proceeded down the Ohio, occasionally stopping to hunt a few days, till we arrived at the mouth of Scioto river; where they established their winter quarters, and continued hunting till the ensuing spring, in the adjacent wilderness. While at that place I went with

the other children to assist the hunters to bring in their game. The forests on the Scioto were well stocked with elk, deer, and other large animals; and the marshes contained large numbers of beaver, muskrat, etc. which made excellent hunting for the Indians; who depended, for their meat, upon their success in taking elk and deer; and for ammunition and clothing, upon the beaver, muskrat, and other furs that they could take in addition to their peltry. The season for hunting being passed, we all returned in the spring to the mouth of the river Shenanjee, to the houses and fields we had left in the fall before. There we again planted our corn, squashes, and beans, on the fields that we occupied the preceding summer.[15]

Deh-he-wä-mis later talked about women's work during the first "four summers and four winters" of her captivity:

In the summer season, we planted, tended and harvested our corn, and generally had all our children with us; but had no master to oversee or drive us, so that we could work as leisurely as we pleased. We had no ploughs on the Ohio; but performed the whole process of planting and hoeing with a small tool that resembled, in some respects, a hoe with a very short handle. Our cooking consisted in pounding our corn into samp or hommany, boiling the hommany, making now and then a cake and baking it in the ashes, and in boiling or roasting our venison. As our cooking and eating utensils consisted of a hommany block and pestle, a small kettle, a knife or two, and a few vessels of bark or wood, it required but little time to keep them in order for use. . . . In the season of hunting, it was our business, in addition to our cooking, to bring home the game that was taken by the Indians, dress it, and carefully preserve the eatable meat, and prepare or dress the skins. Our clothing was fastened together with strings of deer skin, and tied on with the same.[16]

In September 1748, the Commissioners for Trade and Plantations endorsed the Ohio Company's plan to settle the western side of the Great Mountains in a report to the Privy Council. After review the Lords Commissioners concurred with the petitioners "for settling the Countries upon the Ohio and extending the British Trade beyond the Mountains on the Western confines of Virginia."[17] The Crown issued a royal charter to the Ohio Company, granting it five hundred thousand acres of land west of the Appalachian Mountains between Romanetto's Creek [or Kiskomenetto Creek] and Buffalo's Creek south of the Allegheny River, the headwaters of the Ohio River, and between the Two Creeks and the Yellow Creek north of the river. "Settling the Countries upon the Ohio," conceded Whitehall's tacit acknowledgment that nations existed there.[18]

Finding the Ohio Company's petition both beneficial and advantageous to the Crown, since this was the "center of the British Dominions" for producing revenues, encouraging commerce with the Native traders, and checking the encroachment of the French, the Lords of Trade instructed Gooch to grant the requested acreage and to build a fort to secure better the western settlements. Referencing their application, the commissioners recommended including resident landholders in their plan and allowing them four years to survey the land, pay for the rights to it, and to return plans to the secretary's office. Authorization to the two-hundred-thousand-acre land grant carried a caveat: the Crown would forgive quitrents for four years, barring current property owners unless they provide "security for continuing the payment of the quit rents."[19]

Receiving permission, Hanbury and the Ohio Company immediately set out to establish trade relations with the Native nations but found them reticent, both harnessing a temperament of "jealousy" and fearing the English intended their "ruin, not trade." The company averred that this was not the case when the Ohio Company had earlier presented their petition. Abused by the French, the Myaamia had migrated from the lakes watered by the St. Lawrence, shortly before the end of King George's War (1740–48), with the intention of joining the English, who had invited them to make war on the French. They now refused to return to the lakes, having befriended the Haudenosaunee. Hanbury insisted all in the region were friends, but "friendship with these people must be kept firm by presents, which make way for trade."[20]

If speculators continued to have enthusiasm for the Dismal Swamp, they were crazy about Ohio. The enormity and diversity of this territory prompted the council to commission Joshua Fry and Peter Jefferson to extend the Virginia boundary line westward just as an earlier council had commissioned Byrd to find the dividing line between North Carolina and Virginia.[21] Unfortunately, Fry's *Account of the Bounds of the Colony of Virginia & of Its Back Settlements, & of the Lands towards the Mountins & Lakes*, 8 May 1751, was "absolutely silent" about Ohio country northwest of Virginia. The accompanying map and *A Brief Account of the Travels of John Peter Salley, a German who Lives in the County of Augusta in Virginia*, together like Fry's narrative demonstrated ignorance of Native homelands, French encroachments, and the Ohio Company advances."[22]

Toward this end in the lower Ohio River Valley, the Loyal Land Company on December 12, 1749, commissioned Dr. Thomas Walker "to go to the Westward in order to discover a proper Place for a Settlement." Through his 1741 marriage to Mildred Thornton Meriwether, the wealthy widow of Nicholas Meriwether II, Walker had just entered the great planter class by obtaining eighty-six enslaved people on a fifteen-thousand-acre estate known as Castle Hill in Albemarle, "which County includes the Chief of the head branches of James River on the East side of the Blue Ridge."[23]

Now Walker, accompanied by Ambrose Powell, William Tomlinson, Colby Chew, Henry Lawless, and John Hughes, set off from his home in Louisa County on March 6, 1750, and spent their first night at mapmaker and fellow Loyal Company stakeholder Col. Joshua Fry's home in Albemarle. They then visited other planters, including the Rev. Robert Rose on the Tye River, en route to Samuel Stalnaker's homestead on the Middle Fork of Holston River, which then marked the westernmost English locale on the 1749 Fry–Jefferson map of the dividing line between Virginia and North Carolina. Walker's party arrived at Stalnaker's land on March 24, where they helped him to raise his house. They expected Stalnaker, a trapper and trader to the Ani'-Yun-wiya, to pilot them on the Indian Road, since he had traveled the year before through Shawnee country to Ani'-Yun-wiya country; however, Stalnaker gave them directions on the Indian Road to the pass through the mountains but did not accompany them. The Shawnee traveled the well-trod western route of the Great Warriors' Path, which they called Athawominee or the "Path of the Armed Ones," from the Ohio River to the Cumberland Gap and into Kentucky, or *Kenta Aki*, the name in Shawnee folklore meaning "The Land of Our Fathers."[24]

Unlike Christopher Gist, who detailed the Native people and places he visited, Walker did not mention encountering any live Native people in real time. His journal entries are a prototype of the "vanishing Indian" trope. Although a medical doctor, his entries read more like a pathologist's autopsy than a physician's diagnosis. When he does note a Native presence, it is disparaged, decayed, or dead. For example, on March 30, 1750, he journaled, he "discovered the tracks of about 20 Indians, that had gone up the Creek between the time we camped last night and set off this morning. We suppose they made our Dogs so restless last night." The next day at "the Fork between the Holston's and the North River," Walker observed nine "Indian Houses built with logs and covered with bark," and the detritus around their settlement included an "abundance of Bones, some whole Pots and Pans some broken, and many pieces of mats and Cloth."[25]

That evening his party then camped on a Holston riverbank "opposite to a large Indian Fort," yet again no mention was made of any Native people. On April 24 the party "came on a fresh track of 7 or 8 Indians but could not overtake them." Going down the Cumberland River on May 3, Walker's party happened by "an Indian Camp, that had been built this Spring, and in it we took up our Quarters." On June 6, Walker said, they never saw any Native people on a tributary that he called Rapid Creek. "After we had gone eight miles, we could not ford, and we camped in the low Ground. There is a great sign of Indians on this Creek."[26]

On April 11 the Walker expedition traveled through a pass in High Mountain, which he called Cave Gap because of a large limestone cave in the vicinity. On the other side they found a junction connecting Ani'-Yun-wiya towns on the Tennessee River to Shawnee towns on the Ohio River. The Shawnee called the mountain range Wasioto [Waseoto], meaning "the mountains where the deer are plentiful," and the river the Shawanoe after themselves. Not unlike the Powhatan River, which the early settlers renamed the James after King James I of England, Walker renamed the Shawnee River the Cumberland after the Duke of Cumberland, William Augustus, the second son of King George II of England. The party later rechristened Cave Gap the Cumberland Gap to complement the river.[27]

By April 13 Walker's party reached "a Plain Indian Road. On the top of the Ridge are Laurel Trees marked with Crosses, other Blazed and several Figures on them." Not to be outdone by these Native glyphs, Walker carved his name into a tree. "As I went down the other Side, I soon came to some Laurel in the head of the Branch. A Beech stands on the left hand, on which I cut my name." They continued trekking the Indian Road for a week, on April 18 coming to a place where, he wrote, "Indians have lived about this Ford some years ago," which perhaps proves the provenance of the place-name *Kenta Aki*.[28] On April 23, Walker, Powell, and Chew searched out the northern Cumberland mountains for meadowlands in which to settle but instead found "the Land poor and the Woods very thick beyond them, and Laurel and Ivy in and near the Branches." Unaware of the cultivable lands within the region, he situated a spot on the north side of the Cumberland River, where they would build a house. Unlike the Native log houses covered in bark he had observed along the Holston River, Walker's team built this one-room log cabin in the European style out of "round logs with wide chinked joints and a small end chimney." Walker, Powell, and Chew continued the journey, "leaving the others to provide and salt some Bear, build a house, and plant some peach stones and Corn."[29]

Skirting a great meadow within reach, they missed seeing the land that opened into the bluegrass region, which offers the other candidate for the provenance of the place-name *Kentucky: Kenhatà:ke*, from the Mohawk word meaning "on the meadow."[30] Giving further credence to the Shawnee etymological origins, though, Walker observed on April 27 the remnants of an ancient Native town complete with a burial mound: "We crossed Indian Creek and went down Meadow Creek to the River. There comes in another from the Southward as big as this one we are on. Below the mouth of this Creek, and above the Mouth are the remains of several Indian Cabbins amongst them a round Hill made by Art about 20 feet high and 60 over the Top."[31]

Walker's only mentions of Native-made objects, besides the Indian Road, were the moccasins and tomahawks the party needed to make for itself. On April 16 Walker made new moccasins because "those [shoes] I brought out [were now] bad," and again a month later, on May 14, "ours being quite worn out," the party cut new moccasins out of "elk skin." On June 13 the Walker party bushwhacked their way through thickets "so covered with ivy and the sides so steep and stony, that we were obliged to cut our way through with our Tomahawks." At the end of his journey near Hot Springs, where he saw six "invalids" bathe in its waters, "very Clear and warmer than New Milk," Walker "Shaved, Shifted, and made New shoes" for his visits first to Walker Johnson and then to Robert Armstrong's homes. While complimenting the generosity of his hosts, Walker made his final jab, ridiculing the rapacity of the Native people: "The People here are very Hospitable and would be better able to support Travellers was it not for the great number of Indian Warriors that frequently take what they want from them, much to their prejudice."[32]

After he disparaged the ungratefulness of the Native people, Walker bragged about the land's bounty and their hunting prowess. "We killed in the journey 13 Buffaloes, 8 Elks, 53 Bears, 20 Deer, 4 wild Geese, and about 150 Turkeys, besides small game. We might have killed three times as much meat if we had wanted it." Yet as he cast aspersions on Native people, he acknowledged what he had attempted to erase: the presence of a "great number of Indian Warriors." That erasure would soon come with the settlers moving into the region and changing the name of the Great Warriors' Path to the Wilderness Trail. Although settler colonialism aggressively engaged in the erasure of Indigenous culture, complete cultural obliteration is phenomenologically difficult. Historian and founding curator at the Smithsonian National Museum of the American Indians, Gabriella Tayac (Piscataway), argues that the key to understanding the material culture of Native people is their kinship and connectivity to sacred ancestral objects. At first colonizers dealt with Native-made objects as curios and displayed them in "cabinets of curiosity." Later, in the spirit of scientific classification, they categorized Native peoples and objects with natural history in museums.[33]

At the Rivanna River, a young Thomas Jefferson whetted his appetite for Native culture when he observed in 1754 a party of Monacan cultural custodians visiting a mound near an abandoned Native town.[34] Later, in 1783, he conducted a pioneering archaeological dig there, about which he published in *Notes on the State of Virginia*.[35] In 1790 a farmer plowing his field near the Cumberland River tilled up the two-foot "Kneeling Woman" sculpture (Middle Cumberland Culture, ca. 1400) that Judge Henry Innes gifted to Jefferson. An exchange of letters between Innes and Jefferson in 1790 reveals the settler-colonial thought process involved in appropriating Native objects. Innes, who had worked for Jefferson as a surveyor and claims adjuster in western Virginia from 1777 until 1780, notified his old acquaintance that a "settler" had unearthed a "curiosity . . . ploughing his Corn field" near the Cumberland River. Innes's informant described the statue as "carved of Stone of a naked Woman kneeling; it is roughly executed, but from the coarseness of the Stone the instrument with which it was probably carved and its antiquity I think shews the maker to have had some talent in that way, the design being good." Innes also recognized the object likely came from an ancient Native settlement. "I have desired my Informer to examine the place and see if he can discover any appearances of a Settlement having been made there, and if so to cut down a Tree and ascertain the age thereof." Innes also enclosed a "Plan of an old Fortification" in this "Western Country" [Kentucky], which he concluded was built "by Inhabitants and not by European Adventurers as some writers have suggested; I am the more confirmed in this opinion from the Burying Grounds which are large and contiguous to some of these Fortifications."[36]

Affirming the renewal of their acquaintance, Jefferson on March 7, 1791, thanked Innes for his gift and welcomed their continued correspondence, which promised "the line of Natural history . . . my passion." He agreed with Innes not only "that the remains of fortifications found in the Western country have been the works of the natives," but also that the object's quality was "the best piece of workmanship I ever saw from their hands." He did impose a judgment on the object: "If the artist did not intend it, he has very happily hit on the representation of a woman in the first moments of parturition." Innes was closer to the mark than Jefferson, who thought it represented a woman giving birth.[37]

Jefferson donated "Kneeling Woman" to the American Philosophical Association. With this donation the society "began to turn the modest cabinet of curiosities into a museum of natural history worthy of international attention." Under Jefferson's leadership—he became its president in 1796—the society began methodically making a moral equivalency between the natural history of Native people and their "ancient Fortifications, Tumuli, and other Indian works of art" and flora and fauna and vertebrate paleontology, displaying their taken objects in the Museum at Philosophical Hall.[38]

FIGURE 21. Anonymous, "Kneeling Woman." Native American effigy. Middle Cumberland Culture, ca. 1400. Image courtesy of Granger Historical Picture Archive.

CHAPTER 15

Buy Land and Contract
for the Settling Thereof

The Virginia planters, Dr. John Mitchell noted, were motivated to expand into Native country for new fields out of necessity. The economies of scale with enslaved labor on tobacco plantations

> requires richer land, or more manure. . . . [Since the] best is the fresh woodlands . . . of rich black mould, . . . the tobacco planters [are] more solicitous for new land than any other people in America. . . . When they have exhausted their grounds, [they] will sell them to new settlers for corn-fields, and move backwards with their negroes, cattle, and tools, to take up fresh land for tobacco. . . . This is the system of business which made some, so long ago as 1750, move over the Allegany mountains, and settle not far from the Ohio, where their tobacco was to be carried by land some distance, which is a heavy burden on so bulky a commodity, but answered by the superior crops they gained.[1]

Any aspiration in Ohio would come to naught without Haudenosaunee sanction. Thomas Lee, president of the Virginia Council, was "sensible of the great importance it is to preserve the Amity and good friendship of the neighboring Indians, particularly the Six Nations, so powerful in themselves, who have been so long considered as his Majesties Subjects and who possess so large a Tract of Country bordering upon his Majesty's Settlements." "Much concerned" to learn that the Haudenosaunee were "engaged in a design to extirpate the Catawba, a People so well affected to the British Interest," Whitehall credited Lee for his prudence in "giving Intelligence" to the yeh is-WAH h'reh regarding the design. In order to achieve these ends, Lee should not only make presents to the nations "seated on the Ohio River" but also cultivate relations with the Haudenosaunee and dissuade them from aligning with the French. Lee was glad twice, first to learn the French had failed in their "unjustifiable attempt to stir up the Indians on the Ohio" and second to be in receipt of presents for the Ohio nations. At the same time, Whitehall expressed its desire that the French would not dissuade the Haudenosaunee from carrying out in a "very prudent" manner the conveyance of lands purchased by the Crown in the Treaty of Lancaster (1744). Lee's planned hosting of the Haudenosaunee in Fredericksburg and "inviting" the yeh is-WAH h'reh to make peace "answered" the requisite for the Albany meeting. Giving presents and using "all Means of Persuasion" promoted British interest and protected settlers.[2]

Benjamin Franklin included an answer to this question as an example of Haudenosaunee honor: "I would only observe that the Six Nations, as a Body, have kept Faith with the English ever since we knew them, now near a Hundred Years; and that the governing Part of those People have had Notions of Honor." For example, in 1751, when six yeh is-WAH h'reh ambassadors traveled through Mohawk country under the cover of British security "to sue for and treat of Peace for their Nation, they soon found the Six Nations highly exasperated, and the Peace at that Time impracticable." Fearful they would be murdered on their return to New York, they sought assistance from Governor Bull, who in turn made their concerns known to the Haudenosaunee. Upon the order of the Onondaga Council, a spokesman addressed them:

> Strangers and Enemies. While you are in this Country, blow away all Fear out of your Breasts; change the black Streak of Pain on your Cheek for a red One, and let your Faces shine with Bear's-Grease: You are safer here than if you were at home. The Six Nations will not defile their own Land with the Blood of Men that come unarmed to ask for Peace. We shall send a Guard with you, to see you safe out of our Territories. So far you shall have Peace, but no farther. Get home to your own Country, and there take Care of yourselves, for there we intend to come and kill you.[3]

Following Thomas Lee, who died in November 1750, as president of the Ohio Company, Lawrence Washington began reaching out to Rotterdam for Protestant immigrants and to England for goods compatible with the Native trade. He also recruited Christopher Gist, who lived near the dividing line between Virginia and North Carolina. He instructed Gist to explore the mountain passes into Ohio, gauge the military might of the Native nations and their trade networks, assess the Ohio River and its tributaries westward to the Great Falls, appraise the soil's suitability for cultivation, and survey the metes and bounds of the land.[4] John Tayloe expressed his confusion over Gist's mission to Richard Lee: "I am very well satisfied with the resolutions of the Committee but I understood Guiest's [Gist's] business was to buy Land and contract for the settling thereof not barely to discover it."[5] In May 1751 the Ohio Company found it advantageous to open a plantation on the company's land at the mouth of Wills Creek for domestic stock and for watermen to transport skins and other trade items listed in the company's account, and tasked George Mason with acquiring "as soon as he can conveniently purchase . . . three likely able men Slaves who are used to the Country Business and two new Negro women upon the best terms he can for that purpose."[6]

Meanwhile in Virginia, John Mercer, the Ohio Company secretary and general counsel, commissioned a map generated from Gist's "Plan . . . of the Country you pass thro[ugh] of . . . my own drawing and my instructions by which I drew; it cost the company above £600." He sent his son George, armed with Gist's journal and a map of "part of the Ohio River, showing the falls," to London to lobby for a two-hundred-thousand-acre land grant on behalf of the company. On November 6, 1752, Mercer also petitioned the council on behalf of the company and shared his map with fellow company member Governor Dinwiddie with the stipulation that he honor proprietary information. Despite incurring Mercer's umbrage, Dinwiddie circulated it among the councilors, including Cols. Corbin and Ludwell, who "were measuring the distances and taking notes [from the map] in writing." Preempting Mercer's company's petition, the council on June 15, 1753, summarily certified three grants totaling 190,000 acres on the south side of the Ohio River inside the bounds of the company's grant to Corbin and two dozen "signed names in Trust for Councilors." To contravene the Ohio Company grant, Corbin's petition substituted "the Waters of Mississippi" for the Ohio River and stipulated fifty thousand acres from Fishing Creek, forty thousand acres from Buffalo Creek, and one hundred thousand acres from the New River. "I told them this was not fair for the Map belonged to me," Mercer lamented, "but they had done their business, their Entries [for grants] were entered in the Council Books before they left the Room, so that Corbin and Co. in 3 hours' time without a shilling charge or Expense except the Clerk of the Council's fee (which I suppose he dared not charge him) had leave to take up more land than the Ohio Company could obtain in 20 y[ea]rs Solicitation and after £10.000 expense."[7]

Although Mercer rightly judged this land grab as an intrusion on the Ohio Company's jurisdiction, the petitioners included a quarter of the family names of the original investors: Lee, Nelson, Tayloe, Ludwell, and Corbin. Since the subscription list of the Ohio Company in 1749 was limited to twenty subscribers who invested four thousand pounds for the capitalization of the company, this action created a windfall for great planter families not involved with the initial offering. Three-quarters of the twenty-four petitioners belonged to Virginia's twenty-one great planter families. Trying to make sense of Ohio Company boundaries, George Mason IV, Richard and Thomas Lee, and John Mercer discussed the unfairness of Beverley's interdiction of the Ohio Company with John Tayloe II. After serving fourteen years as a burgess from 1736 until 1749, Beverley had finally, following the

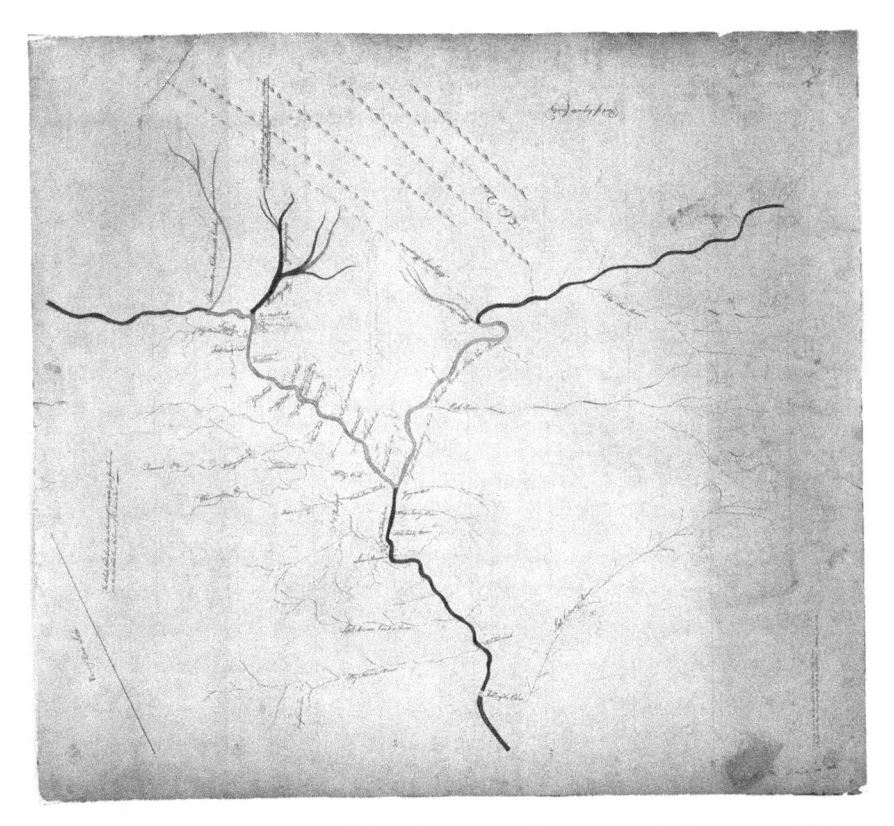

FIGURE 22. John Mercer, *Part of the Ohio River, Showing the Falls*, map of Ohio Company lands made before November 6, 1752. Archives and Special Collections, University of Pittsburgh Library System. Image courtesy of University of Pittsburgh.

death of John Custis IV in 1750, secured his coveted council seat, which he held from 1752 until his death in 1756.[8]

Mercer also learned that Hanbury had intelligence that Beverley, who had patented 130,000 acres in Augusta with the plan to sell or lease the land to "people from the Northward," through his attorney William Russell "interrupted and drove off the Ohio Company's Settlers sealed [seated?] by Gist to encourage Beverley's market." Beverley had dodged the sheriff, avoiding payment of quitrents on unsold and "barren" tracts, which offered fodder to the Ohio Company if they planned to challenge the bounds of Beverley's manor.[9]

To be sure, Gist would pay close attention to Native old fields, the soil already cultivated and left fallow,[10] the meadows already cleared, and the towns already sited by the Indigenous Ohioans. What was less sure was how the company intended to acquire the land. The English settlers sought out the

Ohioans' intentionally cleared meadows for pasturelands, plotted their farms for plantations, and sited their trading towns for their townships. Conflict was not accidental, when the Native travelers returned to these familiar places during the annual raiding parties, like Jonhaty's in 1742. The English colonists settled not only alongside rivers and creeks, where the Native people had previously cultivated, but also in established Virginia patterns spread, dispersed, and "scattered for the benefits of the best lands."[11]

Representing the Haudenosaunee in Ohio, Tanaghrisson [Tanacharison] was one of a half-dozen Native signatories to a treaty between the president and Council of the Province of Pennsylvania and the Indians of Ohio held in Philadelphia on November 13, 1747. Joining a Haudenosaunee alliance favorable to the British, these nations included the Seneca-Cayuga, the Shawnee, and the Myaamia, who recently defected from the Pays d'en Haut, the Great Lakes region of New France. Onondaga designated Tanaghrisson the following year as the half-king over the Seneca-Cayuga and Lenape migrants to Ohio. A half-king had provincial authority and limited power, likely the etymology of the name. He could negotiate and receive gifts, but the Haudenosaunee had final approval. Tanaghrisson may have been a yeh is-WAH h'reh—born captive from the Carolinas, adopted as a youth by the Seneca, who became a chief of the Ohio nations. His origins made him an apt chief over the nations of the Ohio River Valley.[12] Tanaghrisson established his headquarters at Logstown, the Seneca-Cayuga's westernmost town. Although Gist thought the town was Lenape, Logstown was home to a diversity of people: Lenape, Shawnee, and Seneca-Cayuga. At a conference held at Logstown in April 1748, George Croghan representing Pennsylvania and Johann Conrad Weiser representing Virginia gifted Tanaghrisson. He was also the Haudenosaunee spokesman at a conference held at Logstown accommodated by Croghan in May 1751 and at another in June 1752, when Virginia sought ratification of a "land cession."[13]

By 1749, when Pierre-Joseph Céloron de Blainville visited, Lower Shawnee Town had developed into a "considerable village." The purpose of his visit, as indicated on the plaque he buried at the confluence of the Kanawha and the Ohio Rivers, was to restore tranquility in some "savage" villages in these provinces and to mark the renewal "of the possession we have taken of the said River Ohio, and of all those which empty into it."[14] Rather than savagery, he found a cosmopolitan town comprising Shawnee, Haudenosaunee, "more than thirty" Mohawks from the Sault-Saint-Louis, "some from the lake of the Two Mountains, some Loups from the Miami, and nearly all the nations" from the Pays d'en Haut, the Native country of the Nippissing, the Abenaki, and the Ontario from the Ohio Valley to the Great Lakes,

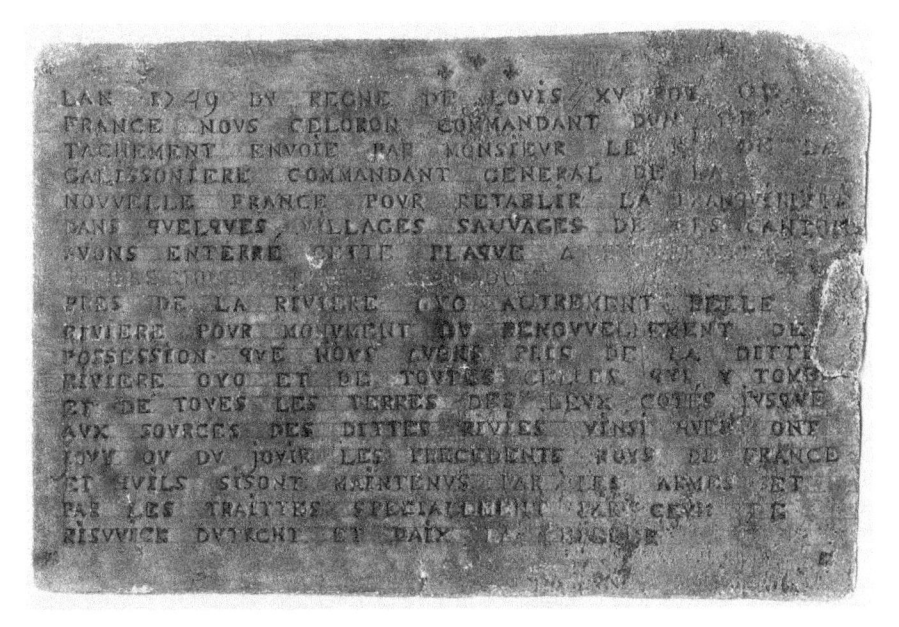

FIGURE 23. Lead marker, Céloron Plate (1749). Image courtesy of Virginia Museum of History and Culture.

which New France claimed. An eighty-man honor guard saluted an anxious Céloron on his arrival at Lower Shawnee Town, firing their rifles into the air, the gunpowder and arms both a result of the trade with the English. No wonder Céloron felt that the Shawnee were "entirely devoted to the English." He reasoned that they "had destroyed the abundance of game; the cheap merchandise which the English furnished was a very seducing motive for them to remain attached to the latter."[15]

Anxious and suspicious of the French intentions, the Shawnee warily watched them poaching their subjects, burying markers on their land, and dotting forts on their rivers. Also anxious and suspicious of Virginia's intentions following the founding of the Ohio Company of Virginia in 1747, the Shawnee sensed that their lands negotiated by the Haudenosaunee in the treaties were in jeopardy.[16] "After 1740 the Ohio country figured prominently in "Iroquois League interests as a hunting preserves for young men and their families," writes Parmenter. "Iroquois League leaders neither contested the movement of their population to Ohio nor responded to colonial officials' demands to return the residents of these villages to traditional Iroquois League homelands."[17]

About the same time in 1750 or 1751, Croghan remembered that while he was trading at Lower Shawnee Town at the mouth of the Scioto River, a party of Shawnee and Ani'-Yun-wiya came over the Allegheny Mountains from Ani'-Yun-wiya country. His recollection underscored not only the pattern of pan-Native council meetings but also questions of sovereignty in the region. The Shawnee reported to their elders that they had left their women and children with the young men acting as guardians at Blue Licks on the Kentucky River, where they intended "to reside and Hunt that Season." They also told their sachems that they had attended a council meeting of "all Indians thereabouts," including Ani'-Yun-wiya, Lenape, Haudenosaunee, and "several" Wyandot. Wary of the Wyandot, the fifty or sixty Ani'-Yun-wiya accompanying them had come to ask the Shawnee "to make up a difference— subsisting between them and the Wyandots." Although Scioto was a Shawnee town, the Ani'-Yun-wiya asked the Haudenosaunee if they "might have liberty to Hunt between the Allegheny Mountain and the Ohio for that Season, as they knew the Country Belonged to them."[18]

When Gist arrived in Logstown in November 1750, he found the chiefs away engaged in a hunt and "scarce anybody but a parcel of reprobate traders." Of Logstown, Gist wrote, "This is the last Town of the Delawares [Lenape] to the Westward. The Delaware Indians by the best Accounts I could gather consist of about 500 fighting Men all firmly attached to the English Interest. They are not properly a Part of the Six Nations but are scattered about among most of the Indians upon the Ohio, and some of them among the Six Nations, from whom they have Leave to hunt upon their Lands." When the people asked the nature of his business, Gist hesitated, reluctant to state his mission. The residents began to suspect his reticence augured malice and "said that I was come to settle the Indian's Land and they knew I should never go Home again Safe." He escaped their wrath only by stating that "I had a message to deliver [to] the Indians from the King, by order of the President of Virginia."

On January 28, 1751, Gist reported the Lenape of the Ohio Valley gratefully answered the governor of Pennsylvania, prompted by both his instructions and warnings about the French, pledging allegiance only to the English and no one else. Yet they demurred: "We shall be glad to hear what our Brothers have to say to Us at the Loggs Town in the Spring." Whatever the Lenape may have heard about Gist when they conferred with the Haudenosaunee at Logstown that spring, Gist never delivered the diplomatic letter to Tanaghrisson, nor did he present gifts and wampum. Clearly, they thought he was a spy, interested in scoping out their lands and their ability to defend them. Gist also visited one "small" Lenape town on the Scioto Creek inhabited by about twenty families, where "Windaughalah, a great Man and Chief of this Town and Much in the English Interest," hosted him. Much to Gist's notice, Windaughalah owned an enslaved man. "He entertained us very kindly and ordered a Negro Man that belonged to him to feed our Horses well." Although "this Night it snowed, and in the Morning though the Snow was six or seven Inches deep, the wild Rye appeared very green and flourishing through it, and our Horses had fine Feeding."[19]

Nevertheless, at the Logstown treaty meeting the Virginians preferred dealing on both trade and desired land settlement directly with Tanaghrisson, the Onondaga representative to the nations "seated on the Ohio River." Tanaghrisson said on June 11 that the Onondaga Council sanctioned the deeds of land to the governors of Pennsylvania and Virginia in the Treaty of Lancaster (1744). He then said he would need the advice of our Council before answering since they had only learned yesterday of the Virginians' understanding of the boundaries of the "lands sold . . . extend further to the Sun setting than the Hill on the other Side of the Allegany Hill." He concluded: they also understand now the French "design to cheat us out of our Lands," but see their actions as more "mischief" than malice, offering for example their attack on our tributary the Myaamia. What Tanaghrisson called "mischief" Croghan reported as mayhem: thirty Myaamia were killed by the nations loyal to France during the first half of 1751.[20]

Tanaghrisson said that despite Virginia's desire to settle southeast Ohio to assist us, it is not now necessary for the French menace is far away. At the same time, your English residents of Ohio consist only of "warriors and hunters and . . . traders," who "are not all wise Men." He entreated the English to send to Ohio "good" and "fit" men, and they in turn will regulate the behavior of our young men there. Rather than settlement, Tanaghrisson requested that Virginia fortify the fork of the Ohio and the Monongahela Rivers (a request two years later tasked to George Washington) and recognize the authority of the leader they had appointed of "our Cousins" the Lenape. Although Tanaghrisson said the "Strong House" on the Monongahela did not require an English presence, the Virginians had insisted that a fort required an English settlement nearby to grow provisions for it; otherwise, they would have to rely on the more costly supply of Pennsylvania traders. The Native people could provide for themselves, but Council could not give full answer yet, Tanaghrisson said, "although in all our Wars we don't consider Provisions, for we live on one another; but we know it is different with our Brethren, the English."[21]

Governor Dinwiddie complained that a man under Haudenosaunee dominion had murdered "a poor Woman on the New River" and requested extradition for him to stand trial in Virginia with the expectation of death if found guilty. Tanaghrisson said he would alert Onondaga about the alleged murderer, who had lived among the French and was under the influence of "evil spirits." In turn he sought redress for a trader who cut a

Haudenosaunee man's wrist and stole his gun, causing the aggrieved man to "threaten revenge on some of the Traders." The commissioners immediately offered reparations: a new gun and "a thousand Wampum to pay for the Cure," ingratiating him to the English. Recalling earlier complaints about quantity and cost of kegs of "spirituous Liquors among us," Tanaghrisson now was dubious about the reassurances from Johann Conrad Weiser about "cheaper rates." At the end of the day, on Saturday, June 13, 1752, the land negotiations stalemated, with both parties agreeing only to deed "all the Lands *within* the Colony of Virginia, as it was then or hereafter might, be peopled and bounded by his Majesty."[22]

The Myaamia reported that a massacre had occurred on June 21, 1752, which Thomas Burney, one of the two English survivors, carried to Governor Dinwiddie. The Piankashaw, a sept of the Twightwee or Myaamia, were caught completely off guard after the French forces had treated with them, offering a peace belt of wampum and a "fine French Coat." While "all our Warriors and briskest men were out a hunting," leaving behind a skeletal force, a score of men, including 9 English of fighting age, 240 French-aligned warriors, and 2 Frenchmen, sprung a surprise attack while another 30 Frenchmen waited two miles away. They not only seized stores and plundered houses outside the fort but also carried away and killed "six of our brothers" and scalped one of the Englishmen. More significantly, "they killed our great Pianquisha [Piankashaw], whom we called Old Britain, named for his great love to our Brothers the English." The Myaamia sent the governor a scalp and a belt of wampum with a request for arms and ammunition, less for themselves and more to avenge those killed and taken captive. If not received, we "must look upon ourselves as lost."[23]

The Pict [Pekuwe Shawnee] and the Wyandot together sent a distressing message to Dinwiddie. The Pict were "one of the five septs or divisions of Shawnee," and the Wyandot considered the Shawnee "nephew" or "younger brother." Displeased with French policy, the Wyandot chief Orontony had begun moving his people from Canada to Ohio in 1745 after he carped that the French "wou'd always get their Young Men to go to War against their Enemies and wou'd use them . . . like Slaves."[24] The Pekuwe and the Wyandot along with the Myaamia, the Piankashaw, and the Lenape began commerce with the Pennsylvania and the Virginia traders around 1748, irritating the French. The Pekuwe and the Wyandot said that the French had prophesized their deaths in 1749 . They did now realize until 1752 that it was the French who planned to kill them. They lamented that the French had killed five, eating three of them, and left two others languishing in irons. Although the French had always counseled alliance, they now say the Pekuwe and the

Wyandot trade with the English for a "supply of powder, lead, and weapons for war."

The English had assured them last spring that they would not be harmed and could hunt without fear. Now the French tell them "go to the English and . . . let them be our father . . . Now we come crying to our brothers and allies." For this reason, the Pict and the Wyandot, both "Captains and Kings," have gone to war with the French and seek arms from the English. "All our Nation, and the *Citzabuse, Makuty, Twightwees, Shandaws, Doutows,* and five Nations," unite against the French, who said they will come and take our land. The Pict and the Wyandot stressed their departure from the French and underscored their loyalty to the English by giving notice of cannibalism to Governor Dinwiddie: they had killed and eaten ten Frenchmen and two of "their Negroes."[25]

The Virginia commissioners Joshua Fry, Lunsford Lomax, and James Patton appointed William Trent, a fur trader and land speculator in Ohio, to deliver presents to the Native sachems at Logstown and to the Myaamia at Pinkwaawilenionki. Trent chronicled his 1752 trip in the *Journal of Captain William Trent from Logstown to Pickawillany.* On June 25 he learned from a white man who thirteen days earlier at Pinkwaawilenionki witnessed Native people allied with the French had visited there and left with twenty-five Picts. On June 27 Trent learned more about Myaamia families going to the French. Powell, a Seneca-Cayuga who had returned from Fort Detroit to Pinkwaawilenionki the week before the departure, told him that three hundred French and their Native allies had set off the month before either to "persuade" the families to return with them or to threaten to "cut them off." Trent arrived on June 29 at Muskingum about 150 miles from Logstown, where he met "some white men from Hochocken or Bottle Creek who said the "town was taken" and "all the white Men killed." The young Shawnee king had escaped the massacre and "brought the News."[26]

On July 2 Trent arrived at Hochocken, where he met Williams Ives, who had "passed the Twightwees town in the Night." Ives said the "white men's houses were all on fire and he heard no noise in the fort, only one Gun fired, and two or three Hollows [excited shouts]." The next day Trent "got back to Mequck, where we heard much the same News." He concluded that he had to go to the lower Shawnee Town with the goods that "we Might know the Certainty." Finally, on July 6, the Shawnee received him "very kindly" at the Shawnee Town, greeting him with a gun salute and the customary "hooping and hollering." They escorted him to the longhouse [council house], where after being given victuals, he inquired into the news, which they said they would tell him tomorrow. On July 6 Trent arrived at the lower Shawnee town, where he met Thomas Burney and Andrew McBryer, the two white survivors of the massacre, at the longhouse.

Confirming the earlier report with greater detail, they said that 240 French-aligned-warriors attacked at 9:00 in the morning on June 21. The Native attackers "surprised" the women working in their cornfields, whom they took captive, and plundered the English traders' storehouse outside the fort of about three thousand pounds worth of goods. Feeling the fort indefensible because only about twenty men and boys remained inside, and with the "majority" of fighting men away on the hunt, they entered into parley. After negotiation the French released the Native women in exchange for the white men, except Burney and McBryer, whom they had hidden. "They killed one Englishman and took six prisoners, one Mingoe and one Shawanees killed, and three Twightwees; one of them, the old Pianguisha [Piankashaw], king, called by the English Old Britain, who, for his attachment to the English, they boiled, and eat him all up."[27]

After deliberating on Trent's journal and the recent events in Virginia, the Board of Trade not only recommended that Virginia collect revenue of two shillings per hogshead of tobacco to appropriate one thousand pounds for presents for "the Twightwees nation of Indians and their allies," but also alerted the Crown about the "hostilities committed by the French and Indians and the forts built by the French on the back of the English settlements."[28]

CHAPTER 16

This Country Belongs to Virginia

Conscious of Virginia's limitations, Governor Gooch reported to the Board of Trade in 1747 that the nations under the dominion of the Haudenosaunee on the colony's northwest are "nearer" to the settlements, unless you count the Dominion's tributary nations, all reduced to "small numbers."[1] The yeh is-WAH h'reh and the Ani'-Yun-wiya reside "within the bounds of the Carolinas to the Southwest, about 400 miles from the Virginia inhabitants," wrote Gooch. Nurturing this relationship, he gifted the "young Cherokee king . . . a suit of Scarlet Clothes laced with gold for himself and a suit of blue Cloth laced with silver for his chief and six blue coats with Brass buttons for his Warriors," because they were "the barrier between us and the more western Indians in League with the French and Spaniards."[2] Gooch's gift to the young king confirmed his efforts to regain trade and diplomatic relations with the Ani'-Yun-wiya, lost principally because of South Carolina's prohibitive duties on Virginia traders.

The Ani'-Yun-wiya tried to shore up their position in the face of Virginia's concern of the French menace and South Carolina's insistence of exclusive trading rights based on the Treaty of 1730. On August 10, 1751, an ambassador of the Ani'-Yun-wiya negotiated with Lewis Burwell, president of the council. The ambassador responded to a query from Burwell with a clear explanation of their intentions. The "principal cause" for their initiative was Governor James Glen's failure to honor a commitment made four years earlier to foster commercial relations with them and to provide them with "Ammunition and other Necessaries." Not only was "the path to Carolina . . . very difficult and incommodious for carrying on a Trade," but also Glen had given aid and comfort to "our Enemies" the Muscogee. "Upon these Considerations our Emperor has sent us to solicit a Confirmation of your Friendship, and to desire, that you will be pleased to send white People amongst us and establish a Commerce between the King of Great-Britain's Subjects, Inhabitants of this Dominion, and the Indians of the Cherokee Nation." After Burwell communicated this message to the council, he said in response that Virginia too sought a "lasting Peace and a flourishing Trade," underscoring this point with a directive of two hundred pounds worth of presents to the emperor and gifts for the Ani'-Yun-wiya negotiators. With gratitude the ambassador said they had traveled from Chota through "Bushes and Briars" to Williamsburg without regret and would return and communicate a "faithful relation" of what was negotiated to their emperor, promising to "make a good road for the people of this Country who shall be disposed to trade with us."[3]

After traveling seven hundred miles to Williamsburg, Amouskositte, recognized by Virginia as "the Emperor of the Cherokee Nation," arrived with his wife and son, an entourage of grandees, and an escort of warriors in November 1752 to negotiate with Governor Dinwiddie. Dinwiddie feted and gifted him and his party and even staged a production of *Othello* in his honor.[4] Presaged in the Ani'-Yun-wiya response to Burwell, Dinwiddie reported to the Board of Trade that "His Errand was to cultivate a Friendship, and encourage a Trade from this Government to His Nation." Hoping to placate Governor Glen, Dinwiddie encouraged Amouskositte to continue his journey to Charles Town and mend fences with the governor, pledging that he would use his influence to that end: "I told Him, I had not Power over our Traders to direct them in their Comerce, but would acquaint them of the Friendship, Protection and Encouragement." To seal the deal, Dinwiddie presented "him, Empress, son, Generals and attendants some fine Cloths and a handsom Present; they went away pleased and fully determined to keep up strict Friendship and Fidelity with the British Nation in General and this Government in Particular."[5]

By 1752, when the Creek War jeopardized the lower town of Keowee on the Keowee River, they moved the town to a more defensible site and permitted the British to build Fort Prince George across the river in 1753. Even though Glen's plan was for the submission of the lower towns to South Carolina, the site of Fort Prince George proved less formidable than he had hoped, and the Ani'-Yun-wiya maintained their sovereignty in the region.[6] De Brahm's map of 1757 evidenced the autonomy of Ani'-Yun-wiya and yeh is-WAH h'reh towns. "A thoroughfare down along the Santee from this place in the blank space in the upper left corner of the map is labeled, simply, 'Path from the Cherokee,'" writes environmental historian Mart A. Stewart. "De Brahm's acknowledgment of Cherokee and Catawba autonomy on the map was six years before a negotiated boundary, the Proclamation of 1763, that added a clear boundary to western settlement and subverted the assumptions about settlement advance that some readers have identified in the blank spaces in the west of this and other maps."[7]

Dinwiddie sought to engage the Ani'-Yun-wiya, now seen as within the British orbit, in a loose alliance with other friendly Native nations against the French and their Native allies. In his May 31, 1753, letter to the "Emperor, Sachems, Warriors of the great Nation of the Cherokee," Dinwiddie said that he was "concerned" to learn that since Amouskositte's visit in November, French-aligned Native people had "disturbed" the Overhill Ani'-Yun-wiya but was relieved that the Haudenosaunee, "our mutual good Friends . . . did

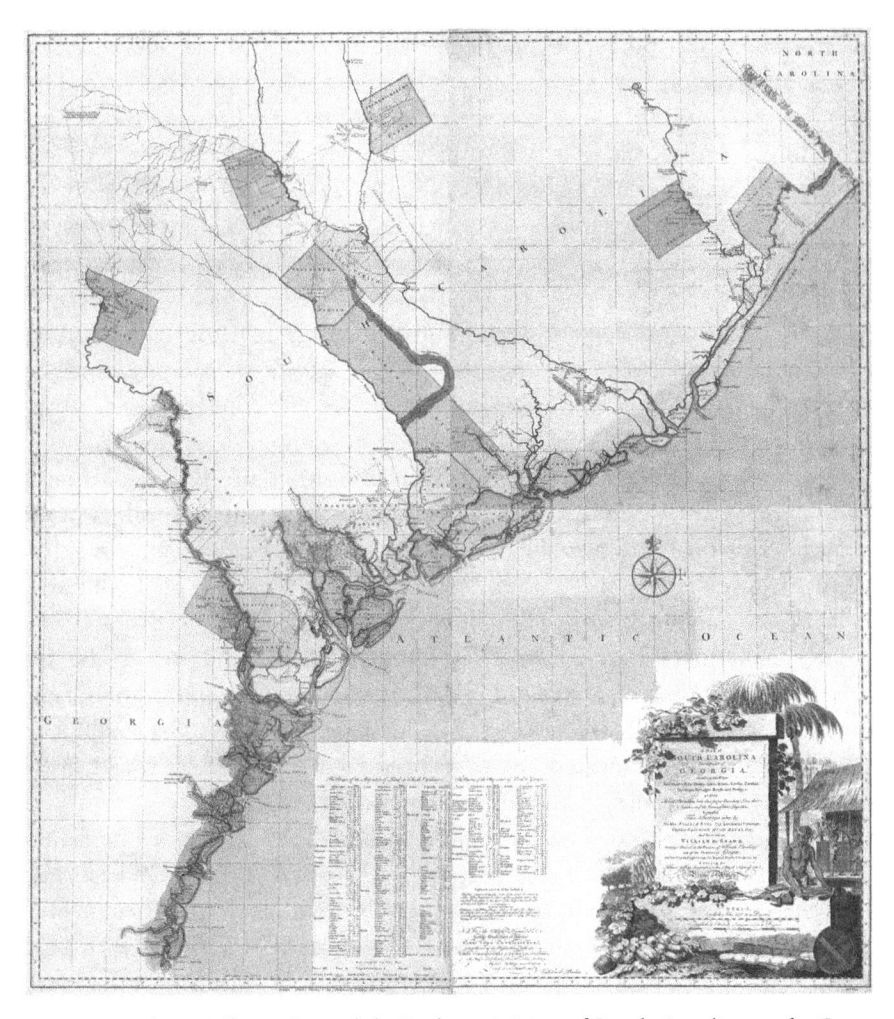

FIGURE 24. John William Gerard de Brahm, *A Map of South Carolina and a Part of Georgia, 1757.* University of Alabama Department of Geography, Wikimedia Commons, CC-PD.

so properly resent it" that they demanded from the governor of Canada the restoration of captives to the Ani'-Yun-wiya. Although resident in Virginia only a couple of years, Dinwiddie drew on Native rhetoric to introduce his envoy Henry Morrie, who was "to let them know that the French have taken up the Hatchet and threaten to strike all the Nations that are in Friendship with the Children of Our King." For this reason he asked that they "bury the tomahoc" with the Muscogee, to which end he has enlisted the aid of the governor of South Carolina. He also promised to give notice of the French threat to the Chikashsha' so that "they be on their guard."[8]

In his January 1755 report on the present state of Virginia, submitted to the Committee of Trade and Plantations, Dinwiddie cited ancient claims that "Virginia runs its ancient Breadth and has no other limits to the West," extending to California. In actuality, he wrote, "the British Subjects have for some years settled within a few Miles of the River Ohio, on the other side of the Allegany Mountains for the western boundaries of Virginia . . . approved by the Six Nations at the Treaty of Lancaster." The English settlement patterns are irregularly "scattered for the Benefit of the best Lands"; the French make no effort at settlement but establish forts strategically as "marks of Possession"; the Native nations dot the Ohio with both towns and farms but build no forts.[9]

Dinwiddie did not mention the coming or going of the Monacan, the Chickahominy, the Mattaponi, the Nansemond, or the Rappahannock. Until midcentury, when settlers advanced toward the central Virginia piedmont, seeking fields Indians had cleared, the Monacan had somehow avoided Williamsburg's attention. Their ancestral homeland was the piedmont and valley regions on both sides of the Blue Ridge at the floodplains of the James and Rappahannock Rivers, where several towns, fields, and burial mounds evidenced their presence. Around 1750 the Chickahominy began migrating back to their ancestral land around the Chickahominy River, King William County, from their relocated homes in New Kent and Charles City Counties, the region that they called Tsenacomoco.[10]

Dinwiddie did recognize the significance of amity with the Haudenosaunee to the north and the Ani'-Yun-wiya, yeh is-WAH h'reh, Chikashsha', and Muscogee to the south, and the "different Nations on the River Ohio, the Picts, Twightwee, and Shawnees to the Westward." He closed with a lament: "This colony has always been happy, and in some Peace with the Indians till lately. The French have, by Threats and fair Promises, seduced some of the Indians from the British Interest, and with great injustice invaded His Majesty's Lands, plundered and robbed many of his Subjects, and carried many of them to Quebec."[11]

After reviewing a petition of merchants of Bristol and Liverpool trading to Virginia concerning an act to settle west of the mountains passed in Virginia in 1752, the Board of Trade on May 28, 1754, approved the draft of a report to the Lords of the Committee of Council. Upon the petition of the House of Burgesses of Virginia, the board endorsed an "indulgence which . . . may be granted to persons who settle to the westward of the Mountains."[12]

By midcentury, British anxiety about French ambition in Ohio stirred the Crown to lay claim to Native country. In 1749 Giles Robert de Vaugondy's *Nouvelle Angleterre: Nue York, Nue Jersey, Pennsylvanie, Mariland et Virginie*, the most prominent French North American map of the time, placed the

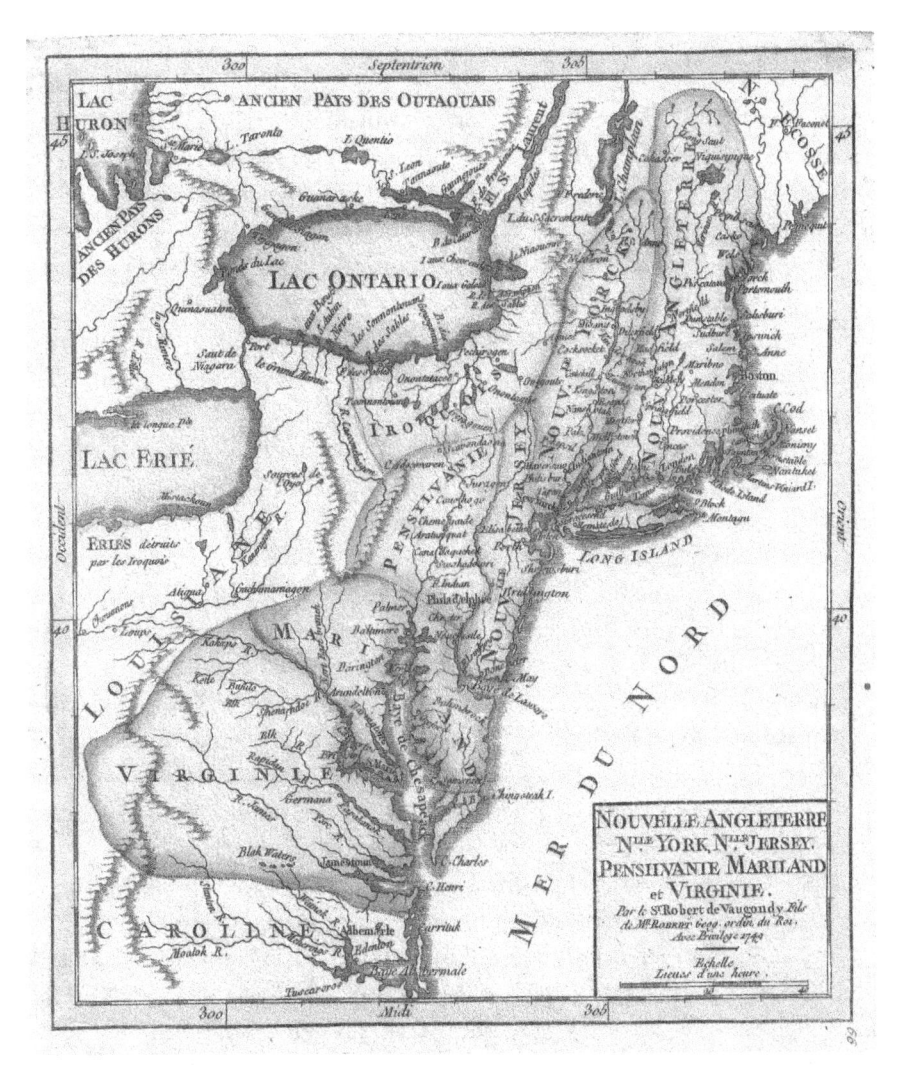

FIGURE 25. Robert de Vaugondy, *Nouvelle Angleterre, Nouvelle York, Nouvelle Jersey. Pensilvanie Mariland et Virginie. Par le Sr. Robert de Vaugondy Fils de Mr. Robert Geog. ordin. du Roi, 1749.* Image courtesy of Geographicus Rare Antique Maps.

Appalachian Mountains as the natural boundary dividing French Louisiana from British America. Surely aware of de Vaugondy's map and conscious of Céloron's expedition, George Montagu-Dunk, Second Earl of Halifax and president of the Board of Trade, pressed for cartographic credentials to the Ohio Valley and tasked Dr. John Mitchell with the responsibility. Mitchell had recently returned to Britain in 1746 after a forty-five-year residence in Virginia. A botanist and physician who corresponded with John Bartram, Mark

Catesby, and Peter Collison, Mitchell published "The Causes of the Different Colors of People in Different Climates" in the Royal Society's *Transactions*, earning himself a fellowship in the society. Mitchell shared Halifax's concern about French activity in Ohio. Yet he submitted a flawed map manuscript of British North America to the Board of Trade in 1750, despite his access to the Board of Trade's map archive.[13]

Revealing the inadequacy of the cartographic repository, this problematic map prompted Halifax to reach out to the colonial governors to find resident mapmakers. Responding to Halifax's call, acting Virginia governor Lewis Burwell commissioned Joshua Fry and Peter Jefferson in January 1751 to construct a Virginia map, which demonstrated Virginia's westward reach into the upper Ohio Valley. In 1749, the same year as de Vaugondy's *Nouvelle Angleterre*, Fry and Jefferson surveyed and extended the dividing line between North Carolina and Virginia ninety miles westward. They then depicted Walker's house on the draft of their unpublished 1751 map. They benefited not only from their earlier 1745 explorations of the Rappahannock and the Potomac Rivers in their Northern Neck surveys of the Fairfax proprietary and Walker's journal to bring up-to-date their map of Virginia, but also from Fry's solicitation on March 26, 1751, of Rev. Robert Rose, who wrote "Rode to Col. Fry's for a visit and lay down Tye River on ye map of Virginia." Fry readied his *Report on the Back Settlements of Virginia*, submitted on May 8, 1751, appended with a map and the travel account of Peter Salley. After reviewing this report for the Board of Trade, which was trying to gauge Virginia's capacity to check the French advance in Ohio country, Mitchell advised the board that the map demonstrated it could.[14]

Fry then contracted in 1752 for Walker's exploration services, witnessed by Jefferson. In exchange for Walker's surveying and selling his share of Loyal Company land, Fry agreed to pay him thirty shillings per one hundred acres plus customary fees and rights due to the surveyors and the secretary's office and to return any plans and certificates of "unsold" acreage he surveyed to the secretary's office. Since he had already been commissioned to survey the company's western land, Walker double-dipped by surveying Fry's landholdings. Fry in turn agreed to deed title to Walker on the above-mentioned acreage once payment was made within five months of registering the certificates.[15] Rev. Peter Fontaine reported to his brothers John and Moses on April 15, 1754, that Walker's company had "an entry on Halifax, beginning on the other side, or properly, west side of the great mountains, upon the line between North Carolina and Virginia, of eight hundred thousand acres of land. . . . Colonel Walker is the chief person in this scheme. They have it quite free for some years and sell it to settlers at £3 the hundred acres. They have about thirty settlements upon it, if the French and their Indians have not routed them lately."[16]

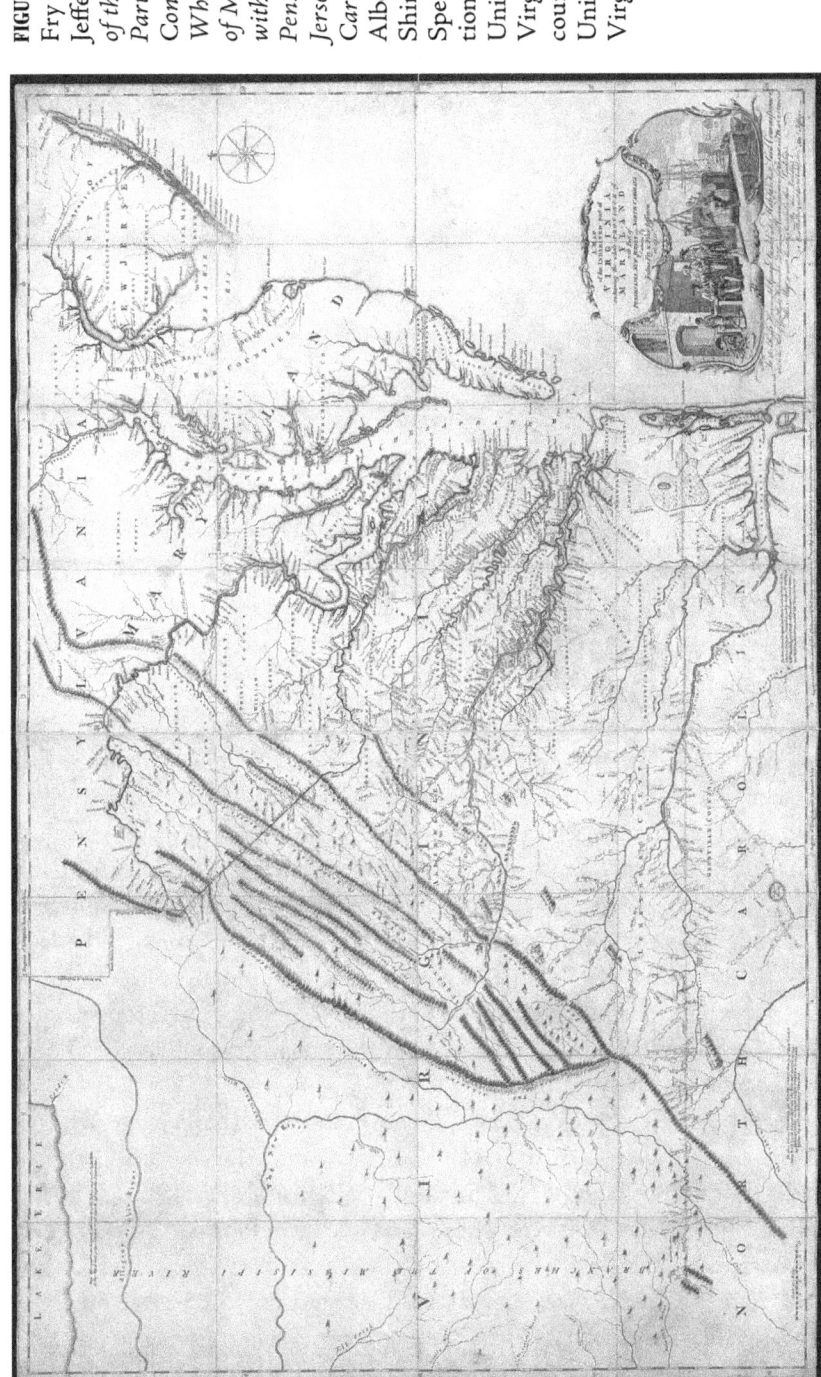

FIGURE 26. Joshua Fry and Peter Jefferson, *A Map of the Inhabited Part of Virginia, Containing the Whole Province of Maryland with Part of Pensilvania, New Jersey and North Carolina (1751).* Albert and Shirley Small Special Collections Library, University of Virginia. Image courtesy of University of Virginia.

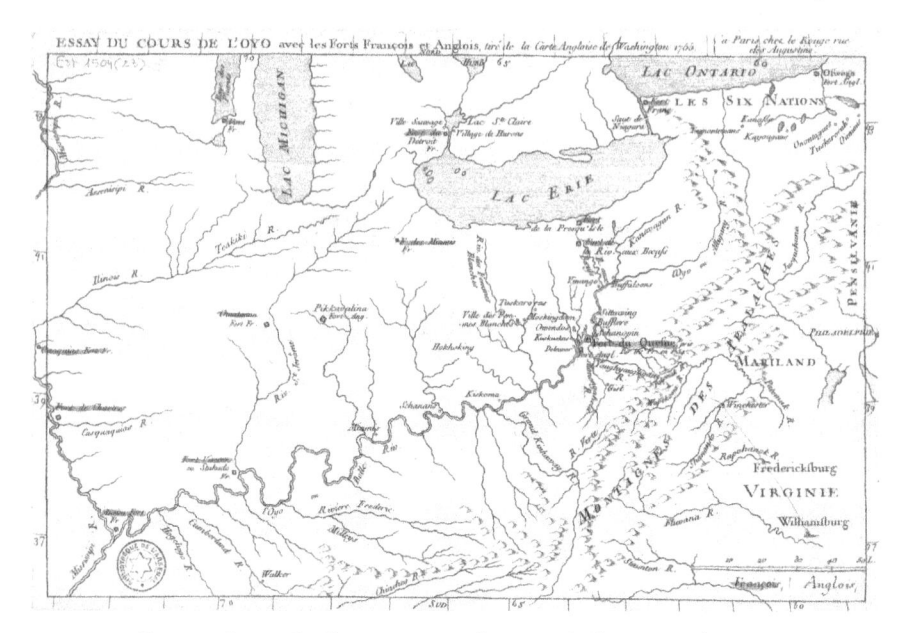

FIGURE 27. Georges-Louis Le Rouge, *Essay du cours de l'Oyo avec les Forts François et Anglois, tiré de la Carte Angloise* (1756). Collection géographique du marquis de Paulmy, Wikimedia Commons.

The published Fry-Jefferson map, cartography scholar William C. Woolridge ascertains, set the pattern for the next generation of Virginia maps. Their map encompassed one hundred thousand square miles stretching from its Atlantic coastal moorings to its western mastheads billowing toward the Mississippi and into the Ohio River. The map centered Virginia in Albemarle, home of its authors, away from Williamsburg, imagining a shift of power away from the locus of the great planter class in the tidewater to a burgeoning middle planter class emerging in the piedmont. This shift in the locus of power coincided with a shift in power from the council to the House of Burgesses, where the speaker began after 1736 to command greater authority. The map's orientation also imaged the growing competition between France and Britain over Native country.[17]

In 1755 French cartographers, following suit after the Fry and Jefferson map, marked off their territory. Robert de Vaugondy reprised his *Carte de la Virginie et du Maryland* (1755). Unlike his earlier Chesapeake map, he bled the English bounds into French Louisiana and even located "Walkers Establiss Anglois en 1750," perhaps a little too far west, as the westernmost English settlement.[18] Likewise, Frenchman George-Louis Le Rouge published *Essay du cours de l'Oyo avec les Forts François et Anglois, tiré de la Carte Angloise*, a map of the Ohio Valley with the French and English forts in 1755.

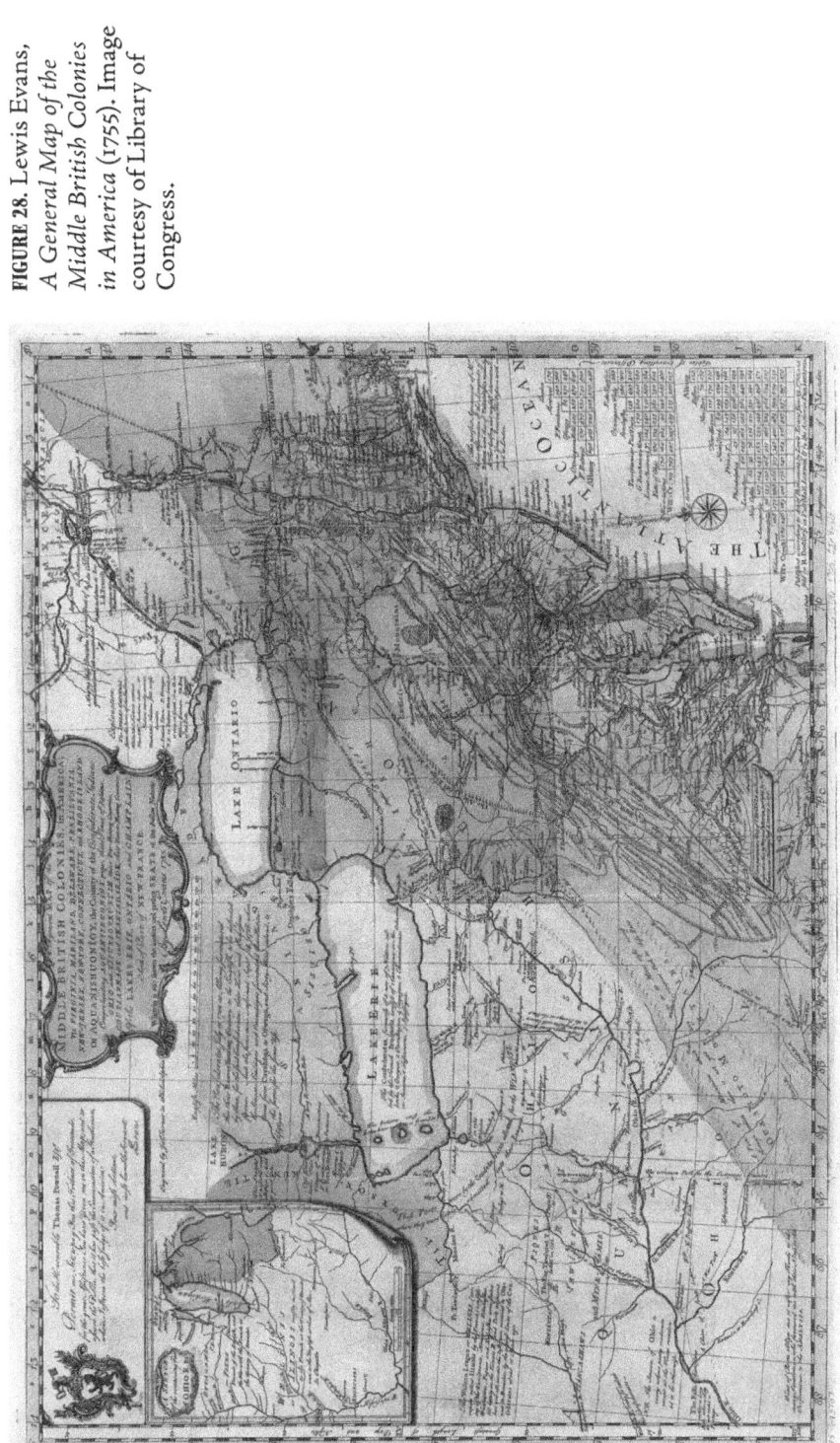

FIGURE 28. Lewis Evans, *A General Map of the Middle British Colonies in America* (1755). Image courtesy of Library of Congress.

Although it designates that it was drawn after the English map of George Washington, it incorporates the geography of Fry and Jefferson, situating Virginia well west of the Appalachian Mountains.[19]

British cartographers Lewis Evans and John Mitchell both published maps in 1755 that drew heavily on the Fry-Jefferson map. Evans acknowledged both *A Map of the Inhabited Part of Virginia* and Walker's contribution for his *General Map of the Middle British Colonies*: "The greatest part of Virginia is composed with the assistance of Messrs. Fry and Jefferson's map of it." He did not, however, extend Virginia across the Alleghenies into Ohio but instead retained the Native place-names, marking the region as Native country. He learned of these areas from a Native man who went by the name the Eagle. He also later compared and contrasted his published map with Gist's draft of his journey, which Gist corroborated "agreed so well with the idea he had of the country." Not only did Evans note the 384-mile distance from Lower Shawnee Town on the Ohio River to Fort Duquesne, but he also noted that it was an entrepôt for English traders. On the other hand, Walker had not inquired into any of these names from the Native people during his exploration and gave them new names after the members of his expedition: the Powell, Hughes, Tomlinson, Lawless, and Frederick Rivers, Price's Meadow, and Powell's Valley. Evans credited Walker for these names and directional flow of the rivers and "the branches of the Ohio, which head in the New Virginia."[20]

Mitchell's 1755 map also drew heavily on the Fry-Jefferson map and report of 1751 and, unlike Evans, made use of Gist's journal. Mindful of imperial ambition, Mitchell's map enhanced Virginia's western reach, depicting Walker's house as Virginia's westernmost settlement, and embraced the colony's northwest bounds, especially Ohio country. "Mitchell laid down the entire course of the Ohio River from its headwaters to its confluence with the Mississippi, and Evans's detail for the area north of the river is better," map scholar Henry Taliaferro concludes. "But the January 1755 state of Fry and Jefferson's map is far superior in its scale and depiction of the course of the upper Ohio River."[21] Alert to the outbreak of hostilities with the French, Mitchell paired his map with *A New and Complete History of the British Empire in America* (1755), which provided an account of English primacy in the Ohio Valley. "As this country belongs to Virginia, being within its grant, the inhabitants of that province began pretty early to visit it," he wrote without foundation. "The Virginians, invited by the fertility of the country and friendly behavior of the Indians, continued their visits thither; and although they made no settlements, yet they traded with the natives, and many private persons went and resided among them for the greater conveniency of carrying on that trade."[22]

PART III
Wars

The Indians themselves, when called upon in a public Treaty, to explain the Motives of their Conduct, declare that the Solicitations of the French, joined with the abuses they have suffered from the English, particularly in being cheated and defrauded of their Land, have at length induced them to become our Enemies and to make War upon us. That the French had been active to draw off the Indians, and engage them in their Interest, was not doubted: But as to the Complaints they made of Abuses received from the English, and of their being wronged of their Lands much Pains have been taken to represent them as groundless, and only lame excuses for their late Perfidiousness.

> —Charles Thomson, *An Enquiry into the Causes of the Alienation of the Delaware and Shawanese Indians from the British Interest* (1759)

CHAPTER 17

Commencement of the French Hostilities

Characterized as an "enterprising genius" by the authors of *A Review of the Military Operations in North-America* (1757), Quebec's new governor-general, Michel-Ange de Menneville, marquis de Duquesne (1752–55), was responsible in 1753 for French expansion into Ohio.[1] If Duquesne contended that La Salle's exploration had given New France primacy in Ohio over Virginia's 1609 charter, he also was responding to Virginia's treaty negotiations with the Haudenosaunee, the Ohio Company's speculation, and increasing English settlement. By the time of Duquesne's arrival, "the governor and Council of Virginia had by the end of 1752 conditionally granted about 2,300 square miles (6,000 square km) of land in the Ohio Valley to settlers. As a result, almost every important Virginia family—including members of the Washington, Lee, and Randolph families—was vitally interested in the fate of the Ohio area."[2] Anxious about Virginia's expansion, Duquesne felt compelled to dispatch troops "to go and seize and establish itself on the Belle Riviere [Ohio River], which we are on the verge of losing if I do not make this hasty but indispensable effort."[3]

Alarmed by the French army at the headwaters of the Ohio River, the Lenape, according to custom, sent an envoy with a formal notice to the French commandant, Paul Marin de la Malgue to cease and desist. The French ignored this warning. The Lenape then issued a "second notice" to Father Ontario from "Your Children on Ohio." "We at first heard you came to destroy us; our Women left off planting, and our Warriors prepared for War. We have since heard you came to visit us as Friends, without Design to hurt us; but then we wondered you came with so strong a Body. . . . If you had thought amiss of the English being there; and we invite you to do it now, before you proceed any further."

Marin responded, "Children, we come bearing no ill will," and averred that he did not "carry my Hatchet under my Coat." His troop was "so heavy a Body that the Stream will carry me down . . . to build four strong Houses," at Weningo, Monongahela Forks, Logstown, and Beaver Creek. Of the English presence, the commandant said:

> I have spoken[n] to them [the governments of Pennsylvania and Virginia] and let them know they must go off the Land, and I shall speak

to them again; if they will not hear me, it is their Fault, I will take them by the Arm, and throw them over the Hills. All the Land and Waters on this Side [of the] Allegheny Hills are mine, on the other Side theirs; this is agreed on between the two Crowns over the great Waters. I do not like your selling your Lands to the English; they shall draw you into no more foolish Bargains. I will take Care of your Lands for you, and of you. The English give you no Goods but for Land, we give you our Goods for nothing.[4]

After receiving this response, the Haudenosaunee, the Lenape, and the Shawnee conferred in council at Logstown, where each agreed to send an envoy to Pennsylvania and Virginia and a third notice to the French commandant. Tanaghrisson delivered this notice to Marin:

Of late you have chastised the Twightwees very severely, without telling us the Reason; and now you are come with a strong Band on our Land, and have, contrary to your Engagement, taken up the Hatchet without any previous Parley. These Things are a Breach of the Peace; they are contrary to your own Declarations: Therefore, now I come to forbid you. I will strike over all this Land with my Rod, let it hurt who it will. I tell you, in plain Words, you must go off this Land.

Onondaga tasked Oneida chief Monacatootha [aka Scarouady], "a Person of great Weight in their Councils," to the "Conduct of the Treaty in Virginia" on the "the State of Affairs at Ohio." The "principal Design" of the Ohio nations was first to treat with Virginia at Winchester and afterward to visit Williamsburg, where Dinwiddie had promised them a "hearty Welcome."[5]

The specter of the French settling on the "banks of the Ohio . . . quickly alarmed" the English colonies, especially Virginia, and "immediately concerned" Dinwiddie.[6] Instead of proceeding to Williamsburg, Monacatootha instead went to Carlisle, Pennsylvania, where on September 26, 1753, colonial commissioners Richard Peters, Isaac Norris, and Benjamin Franklin, representing both Pennsylvania and Virginia, hastily convened with the sachems representing the Lenape and the Shawnee. Alluding to the Myaamia and Lenape, "their great Men cut off by the French," and the Odawa, "all the Chiefs . . . being lately dead," Monacatootha said they could "not proceed to Business while the Blood remained on their Garments, and that the Condolences could not be accepted unless the Goods, intended to cover the Graves, were actually spread on the Ground before them."[7] The commissioners responded to the mandate by hastening the wagons in transit, "carrying chiefly fine Cloths, and a few Guns," reassuring that "the Presents of Condolence should be first made to wipe away Tears."[8]

In the meantime the commissioners learned the contents of the Virginia treaty from Croghan and Andrew Montour [aka Sattelihu, Eghnisara, Henry Montour], a *métis* [mixed ancestry] interpreter. Croghan told them that the Virginia government had earlier in the spring supplied the Ohio nations with arms and now, heeding their insistence, at Winchester stored "a suitable Quantity" of ammunition "in a particular Place under the care of Trent, Guest [Gist], and Montour" on the southeast side of the Ohio River. This gesture carried the hope that the other nations "settled at or near Allegheny" would recognize Virginia's "kind Intentions . . . in the Appropriation of a large Sum of Money for the Use of these Indians, in case they should be distressed by their Enemies, and their Hunting and Planting prevented."[9]

Acting free of Onondaga, the Ohio nations prepared to defend themselves; Tanaghrisson had gone to deliver his notice to the French commandant. Monacatootha now opposed building an English strong house at Monongahela. Once negotiations began on October 1, Monacatootha suggested that Dinwiddie's request for them "to build a strong House on Ohio" must have come to the attention of New France's Governor-General Duquesne: "We suppose this caused him to invade our Country," an event that made additional dialogue difficult "because he speaks with two Tongues." "We desire that Pennsylvania and Virginia would at present forbear settling on our Lands, over the Allegheny Hills. We advise you rather to call your People back on this Side the Hills, lest Damage should be done, and you think ill of us. . . . Let none of your People settle beyond where they are now . . . till the Affair is settled between us and the French."[10]

Ignoring his mention of land, the commissioners began to deal with other grievances discussed at Winchester. Demonstrating their earnestness, Virginia and Pennsylvania would solicit the release of the Shawnee captives jailed in Charlestown, "sending by Sea to Charles-Town; and an Express by Land . . . dispatched to Governor Dinwiddie." However, the commissioners put off Monacatootha's planned trip to Williamsburg, despite Shawnee disappointment, which he took in stride. "I will take your Advice, and not go to Virginia at this Time, but go Home, and do every Thing in my Power for the common Good."[11]

Responding to this threat, Governor Dinwiddie on October 31, 1753, penned a diplomatic letter to Marin, who had died two days earlier at Fort Le Boeuf, "complaining of sundry late hostilities: and desiring to know, by what authority an armed force had marched from Canada and invaded a territory indubitably the right of his Britannic Majesty."[12] Dinwiddie commissioned young George Washington, a member of the Ohio Company, to deliver a letter to the French commander in Ohio, which Washington memorialized in his *Journey to the French Commandant*. If Colonel Washington's official purpose was to deliver a letter to the French commandant, he was also unofficially gathering intelligence and courting the Ohio nations to the British side. At Logstown on January 16–17, 1754, Washington met with Tanaghrisson, the Seneca-Cayuga chief representing the Haudenosaunee in Ohio, alerting him about his mission and asking him for an armed escort to the French quarters. The French "had built two Forts, one on Lake Erie, and another on French Creek, near a small Lake about 15 Miles asunder, and a large Wagon Road between," said Tanaghrisson to Washington. "They are both built after the same Model, but different in the Size; that on the Lake the largest; he gave me a Plan of them of his own drawing."[13]

Tanaghrisson also relayed what had happened in his meeting with the French officers. He had met with Marin on September 3, 1753. Their exchange employed familial tropes of dependency, alluding to French fathers and Native children. Tanaghrisson called out the French "Fathers" as the "disturber in this land," taking it by force and building towns. "Both you and the English are White. We live in a Country between; therefore, the Land does not belong either to one or the other, but the GREAT BEING above allowed it to be a Place of residence for us." The Haudenosaunee would never submit to their intrusion. "So Fathers, I desire you to withdraw, as I have done our Brothers the English, for I will keep you at Arm's length . . . and I come now to tell it to you, for I am not afraid to discharge you off this Land."[14] Calling out the French as "White" like the English underscored the "sufficient importance" of Tanaghrisson's animus, for as Rev. Jonathan Boucher observed, the Native people usually only called English "white"—not the French or Spanish, whom they called by their nationality, not their race.[15]

Addressing him in a "stern manner," Marin had dismissed the Native people as pests, like mosquitoes and flies, and Tanaghrisson's threats as groundless. He said, "Child, you talk foolish; you say this Land belongs to you, but [René-Robert Cavelier, Sieur de La Salle, who explored the Ohio country sixty years earlier] saw that Land sooner than you did, before the Shawnesse and you were at War. . . . It is my Land." Consciously changing the terms of familial blandishments, Washington responded fraternally "Brothers, [I am here] by your Brother the Governor, to call upon you, the Sachems of the Six Nations, to inform you of it, and to ask your Advice & Assistance to proceed the nearest & best Road to the French. . . . His Honour likewise desir'd me to apply to you for some of your young Men to conduct and provide Provisions for us on our Way: and to be a Safeguard against those French Indians, that have taken up the Hatchet against us."[16]

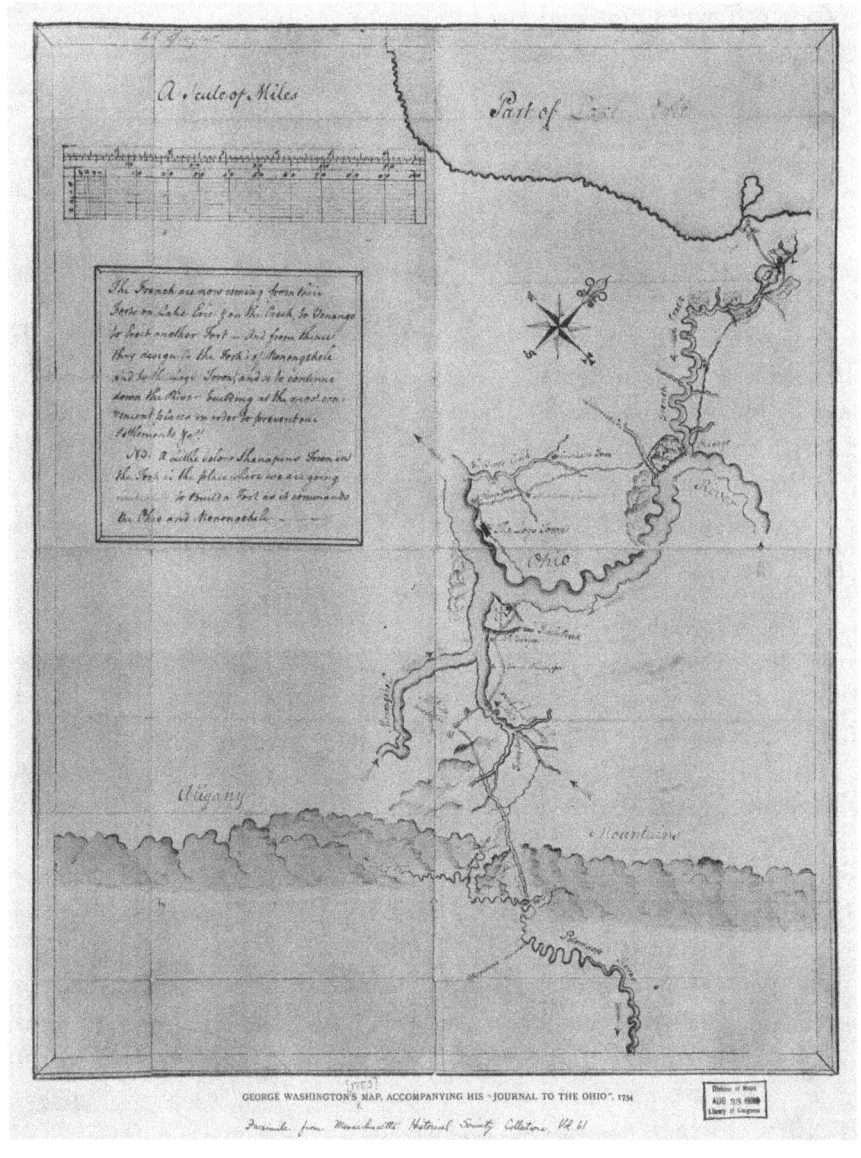

FIGURE 29. *George Washington's map accompanying his "journal to the Ohio,"* 1754. Image courtesy of Library of Congress.

Responding in kind to the fraternal "my brothers," Tanaghrisson said, "I intend to send a Guard of Mingoes, Shawnesse, and Delawar's, that our Brothers may see the Love and Loyalty." He then said that Washington should inform Governor Dinwiddie of French intentions in Ohio. Capt. Philippe Thomas de Joncaire, sieur de Chabert, an interpreter and a member of Céloron's expedition, said in a formal speech delivered to Tanaghrisson that the "three Nations of French Indians," the Ojibwe, the Odawa, and the Adirondack, had "taken up the Hatchet against the English." They intended their advance into Ohio once "they met in full Council with the Shawnesse, and Delaware Chiefs." Joncaire also had news from Venango of the French meeting with the Seneca-Cayuga, Lenape, and others. Although they had planned to come down the Ohio River that fall, the cold weather encouraged them to quarter until spring, when they could advance "with a far greater Number." He expected the fighting to last three years, but if the war stalemated, then he expected the English and the Ohio nations "would join to cut them off and divide the Land between them." Nevertheless, Joncaire believed that despite the recent death of Commandant Marin and "some few of their Soldiers, yet there was Men enough to reinforce, and make them Masters of the Ohio."[17]

Although the Shawnee had yet to arrive, Tanaghrisson felt they should proceed. Before leaving, he gave to Washington the speeches Jeskakake, "one of their old Chiefs," had given to the French commandant, which repeatedly warned the French to leave their land. He also shared their orders to send a "very large String of black and white Wampum . . . immediately up to the Six Nations, if the French refused to quit the Land at this [third and last] Warning." Washington had also asked Tanaghrisson about two English captives taken by the Haudenosaunee. "Child you think it is a very great Hardship that I made Prisoners of those two People at Venango," said Tanaghrisson, reversing the father-child dyad. "Don't you concern yourself with it. We took and carried them to Canada to get Intelligence of what the English were doing in Virginia." In turn, he pressed "very particularly" their concern about the Shawnee jailed in South Carolina.[18]

In another instance, George Mercer recorded that the French-aligned nations had exchanged the captive traders for "Negro boys." In 1753 the Kahnawake [Caughnawaga] had captured on the Kentucky River "our Indian traders" Alexander McGinty, Jabez Evans, David Hendricks, and William Powell, whom they "made Slaves" in Canada. They demanded a "Negro boy" for each or their equivalent value. On June 14, 1754, Orongraguicte, chief of the Falls of St. Louis, thought he should receive at least £20 sterling for each captive, making the point of seeing enslaved white people as equivalent with enslaved Black people. The commissioners of Indian Affairs at Albany bargained for them to "take less" and offered them £72. 5. 3, but the Native people "pretend not to be satisfied."[19]

The new commandant, Jacques Legardeur de Saint-Pierre, received Washington and read Dinwiddie's diplomatic letter of October 31, 1753. Dinwiddie had written that, "the Lands upon the Ohio in the Western Parts of the Colony of Virginia are so notoriously known to be the Property of the Crown of Great Britain, that is a matter of surprise and concern for me to hear that a Body of French Forces are erecting Fortresses and making Settlements upon that River within his Majesty's Dominion." He then stated that their hostile violation of both the law of nations and the treaties existing between the two Christian monarchies have elicited several complaints from British subjects, implicitly including Native peoples, and Britain demanded their "peaceable departure."[20] Responding on December 15, 1753, Legardeur admonished Dinwiddie for not sending Washington to Quebec to present this diplomacy directly to Marquis Duquesne, for he was only authorized "to demonstrate the reality of the King my master's rights to lands situated along the Ohio, and to dispute the pretensions of the King of Great Britain in that respect." Legardeur duly sent the diplomatic pouch forthwith to Duquesne. Likewise, he scoffed at Dinwiddie's directive to withdraw his troops. "I cannot believe myself under any obligation to submit to it. I am here, in virtue of my general's orders."[21]

Returning home, Washington met twenty Haudenosaunee on the road. They had been en route to yeh is-WAH h'reh country on the Great Warriors' Path, where they came across a grisly scene on the Great Kanawha. They found "people killed and Scalped, all but one Woman with very Light Hair . . . lying about the House, and some of them much torn and eat by Hogs." Even though they identified the assailants as the Odawa, aligned with the French, because of the "marks" they left behind, they beat a hasty retreat, fearful they would bear blame for the massacre.[22]

Upon Washington's return to Williamsburg Dinwiddie, immediately reported Legardeur's "resolute answer" to the Crown. Dinwiddie also moved swiftly, for "our common security," partly "by alarming speeches labored to rouse the Virginians into a vigorous opposition," partly by imploring letters intended to persuade "neighboring" governors "for repelling the invasion," and partly by ordering directives designed to fortify the forks of the Ohio. Nevertheless, he was met with opposition of "a profound lethargy, . . . resigned to stupidity and slumbering, [which] appeared insensible of the threatening danger." The colonies other than New York, which raised "5000 £ currency in aid to Virginia, . . . contemned" the danger was overblown. After all, New France was a distant threat. Not only was its settlement insufficient of "their inhabitants" and its intelligence "entirely unacquainted with the situation of the inland country," but also its governance was "inattentive . . . to the inconveniencies of an endless frontier." "The waters of the Ohio, before this period, were scarce known, save to a few Indian traders; and the generality deemed those French settlements too remote to be the object of dread, and a matter of insignificant moment."[23]

Dinwiddie on January 29, 1754, wrote to Gov. James Hamilton of Pennsylvania, reporting on Washington's planned expedition to Ohio and of his efforts to raise troops under Washington's command. To thwart the "intents of the French in settling those Lands," Dinwiddie organized his staging ground at Alexandria at the head of the Potomac. The troops would proceed from there to Will's Creek and then to Ohio. He pressed Hamilton on the need of more support and asked what "supply of forces and men" he could expect from the Pennsylvania Assembly. He suggested drawing on the "considerable number" of Palatines and Germans in Pennsylvania and enclosed Washington's *Journey to the French Commandant.*[24]

In February 1754, the Virginia General Assembly legislated raising ten thousand pounds and dispatching three hundred men to defend western Virginia. Dinwiddie issued a proclamation on February 19, 1754, "encouraging men to enlist for the defense and security" of Virginia. That security required building a fort at the confluence of the Ohio and the Monongahela to stop the "hostile attempts of the French and the French-aligned nations in their interest." For their "voluntary" service, he offered "over and above their pay, two hundred thousand acres . . . on the east side of the river Ohio, within this dominion, (one hundred thousand acres whereof to be contiguous to the said fort, and the other hundred thousand acres to be on, or near the river Ohio)." In addition, "the said lands shall be divided amongst them, immediately after the performance of the said service in a proportion due to their respective merit, as shall be represented to me by their officers, and held and enjoyed by them without paying any rights and also free from the payment of quit rents, for the term of fifteen years."[25]

On February 14, Dinwiddie called an emergency session of the General Assembly because of his "great concern" with the French and aligned nations' depredations in the Ohio River Valley. Once the group had assembled, he delivered a fiery speech. He first reported on Washington's visit to the French commandant on the Ohio River. He witnessed that the French had not only built a fort but also were planning two others. They also had 220 canoes at the ready to transport about 1,500 "regular forces" and their Native allies in the early spring with the intention of erecting more forts, choosing Logstown as the "chief place of their rendezvous." The commandant also answered Washington's query: Why had the French seized English traders? He said they seized their goods and sent them to Quebec because the governor-general had prohibited English traders on the Ohio. For the same reason, they confiscated John Fraser's house, where he had lived for a dozen years. He escaped capture; otherwise, they would have sent him to Quebec. Dinwiddie railed that these actions violated the treaties between the two nations and insulted the Crown. Adding to the insult, the French and Native allies inflicted injury to the settlers. For example, Dinwiddie held the French responsible for the "cruel and barbarous murder" of the family on the Great Kanawha, which Washington had reported. He also blamed the "bloody villains, thievishly lurking about a Man's Plantation" on the south branch of the Potomac River and attacking "like vermin," murdering his infant child.[26]

If the nations aligned with the French committed these "barbarous" acts as alleged, the French were generally "privy and instigators of their Robberies and Murders." He called on the assembly "to Drive away these cruel and treacherous Invaders of your Properties, and Destroyers of your Families . . . in establishing the Security and prosperity in Virginia on the most solid and permanent Foundations."[27] Dinwiddie, who had already received from the Crown "Thirty Pieces of Cannon, Eighty Barrels of Powder, and other Ordnance Stores suitable," sent "Ten of the Cannon, and a Proportion of Ammunition" to Alexandria and dispatched with the council's consent the militia to erect a fort at the fork of the Monongahela and the Ohio Rivers. He also had solicited neighboring governors to contribute to "their common cause." Now he advised the "Act for Making Provision against Invasions and Insurrections" (1748) was inadequate to deal with the present crisis. He deemed "the Pay is very unequally proportioned, being too high for the soldier and too Low for the officer and there is no Provision for a doctor and a commissary of stores and several other Requisites. I think it would be better to pay the Militia in money rather than tobacco, by which there may be a Saving to the Country, and the Men better Satisfied."[28]

Writing to Hamilton on March 21, 1754, Dinwiddie referenced the Great Kanawha atrocity, when giving the reason for the necessity of preempting the French from settling Ohio by building two or three forts toward that end.

> The Incursions of these People [the French] with their Native allies on our present Settlements, will be constantly, and attended with Robberies and Murders, which was the Case last Year when some of their Indians Came to our Frontiers, Murdered a Man, his Wife and five Children, Robbed them of all they had, and left their Bodies to be tore in Pieces by the wild Beasts. This is no more than may be annually expected from them. His Majest'y's Orders to me are to prevent their Settling on his Lands on the Ohio.[29]

Capt. William Trent tasked Ensign Edward Ward to revisit building the strong house, which Monacatootha had opposed in October, for precipitating the French invasion. Ward assembled the Chiefs and Deputies of the Six Nations and requested of them permission to Erect a Trading House at the Junction of the Allegheny and Monongahela Rivers, to carry on a Free and open Trade with the Six Nations and their dependents: which was granted by the said deputies with this restriction, that he was to form no Settlements or improvements on the said Land, but on the Contrary to Evacuate the same when required by the Six Nations.

Under these terms, Trent ordered thirty-three men to begin building the fort; however, on April 17, before they could finish, Ward, who had assumed command in Trent's absence, surrendered it to a "superior" French force in the presence of Tanaghrisson and a "number of the Six Nations, in the English Interests."[30]

Dinwiddie had on March 31, 1754, commissioned George Washington lieutenant colonel of the Virginia Regiment with orders "to march with them towards the *Ohio*, there to help Captain Trent to build Forts, and to defend the Possessions of his Majesty against the Attempts and Hostilities of the French."[31] By the time Washington arrived on April 20, he found that the French had ferried a detachment of one thousand men on sixty bateaux and three hundred dugouts and had forced under the threat of bombardment the surrender of a fort and the departure of its garrison. Washington also found that the Ohio nations had held "steadfastly" to the British line. For example, Tanaghrisson sent a speech "for the Governors of Virginia and Pennsylvania" reporting on how the French had treated them and intended "to use us. . . . We are now ready to fall upon them, waiting only for your Succor." On the other hand, "If you do not come to our Assistance now, we are entirely undone, and imagine we shall never meet together again."[32] Ward remembered "that the Deputies of the Six Nations after the surrender Joined the Virginia Forces, Commanded by Colonel George Washington, who was then on his march, at the Little Meadows, and continued with him, in the service of Virginia till after the defeat of Monsieur La Force, and a party of French Troops under his Command."[33]

After learning that six hundred Odawa and Chippewa warriors were winding down Scioto River to rendezvous with the French in Ohio, Washington thought it advisable to request the assistance of the Ani'-Yun-wiya, yeh is-WAH h'reh, and Chikashsha' with the caveat that the Haudenosaunee first make peace with these southern nations before they engaged in Ohio to avoid a "great Disorder." At the same time, Washington had to shore up the Ohio nations, ever mindful of their tributary relationship to Onondaga. If he was able to persuade King Shingas of the Lenape to send out scouts to surveil the French movements, he was still unable to persuade him to decamp the Lenape families with his troops, fearful of Onondaga reaction. Shingas counseled Washington on how best to request their aid. He must "prepare a great War-Belt, to invite all those Warriors who would receive it, to act independently from their King and Council; and King Shingas promised to take privately the most subtil Methods to make the Affair succeed, though he did not dare to do it openly."[34]

The sachems of the Ohio nations, the Pekuwe, the Myaamia, and the Shawnee, had failed to convene a scheduled meeting with Dinwiddie at Winchester "but sent [him] Strings of Wampum, with a Speech, that the French had invaded their Lands." At first they could not "leave their young Men," but now "they were marching to join our Forces under Colo. Washington." If they joined with "with some of our Forces . . . they could cut . . . off . . . the French from the Fort, . . . hankering about our Camp." Perhaps the British could have "dislodged" the French from Fort Duquesne if the colonial governors had provided the supplies ordered by the Crown. "Colo. Washington immediately marched in the Night with Forty Men; being dark and rainy, they lost Seven of their Men in the Woods; in the morning they joined the HalfKing."[35]

Meanwhile Washington's troops embarked on May 1 and "skirmished" with the French and their Native allies on May 28, killing ten and taking twenty prisoners. Washington explained what happened to Dinwiddie in a letter dated May 29, 1754. After receiving intelligence of a fifty-man French approach, Washington dispatched seventy-five of his militia to check their advance. He soon learned in an "express" from Tanaghrisson, bivouacked about six miles away, that he had espied two scouts, believing the rest of the French troop nearby. Following this intelligence, Washington led another forty men to join Tanaghrisson's warriors at his encampment. All this activity happened between nine and ten o'clock that "dark night" in a "heavy rain," together blurring the path. Once there Washington counseled Tanaghrisson, together with Monacatootha, to join him in attacking the French. They engaged the French in a fifteen-minute battle, killing ten, including M. de Jumonville, wounding one, and taking twenty-one prisoners. Washington's militia suffered only two or three wounded and one killed, "a most miraculous escape." "Principal Officers taken [were] Monsieur Druillong and Monsr Laforc," among other prisoners. Although they claimed they were a delegation, Washington discerned from their "insolent" summons that they had sought Washington's position and a "skulking place." Rather than dispatching scouts to deliver a diplomacy, they "sent Spies to Reconnoiter our Camp."[36]

Washington's militia had warily approached the French encampment, Dinwiddie reported to the Board of Trade on June 20, 1754. When the French discovered them in the distance, they hurried to their arms and a scrimmage began. The British casualties included one dead and another wounded; the British killed a dozen French and captured twenty-one, now imprisoned in Williamsburg. In the Native mode of warfare, Tanaghrisson's forces scalped the French dead. Now if Onondaga "declared against the French, it will give proper Spirit to the other Nations of Indians."[37]

Dinwiddie failed to appreciate Onondaga's perspective of what had transpired. After Tanaghrisson learned of the "mere pretense" and the "hostile manner" of the French mission, he declared he would not continue his alliance with Virginia if Washington let these prisoners go. Receptive of Dinwiddie's speech but fearful for his people, he went to secure them with an assist of thirty men and twenty horse. "He has declar'd to send these Frenchmen's Scalps with a Hatchet to all the Nations of Indian's in union with them, and did that very day give a Hatchet and a large Belt of Wampum to a Delaware Man to carry to Shingas: he promised me to send down the River for all the Mingo's and Shawnesse to our camp, where I expect him to Morrow with 30 or 40 Men with their wives and Children, to confirm what he has said here, he has sent your Honor a String of Wampum."[38]

Military historian David Preston's discovery and interpretation of "A Treaty with the Indians at Camp Mount Pleasant October 18th, 1754," sheds new light on what happened at Jumonville Glen from a Native perspective.[39] An unidentified "chief warrior" spoke at length and in detail about the event, especially about Washington's culpability. French accounts had cast aspersions on the young Washington's expedition for attacking a diplomatic mission and assassinating its leader, Ensign Joseph Coulon de Jumonville. Other accounts blamed Tanaghrisson for the murder of Jumonville, even quoting him as saying, "Tu n'es pas encore mort, mon père"— "You are not yet dead, my father," as he tomahawked the Frenchman's head. The chief warrior's speech, taken down verbatim at Camp Mount Pleasant, expressed the Native point of view. First, the interlocutor said that the Ohio nations believed that the English and the French had colluded to seize Native country and divide it between themselves. The chief warrior described Washington as a brash young chief. He recalled accompanying Washington from his meeting with the French commandant in 1753. In his haste to deliver the commandant's response to Dinwiddie, not only had Washington failed to convey to the Ohio nations what had happened between him and the French, but he also was loath to curry friendship with them.

He then related a story that Preston interprets as the rationale for revenge at Jumonville Glen. During the English and the Ohio people's surrender to the French at Trent's Fort in April 1754, Tanaghrisson remained obstinate, calling out the French as invaders and telling them that the Haudenosaunee had permitted the English trading post there. During the crisis French officer La Force [aka Michel Pépin] had humiliated Tanaghrisson in front of his people and threatened to kill them within three weeks. Consequently, Tanaghrisson's motives in striking the French at Jumonville were partly preemptive and partly vindictive. The Native chiefs had advised Washington where to approach the French in an ambuscade about fifty yards from their camp, where he opened fire, signaling the skirmish. This account squarely places the onus for initiating the attack on Washington. The chief warrior repeatedly called out the name La Force, the familiar name of Michel Pépin, the French commissary of stores on the upper Ohio, rather than Jumonville as the targeted French officer. Here Tanaghrisson tried in vain to revenge himself on La Force, but Washington protected him.[40]

Colonel Washington and Capt. James Mackay reported to Dinwiddie "the late Action between them and the French, at the Great Meadows in the Western Parts of this Dominion." Hearing at nine in the morning on July 3, 1754, that the two hundred French and Native warriors were marching with seven hundred reinforcements from the Monongahela line, Washington had his force of three hundred prepare for their defense by "throwing up a small Intrenchment." Two hours later, the enemy had reached their line of defense. As it turns out, Washington had selected an indefensible place where the French and their allies were positioned to lay siege. "An Enemy sheltered behind the Trees, ourselves without Shelter, in Trenches full of Water, in a settled Rain," Washington lamented, "and the Enemy galling us on all Sides incessantly from the Woods."

The next morning another one hundred Native warriors joined the French deployment, "who hardly restrained from attacking us, and did us considerable Damage by pilfering our Baggage." In retreat, the Virginians abandoned their stores and supplies. Washington estimated his death toll at thirty and another seventy wounded. Relying on "uncertain information" obtained from "some Dutch in their Service," he estimated the enemy's dead at three hundred, including "an Officer of distinguishable Rank," which, despite their recognition of the dire straits the Virginians were in, he ascertained "induced them to call first for a Parley." Shifting blame from his command to the lack of British reinforcements, despite HMS orders, Washington complained that this negligence contributed mightily to their defeat. "Thus have a few Men been exposed, to be butchered, by the Negligence of those who, in Obedience to their Sovereign's Command, ought to have been with them many Months" before; and it is evidently certain, that had the Companies from New York been as expeditious as Capt. Maccay's from South-Carolina, our Camp would have been secure from the Insults of the French, and our brave Men still alive to serve their King and Country."[41]

At the same time both the Haudenosaunee and the Ohio nations were reluctant to engage the French and their Native allies. Albany had issued invitations convening a congress at Albany for the colonial commissions to meet with the Haudenosaunee in order "to concert a scheme for a general union of the British colonies." The negotiations beginning on June 18, 1754, were "conducted with great solemnity," and the sachems of the Six Nations, the Mohawk, Oneida, Onondaga, Cayuga, Seneca, and Tuscarora, "appeared well pleased" with the presents of "immense value." Nevertheless, the Haudenosaunee were reticent to commit their allegiance and were dismissed. Smith, Livingstone, and Scott's *Review of the Military Operations* gave their reasoning: they had "recriminated upon us the desertion of our fort at Saratoga the last war; lamented the defenseless condition of our frontier city of Albany; and extoled the better conduct of the French, in fortifying and maintaining their garrisons."[42] The *Review* pithily summed up the battle at Great Meadows. "Alarmed" to learn in July "that 900 French and 200 Native warriors were advancing from the Ohio," Washington began building a palisaded fort and bivouacked his army of "three hundred effective men" at Fort Necessity, where he engaged a superior force. Despite killing "near two hundred of the French and their Indian allies," Washington recognized the futility of his situation. After a loss of thirty dead and fifty wounded and "hemmed him in on all quarters," Washington surrendered, "submitting to the disagreeable terms that were offered him."[43]

Maj. Edward Ward recalled that after "the defeat of Colo: Washington at the great Meadows, the Shawanese, Delawares, many of the Western Tribes of Indians, and an inconsiderable number of Renegades of the Seneca Tribe, one of the Six Nations, Joined the French, and Prosecuted a War against the Frontiers of the States of Virginia, Maryland and Pennsylvania, till the conclusion of the Peace with the Indians in the year 1759; but that he ever understood the Body of the Six Nations continued the firm Friends of the English."[44]

Washington's military shortcomings coming on the heels of both English trade abuses and encroachments on their land caused the Ohio nations to waver in their English support.

"It was very unfortunate for the *English* interest, that at the same Time the Affections of the *Indians* were alienated from us by the Abuses committed in Trade, and by our dispossessing them of their Lands, their Opinion of our military Abilities was very much lessened." Washington's "conduct and behavior" at the Meadows gave Tanaghrisson pause. He removed thirty families under his command out of harm's way to Aughwick Old Town, near Fort Shirley, where he placed his wife and children, leaving Washington and his militia behind to deal with the French and their Native allies. So did other Native people before the battle began, because "Col. Washington would never listen to them, but was always driving them on to fight by his Directions."[45]

Tanaghrisson accompanied Conrad Weiser, who kept a journal of the proceedings. Although he had broached the topic of Washington's conduct at Monongahela on August 31, they did not have a chance to speak about it until September 3, giving Tanaghrisson time to compose his thoughts. Signifying both his interest in maintaining relations with the English and his familiarity with an elite Virginia vernacular, Tanaghrisson voiced his disfavor of Washington's capabilities in a "very modest manner." He characterized him as "a good-natured man but had no Experience . . . he took upon him to command the Indians as his Slaves." He was unwilling to listen to their counsel, even though they knew the lay of the land and had experience in forest warfare. He arrogantly commanded them not only to scout out the enemy but also "to attack the Enemy by themselves." He demonstrated his inexperience by bivouacking at "that little thing upon the Meadow [for] a full moon," believing "the French would come up to him in open Field." Had Washington fortified the meadow as he counseled, Tanaghrisson was confident that "he would have certainly beat the French off." At length, "the French had acted as great Cowards, and the English as Fools in that Engagement."[46]

CHAPTER 18

Defend Our Lands and Hinder the French

On September 5, 1754, Governor Dinwiddie again called a special session of the General Assembly because of the "impending danger from the violent Incursions of the French, their Threats and Depredations." He expressed his surprise at the indifference of the legislators to the threat, despite their rhetorical flourish, both acknowledging the danger and professing their "Zeal for her Service." He chastised them for failing to financially support the militia already called, clothed, and compensated. Prognosticating that the burgesses would appear in a "bad light" to both the Crown and other colonies, he recessed the assembly for their lack of resolve.[1] When the General Assembly finally found its resolve, William Fairfax notified his friend Washington of the efforts of the burgesses to raise war funds. Some wanted a lottery "as the most probable Means" of defraying the costs, and others put forth a land tax "would be more Effectual."

Unable to choose one way over the other, they joined them together and then added the tried-and-true tax on Black people to boot. First, the General Assembly passed "An Act for Raising the Sum of Six Thousand Pounds by a Lottery, for the Further Protection of His Majesty's Subjects against the Insults and Encroachments of the French." Then they passed "An Act to Explain an act, Intituled, An act for Raising the Sum of Twenty Thousand Pounds, for the Protection of His Majesty's Subjects, against the Insults and Encroachments of the French" [May 1755]. This anti-French measure added revenue for military defense by laying a duty on enslaved people: two shillings on each tithable enslaved person plus an extra duty of 10 percent on captives imported during the next three years. The legislation also laid a tax of one shilling and three pence per one hundred acres throughout the colony and singled out Fairfax "by enabling the sheriffs to collect the said land tax, from the proprietors of land, within the territory of the right honorable Thomas Lord Fairfax." Fairfax expressed his concerns and hopes to his friend Washington: "We shall be a little impatient till We can know You have passed the rugged, and Sometimes thought, impassable Mountains called the Allegany and have descended into the fertile Plains of the Ohio, driving back the French to their narrow Limits in Canada."[2]

Under a counsel of "misrepresentations," likely coming from Dinwiddie, Major General Edward Braddock had chosen to march immediately from Alexandria to Fort Duquesne. Dinwiddie had publicly supported erecting a fort at the fork of the Ohio and Monongahela Rivers, where the Ohio Company speculation and Christopher Gist's plantation had established settlements of about twenty families, both considered within the legal boundaries of Virginia.[3] Braddock clearly did not take his volunteer aide Washington's advice. After two recent expeditions to Ohio over the past two years, the young officer recognized the foolhardiness of the plan.[4] Smith, Livingstone, and Scott's *Review of the Military Operations in North-America* concurred: "Those who were well acquainted with the country, could not help observing, that a march from Potomac, across the Allegheny mountains, must be attended with incredible difficulty, hazard, and expense." The more advantageous and strategic course initiated the march in New York, where "its fort of Oswego on Lake Ontario—together with the advantages of water carriage"—forced the French to defend their own turf in Canada.[5]

Seeking to curtail vice and maintain discipline as they prepared to go to the Alexandria staging grounds, Braddock forbade both spirituous liquors and gaming to regulars and discussed with Washington women accompanying the troops as laundresses. More important, Braddock's order book made mention of the cancellation of the proposed pan-Native conference, perhaps as costly a mistake as his choice of march route.[6] Surely Braddock was aware of the map drawn around 1755 by Chegeree, an Indigenous man "who says he has travelled through the country," conveyed to an unidentified British agent. His knowledge of the environs of Lake Erie to the mouth of the Ohio River led to his creating a map "oriented with north toward the upper right," its notations showing areas of French military preparedness, locations of Native towns, and "distances to a 'French Fort,' i.e., Fort Duquesne." Chegeree included six Myaamia [towns not in amity with the French, perhaps jockeying for an alliance with the British ally in Ohio country.[7]

Surely, Washington had advised Braddock on the necessity of a Native alliance, recalling Shingas's subtle counsel on how best to request Native aid. Instead, Shingas and two chiefs each representing the Shawnee and Seneca-Cayuga had approached Braddock and asked him "what he intended to do with the Land if he Could drive the French and their Indians away." Braddock responded: "The English Should Inhabit and Inherit the Land." Shingas asked Braddock "whether the Indians that were Friends to the English might not be Permitted to Live and Trade Among the English and have Hunting Ground sufficient To Support themselves and Families as they had nowhere to Flee To But into the Hands of the French and their

Indians who were their Enemies." Braddock said, "No Savage Should Inherit the Land." After repairing to their people, they returned the next morning and reiterated their concerns and repeated their queries, only to receive the same responses. Shingas and the other chiefs answered, "If they might not have Liberty to Live on the Land, they would not Fight for it." Braddock answered, "He did not need their help and had No doubt of driving the French and their Indians away." After Shingas and the other chiefs communicated what Braddock had said, "a Party of them went Immediately upon it and Joined the French But the Greater Part remained neuter till they saw How Things would go Between Braddock and the French in their Engagement."[8]

On June 10, 1755, Braddock began his march "towards the Ohio, at the head of about 2,200 men, in order to invest Fort Duquesne, and drive the French from their encroachments on the settlements of Virginia and Pennsylvania." The landscape did not offer the well-trod lines of march of European warfare where Braddock cut his teeth; his army had "to surmount, in a country rugged, pathless, and unknown, across the Allegheny mountains, thro' unfrequented woods, and dangerous defiles." Braddock divided his forces into two divisions. He commanded the lead troop of fourteen hundred men, carrying "the greatest part of the ammunition and artillery." Bringing up the rear, Colonel Thomas Dunbar commanded the remaining eight hundred men and the commissary "with the provisions, stores, and heavy baggage." After receiving intelligence that five hundred French reinforcements were en route to Fort Duquesne, Braddock ordered his troops to increase their pace in "forced marches, which fatigued the soldiers, weakened his horses, and left his second division near forty miles in the rear."[9]

After passing the Monongahela settlement and within seven miles of Fort Duquesne, around noon on July 9, 1755, about thirty French regulars and a combined force of five hundred to six hundred Native warriors, including the French-aligned Odawa, Myaamia, and Wyandot and the English-disaffected Lenape, Shawnee, and Seneca-Cayuga, attacked the "vanguard under Lieut. Col. Gage . . . with quick and heavy fire." When the soldiers from the main body rushed to defend their flank, their officers called them back to "form into battalia," an arrangement of troops more suitable to the European field of battle than the American forest, engulfing the entire army into "a general panic. During this scene of confusion, they expended their ammunition in the wildest and most unmeaning fire. Some discharging their pieces on our own parties, who were advanced from the main body for the recovery of the cannon." Finally, after three hours of "enduring a terrible slaughter, from (it may be said) an invisible foe," the surviving officers ordered a retreat. Most of the men took "immediate flight," dropping their arms and gear, only relaxing their stride three miles distant, and "leaving behind them all the artillery,

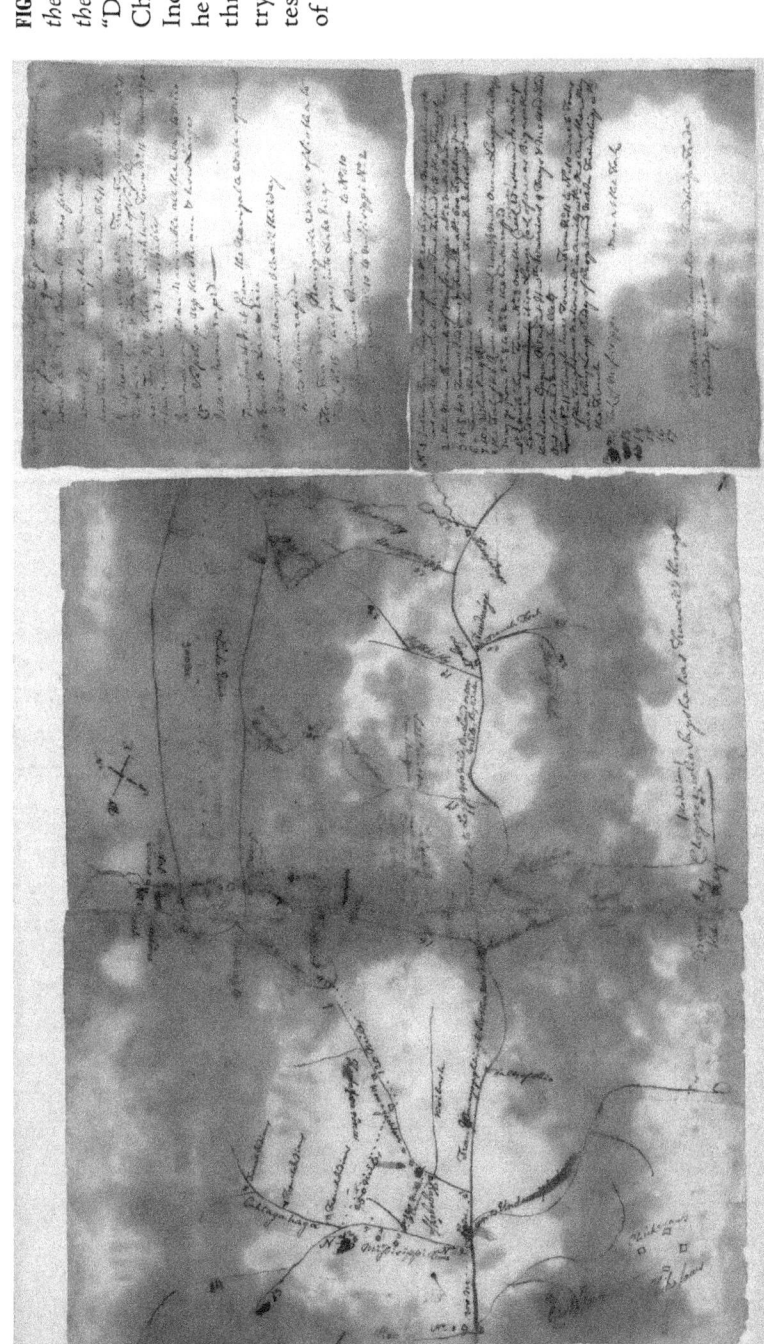

FIGURE 30. *Map of the Country about the Mississippi.* "Drawn by Chegeree (the Indian) who says he has travelled through the country." Image courtesy of Library of Congress.

provisions, ammunition, baggage, military chest, together with the general's cabinet, containing his instructions and other papers of consequence."[10] Only about one hundred men beat an orderly retreat. The "routed" army reached Colonel Dunbar's troop forty miles in the rear, yet "fearful of an unpursuing foe, all the ammunition, and so much of the provisions were destroyed, for accelerating their flight, that Dunbar was actually obliged to send for thirty horse loads of the latter, before he reached Fort Cumberland—where he arrived a very few days after, with the shattered remains of the English troops."[11]

Braddock received universal condemnation. In an excited utterance, the botanist John Bartram expressed the "astonishment" of 'his defeat to Peter Collinson in a letter of around July 10, 1755: "Both Town and countrey [were] moved as the leaves on the trees with A wind and sea in a storm. . . . General Braddock is overthrown 600 of his men slain and wounded most of his officers killed and ye artillery taken by 300 Indians Oh Stupid obstinate Briton."[12] Smith, Livingstone, and Scott's *Review of the Military Operations in North-America* concluded that the cocksure Braddock was blameworthy for neglecting both the aid of Native allies and their methods of conducting warfare:

> In fine, that the provincials had disheartened them, by repeated suggestions of their fears of a defeat, should they be attacked by Indians; in which case the European method of fighting would be entirely unavailing. But, my Lord, however censurable the conduct of the soldiery may be thought, Mr. Braddock, too sanguine in his prospects, was generally blamed for neglecting to cultivate the friendship of the Indians, who offered their assistance; and who, it is certain, had a number of them preceded the army, would have seasonably discovered the enemy's ambuscade.[13]

In his memoirs George Washington concurred: "The folly and consequence of opposing compact bodies to the sparse manner of Indian fighting, in woods, which had in a manner been predicted, was now so clearly verified that from hence forward another mode obtained in all future operations."[14]

Evidently under Onondaga instructions, Monacatootha had accompanied Braddock with about a dozen warriors. Meeting in Philadelphia with a delegation of English and Native nations on August 22, 1755, he wanted it known to "all the English on this Continent" that he had constantly counseled Braddock about the "danger he was in with his Soldiers," however, his "pride and ignorance" prevailed. "He looked upon us as dogs and would never hear anything what was said to him. . . . He never appeared pleased with us, and that was the reason that a great many of our Warriors left him and would not be under his Command." Nevertheless, Monacatootha advised the English not to surrender, reminding them that "you are very numerous" and that the seaboard governors could raise enough soldiers, rather than rely on the British soldiers who "come over on the great seas; . . . they are unfit to fight in the woods. Let us go ourselves, we that came out of this Ground, we may be assured to conquer the French."[15]

After Braddock's "unhappy catastrophe," the Crown appointed Governor William Shirley of Massachusettsas major general. He quickly moved the theater of war from the southwest to the northeast, sending sixteen thousand troops from Albany to Philadelphia and "leaving behind the Virginia and Maryland companies, and about 400 wounded. At this sudden departure of forces, the Virginians were extremely disobliged, as not only exposing their frontiers, and occasioning the daily desertion of their provincials; but because the enemy, in flying parties penetrated into the province, and on many of the inhabitants, committed robberies and murder."[16] As the war strategy shifted to the northeast, the English considered Oswego "of the greatest importance for securing the frontiers of the western colonies, maintaining the British dominion over the great lakes, and the country beyond the Appalachian Mountains."[17] "As to Virginia—now equally open to the eruptions of the enemy, four companies of rangers were ordered out, and the assembly voted 40,000£ for furnishing a thousand men for the frontier defense. . . . Virginia chose to be entirely upon the defensive."[18]

The Haudenosaunee continued their allegiance to the English, but despite sending threatening directives to their dependencies, they were unable to keep them from joining the French.[19] After Braddock's defeat the French "immediately compelled" the neutral Ohio nations to join them. At the same time, the Ohioans' attachment to the English began to wane. So compromised, the Lenape, the Shawnee, and the Seneca-Cayuga reticently joined the French and retentively reached out to the English by seeking a treaty in Philadelphia. Unable to receive the "necessary Encouragement the Indians agreed To Come out with the French and their Indians in Parties to Destroy the English Settlements."[20] Joseph Nicholas recalled that a year after Braddock's defeat, he was captured by a party of Shawnee and Lenape, who in turn transported him to the Cayuga. Although he acknowledged the Cayuga as "greatly mixed with other nations," the Haudenosaunee who held him "spoke the Kayuga Language and resided in that Nation," where he was held captive for seven years. "He knew several of the said Tribe to go with other Parties against the Settlements, and that he saw several small, parties of the Seneca Tribe, on their way to war against the Inhabitants—that it was always denied by the Chiefs of the Six Nations that they were at war with the white people."[21]

The French then deployed the Ohio nations in roving bands to that end, beginning on the south branch of the Potomac near Fort Cumberland and spreading out from Fort Duquesne, attacking settlements, where they inflicted terror and made captives. The means of continual encroachment in Ohio and of an absence of a response to their request for military stores proved the Lenape's suspicions of English ends. Partly because of their anger at Pennsylvania-Haudenosaunee collusion, which had deprived them of their land in the Walking Purchase of 1737, and partly because of the humiliation they had received at the treaty at Philadelphia in 1742, and partly because Virginia and General Braddock had cast aspersions on them and refused to honor their dominion over Ohio, the Lenape attacked the English during the fall of 1755.[22]

After dividing his forces into two troops, Shingas grudgingly carried the war against the English. After days of killing and plunder, on November 3, 1755, they divided their spoils and split into two companies: the Shawnee under Capt. John Peter and the Lenape and Seneca-Cayuga under Shingas. "Captivated" in Cumberland County, Pennsylvania, on October 29, 1755, Charles Stuart heard Shingas a week later (November 8) gravely address his captives. Shingas, the chief judge, opposed the council-in-general's recommendation for a torturous death for the captives. In doing so he recalled his earlier relationship with settlers, singling out Stuart's people: he "had Always been supplied with Provisions and what they wanted Both for themselves, and [for their] Creatures without Ever Charging them Anything for it." Shingas then said they did not want to continue the war with the English. He proposed returning the captives and their possessions provided the English met two conditions for peace, both involving cooperative living and the English transfer of trades.[23]

In the first instance, Shingas proposed the English send five artisans to live among the Native people, who would work without wages other than the expense of their maintenance. They would be employed not only making gunpowder and smelting lead and iron but also "making and mending guns for them." In exchange they would locate lead mines and sources for "every other metal that was necessary." In the second instance, he proposed the English with their families would come and settle among the Native people and promote spinning and other trades "that they might be Supplied with what they want near home." Although Shingas called for harmonious relations, even the notion that they should "Become One People and Live Together in Love and Friendship," Stuart was quick to note, he did not encourage intermarriage. Shingas and Captain Peter left the dispatch in a split stick that they put into the ground near an English fort. Upon receipt of the proposal, Pennsylvania governor Robert Hunter Morris responded that the English "People were Born free and that tho' he cou'd persuade them to Come and Live among the Indians yet he cou'd not oblige them to do it." The following day, Shingas dispersed the captives among his people, and the proposition came to naught.[24]

Simon Girty's captivity revealed to him, as his deposition indicated, how completely the Haudenosaunee and their dependencies had aligned with the French. A party of Lenape and Shawnee captured him and delivered him to the French, who imprisoned him at Fort Duquesne. He was then taken to Kittanning, "inhabited" by the Lenape and the Seneca-Cayuga, and later taken to Seneca country, "where he continued a considerable time." He "always understood" that a French-aligned party of Wyandot, Seneca, Lenape, Shawnee, and Odawa "defeated" General Grant on September 14, 1758, at the Battle of Fort Duquesne. He said Guyasuta, the Seneca chief, was not only among them but also later led a Native party of fifty-five, principally Seneca, on May 22, 1759, to victory against a troop of one hundred Virginians commanded by Capt. Thomas Bullitt on the Forbes Road near Fort Ligonier. Girty remained a prisoner at Kittanning until "it was destroyed by the English."[25]

Mary Jemison was twelve years old in 1755 when a party of six Shawnee and four French captured and massacred her settler family. "My two brothers, Thomas and John, being at the barn, escaped and went to Virginia, where my grandfather Erwin then lived."[26] Her uncle John Jemison had served under Washington at Great Meadows or Fort Necessity, where he had been killed in battle, which in a sense foreshadowed her fate, for she was adopted by a family that had lost a relation to warfare with the English. The Shawnee took her to Fort Duquesne. Before she arrived, "the Indians combed the hair of the young man, the boy and myself, and then painted our faces and hair red, in the finest Indian style."[27] She was given to two Native women who carried her down the Ohio River past a Shawnee town to a Seneca town, where she experienced an adoption ceremony "to supply the place of their brother in the family."[28]

Oh, our brother! Alas! He is dead—he has gone; he will never return! Friendless he died on the field of the slain, where his bones are yet lying unburied! Oh, who will not mourn his sad fate? No tears dropped around him; oh, no! No tears of his sisters were there! He fell in his prime, when his arm was most needed to keep us from danger! Alas! he has gone! and left us in sorrow, his loss to bewail: Oh, where is his spirit? His spirit went naked, and hungry it wanders, and thirsty and wounded it groans to return! Oh, helpless and wretched, our brother has gone! No blanket nor food to nourish and warm him; nor candles to light him, nor weapons of war: —Oh, none of those comforts had he! But well, we remember his deeds! —The deer he could take on the chase! The panther shrunk back at the sight of his strength! His enemies fell at his feet! He was brave and courageous in war! . . . Though he fell on the field of the slain, with glory he fell, and his spirit went up to the land of his fathers in war! Then why do we mourn? With transports of joy, they received him and fed him, and clothed him, and welcomed him there! Oh friends, he is happy; then dry up your tears! His spirit has seen our distress and sent us a helper whom with pleasure we greet. Deh-he-wä-mis has come then let us receive her with joy! She is handsome and pleasant! Oh! she is our sister, and gladly we welcome her here. In the place of our brother, she stands in our tribe. With care we will guard her from trouble; and may she be happy till her spirit shall leave us.[29]

"Surprised" to hear of Braddock's defeat, Dinwiddie's first impulse was not to defend the settlements but to guard against an insurrection of the enslaved, for "the Villainy of the Negroes on any Emergency of Government is what I always feared." Reacting to the massing of Black people near Charles Carter's son's house, he wrote to him on July 18, 1755, that it was "absolutely necessary" to muster the county militias and immediately to recall to him "their Numbers and Arms, Powder, etc., and keep Patrollers our for the Peace of Your County." "I greatly approve your sending the Sheriffs with proper strength to take up those who appeared in a Body at your Son's house, and if found Guilty of the Expressions mentioned I expect You will send for a Com'o. [court of oyer and terminer] to try them, and an Example of one or two at first may prevent those Creatures entering into Combinations and wicked Designs against the Subjects."[30] A month late, Dinwiddie reported that the slaveholders feared the more than eleven hundred "neutral" Arcadian refugees from Nova Scotia distributed to Virginia would corrupt the enslaved people. Drawing upon tropes of "papists and priests" to revile the French-speaking Catholics, the planters thought them an "intestine" fifth column, "corrupting their Negro slaves." "I am very well convinc'd so debauch the minds of the People and have too much influence amongst the Slaves," Dinwiddie said to Col. William Fitzhugh on August 30, 1755, "and it's a Pity Y'r Legislature do not take some Method to expunge those Vermin who are a Pest to Society."[31]

Dinwiddie had sent a message on August 5, 1755, to the House of Burgesses on call for a special session. He informed them that he had news from Mr. Orme, aide-de-camp Braddock and Col. Washington, of Braddock's "fatal Defeat . . . threatening this colony with the most fatal consequences."[32]

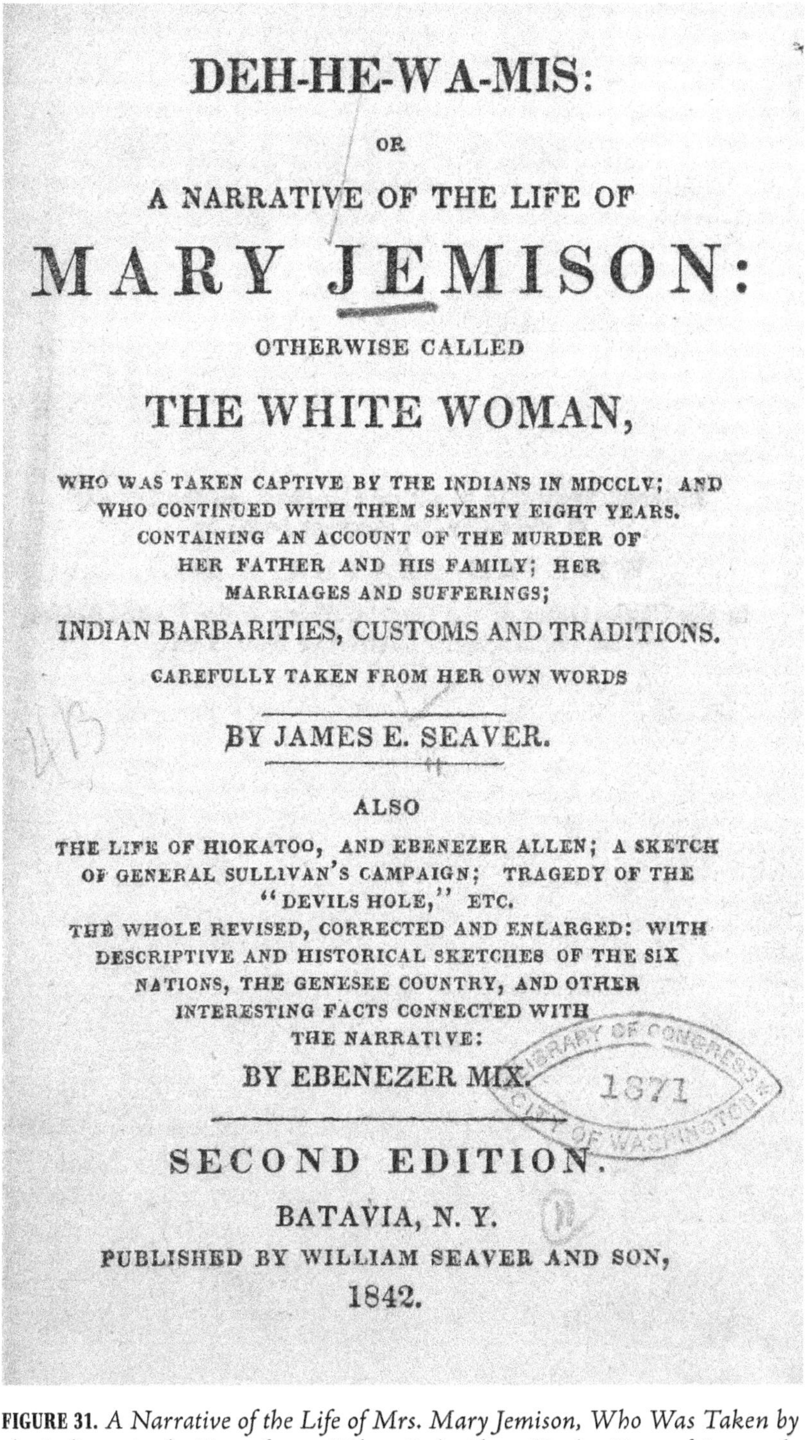

DEH-HE-WA-MIS:

OR

A NARRATIVE OF THE LIFE OF

MARY JEMISON:

OTHERWISE CALLED

THE WHITE WOMAN,

WHO WAS TAKEN CAPTIVE BY THE INDIANS IN MDCCLV; AND
WHO CONTINUED WITH THEM SEVENTY EIGHT YEARS.
CONTAINING AN ACCOUNT OF THE MURDER OF
HER FATHER AND HIS FAMILY; HER
MARRIAGES AND SUFFERINGS;

INDIAN BARBARITIES, CUSTOMS AND TRADITIONS.

CAREFULLY TAKEN FROM HER OWN WORDS

BY JAMES E. SEAVER.

ALSO

THE LIFE OF HIOKATOO, AND EBENEZER ALLEN; A SKETCH
OF GENERAL SULLIVAN'S CAMPAIGN; TRAGEDY OF THE
"DEVILS HOLE," ETC.
THE WHOLE REVISED, CORRECTED AND ENLARGED: WITH
DESCRIPTIVE AND HISTORICAL SKETCHES OF THE SIX
NATIONS, THE GENESEE COUNTRY, AND OTHER
INTERESTING FACTS CONNECTED WITH
THE NARRATIVE:

BY EBENEZER MIX.

SECOND EDITION.

BATAVIA, N. Y.
PUBLISHED BY WILLIAM SEAVER AND SON,
1842.

FIGURE 31. *A Narrative of the Life of Mrs. Mary Jemison, Who Was Taken by the Indians, in the Year of 1755, When Only About Twelve Years of Age, and Who Has Continued to Reside amongst Them to the Present Time . . . and Other Entertaining Matter* (1824). Image courtesy of Library of Congress.

He had deployed three companies of rangers to the "three Frontier Counties" to check the advance and urged the assembly to pass acts to prepare the militia for this dire threat. Washington had written: "I Tremble at the consequences that this defeat may have upon our back settlers, who I suppose will all leave their habitation's unless there are proper measures taken for their security."[33]

CHAPTER 19

Assure Them of a Right to the Lands

In July 1756 Teedyuscung, king of the Lenape, immediately responded to the English invitation to the council fire, saying he represented ten nations, all "desirous to hear what will be Said and done." Unfortunately, they had too many kings, which "raised clouds and caused confusion," he said, but now they had all united under two kings and had the authority of the Haudenosaunee "to treat with you." Employing the self-deprecative decorum of Haudenosaunee discourse, Teedyuscung acknowledged that the sexualized insult issued earlier by Onondaga carried more weight than name-calling. The Onondaga uncles, an honorific recognition of their role as hegemons, "have renewed their Covenants with us and told us that as they formerly called us Women and treated us as such, they employed us only in women's business, they would now putt us in Man's business, and if we can do the business, they will make Men of us."[1]

Charles Thomson joined the Quaker opposition to Pennsylvania's Native policy. To that end he penned *An Enquiry into the Causes of the Alienation of the Delaware and Shawanese Indians from the British Interest* (1759). Finding succor with the French when the hostilities started, the Lenape, he wrote, "took severe Revenge on the Province, by laying Waste their Frontiers, and paid so little Regard to a menacing Message the Six Nations sent them, that they in Turn threatened to turn their Arms against them, and at last, forced them to acknowledge they were Men, that is, a free independent Nation."[2] Responding to the conflicts of 1755, the Lenape retaliated against both the English and the Haudenosaunee, metamorphosizing into men. Thomson's interpretation of the Lenape becoming men after the Haudenosaunee had called them women fits within the framework of what ethnologist Jay Miller tags as the anthropological theory of transformation or cultural shifting. Rather than emasculation or sexual shaming, the designation of the Lenape as women shielded them from constant interactions with the English, a role assumed by the Haudenosaunee, who acted in their own interests. This declaration is consistent with Richter's interpretation of an earlier description of women and land alienation in the treaty minutes of 1684. "The consent of the women . . . was crucial to a transaction involving the transfer of land, which belonged to them rather than to the men."[3] Drawing on the oral traditions of both the Haudenosaunee and the Lenape, historian Leroy V. Eid argues that since the Haudenosaunee had never conquered the Lenape, their designation

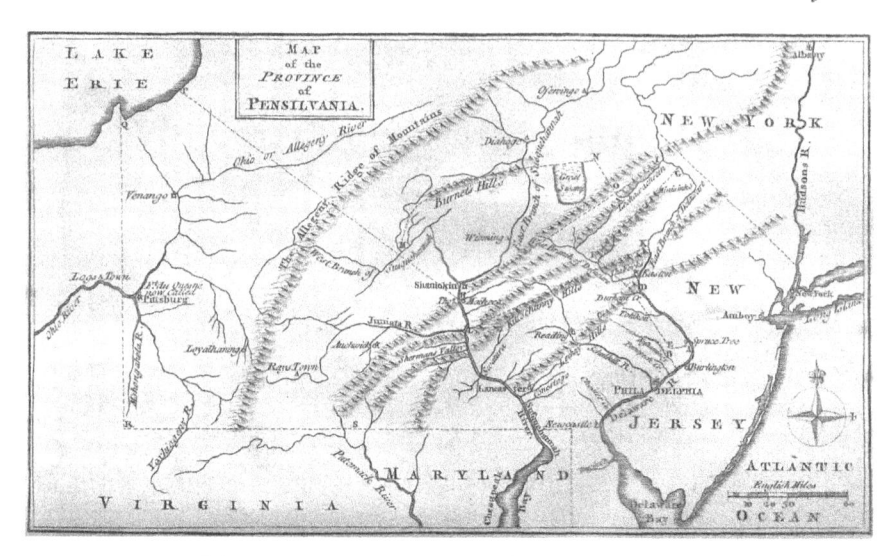

FIGURE 32. *Map of the Province of Pensilvania,* (1759 [1756]), printed for
T. Kinnersly. Image courtesy of Historical Maps of Pennsylvania (mapsofpa.com).

as women more likely fits within the schematic of matrilineality of both nations. Their "role as 'women'" fits within the Haudenosaunee honorific of the
"Peace Queen" of Kienuka, rather than a sexual slur.[4]

On the other hand, the Native people could have understood the sexual dynamic not as one-dimensional, just as the English could categorize
a woman as a whore or witch and at the same time see her as the guard-
ian of virtue. Certainly, sexual disparaging, as indicated earlier, is how the
Haudenosaunee understood the yeh is-WAH h'reh slur of being double men
with two penises willing to make women of them and Canassatego's insult
of the Lenape for selling land without their permission. The English interpreted this arrangement as a putdown and used it as a strategy to divide
and conquer. Perhaps what Thomson missed is a gendered perspective of
sexual shaming, or what feminist scholar Lynda E. Boose in another context
has called the creation of a "personae who has been emasculated—hence de-
potentiated into the feminine."[5]

Cultural shifting or not, Teedyuscung emerged as an envoy of the
Haudenosaunee. "I have the appointment of ten Nations, among which are
my Uncles the Six Nations," he said on November 13, 1756, at the condolence
ceremony, "authorizing me to transact Business for my own Nation." Still,
Teedyuscung asserted, he was simply a messenger who could respond to certain of the English inquiries and deliver to Onondaga what the English had
to say. "The Main thing I am authorized to Say depends on what the Governor may Say and then according to what he Should hear he might Speak

further." Under these ground rules, Teedyuscung mapped European-Native relations in roads and shapes reminiscent of the "Catawba deerskin" map discussed earlier: the French and the English each stood at one end of a "line or road to the Middle, where was a large Square describing the Indian Land." He wanted to see Native country remain free of Europeans, "alluding to the Expectation the Indians have, that if the English are Really their Friends, they will Assure them of a right to the Lands between the English Plantations and Canada and . . . Support them in the possession of them."[6]

Smith, Livingstone, and Scott's *Review* found the Native nations allied with the French included "a considerable number, . . . who had been long in the English alliance, not a few of them," the Haudenosaunee, the Lenape, and the Shawnee. Upon Washington's surrender at Fort Necessity, the French-aligned nations plundered the camp, "shot some of the horses and cattle, and scalped two of the wounded" to the delight of the Canadians' bloodlust. The review concluded that this initial campaign, which "advantaged" the French in their "quiet possession of that fertile country," had had a twofold effect. French success not only "exposed, through the parsimony of the provinces," the weakness of English western defenses, but also "riveted" Native recognition of French mastery in the field of battle. The English realized the remedy required both the "expediency of uniting the power of the British colonies" and of enacting the "absolutely requisite . . . measures . . . for supporting our Indian interest and preventing their total declension."[7]

Preventing their total declension was the point of Thomson's *Enquiry into the Causes of the Alienation of the Delaware and Shawanese Indians*. He raised the question: Why do the English have "so few" Native allies and are unsuccessful in securing Native allies? The Native nations answered: "The Solicitations of the French, joined with the abuses they have suffered from the *English*, particularly in being cheated and defrauded of their Land, have at length induced them to become our Enemies and to make War upon us." The English acknowledged the efforts of the French to "draw off the Indians, and engage them in their Interest," but disavowed the accusation of English abuses and the Native nations "being wronged of their Lands . . . as groundless, and only lame excuses for their late Perfidiousness."[8]

If the council treaty was a rehearsal for the Easton treaty and Teedyuscung had the lead role, the Haudenosaunee now cast him as an understudy at the Easton conference in October 1758. The Haudenosaunee, presenting a united front of fifteen nations, and the British, led by Sir William Johnson, Bart, superintendent of Indian Affairs, and influenced by the Friendly Association for Regaining and Preserving Peace with the Indians by Pacific Measures, treated together in the diplomatic discourse of the Covenant Chain. Using the metaphor of removing and burying the hatchet, the

Haudenosaunee counseled the process of "healing" the relationship between the British and the Natives.[9]

Speaking at the "request of Teedyuscung," Tagashata, the Seneca chief, said: "Teedyuscung told us that the Cause of the War was, that their foolish young Men had been persuaded by the false-hearted French King, to strike their Brethren the English." The Lenape had "unfortunately" stuck the "French hatchet" in the British head. Blaming their action on the instigation of the French, they now removed and buried the hatchet. The Mohawk, Seneca, and Onondaga advised the Munsee Lenape [Minisink] and "those likewise of our own Nations who are on the Ohio, under the Influence of the French, to "lay down the hatchet" and make amends to the British. Likewise, Toka aio, the Cayuga chief, advised the Cayuga, Oneida, Tuscarora, Tutelo, Nanticoke, and Piscataway—the "younger Nations" under Haudenosaunee dominion—that they must together treat for peace with the British. They established two key talking points. First, the two sides planned to establish a fixed boundary along the Allegheny Mountains between the British settlements and the Haudenosaunee dominions, reserving Ohio as Native country. Second, the Native nations agreed to withdraw their support for the French in the Ohio Valley.[10]

Speaking for the "United Nations" on October 18, 1758, Nichas, the Mohawk chief, said to the governors that the warriors had caucused and deliberated upon the "information given by the several Indians now present, who were acquainted with the Facts." Their interpreter Thomas King would "deliver their words as Matters of great Consequences" in the relations between the British and the Native nations. The key questions raised by the British concerned the causation of the war and the alliance with the French of the nations, formerly aligned with the English. In each case the Shawnee, Seneca, and the Ohio nations first felt wronged by the English before they turned toward the French and then felt "wrongfully" charged with attacking the English without cause. The Shawnee said that during the period of "profound peace" with the English, Shawnee warriors were passing through South Carolina on their annual raids with their enemies, when the English "persuaded [them] in a friendly way into their Houses," where they waylaid them. The English imprisoned them, treated them "severely," and killed their leader. Hearing their story, the French, who came shortly after this to "settle on the Ohio, . . . made artful use of it, set them against the English, and gave them the hatchet." The Shawnee then reached out to their "grandfathers," the Lenape, to help them avenge the affront and the loss of their chief.[11]

Likewise, the Seneca said the English had also abused them about three years earlier, when "upon their Warriors Road, and we were in perfect Peace." At Green Briar they met a troop of about 150 soldiers, who "kindly" offered provisions from their store. After traveling together in a "friendly manner" for two days, the English disarmed them once they arrived at the storehouse. "The head Man cried out, here is Death, defend yourselves as well as you can; which they did, and Two of them were killed on the Spot; and one, a young Boy [Squissatego] was taken Prisoner." This offense "provoked us to such a Degree that we could not get over it." Finally, the Ohioans said the English had also offended them. They had immediately alerted the English of the French arrival in Ohio, asking for their presence to combat the French and arms, "intending to defend our Lands, and hinder the French from taking the Possession of them." Ignoring their request, "perhaps they thought there was no Foundation for our Intelligence," the English traders had abandoned the country. When the French became "our Neighbors," out of necessity the Natives traded with them. Adding grievance, "the Governor of Virginia took Care to settle on our Lands for his own Benefit; but when we wanted his Assistance against the French, he disregarded us."[12]

Acknowledging the "true Cause of the Bitterness of your Hearts towards us, and the Reasons which induced some of your young Men first to strike us, and others to side with the French on the Ohio," Pennsylvania governor William Denny promised to "guard against any Breach of Friendship between us for the future." He also promised to make inquiries to Virginia governor Dinwiddie immediately about Squissatego, whom "you say was left a Prisoner in his Country; and if he is alive, you may depend on his being returned to you."[13] Nevertheless, the Native people were wary of the English intentions, and for good reason. They were certainly aware of the worsening attitude toward them. For example, George Washington's uncle Joseph Ball, who had two plantations in the Rappahannock River region, in his letter to a merchant in Liverpool, September 21, 1758, which had nothing to do with the war, excitedly uttered: "Dam the Indian, cut them of[f] Root and Branch. Such Rascals Friendship is not worth having."[14]

Toka aio called out the governors of Pennsylvania, Carolina, and Virginia by name on their straightforwardness. "They have called us down to this Council Fire, which was kindled for Council Affairs, to renew Treaties of Friendship, and brighten the Chain of Friendship. But here we must hear a Dispute about Land, and our Time is taken up from Day to Day; but they do not come to the chief Point." "The English first began to do Mischief; we told them so: They only thanked us for our Openness and Advice, and said they would take Care for the Future, but healed no Wounds. . . . They ought not thus to treat with Indians on Council Affairs."[15]

When Tagashata and Nichas insisted on seeing the deeds, which the proprietors laid claim to Native lands, they were only able to procure a facsimile,

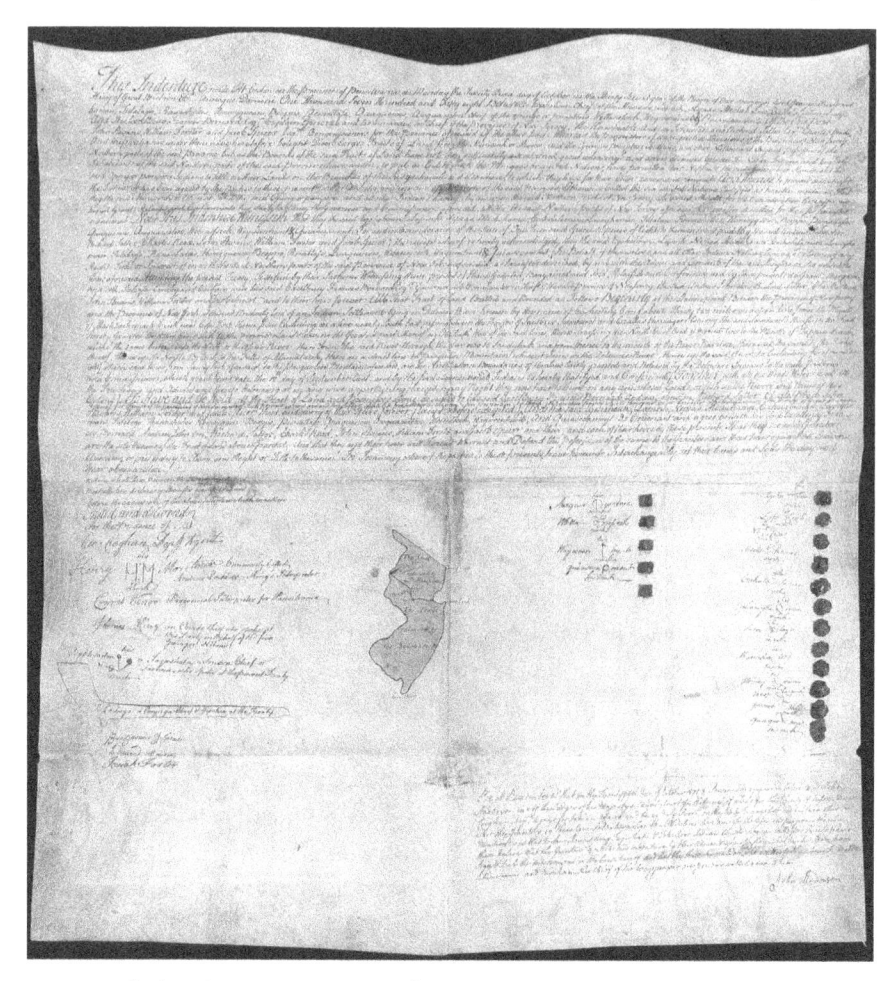

FIGURE 33. *Indian Treaty, Easton Conference, 1758.* Private collection. Image courtesy of Christie's Images/Bridgeman Images.

giving credence to the claim made in 1756 at Easton that the English had taken possession of "some lands . . . by Fraud and Forgery," passed down by the generations. Thomson, who served as secretary to the Lenape, illustrated the two modes of treatment over land by the English and the French:

> The *English*, in order to get their lands, drive them as far from them as possible, nor seem to care what becomes of them, provided they can get them removed out of the Way for their present Settlements, whereas the *French*, considering that they can never want Land in America, who enjoy the Friendship of the Indians, use all the Means in their Power to draw as many into their Alliance as possible; and, to secure their

Affections, invite as many as can to come and live near them, and to make their Towns as near the French Settlements as they can.[16]

The Lenape were still "dissatisfied" with the land deal and "desirous that Part of it should be reserved for them." At the 1755 Albany treaty meeting hosted by Sir William Johnson, Superintendent of Indian Affairs, they had addressed the discontented sachems and had dealt with the terms of the sale of lands west of the Allegany or Appalachian Mountains. In their defense the English contested that the proprietors had only agreed to pay "One Thousand Pieces of Eight" once the English had settled there. Nevertheless, at this request the English "cheerfully" relinquished "all that Part of the Purchase you have reclaimed." Now the parties needed "to settle the Boundaries between you, that they may release the Lands to you accordingly, before you leave this Place, and set your Minds at Ease." In response to the query of whether the Native nations would join General John Forbes in the Western campaign, they said that they

would by no Means advise this Government so soon to press them to take up the Hatchet, because their Wounds were not yet healed, nor Peace made, which must first be done. They said further, that as the French had many Indians fighting for them, and they by Intermarriages were related to the Indians who sent the Messages, it could not be expected they would easily be persuaded to join the English, lest they should kill their own Flesh and Blood. . . . [The] only proper Measure, that could now be taken, was to advise them to sit still and keep out of the Way.[17]

CHAPTER 20
Experience Has Taught Them Wisdom

Concerned that Williamsburg little understood the instability of the settlements, Rev. James Maury in 1756 reported to Philip Ludwell III, a member of the council, that the region is "almost totally depopulated." Settlers are leaving the valleys on both sides of the Alleghany Mountains not because of the "heavy taxes" but because of the depredations by the French-aligned nations. A war party of "only fifty . . . Indians made such havoc and desolation, drove off upwards of 2,000 head of cattle and horses to support themselves and the enemy at Fort Duquesne, besides what they wantonly destroyed." If he could not fathom what a larger scale invasion might accomplish, "certain it is, should that be attempted and no effectual methods pursued to defeat the attempt, many parts of this Colony, now several miles within the frontier, will shortly become frontier in their turn."[1]

At the same time, Maury opined, the governor had not properly allocated the revenue collected for security; rather deploying fifty rangers under Major Lewis to search out the Shawnee was an exercise in futility. "The Shawanese nevertheless continued their eruptions into that province: and Governor Dinwiddie was obliged to draft the militia, to oppose their progress, and preserve the town of Winchester."[2] The depredations and departures persisted into the fall of 1757, when William Allason reported from Rappahannock that in October the French-aligned nations came within ten miles of Winchester, "where the Virga regiment lys," and "scalped and carried off forty persons. The back Inhabitants are move downward daily."[3] Thousands of settlers had become "voluntary exiles" headed for Carolina, their number drawn from "the honest and industrious, men of worth and property." Fearful that the paltry expeditionary force might fail, leaving the mountain passes defenseless, they concluded that a better course of action was to seek cover with the yeh is-WAH h'reh and the Ani'-Yun-wiya in western Carolina, where "the French Indians will . . . scarce think proper to make any inroads."[4]

Dinwiddie had curried favor with the Ani'-Yun-wiya and the yeh is-WAH h'reh in 1753. In a letter to the "Indian trader" Richard Pearis [Paris], he said he had received a letter from the head of the Ani'-Yun-wiya. He expressed surprise that the Ani'-Yun-wiya, who "constantly declare themselves brothers to the English," were willing to attend conferences with the "perfidious" French.

I hope the Cherokee and Catawba will prevent the French building any Forts at Choto [Chota]; or Holstein's River; we never build any Forts but by the Consent and Approbat'n of the Ind'n Nat'ns, for if they allow them, [the French] it's giving them leave to take their Lands by Force of Arms. The one building so near Choto; they sh'd immediately destroy. They are two brave Nat's, and they can, if they will, prevent, or destroy it if built. . . . I had a Visit from the King of the Catawbas and some Cherokee. I rec'd them as Bro's, and entertain'd them well, gave them some Pres'ts; and order'd them some Powder and Lead. . . . I always (till now) understood the Emperor was their Chief Man. If Old Hop [Connecorte] is a greater Man, I shall hereafter notice him as such. I shall be glad if you can spirit them up with resentm't ag'st the French, who are now endeavouring by Force of Arms to take all their Lands from them, the back of our Settlem'ts, and if they w'd take a Hunt the end of this Mo., or beginning of next, towards the Ohio, where probably they will meet a great Number of our Forces.[5]

On August 5, 1754, Dinwiddie wrote to Governor Glen that about a year ago the Ani'-Yun-wiya and yeh is-WAH h'reh had written to him and pledged eight hundred warriors to defend "their Hunting Grounds and our Lands" if the French invade. Dinwiddie's effort to distinguish their lands as hunting grounds and not homelands is noteworthy. "They were ready" to go once he sent ammunition, but they said the governor of South Carolina advised them "to remain home, take care of their Families and Hunting," for Virginia was "only going to build a Fort, which he could do without their assistance." If true, he said, Glen's opinion was ill-advised, for Virginia had no treaty with any Native nation, for they were "Allies of Great Britain."[6]

A year later Dinwiddie did an about-face and dispatched Peter Randolph and William Byrd III on December 23, 1755, to negotiate a treaty with the yeh is-WAH h'reh and the Ani'-Yun-wiya. He instructed them to negotiate in the customary manner of the Native nations by throwing ceremonials, giving presents, and addressing them as *brother* and George III as *father*. Tell them that "their brother, the governor of Virginia is going to speak to them" through the speeches Randolph and Byrd carried with them. Dinwiddie wanted them to raise an army to fight the French. During the negotiations they should gauge what they wanted in return for supplying warriors. "Do all you can to raise their resentment against the French and their Indians and that they may discourage and hinder their coming into the Nation." Dinwiddie gave the two envoys the heads-up for their negotiations with the two nations: "The Catawba had complained being long confined by the English settling their land; that they wanted to sell their land and go further to the westward," he said. If they raise this issue in the negotiations, he advised, assure them that he would coordinate their concerns with his fellow Carolina governors.

The Ani'-Yun-wiya had concerns about the arms promised them. "Make an excuse for not sending them arms, let them know they were not to be had here," Dinwiddie advised, "but we will endeavour to provide some for them." At the same time, show them "hardy thanks" for sending warriors against the Shawnee. Dinwiddie rattled off a series of imperatives for when negotiating with the Ani'-Yun-wiya: remember that they are a "much more numerous and more extensive" nation than the yeh is-WAH h'reh, reportedly outnumbering them ten to one. The French had long courted them and desired building a fort in Ani'-Yun-wiya country. If they had built it, Randolph and Byrd were to encourage them "to destroy it and by no means allow them any settlement in their Nation and if possible, to hinder any of the French or their Indians having any consultations with them, unless they bring a certificate or message by one of the Six Nations or their brothers the English other ways. . . . Persuade them to take great care of the passes over the mountains to the upper Cherokee to prevent any surprise."[7]

Virginia negotiated a treaty with the yeh is-WAH h'reh at the Catawba town and the Ani'-Yun-wiya at Broad River in the months of February and March, respectively. At the Catawba town on February 20, 1756, William Giles, the interpreter, read Dinwiddie's letter to King Hagler and the assembled sachems and warriors of yeh is-WAH h'reh. Dinwiddie advised his brothers the yeh is-WAH h'reh should "guard against their invidious Insinuations" of the French, who were recruiting "our friendly Indians to their Interest." The Haudenosaunee, who had joined the British in opposing the French invasion, had "handed them a remarkable Defeat, killed many of their People and taken several of their great Officers Prisoners; and I hope next Year they will be able to confine them to the barren Lands of Canada." On the other hand, the Shawnee had joined the French and attacked the settlements. The Ani'-Yun-wiya had come to Virginia's aid against the "perfidious" French and their Native allies. Likewise, Dinwiddie hoped the yeh is-WAH h'reh would also send "a Number of your brave Warriors."[8]

Byrd and Randolph reiterated Dinwiddie's sentiments, calling out both the Lenape and the Shawnee for violating the Logstown treaty and joining the French "to make Incursions on the Frontiers of Virginia, Maryland, and Pennsylvania, to murder in the most inhuman Manner, defenseless Husbandmen at their Labor, weak Women in their Beds, with their tender Infants at their Breasts, resting secure in their own Innocence in Time." They underscored the Haudenosaunee's alliance and assistance in the victory at battle at Lake George in September 1755. "We are desired by the Governor of Virginia, to inform you, That we now stand in need of your Assistance; and from the many Instances of your Friendship, we hope you will join our Forces with such a Number of Warriors, as you think you may with Safety to yourselves spare, whenever there may be Occasion for them, of which you shall have due Notice." For their assistance Virginia promised "that your Men shall be supplied with Arms, Ammunition, and everything necessary for War."[9]

Renewing his pledge to assist the governor of Virginia, whom he had visited last year, Hagler promised he would "hold my Warriors in Readiness, not doubting, but that he should have Occasion for them soon." He had honored "repeated requests of the Northern governors" to make peace with their Native allies, including their ancestral enemy the Haudenosaunee, a bitter pill for the yeh is-WAH h'reh to swallow. Although he only had forty warriors at the ready, the others being out at the hunt, Hagler said, "It is my Resolution to lead them on whenever the Governor of Virginia thinks proper." He asserted "perfect Amity" with the Ani'-Yun-wiya, Chahtas, and Chikashsha'. "The Cherokee have ever been our Friends," and underscoring what Dinwiddie had noted in his instructions, "as they are a numerous Nation, we acknowledge them to be our elder Brother."[10]

Byrd and Randolph then headed to Ani'-Yun-wiya, where on March 13 they read Dinwiddie's Ani'-Yun-wiya letter addressed to Old Hop and other sachems. Dinwiddie had addressed the letter to Connecorte, also called Old Hop, because he had learned that he was considered a "greater man" than their emperor Amouskositte.[11] Dinwiddie cautioned the Ani'-Yun-wiya to be wary of the French, who were trying "to poison the Minds of our friendly Indians . . . to withdraw them from their Brothers the English . . . and by no Means allow them to build any Forts on the River Hogohegee [later called the Holston], in the Upper Cherokee Country." As he had with the yeh is-WAH h'reh, Dinwiddie touted the alliance with the Haudenosaunee and their victory together over the French at Lake George. The proposed treaty sought an alliance between the Ani'-Yun-wiya against the French and their Native nations and "the Commissioners will deliver you some Powder, Lead, and other Goods."

More than doubling the length of their speeches to the yeh is-WAH h'reh, the commissioners gave a full-throated amplification of Virginia's needs in their pleadings to the more considerable Ani'-Yun-wiya nation, underscoring their recognition of their importance. Since the Ani'-Yun-wiya had already come to the aid of the English, after the customary blandishments "brightening and strengthening the Chain of Friendship," the commissioners, as instructed by Dinwiddie, immediately apologized for Virginia's inability "to procure a sufficient Number of such fireArms," a situation they meant to rectify soon. Additionally, "the King your Father, that He always disposed to reward his dutiful Children, has ordered a Present of Goods to be sent to you." The commissioners then insisted they not allow the French to build "any Forts on the River Hogohegee, in the Upper Ani'-Yun-wiya Country." He drew their attention to the allegiance of the Haudenosaunee and their great victory together and of the "skulking Parties" of the Lenape and the Shawnee "not observing the most solemn Treaties," who, despite having a "large Share of the Royal Bounty," had "withdrawn from their Allegiance." On the other hand, for the Ani'-Yun-wiya's allegiance "the Commissioners will deliver you some Powder, Lead, and other Goods, from your Father and your Brothers of this Dominion, to convince you of our sincere Friendship to your Nation."[12]

The commissioners continued to cast aspersions on "the treacherous and most perfidious" French, who "contrary to the Law of Nature and Nations, are forever pushing on our own Allies to destroy us," including using "every Artifice in their Power to win the Six Nations to their Interest." Nor would they stop their aggression with British settlements, for they had usurped Natchez lands and continued to deprecate the Chikashsha'. "Unless you take the necessary Steps to prevent it you will likewise be involved in the same Calamity. That we may never be again exposed to the Treachery and Deceit of those cruel Savages, we have resolved to cut them off from the Race of Mankind, and we do on Behalf of the People we represent. . . . The French, who have nothing less in View than universal Monarchy, and are forever encroaching upon the Lands of not only the English, but of all the Indian Nations in America, have built Forts upon our Lands." Finally, in addition to the arms and ammunition and proffered presents, to sweeten the pot the commissioners offered "to send some of your Boys to Virginia, where we have a School erected for their Education. We promise you that all due Care shall be taken of them, both with Respect to their Cloaths and Learning. When they come to be Men, they will be acquainted with the Manners and Customs of us both, and our Children will naturally place such a Confidence in them, as to employ them in settling any Disputes that may hereafter arise." In exchange for the allegiance of the Ani'-Yun-wiya and their allies, modeled by the Haudenosaunee and theirs, "the King your Father, and your Love to your Brethren. For that Purpose, you shall be furnished with Arms and Ammunition, Cloathing and Provision."[13]

Speaking for the Ani'-Yun-wiya, Oukanaekah [aka Otterle-Culloughculla, Attakullakulla, or the Little Carpenter] answered the commissioners' speech on March 15, 1756. Referring to the Virginians as their "eldest Brothers," he first remarked on his visit to England and his audience with the Great King, who "acknowledged the *Cherokee* to be his children as well as the *English*." Expressing his "greatest concern" for the murderous attacks on the Virginia settlements, he offered that the Ani'-Yun-wiya upper towns, which are "as much exposed to the Incursions of the French and Indians, as your Frontier Inhabitants," were in the best position to assist. However, without the fort promised by Governor Glen of South Carolina in the Saluda Treaty of July 2, 1755, for the protection of their women and children, it was too perilous to leave them. Since he was wary that Glen would honor his word, he could not commit forces without the concomitant security for their families. If Dinwiddie had cause for meeting the commissioners again, he recommended they meet on the Northward Path, which was more conveniently situated than the Southern Path, and he would meet anytime with the governor at Stalnaker's settlement on the Middle Fork of the Holston River.[14]

The willingness of the united nations to sit out the remainder of the war meant that Virginia's alliance with the southern nations took on greater import. Col. Charles Pickney, attorney, plantation owner, and father to his more famous namesake, was especially concerned about the progress of the French in the "back of Virginia." He reported to the Lords Commissioners of Trade and Plantations in June 1754 that erecting a fort in upper Ani'-Yun-wiya country was essential to British interest. He believed that the French desire to build a fort there was a "matter of the greatest consequence." Not only would it drive away the English traders from Ohio country, but it would also expel the English from a great part of Ani'-Yun-wiya country. The French had made overtures by sending their colors and an invitation to the Ani'-Yun-wiya to negotiate an alliance. The Ani'-Yun-wiya responded by burning their colors and rejecting their invitation. The Ani'-Yun-wiya had every expectation that in consequence of their response the Native Ohio nations aligned with the French would attack them. The Ani'-Yun-wiya, he contended, would not be able to withstand the attack without the presence of British forts in Ani'-Yun-wiya country to support them and thwart the French efforts.[15] "Some hopes indeed were entertained of the fidelity of the Cherokee—a people warlike and powerful," opined Smith, Livingstone, and Scott in *A Review of the Military Operations*, "in whose territories the Virginians were erecting a fortress."[16]

For the nine-year period of the misnamed Seven Years' War (1754–63), Pickney, Dinwiddie, and others believed the Ani'-Yun-wiya were key to both a defensive and an offensive strategy. First, the Ani'-Yun-wiya were a backstop protecting the Virginia settlements from the northeast attacks of the French and their aligned Native nations. Their position of holding the line in the southern Appalachians also buffered the Carolinas and Georgia. Without the Ani'-Yun-wiya's first line of defense, the southern colonies of Virginia, the Carolinas, and Georgia, Pickney warned, were at risk of both foreign invasion and slave insurrection. He laid out the scenario of risk for the Lords Commissioners:

> The dangers to Carolina and Georgia, from the present Army of French Regulars and Indians on the backs of Virginia, and these which it is said are to join them from the Mississippi and the French Settlements of Louisiana are very great, should they, as in all probability they will, when they have beat the English from their Forts and Settlements on the Ohio, march southerly into the Cherokee Countrys and make themselves Masters there. . . . Once the French have fixed themselves in the Cherokee they will according to their known practice strongly enfort themselves there, and then march more Southerly and make themselves masters of the Chickasaws and upper Creeks, from whence they may too easily extend their conquests thro the lower Creeks and lower Cherokee, which will bring them within a few days march of the Capitals of both Provinces, which means our Trade and intercourse with all the Indians, the small Tribe of Catawbas, will be entirely cut off, our out settlements broke up and driven in, our Negro Slaves encouraged to rise in rebellion against us, and our Planters shut up in the Towns Sea Coast, and at length, unless they have a very extraordinary protection, the whole of the two Colonies must inevitably be push into the Sea.[17]

Of the two colonies, Virginia more than South Carolina was keen to use the Ani'-Yun-wiya warriors in Ohio, a push to protect their interests there. The Ani'-Yun-wiya also preferred to go on offense, which necessitated the building and garrisoning of forts to protect their loved ones while they were abroad on a combat mission. The Ani'-Yun-wiya were impressed with the Virginians' skill in building fortifications, which would free them to go to war and to garner both prestige and presents. Dinwiddie strongly believed that Braddock's march to Fort Duquesne would have benefited mightily from the Ani'-Yun-wiya. They were reticent partly because Virginia had not allowed their requested trading town on the Roanoke River and partly because Virginia held out an empty promise of a fort in Overhill, named so because of its location over the mountains. They held back because Governor Glen of South Carolina selfishly siphoned five hundred of them off with an invitation to a congress at Saluda, with the lure of building a fort in the lower towns in a ploy to take their land. Their absence not only contributed to Braddock's defeat but also put Virginia at risk of slave insurrection. Now even more motivated, Governor Francis Fauquier encouraged their participation, but he was hampered by unfulfilled promises to build and garrison the fort at Chota.[18]

Virginia settlers had begun to occupy the basin between the New and the Holston Rivers but had not yet demonstrated the pressure on Overhill that South Carolina settlers had made on lower towns. Honoring the treaty of Broad River, the English began in August 1756 construction of a log fort under the engineering direction of John Gerrard William De Brahm on the Little Tennessee River in Overhill and placed it under the command of Capt. Raymond Demeré. Virginia traders also began buying deerskins, offering another trade route to the Ani'-Yun-wiya, much to the chagrin of Governor Glen. The Virginia traders engaged in duplicitous trading practices with "false weights and measures," shorting Ani'-Yun-wiya vendors. "As more and more Virginians appeared," historian John Stuart Oliphant writes, "the returns on skins dwindled in the face of overhunting and advancing settlement."[19]

Sensitive to this drift in relations, Louis de Keleréc, governor of Louisiana, once again encouraged the Ani'-Yun-wiya to join the colony in an alliance with the Shawnee and the Muscogee nations. Knowing that the Ani'-Yun-wiya were cognizant of how slaveholders treated Africans, the French sent rumormongers into the Ani'-Yun-wiya towns who said that the British promise of a fort for security was a ruse. The British had yet to garrison the fort, still under construction. Rather, they said, the British planned to use the site as a slaving ground for the defenseless Ani'-Yun-wiya women and children; the imported iron was not for construction but for the men's shackles. So primed, the Ani'-Yun-wiya were well disposed to the French invitation to talks.[20] Keleréc appointed Louis de Lantagnac ambassador to carry out this mission at Fort Toulouse. Lantagnac was well placed to represent French interest. As a youth stationed at Fort Toulouse, the most eastern French outpost built at the sufferance of the Muscogee nation in Alabama as a bulwark against British expansion, Lantagnac was captured by the Chikashsha', who then sold him to Charles Town. After gaining the confidence of Glen, he became a licensed trader to the Ani'-Yun-wiya and lived among them with his Ani'-Yun-wiya woman and their son at Great Tellico. Eventually he found his way back to Fort Toulouse, where he invited the Ani'-Yun-wiya for a negotiation.

In October 1756 Great Tellico sent Usteneka [Ostenaco] of Tomotley, the Mankiller, a name denoting his military rank, with a formal delegation of two dozen Overhill emissaries to meet with Lantagnac at Fort Toulouse. France had established a stronghold about a dozen miles below the mouth of the Ani'-Yun-wiya [Tennessee] River. He promised them both the protection of a new fort at Hiwassee on the river and access to the Mississippi market, which they had previously raided. Unsurprisingly, their traditional enemy

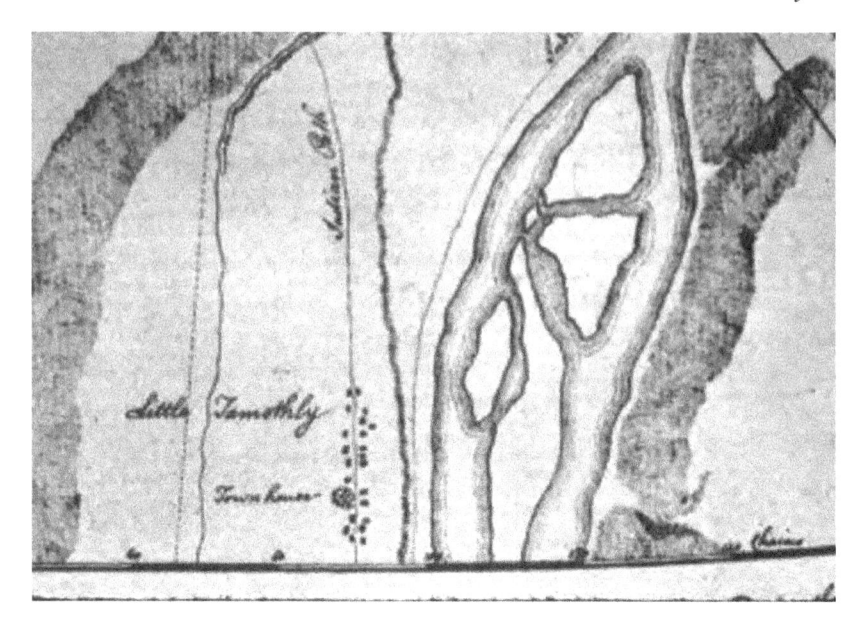

FIGURE 34. John Gerrard William De Brahm, *Detail of map indicating the Overhill Cherokee Village of Tomotley*, ca. 1756. Repository Frank H. McClung Museum Photographic Collection x, University of Tennessee, Knoxville. Image courtesy of University of Tennessee Libraries.

the Muscogee shut the door on this plan. After the meeting Usteneka returned home, but a handful of his embassy continued onto Mobile and then to New Orleans. At the same time, the Shawnee traveled to Great Tellico to treat with the Ani'-Yun-wiya, likely with the go-ahead of Connecorte and Oukanaekah, telegraphing to Virginia that something was amiss and panicking Capt. Raymond Demeré, who instantly recognized that the undermanned Virginia fort was encircled. Because France did not come up with the promised presents and weapons, the proposed Franco–Ani'-Yun-wiya alliance was dead in the water even before Virginia learned of the proposed treaty after a British sloop intercepted at sea the diplomatic pouch en route to Versailles.[21]

In "An Act for Establishing a Trade with the Indians in Alliance with His Majesty," passed in April 1757, the assembly moved for the Dominion to establish trade "upon reasonable terms" with aligned nations directly because they could not depend on private traders during wartime—"judged the best method to preserve the friendship of such Indians, and to draw others off from the French interest, and it may be very beneficial to this colony to purchase from such Indians the skins and furs which they are now obliged to sell to the French." The assembly assigned as directors Peter Randolph, William

OUTACITE,
Chief of the CHEROKEES.

Reynolds Pinx.

FIGURE 35. *Outacite [Usteneka], Chief of the Cherokee* (1762). Unidentified artist copy after Joshua Reynolds (1723–92). Smithsonian National Portrait Gallery, Washington, DC.

Randolph, Richard Bland, Archibald Cary, and Thomas Walker, "for the better managing and carrying on such Indian trade for, and purchase a cargo of goods, such as may best answer the wants and occasions of the Indians, and cause or procure the goods so to be sent for or purchased to be carried with all convenient speed and safety to some fortress built or to be built for the defence of the south-western frontiers of this colony, or to any Indian nation, town or other place they shall judge most convenient for carrying on the said trade."[22]

Fearing a French and Shawnee attack and desiring to placate the Ani'-Yun-wiya, Demeré increased his garrison to 260 in January 1757 and completed construction on Fort Loudon near Chota in the summer.[23]

Meanwhile, Dinwiddie continued to woo the Ani'-Yun-wiya, seeking their aid in a spring 1757 campaign. Trying to fend off trade concerns, he convinced the assembly to subsidize the Ani'-Yun-wiya trade goods below market prices. The Ani'-Yun-wiya were wary of sending their warriors to Ohio country, fearful of offending the Haudenosaunee. In May Usteneka traveled to Williamsburg, and then in June he met with Edmond Atkin in Winchester and showed him diplomatic letters from Williamsburg. Atkin feted and gifted Usteneka at Winchester, but the garrison was still undermanned. Yet Dinwiddie dragged his feet on garrisoning the fort. He did try to solve the trade crisis by getting the House of Burgesses to agree to subsidize trade goods to the Ani'-Yun-wiya to forestall the French.

The Ani'-Yun-wiya went to war with the Shawnee and the Myaamia during campaigns in 1757 and 1758, while pursuing nonaggression pacts with the Lenape and Haudenosaunee. The Ani'-Yun-wiya–British alliance to protect the southern Appalachians shielded the Virginia settlements. The Ani'-Yun-wiya numbered about two-thirds of the four hundred warriors in the Ohio campaigns in the spring and summer of 1757. These Ani'-Yun-wiya mainly came from the lower towns under Wawatchee [Wohatchee] of Keowee. Gifting had "magnified importance" in the summer of 1757 when two-thirds of the warriors went without gifts, their service unrequited. "Gift giving was part of the essential protocol of friendship and treaty making symbols of ratification and good faith," writes Oliphant. The Native warriors "who went to Virginia in 1757 were in a suspicious mood, and only presents could give them full confidence in British honesty."[24]

Tensions flared up between Virginia and Ani'-Yun-wiya in the spring and summer of 1758 when Ani'-Yun-wiya warriors, returning from their service in Ohio, were angered for not receiving promised presents. They raided Bedford and Halifax Counties and stole settlers' horses. The settlers responded by killing thirty to forty Ani'-Yun-wiya. More than a few Ani'-Yun-wiya wanted revenge, and the Virginia settlers wanted reassurance, but both Tellico and

Williamsburg advised restraint. Willinawaw, chief of Toqua and Ouka-naekah's brother, conceded that the Ani'-Yun-wiya were at fault for initiating the conflict. Connecorte and Oukanaekah both counseled restraint and accorded individual rather than national responsibility. Apologetic to Byrd both about the losses of life, which fault he accorded his people, and about his delay in meeting him at Winchester, Oukanaekah explained that he was late because "the path from Keowee was bad at mid-point." He pledged his loyalty to the "grate King George, our father," and expressed his disdain for the French. "The French I have always looked upon, as our greatest enemies, and they live very near our Nation, likewise the Creeks, and the Chickasaw is likely to brake war with us." On white people, he explained, he was in a bind with respect to restraining the younger generation. "I always desire our young fellows, not to hurt the w[h]ite people, nor kill any of our friend Indians, but now they have done both, which makes me very uneasy, for my people kill their friends as well as their enemies; so, I can't say which way to turn myself." Appreciative of the "great presents" he had received, he said, he would tell his people not to hurt the English.[25]

By April 8, 1758, council president Blair advised Captain Abraham Bosomworth that since "a large body of Southern Indians are already come to our assistance, and many more daily expected, and consequently the Service you were appointed to in the Cherokee Nation [is] in a great measure affected," he should proceed to Winchester.[26] Delayed in Williamsburg waiting for a guide to Ani'-Yun-wiya country, Bosomworth in turn wrote to General James Abercrombie that because of his "involuntary detention," he was anxious to go to Winchester without delay and "meet with their Chiefs and Warriors. . . . I flatter myself from the knowledge and experience I have already had of Indian Warfare that I have some Influence and ascendancy in their Councils and can thereby easily remove any Insinuation of his Majesty's Enemies." To "gain the desired End of preserving their friendship and alliance," it was "absolutely necessary . . . [to] furnish them with Sundry presents and Implements of War."

> Although already a considerable body of Cherokee, Creek and Catawba Indians arrived at Winchester and other parts to engage those Indians who are already arrived the firmer in our Interest which I shall next the utmost of my abilities employ them in Scouting, Ranging, and gaining Intelligence of the enemies motions till the Expedition goes on, least a service so apparently to the present Campaign should by any means suffer or the Indians Return to the Nation should be any ways endangered by a Neglect thereof which must be productive of dangerous Consequences.[27]

Forbes found the Ani'-Yun-wiya "in want of everything" when he arrived in Winchester two weeks later. "I have made a demand case of three hundred light horses to send them (in the meantime) with some ammunition," he said, "and I see that I shall be obliged to provide them in all their necessaries and presents which will not admit or thereof delay as of temporizing. . . . I find they begin to show some uneasiness in not having things ready provided for them."[28] He felt that the six hundred Ani'-Yun-wiya at Winchester "rightly looked after may be of infinite service."[29]

A month later the Ani'-Yun-wiya chiefs Techtama and Homwhyowa, or the Wolf King, sent a message to the Lenape chief Teedyuscung, which was translated on June 20, 1758. In the message the Ani'-Yun-wiya affirmed their alliance with the English. Disabusing the Lenape of any personal ill will toward them from the Ani'-Yun-wiya's accompanying British Maj. Gen. James Abercrombie in his Ohio expedition against the French and their allied Native nations, they intended not to attack northern nations allied with the English. Even though both the Shawnee and the Lenape had engaged in raids against the English settlements, they desired a permanent peace and friendship with them. They also warned that any Lenape resident on the Ohio among the French should relocate. They sent a similar message to the Haudenosaunee.[30]

Hoping for deescalation, the Virginia General Assembly in September 1758 rescinded its thirty-pound scalp bounty legislated six months earlier to prevent "hostile incursions," and the House of Burgesses ignored Bedford's petition asking for permission to kill Ani'-Yun-wiya. About the same time, in September, Forbes wrote to Abercrombie that he expected the Virginians to arrive at Winchester tomorrow, and he would judge "by their countenances, what is in their hearts, and proceed accordingly."[31] Governor William Henry Lyttelton of South Carolina proffered gifts to indemnify the relatives of the dead, waxing rhetorical, perhaps patronizingly, in the Native manner in his condolence, "sufficient to hide the bones of the dead Men and wipe away the tears from the eyes of their friends." He also said, "I gave the Indians full time of being sensible of their Errors and of their reconciling themselves at this treaty now holding at Easton which I most earnestly labored to bring about being thoroughly sensitive of the insurmountable difficulties . . . as the Virginians join me here tomorrow."[32]

Maj. Edward Ward recalled that upon the heels of the Easton Treaty and the evacuation of Fort Duquesne by the French on the approach of the British army in 1758, General Forbes, by one of the deputy agents for Indian Affairs, "made a requisition to the Chiefs of the Six Nations for Permission to re-establish a Fort at the same place, for the purposes aforesaid, and to prevent the French from returning, which was Granted, a Fort Executed and

Garrisoned." John Stanwix was promoted to major general and built Fort Pitt in 1759. He called

> a Council of the Six Nations, Shawanese, Delawares and other western Indians, when the General by the Deputy Agent Informed the Indians Assembled that he was then going to erect a strong Fort, and asked the permission of the Six Nations, for that purpose, which was granted upon a promise of a fair and open Trade, and a reservation of the right of the Lands to the Six Nations, and that it should be abandoned at any time when required by them.[33]

Reflecting on his *Travels through the Middle Settlements* in 1759 to 1760, Andrew Burnaby gave a devastating critique of the security in the southern colonies, explaining that in addition to the insurrection anxiety engendered by having a Black fifth column in their rank, the Native nations on their flank were a greater risk to them. The enslaved Black people "cannot but be a subject of terror to those who so inhumanly tyrannize over them," he wrote. The southern nations, including the Ani'-Yun-wiya, Muscogee, Chikashsha', and the yeh is-WAH h'reh, "are numerous, and are governed by a sounder policy than formerly; experience has taught them wisdom. They never make war with the colonists without carrying terror and devastation along with them."[34]

Governor William Bull II of South Carolina also recognized the twin threat of Native invasion and Black insurrection. On May 8, 1760, he reported to the Lords Commissioners for Trade and Plantations that he feared the Ani'-Yun-wiya's unpredictability, and the evacuation of Fort Loudon would lay bare the southern countryside. He had intelligence from Fort Loudon that on April 5, 1760, the Ani'-Yun-wiya's "trifling" peace initiatives were simply a stall until they could learn the success of their several embassies while eyeing the Muscogee's disposition toward the war. Hedging their bet, the Ani'-Yun-wiya had sent emissaries to the "Ottaways, Nuntooyas [*Nunta-neuc*], and other French Indians" and to Alabama Fort (Fort Toulouse) and from there to New Orleans. Strategically situated to thwart the French advance, the loss of Fort Loudon would open the passage for the French effort to coordinate their advance on a Native town midway between the Alabama fort and the Telligus near the head of the Alabama River. If the Ani'-Yun-wiya in the unlikely event were "extirpated," or "only exterminated, and driven into the Countries of the French," then the British countryside would lose its buffer and become vulnerable to the French and their Native allies. What was worse, the valleys shadowed by the mountains would become refuge for Black runaways. The British authorities knew the militia was needed for

FIGURE 36. Military commission granted to Chief Okana-Stoté (Oconostota) of the Cherokee by Governor Louis Billouart, Chevalier de Kerlérec, February 27 1761. Courtesy of National Archives and Records Administration.

their subjugation. The mountains would afford a "secure Refuge" to fugitives from South Carolina and Virginia, "who might be more troublesome and more difficult to reduce than the Negroes in the Mountains of Jamaica."[35]

The French likewise recognized at this critical juncture in a continental war the significance of the Ani'-Yun-wiya. For this reason, in exchange for his leadership and the fidelity of the Ani'-Yun-wiya nation, Louis de Kerlérec, governor of the Province of Louisiana, offered Oconostota a commission as captain "to be recognized in this capacity in his nation, and to cause him to enjoy the honors and prerogatives attached to this grade, and with which the King favors the commanders of detachments who serve him faithfully. Furthermore, we command all officers of the regular troops, of the militia appoint him captain and great medal chief of all the detachments which shall go to war against the enemy and in the service of the French Nation."[36]

On July 17, 1761, Oukanaekah sent a talk to William Byrd III.[37] He opened by acknowledging that he had received Byrd's enclosed talk and sent it by messenger to the Ani'-Yun-wiya headmen as requested. He then addressed the Ani'-Yun-wiya's position on "the present war, of all Their Transactions, and News Stirring among them." Two days before he began his journey from Keowee to Chota, two envoys returned from their conference with the "Northward Nations." "They intended to Strike the white people again and were Desirous that all the Red people might unite," including the Ani'-Yun-wiya, the Muscogee, the Chahta, and the Chikashsha'. Their plan was to attack the former French forts now under English control. Oukanaekah also reported that Lt. Col. James Grant messaged for him to wait for him at Keowee, where he would give him something "material." He also promised to go to Chota in the summer and meet with the Ani'-Yun-wiya headmen. Grant promised not to "molest" the Ani'-Yun-wiya if they ceased their attacks on the settlers. He went home to Tuskeegee on the Little Tennessee River and then to Chota, where he told Oconostota and the other Overhill headmen what Grant had said to him. The councilors "confessed" that they could trust the English and that they should not go to war with them. "If they Did they would Loose all Their trade be Naked for want of Cloaths, and in fine be all Cut off."[38]

While on the road to meet Grant, Oukanaekah ran into a man from the lower towns who told him that "I might save myself The Trouble," for a party of Ani'-Yun-wiya had attacked the settlers.

> I have since understood that it was Beemers [James Beamer, trader to the Ani'-Yun-wiya] Son in Law who Attacd. The white People, That he took a Little Flower from Them which was on Horses, but upon the coming up of Col. Grants Indians Immediately Run away with the Loss of Four Men and two women Kill'd, . . . all The Indians below the Valley betook Themselves to The woods whose Towns Col Grant Intirely Destroy'd. . . . The People are so starv'd for Provision That Several have been found Dead in The Paths, and were Reduc'd to kill Their Horses for Subsistance.

At Keowee Oukanaekah met with a northern Native man, perhaps a Mohawk and Stockbridge scout, accompanying Grant's army. Offering him tobacco as a physick for the Ani'-Yun-wiya in distress "will Soon make Them well, bring Their Senses to Them again, and will make Them Think of The English as I do." He later told him that "the great Warrior and Some Others had been to Visit The French talk'd Humorously of Their Poverty giving Them Buffaloe Skins instead of Cloathing, That a French Governer (I Sopose Orleans) Advis'd Them as his Children to come and see him after but above all things not to War with either the English or them, and it was Their Interest to Remain in peace."[39]

In mid-November 1761, the Virginia Regiment under Col. Adam Stephen had bivouacked on the big island in the Holston River, where they were approached by a Native party. Hoping to head the Virginians off, the Overhill Ani'-Yun-wiya proffered a peace offering. Accepting their entreaty, Stephen proffered gifts to seal the deal, but the Native representatives insisted that an officer return with them to Ani'-Yun-wiya country with the gifts to demonstrate the genuineness of the accord. Sensing the danger of sending an envoy into Ani'-Yun-wiya country, Stephen balked at their request. Ensign Timberlake, recognizing the gravity of the moment, volunteered to go to Ani'-Yun-wiya, which Stephen agreed to reluctantly.

Approaching the Cherokee [Tennessee] River, the peace party became fearful that they were being shadowed by Native enemies. They were apprehensive when they faced an elderly Ani'-Yun-wiya called the Slave Catcher of Tennessee, accompanied by about a dozen armed men. Slave catcher was the title of the first rank attained in the Ani'-Yun-wiya military, followed by raven, then mankiller, and finally the prestigious rank of warrior.[40] Slave Catcher "agreeably surprised us, by asking, in the Cherokee language, to what town we belonged? To which our interpreter replied, To the English camp; that the English and Cherokee having made a peace, I was then carrying the articles to their countrymen." After ascertaining that Timberlake was indeed carrying articles of peace to the Overhill Ani'-Yun-wiya, Slave Catcher not only deviated from his planned hunt but also "invited us to his camp, where he treated us with dried venison, hominy, and boiled corn." We then immediately repaired to "his house, opposite the mouth of Tellequo [Tellico] river," where his woman prepared a feast of "roast, boiled, and fried meats of several kinds, and very good Indian bread."

The following morning the English camp crossed the river into the town of Tomotley, where Chief Usteneka and his wife entertained the diplomatic party at his house. After engaging in the customary smoke and discourse, Timberlake "delivered a letter from Colonel Stephen, and another from Captain M'Neil, with some presents from each," which Usteneka gratefully accepted. "Some days after, the headmen of each town were assembled in the town-house of Chote [Chota], the metropolis of the country, to hear the articles of peace read." After sharing the terms to the satisfaction of the assembly and passing the peace pipe around the hall, Usteneka spoke:

> The bloody tomahawk, so long lifted against our brethren the English, must now be buried deep, deep in the ground, never to be raised again; and whoever shall act contrary to any of these articles, must expect a punishment equal to his offence. Should a strict observance of them be

neglected, a war must necessarily follow, and a second peace may not be so easily obtained. I therefore once more recommend to you, to take particular care of your behavior towards the English, whom we must now look upon as ourselves; they have the French and Spaniards to fight, and we enough of our own color, without meddling with either nation. I desire likewise, that the white warrior, who has ventured himself here with us, may be well used and respected by all, wherever he goes amongst us.[41]

The meeting concluded with feasting on "venison, bear, and buffalo . . . potatoes, pumpkins, hominy, boiled corn, beans, and pease," and dancing, much to the chagrin of the "fatigued."[42] After a respite of a "short nap," Timberlake resumed talks at the townhouse, where the gathered chiefs "desired [him] to write a letter for them to the Governor of South Carolina, which signified their desire of living in peace with the English, as long as the sun shone, or grass grew, and desired that a trade might be opened between them." He obliged them and enclosed with their letter "wampum and beads in the inside." Considering the late treaty to mend relations between the colony and the Ani'-Yun-wiya, Gov. Thomas Boone recommended on December 16, 1761, that the assembly pass legislation "framing" the Native trade.[43]

In his May 1, 1762, letter to the LCTP, Fauquier wrongly identified the chief warrior en route to Williamsburg as "Conogotocko, who is old," rather than their "chief Warrior *Skiagusta* Oconostota . . . who came here to confirm the peace. . . . This Chief is a Man of great Influence among them being reputed the boldest Warrior of the Nation, and a Man of Integrity." If Fauquier misunderstood which of the chiefs was coming to Williamsburg, he did comprehend that the Ani'-Yun-wiya did not speak with one voice. They diplomatically divided into opposing roles of advocacy: Oconostota, the great warrior, and Oukanaekah, the peace chief. However, Fauquier comprehended this distinction as factions or parties, not unlike the British both at home and abroad. They headed "different parties," said Fauquier. Oconostota was "one of the last" to agree to the peace accords, although he has been the foremost to treat our prisoners with humanity, and to release them."[44]

Oconostota expressed his desire to go to England in part to see whether what he had been told by Oukanaekah was true and in part to bring attention to "daily" settler encroachment into their hunting grounds. He also wanted to recruit "skillful" persons to assist them in working the "very rich mines of gold, silver, lead, and copper" in their country and to teach their youth "religion, reading and writing." Fauquier warned him of the risks of

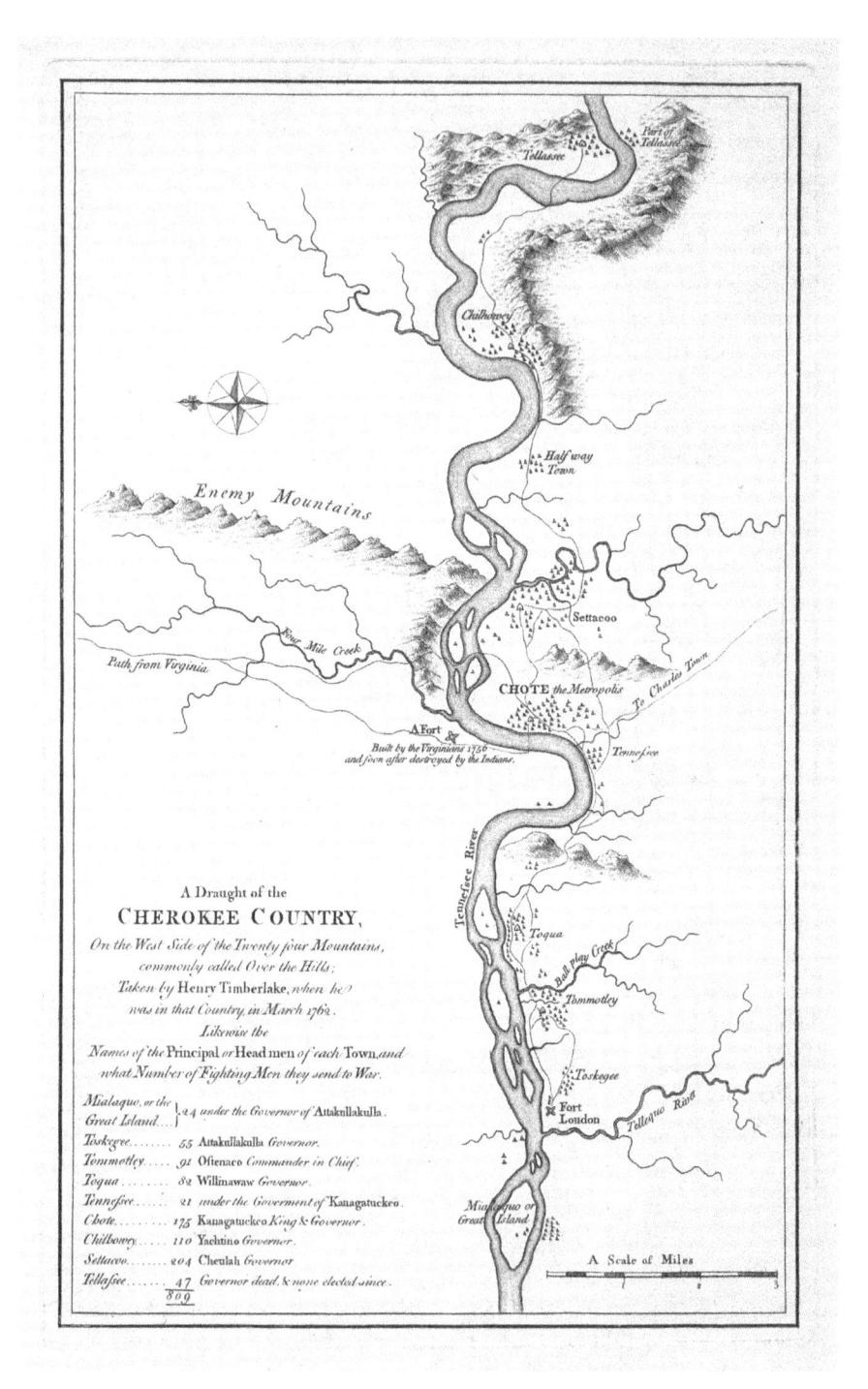

FIGURE 37. *A Draught of the Cherokee Country on the West Side of the Twenty-four Mountains, commonly called Over the Hills; Taken by Henry Timberlake, When He Was in That Country in March 1762.* Courtesy of Museum of Early Southern Decorative Arts.

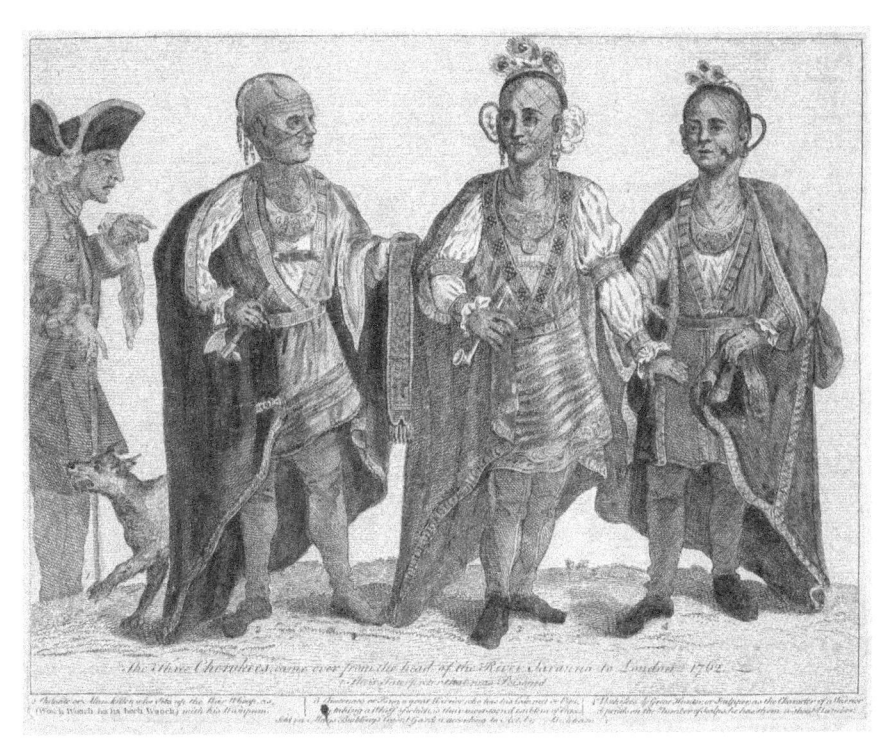

FIGURE 38. George Bickham the younger, *The Three Cherokees Came Over from the Head of the River Savanna to London*, accession no. 3576.429. Courtesy of Gilcrease Museum.

travel, mindful of the discord that might follow his death abroad. On the other hand, the council thought a royal visit could be of "very great utility" to Virginia colonialism. Seeing the majesty of the Crown and the strength of the kingdom could curb Oconostota's future behavior. Moving quickly on this proposition, Fauquier found passage for him with "Captain Blake of his Majesty's Sloop *L'Epreuve* now ready to sail with a few Ships under his Convoy." He assigned Lieutenant Timberlake, a man "much respected" by Ani'-Yun-wiya, to accompany the delegation to England.[45]

Three Ani'-Yun-wiya ambassadors journeyed from the headwaters of the Savannah River at the southern tip of the Blue Ridge Mountains to London in 1762. The Crown not only paid their expenses for their passage through the agent for Virginia but also provided them a "small present on their departure." After learning of his Crown's order, Lieutenant Timberlake decided to host them "for a few days longer" and directed the secretary to invite the agent of Virginia to a reception the next day.[46]

CHAPTER 21

Convert Them into Free Men, Useful Subjects, and Good Christians

With the war apparently ending, the Ohio Company began to re-envision both its land and trade options in Ohio, even hearkening back to Native trade activities from 1708 to 1712 referenced in the Memorial of the Virginia Indian Company.[1] Imperial efforts, however, forestalled Virginia's desire to settle Ohio. Forced out after 1754, the Ohio Company in 1760 put out feelers to Fort Pitt commander Col. Henry Bouquet of their intention to return to the Ohio Valley. Bouquet responded that the Treaty of Easton (1758) settled with the Lenape for no trans-Appalachian settlement also applied to the Ohio Valley, even though Virginia and Maryland were not signatories. To emphasize the point, Bouquet issued a proclamation on October 31, 1761, banning trans-Appalachian settlement. On behalf of the company, Governor Fauquier pleaded to no avail with Bouquet for resettlement of previously patented lands vacated during the war.[2] Nevertheless, Maj. Edward Wood noted, by 1762 "several settlements were formed by Emigrants from the different parts of America, by Permission of the Commanding Officer, for the purpose of accommodating Travellers on the Public Roads. That a Settlement and Improvement was formed about four miles above the Fort, on the South Eastside of the Allegheny River by Col. Croghan, in consequence of a Grant from the Six Nations."[3]

The Virginia commissioners were concerned with two points: Did the Six Nations have the proprietary rights to the land, which they claimed by the right of conquest? And had they forfeited that right because they had been defeated by the British? If defeated, then the right of conquest gave Britain proprietary right. For this reason they asked if he knew which Native nations "attacked and were defeated" by Col. Henry Bouquet at the Battle of Bushy Run. He had only "heard . . . that a few of the Six Nations of the Seneca Tribe Joined the Delawares and Shawanese." Colonel Bouquet's reports of the Battle of Bushy Run to Gen. Jeffrey Amherst gave them reason for their query. Bouquet had with disdain labeled the Native enemy "savages," never distinguishing their nationality.[4]

Virginia also sent George Mercer as its agent to lobby its cause. Mercer joined the Ohio Company in 1761 and succeeded John Hanbury in 1763 as agent acting for the company in London. His father, John Mercer, had been secretary and general counsel to the Ohio Company. George was a veteran of the Seven Years' War, serving at the Battle of Fort Necessity in July 1754, the Battle of the Monongahela in July 1755, and as Washington's aide-de-camp for nearly three years. He was promoted to lieutenant colonel of the newly formed Second Virginia Regiment, which accompanied Gen. John Forbes's expedition to capture Fort Duquesne in 1758.[5] In 1763 the Ohio Company sent enslaved laborers to a new plantation on the company's land at the mouth of Wills Creek, both as watermen to transport skins and other trade items and as "breeders" to reproduce themselves. They were listed in the company's account as "three likely able men Slaves who are used to the Country Business and two new Negro women upon the best terms he can for that purpose."[6]

The western settlements of Virginia in 1763 were still fraught with danger. On July 10, 1763, William Allason wrote from Falmouth, Virginia, "Am well informed by officers of pretty high rank that the Indians are sufficiently supplied with ammunition for seven years by their extraordinary husbanding the supplies granted to them by the French during the War, with is what has been since furnished by the Traders."[7] Likewise, Dr. William Fleming wrote to Fauquier from Staunton that he deplored the quality of the militia in defending the mountains against either Native incursions or Black insurrection. Not only were the settlers in the region remote and "destitute of Arms and Ammunition," but they also lacked quality officers. The militia officers were too busy with the harvest or "unfit or unwilling, not to say afraid." Fleming wrote that in their latest incursion, the Native nations caused a "general Consternation," greater than any during his eight years of service as a surgeon in the Virginia Regiment. "Without protection and without a person to Head them," the settlers "fly" away, fearing another attack will desolate the county. The first attack was a "sudden, unexpected, and great Slaughter of the People." At the same time, the Native nations are "saving and Caressing" all Black fugitives they take in. Insurrection will have the "most serious consequences."[8]

Oddly, Henry McCulloh, who had extensive land grants in western North Carolina, said nothing about slavery or the slave trade in his *Miscellaneous Representations Relative to Our Concerns in America*, submitted in 1761 to the Earl of Bute. What concerned McCulloh most in America was maintaining the trade to Native country in Ohio. Even if the French surrendered Canada to the British, they were still poised in Louisiana

> to annoy us, and to carry on a large and extensive Trade with the Indian Nations which border upon the Five Great Lakes, as well as those which lie between the Mississippi and the Appalachian Mountains. . . .

Considering the great Enmity that has always subsisted between the Nations of Indians in their Interest, and in ours, it is more than probable that the French would be still able to continue the said Indians in their Interest; and to make use of them in annoying our Frontier Settlements.[9]

John Bartram echoed this sentiment to Peter Collinson on December 3, 1762: "I shall be glad of an honourable peace but if Louisianna be not delivered to us we on ye continent can hardly call it A peace for the French will directly [by] encouraging and supplying ye Indians set them against us etc also incroaching them selves which will soon cause first quarreling and next A war."[10] What led to the war with France, McCulloh said, was the lack of a system with "wise and proper regulations" of the Native nations, which by "right belonged" to the Haudenosaunee. Consequently, all the British colonies must unify one system and raise funds "to make Presents to the Indians, and to put those Concerns upon a proper Footing." To pay for these presents, McCulloh recommended that it would "be absolutely necessary to establish proper Funds in America, by a Stamp Duty on Vellum and Paper; and also, by regulating and lowering the Duties upon French Rum and Molasses."[11]

With McCulloh's recommendation in mind, the Council of Trade and Plantations began planning for the postwar period in April 1762. After reading a letter from Dinwiddie dated November 30, 1761, concerning "the settlement of lands to the westward of the Alleghany Mountains," the LCTP proposed tasking joint commissions representing Virginia and Pennsylvania to determine the "boundary line" both between their respective colonies and Maryland. Looking backward, the commissions sought the "release from the Indians of the Six Nations of all the lands in Virginia, made at the Treaty at Lancaster in 1744," and the confirmation of the deed of release by the Ohio nations at Logstown in 1752. Looking forward, they proposed a "conference between the King's generals, governors, etc., and the Western Indians since the Treaty at Easton."[12]

To unify into one system, John Stuart, royal superintendent of Indian Affairs for the Southern Districts of North America, convened a "Southern Congress" at Augusta, Georgia, to find comity between the colonies of Georgia, South Carolina, North Carolina, and Virginia and the nations of the Muscogee, Ani'-Yun-wiya, Chahta, Chikashsha', and yeh is-WAH h'reh. More so than in earlier treaty talks, racial references reigned supreme. Both the British and the Native speakers distinguished between the "white" and the "red" people. The colonial governors met together first to find common cause before meeting with the sachems of the southern nations. Stuart opened the meeting on October 15, 1763, with the familiar rhetoric of the Covenant Chain. He said their intentions were to "brighten the chain of friendship between the White and Red Men" in accordance with the instructions of the "Great King our Common Father" and to "hold fast" to the links of friendship that bind them together. Then he got to the point. He exhorted the Native attendees to disregard any "evil news" bantered about that the British plan to "possess your lands." The purpose of the congress was to openly spell out that "your lands will not be taken from you."[13]

The Muscogee demanded to hear from of Georgia what claim they had to the land on the Tugaloo River; Georgia responded that the Ani'-Yun-wiya had ceded them the land. The Muscogee threatened to hold up the congress "unless the Georgians consented to annul the secret treaty with the Cherokee and receive that territory immediately from them." Georgia "complied, though violently extorted from the Cherokee, contrary to right and sanction of treaties." William Bartram, who attended the congress, used this episode to illuminate the stoic nature of the Ani'-Yun-wiya character, even in the face of humiliation. The Ani'-Yun-wiya had come into possession of this formerly Muscogee land in 1717 after the Muscogee had supported the Yamasee and lost. Since "the Savanna river and its waters were acknowledged to be the natural and just bounds" separating the Ani'-Yun-wiya and Muscogee nations, Bartram reasoned, the Ani'-Yun-wiya had a right to sell the land. This transaction, however, was "unknown" to the Muscogee, and they "lashed" out at the Ani'-Yun-wiya, who paid "homage" to them.

> A chief and warrior started up, and with an agitated and terrific countenance, frowning menaces and disdain, fixed his eyes on the Cherokee chiefs, asked them what right they had to give away their lands, calling them old women, and saying that they had long ago obliged them to wear the petticoat; a most humiliating and degrading stroke, in the presence of the chiefs of the whole Creek confederacy, of the Chickasaws, principle men and citizens of Georgia, Carolina, Virginia, Maryland and Pennsylvania, in the face of their own chiefs and citizens, and amidst the laugh and jeers of the assembly, especially the young men of Virginia, their old enemy and dreaded neighbour: but humiliating as it really was, they were obliged to bear the stigma passively, and even without a reply.[14]

Recouping the Ani'-Yun-wiya's honor on November 5, Usteneka, recently returned the year before from his embassy to London, made the salutation to the gathered "beloved men" and "presented a pipe and some Tobacco as a Testimony of Friendship between the Cherokee and White People." Oukanaekah then took the lead in speaking for the Ani'-Yun-wiya delegation.

He opened his discussion, professing "friendship for the White People" and pointing out a string of beads to underscore this proposition. He "remembered" all that had passed between them, presenting a belt of wampum. Yes, "some" of the Ani'-Yun-wiya youth had behaved badly, but he prayed the governors would forgive their transgression. Again, presenting a belt of wampum, he hoped that the governors would remember the losses of men from both the Lower and Overhill towns, and he promised "reparation for future Injuries and hopes you will do the same." He desired that their children would know peace. He then proceeded to his point: trade. The Ani'-Yun-wiya had returned to their hunting grounds, but it was rare to find traders with goods at Chota. If any harm should come to them, it was not by the Ani'-Yun-wiya but by the "northward" nations, who were their "enemies as well as [that of] the White People." He now sought agreement that the Virginians set a fair price on the exchange of their goods. Taking advantage of their "distress, . . . some people did come from Virginia but had exorbitant prices and got their Skins almost for nothing."

The governors claimed they already had given orders for fair trade, but Oukanaekah wanted the "matter cleared up," and he advertised that Chota was open to trade. Although he gave primacy to the Virginia traders, he said he would allow access to the other three colonies as well.[15] On November 8, Oukanaekah addressed the boundaries issue. He said that the "White People settled beyond the long Canes . . . may stay there but must proceed no farther. . . . The Lands towards Virginia must not be settled nearer the Cherokee than the Southward of New River. Hunting is their Trade, and they have no other way of getting a living."[16]

The superintendent and the governors saluted the Native spokesmen's "good disposition" and appreciated their sense of the "Great King's kind and fatherly Intentions to you and all his Red People and children." They then addressed the two areas of contention: trade and settlements. On trade they said the prices on trade goods were subject to market conditions. If the traders could not profit, they would not carry goods into Ani'-Yun-wiya towns, a presumption applicable to them as well. In the case of the South Carolina trade, a reconciliation of lower than market prices applied; because of "the madness of your young men and the misbehavior of our Traders a Factory was settled at Keowee." This adjustment would stay in effect until the king lifts the sanctions.

> And as to Virginia the Traders there are free to carry up their Goods or not as they find their advantage. There are no Laws to compel them to go or to restrain them from going. Every man carries up his goods as he thinks proper and sets such prices upon them as he judges will answer

his Expense in carrying them up into your Towns. You are also free to purchase them or not as you approve of the prices set upon them. And all we have to add on this subject is that the Government of Virginia sets no Prices on the Goods sent up to you but leaves you and the Traders to agree upon the Price in such manner as is suitable to you both.

On the boundaries and settlement of lands, the colonial representative explained that all their settlements complied with the Great King's instructions, which they have distributed copies to them. They readily dispensed with the case of the Long Canes settlements and South Carolina, which Oukanaekah had already conceded. "Those Settlements were allowed and agreed to in the Treaty of Peace signed at the close of the last War by Lieut. Gov. Bull and Oukanaekah between the White People and your Nation." They then addressed the pertinent issues related to Virginia. First, they dealt with the Ani'-Yun-wiya's admonition that no new settlements be established west of the New River. Twenty years ago Gooch had awarded Col. James Patton a land grant, which "you have acquiesced without complaint to this Time as they are at a great distance from your Country." Second, the Great King gave "another large grant" on the eve of the war with the French before settlers could move there. The king had subsequently instructed "the Governor of Virginia no land can be granted even as far as the Eastern Banks of that River [Kanawha] and in obedience to that Instruction not a foot has been since granted upon that River so that you have nothing further to apprehend on that account." Finally, they promised that Governor Fauquier would "punctually" observe all treaties and preserve their security and treat them justly. "The Cherokee of their own accord . . . had claimed more than were their Hunting Grounds and what they now desired was that they might not be molested in hunting as far as the Spring Head of Holstein [Holston] River."[17]

On November 10 the British drew up "A Treaty for the Preservation . . . of a firm and perfect Peace and Friendship" to solidify the proceedings. Boundaries and lines from the newly ceded French and Spanish territories were spelled out in detail between settler colonies of South Carolina and Georgia and the Native nations of the yeh is-WAH h'reh, the Muscogee, the Chikashsha', and the Chahta. Curiously, neither the trade stipulations nor boundaries agreed to by the Ani'-Yun-wiya and Virginia, nor any stipulations for North Carolina, which bordered Middle Ani'-Yun-wiya country, were included in the formal agreement. Although throughout the treaty negotiations both parties as translated into the minutes referred to each other in binary terms as white and red people, article 2 in the formal treaty stipulated that for the sake of jurisdiction "the Subjects of the Great King

George and the aforesaid several Nations of Indians shall forever hereafter be looked upon as one People." At first glance one might see the equivalence of Native and British humanity, but on further reflection, the declaration effectively subordinates Native people to British law and undermines Native sovereignty.[18]

Whether or not the Native and British subjects could be one people troubled colonial thinkers. Intermarriage with Native people was often compared to that with Black people. William Byrd II discussed in *The History of the Dividing Line* the "whitening" of Black and Native peoples. Alluding to the Jamaican law that recognized creolization and miscegenation and deemphasized racial origins, he wrote: "Nor would the shade of skin have been any reproach at this day, for if a Moor may be washt white in three generations, surely an Indian might have been blanch in two."[19] Following this same reasoning, in *Howell v. Netherland* (1770) Thomas Jefferson argued that the indentured status passed on to Samuel Howell, the progeny of a Black grandfather and a white grandmother, should not be extended to the third generation. He submitted that according to "the law of nature . . . we are all born free." Jefferson did not win this case.[20]

Reverend Fontaine's thoughts on interracial sex and marriage are revelatory. He thought the English "ought to intermarry" with Native people to ease their access to Indigenous land, "because it would have incorporated us with them effectually, and made of them stanch friends, and which is of still more consequence, made many of them good Christians." On the other hand, English traders treat Native women like "whores" and "leave their offspring like bulls or boars to be provided for at random by their mothers. As might be expected, some of these bastards have been the leading men or war captains that have done us so much mischief. This ill treatment was sufficient to create jealousy in the natural man's breast, and made the Indians look upon us as false and deceitful friends and cause all our endeavors to convert them to be ineffectual."[21]

About the same time, on December 15, 1757, John Bartram conveyed similar thoughts to his fellow botanist Peter Collinson about interracial marriage. He also reached similar conclusions about the horrendous treatment of Native women by the English traders.

> I don't remember to have known any English man to have married an Indian nymph. It would be reconed a horrid crime with us but indeed if thay was well dressed and as cleanly as our women they would make as handsom dutiful loving and faithfull wives as many of our own women if we could whiten their skin a little and persuade or compel them not to use strong drink but most of our Indian traders debaucheth them

shamefully which is one cause of many that hath alienated their respect from us ye young girls and women are generally very modest unless debauched by Europeans.[22]

If Fontaine thought that reconciliation with Indigenous people could be achieved through intermarriage, he had an obverse view of relations with African-descended women. If he thought English traders had mistreated Native women and their offspring, he believed white Virginians were "guilty of much more heinous practices, more unjustifiable in the sight of God and man, . . . for many base wretches amongst us take up with negro women, by which means the country swarms with mulatto bastards." Yet rather than promote interracial marital relations, he lamented the law in Virginia that allowed mixed ancestry people to pass into the white race after three generations and "intermarry with the white people, and actually do every day so marry. Now, if, instead of this abominable practice which hath polluted the blood of many amongst us, we had taken Indian wives in the first place, it would have made them some compensation for their lands. They are a free people, and the offspring would not be born in a state of slavery. We should become rightful heirs to their lands."[23]

Rev. Jonathan Boucher assessed the current problem in 1763 to be the "general passion" of itinerant settlers constantly searching for "fresh lands," which more so than anything else keeps us involved in Indian wars. Like Fontaine, Boucher proposed cultural genocide as a way to quell friction and access Native land. "We shall endeavor to diffuse political security and happiness to the Indian nations with whom we have any intercourse; and to convert them into free men, useful subjects, and good Christians." The remedy was not to rein in that "vagrant and unsettled way of life" but to "civilize" the Native people "who already have a better title to any of our unlocated lands, than we can possibly give any newcomers."[24]

Fauquier's assessment of the civilizing mission to the Virginia tributaries that same year underscored cultural genocide. Their remnants, including along the Eastern Shore, were so assimilated as to "wear European dress, and in part follow the Customs of the common Planters." The Pamunkey and the Nottoway fighting force were "reduced and inconsiderable." Although Nottoway, Meherrin, Tuscarora, and Saponi continued to follow their Native traditions, they were severely compromised and their number in decline. Fauquier's observed "their great Fondness for Rum," more likely an effect rather than a cause of their demise.[25]

Dr. John Mitchell, a resident of Urbanna, Virginia, employed the civility/nudity trope as scientific treatise. The naturalist Mitchell earned his scientific bona fides and fellowship in the Royal Society with his article "The

Causes of the Different Colors of People in Different Climates," published in 1744 in *Philosophical Transactions*. Offering an environmental explanation for darker pigmentation and curlier hair, he noted the descendants of Spaniards inhabiting the torrid zone "are become as dark coloured as our native Indians of Virginia . . . Surely the minds of the Spaniards did not change with their complexions!" He combined an environmental and cultural hypothesis and deduced an explanation for darker skin pigmentation. The Africans' skin was darker owing to their not wearing clothing or covering their bodies in the torrid zone.[26]

Likewise, John Bartram confidently stated that since the population of the New World had grown in isolation from Europe, the principal divide is "colour, manner, and language," which seem "irreconcilable."

> But are the Negroes in Guinea more similar in these respects, to the rest of the world? Let any one tell me, why most of the Africans are black and woolly-pated, and I will shew him why the Americans are red and without hair on their chins, and many parts of their bodies. After all are we sufficiently acquainted with the utmost powers of nature? to be sure the offspring of the same pair in 3 or 4000 years might without a super[na]tural interposition become of various complexions, and suppose we were convinced of this, may not the infinite power that created our first parents, and miraculously wrought the confusion of tongues, have thus distinguished their posterity for-purposes only known to his infinite wisdom.[27]

Bartram explained the peace and the rationale for the destruction of Native people to Collinson on March 4, 1764:

> I think *our* Indians received A full value for that cheating walk [Walking Purchase of 1737] and pretended to be fully satisfied with what they received above ye first agreement and for Pittsburg they let ye French settle and build there then why may not ye English after thay have drove ye French out, keep possession of it and as ye Indians have committed such barbarous destruction on our people, we have more reason to destroy them and possess their land thewn you have to keep Canada and must all our Provinces suffer a Prodigious yearly expence and have thousands of our innocent people be barbarously murdered because some of our traders made them drunk to get a scin cheap, or an Irishman settles on A bit of thair land which they will never make use of.[28]

Boucher elaborated on Adam Smith's categorization of Indigenous people in *The Theory of Moral Sentiments* as a people possessing a "Spartan discipline." Ignoring their agricultural pursuits, Boucher maintained that the group's defining characteristics classified them as "warrior and savages."[29] Their chieftains, invasions, and conquests are not unlike the histories of Rome or Greece, but the Indigenous people had not produced a Thucydides or Pericles to chronicle their achievements. Yet modern polities had gestated from the embryonic warrior state to become refined nations. "What else is the early history of nations now the most polished, but the history of Indians? The brief character of uncultivated man is *to neglect agriculture, to practice hunting, and to delight in war,*" not unlike "Britons in ancient times." Yet it was not enough simply to pacify the Indigenous people.

> It would seem, then, that we have only to wean Indians from the chase, to tame them. Every other effort to mollify and humanize their stubborn spirits, without this preliminary requisite, will continue to be made to little purpose. They may make talks; they may give strings of wampum; nay, they may even be baptized, and be called Christians: but as long as they live by hunting, they will still be Indians. The putting an end to hunting is the first step in the progress of civilization.[30]

He could have added "and the vanishing of the Indians." Deh-he-wä-mis [Mary Jemison], captured and adopted by the Seneca, cautioned against this civilizing impulse.

> The attempts which have been made to civilize and christianize them by the white people, has constantly made them worse and worse; increased their vices, and robbed them of many of their virtues; and will ultimately produce their extermination. I have seen, in a number of instances, the effects of education upon some of our Indians, who were taken when young, from their families, and placed at school before they had had an opportunity to contract many Indian habits, and there kept till they arrived to manhood; but I have never seen one of those but what was an Indian in every respect after he returned. Indians must and will be Indians, in spite of all the means that can be used for their cultivation in the sciences and arts.[31]

If Boucher maintained that Native men gravitated to the martial arts, then he exaggerated preternatural maternal instinct supposedly in Native women. For example, he gave a "Transmontane anecdote" of a Native woman "of some note, from her dress being composed almost entirely of silk hand-kerchiefs." In this story he cast the settlers as savages who shot and scalped her and her infant child as she tried to shield the baby with her body. After a skirmish provoked by English encroachment, when Indians brandishing tomahawks were overwhelmed by riflemen, she hid in the marsh until she was discovered by the "chieftain" of the white settlers. "Her last and only care was, if possible, to preserve her babe. With this hope, she instantly turned it from her back to her breast; that she alone might receive the ball. And even when she fell, by a kind instinct of nature (of the true force of which in such a case mothers only are, perhaps, the proper judges) she was anxious and careful so to fall as that her child might not be hurt." Boucher challenged the classicists to offer a comparable story of "any instance in which the force of nature is more forcibly displayed."[32]

Benjamin Franklin also railed against the aspersions "lately" cast on the colonists by Adam Smith. "The gentle terms of republican race, mixed rabble of Scotch, Irish and foreign vagabonds, descendants of convicts, ungrateful rebels etc. are some of the sweet flowers of English rhetoric, with which our colonists have of late been regaled."[33] He could have been replying directly to Smith when he criticized this characterization of the Chesapeake colonies:

> But it seems the Inhabitants of Virginia and Maryland, who are de-scended from the Royalists of the Church of England, driven hence by those very Oliverian Stiff Rumps, and never tinctured with Fanaticism, are, in the present Case, as stiff rump'd as the others, and even led the Way in asserting what "'they call their Rights.'" So that this Hypothesis of Fanaticism appears insufficient to account for the Opposition uni-versally given to the Stamp Act in America; and I fancy the Gentleman thought so himself, as he mends it a little after, by lumping all the Ameri-cans under the general Character of "'House breakers and Felons.'"[34]

About the same time, Franklin used the trope of honor among bar-barians, giving examples of both the Haudenosaunee (discussed above) in dealing with their ancestral enemy the yeh is-WAH h'reh and Cudjoe, the caboceer of Cape Coast Castle, offering sanctuary to an English seaman. The Haudenosaunee recoiled at the thought that they might harm an embassy of yeh is-WAH h'reh en route through Mohawk country after giving their word of safe passage. Captain Seagrave had left "second Mate, William Murray, sick on Shore," at Cudjoe's house to recuperate. In the meantime a Dutch ship "treacherously seized" Africans negotiating on board. Their people wanted to take revenge on Murray, but Cudjoe took umbrage and protected him. "I relate this, says Captain Seagrave, to show, that some among these

FIGURE 39. Arthur Lee, portrait by Charles Willson Peale. Courtesy of Virginia Museum of History and Culture.

dark People have a strong Sense of Justice and Honour, and that even the most brutal among them are capable of feeling the Force of Reason, and of being influenced by a Fear of God (if the Knowledge of the true God could be introduced among them) since even the Fear of a false God, when their Rage subsided, was not without its good Effect."[35]

If Adam Smith's castigation of the slavers as European refuse raised the rancor of Franklin, it along with his attribution of valor to enslaved Africans raised the ire of Arthur Lee. Matriculating as a medical student at the University of Edinburgh, Lee reproached Smith for not condemning the slave trade. Taking the bait, as Smith suggested is the wont of the civilized, Lee justified his fellow colonials in *An Essay in Vindication of the Continental Colonies of America* (1764). Lee knocked the trope of the jailbird origins of the slaveholders' alleged by Smith, promoting instead the myth of their cavalier origins.[36]

Indeed, Lee chided Smith for not using his expertise and his exalted stature to attack the slave trade rather than libeling the colonials. Taking issue with Smith's stamp of nobility on the enslaved Africans, Lee argued that Black people were devoid of any virtue. Rather by using the example of Native people as a counterweight to Africans, Smith wrote (in an often-cited quotation):

> The savages in North America, we are told, assume upon all occasions the greatest indifference, and would think themselves degraded if they should ever appear in any respect to be overcome, either by love, or grief, or resentment. Their magnanimity and self-command, in this respect, are almost beyond the conception of Europeans. . . . Every savage is said to prepare himself from his earliest youth for this dreadful end. He composes, for this purpose, what they call the song of death, a song which he is to sing when he has fallen into the hands of his enemies and is expiring under the tortures which they inflict upon him. It consists of insults upon his tormentors and expresses the highest contempt of death and pain. The same contempt of death and torture prevails among all other savage nations. There is not a negro from the coast of Africa, who does not, in this respect, possess a degree of magnanimity, which the soul of his sordid master is scarce capable of conceiving. Fortune never exerted more cruelly her empire over mankind, than when she subjected those nations of heroes [Africans] to the refuse of the jails of Europe, *to wretches* [Virginian slavers] who possess the virtues neither of the countries which they come from, nor of those which they go to, and whose levity, brutality, and baseness, expose them to the contempt of the vanquished.[37]

To undermine Smith's argument, Lee set up a straw man first with a sin of omission or, better, an act of erasure by eliminating the transitional reference to Native people in the line "The same contempt of death and torture prevails among all other savage nations." Lee falsified his reading of *Moral Sentiments*, historian Richard K. MacMaster writes, "by wrenching a quotation out of context." The wanting context is a discussion of the fortitude of Native people enduring pain, which leads to the attribution of magnanimity to enslaved Africans, a quality not attributable to their "sordid" masters.[38]

Then by sleight of hand, Lee intentionally substituted one preposition for another and changed Smith's line about lacking the moral sentiments of their countries of origin. In Smith's text "*to* wretches" alludes to the Virginia slavers. In Lee's version, "*of* wretches" alludes to the Africans: "Fortune never exerted more cruelly her empire over mankind, than when she subjected those nations of heroes to the refuse of the jails of Europe, *of* wretches who possess the virtues neither of the countries which they go to, nor of those which they come from, and whose levity, brutality, and baseness, so justly expose them to the contempt of the vanquished."[39]

It Is You Who Are Frequently Passing up and down the Ohio, and Making Settlements upon It

George Washington suggested that John Posey settle his debts, even if it meant starting over in the backcountry. If one cannot maintain one's estate for three to four years until "the Country, I mean the Indebted part of it, can emerge a little from the distress," then "sell immediately . . . beginning with the Sales of such things as can be best spared, and so raising to Negroes, and even Land if requisite." "There is a large Field before you—an opening prospect in the back Country for Adventurers," a great opportunity where an enterprising settler could amass an estate on the shores of the Monongahela. Within twenty years, he would realize a fivefold increase if the history of settling new lands held true. For example, Washington wrote, just look at the success of the Hite family in Frederick County, where Washington had holdings. The Hites had amassed one hundred thousand acres in one generation after arriving in 1732. He asked rhetorically, "Was it not by taking up and purchasing at very low rates the rich back Lands which were thought nothing of in those days, but are now the most valuable Lands we possess?"[1]

Washington detailed efforts to secure Ohio lands under the terms of Dinwiddie's proclamation of 1754. He had patented the land but had yet to improve it properly. He looked forward to securing land in the "King's part," or that land protected for the Native nations by the 1763 proclamation, which he saw only as a "temporary expedient" to placate the Native inhabitants. Rather he believed in a "few years" the Indigenous people would consent to the English settling of these lands. This was why he was keen on "hunting out" the best lands immediately rather than lose that opportunity. For this reason he asked William Crawford to search out a tract of fifteen hundred to two thousand acres of "good land . . . contiguous to your own settlement" near the Virginia-Pennsylvania boundary. He was not interested in poor or middling land far from navigation but rather the "rich" and "level" land near it. He was concerned about missing his opportunity once others learned that "rights" were available. Offering a portion for his effort to Crawford, he asked the latter to keep his activity secret except to recruit his friends into the scheme. It not only might alert competitors but also could alarm the Crown, which could censure him for violating the proclamation line.[2]

John Mercer, who owned one share of Ohio Company stock in 1768, wrote to George, his father, that he could satisfy his quota by himself. He needed settlers to come with "two good hands each." He had "carpenters and very good Smith of my own to build for them and should want for nothing but nails. I yesterday hired Mr Semple twenty-one Negro men, 1 woman and 3 boys and 2 white servants, the man at £12, woman at £6, and boys at £5 the year. Supplies them with 6 pounds of meat per week finds them bedding, tools, and pays their levies and taxes and is to return them completely clothed."[3]

In 1765 a perfect storm of circumstances prompted the Board of Trade to recognize in Virginia the convergence of the murder of "Cherokee and the riots and insurrections on the frontiers; the unlawful settlements on lands to the westward of the Allegany Mountains, and the resolutions and proceedings of the House of Burgesses on the Stamp Act."[4] Fauquier had reported to the board on May 26, 1765, an account of the murder of Ani'-Yun-wiya and settlers from Pennsylvania and the Virginia backcountry moving without permission onto "the waters of the Ohio" to the "umbrage" of the "neighboring" Native people. Fauquier noted that backcountry people had murdered five Ani'-Yun-wiya on the frontier. He could not think of any other measure to assuage the Ani'-Yun-wiya other than invite their chiefs to witness the execution of the perpetrators.[5] Fauquier followed up this message with the recommendation by the assembly to encourage trade with the Ani'-Yun-wiya.[6] The arrest of people for the murder of the Ani'-Yun-wiya provoked "riotous insurrections" on the frontier.[7]

Consequently, the Ani'-Yun-wiya moved directly to settle their affairs with the English, including settling boundary lines and demanding that the governor hang the murderers of their people. The two parties met in Congress at Fort Prince George. On May 8, 1766, Kittagusta said: "We returned yesterday from marking the Boundary Line between South Carolina and our Country, a Sash of Fatigue, but nevertheless agreeable." Cognizant that the white people were "settled on the Frontiers . . . we can never now have any disputes about Land." He repeated their territorial concessions made in October, offering a "straight course" from the South Carolina terminus at the Reedy River to Colonel Chiswell's mines, with the stipulation of "a just Boundary, and the only one we Can Allow." He expressed his anxiety at the number of backcountry settlers from Virginia and North Carolina "upon a great Part of our best lands, and the bold inroads of a few that are within an easy days march from our Towns, are circumstances very alarming to us; therefore, we shall be ready at the end of the Fifth moon [September] from

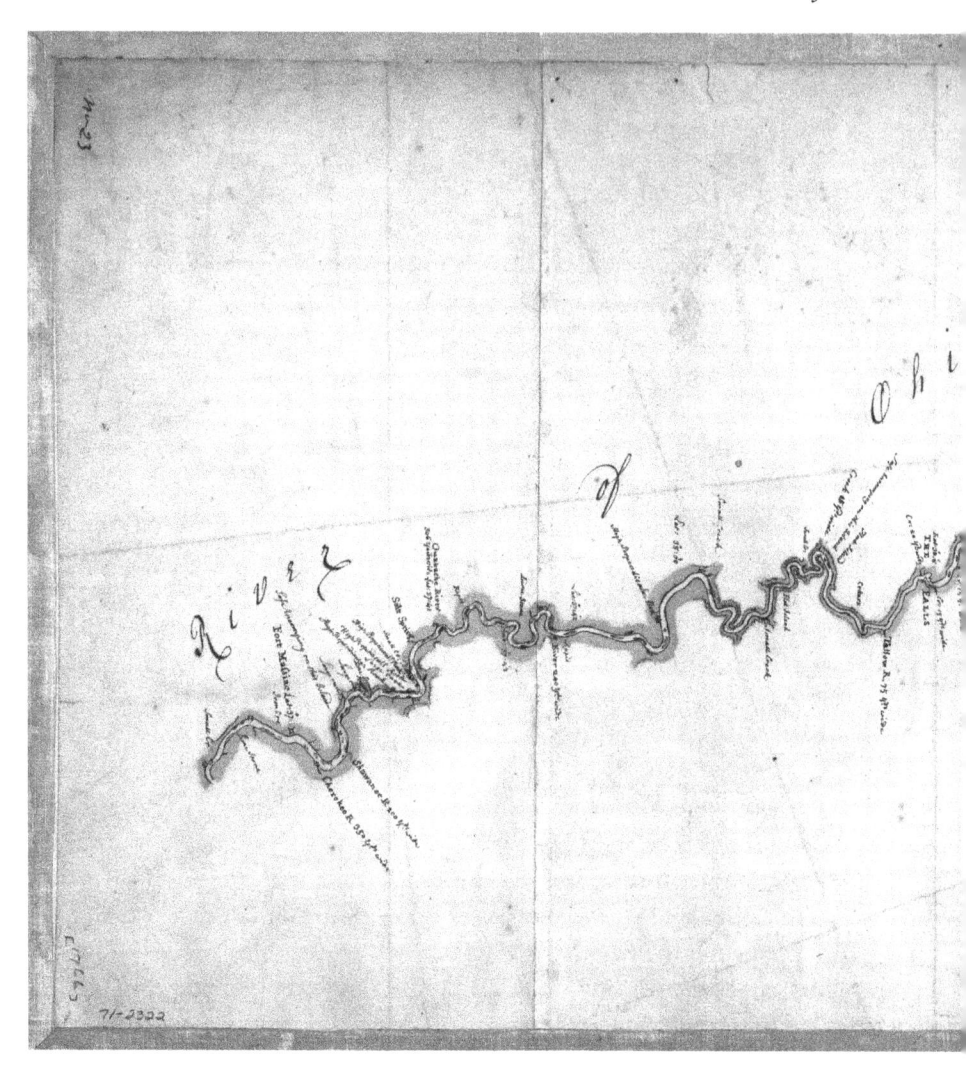

this Time to attend at the marking a Line. Our minds will not be easy till it is Compleated, and if our Brothers [the English] will not be assisting in it, then we must Effect it ourselves."

Kittagusta reminded Stuart that at the congress at Augusta in 1763, attended by the governors of Virginia, Georgia, and the two Carolinas, "we were promised quiet Possession of our Lands, and redress of our Grievances That we might claim the land a great way beyond where we propose to Run the Line, but chuse much Rather to part with it than have any disputes concerning it." Pressing his plea directly to the governors of Virginia and North Carolina for a congress to discuss "the Reasonableness of our demand," he

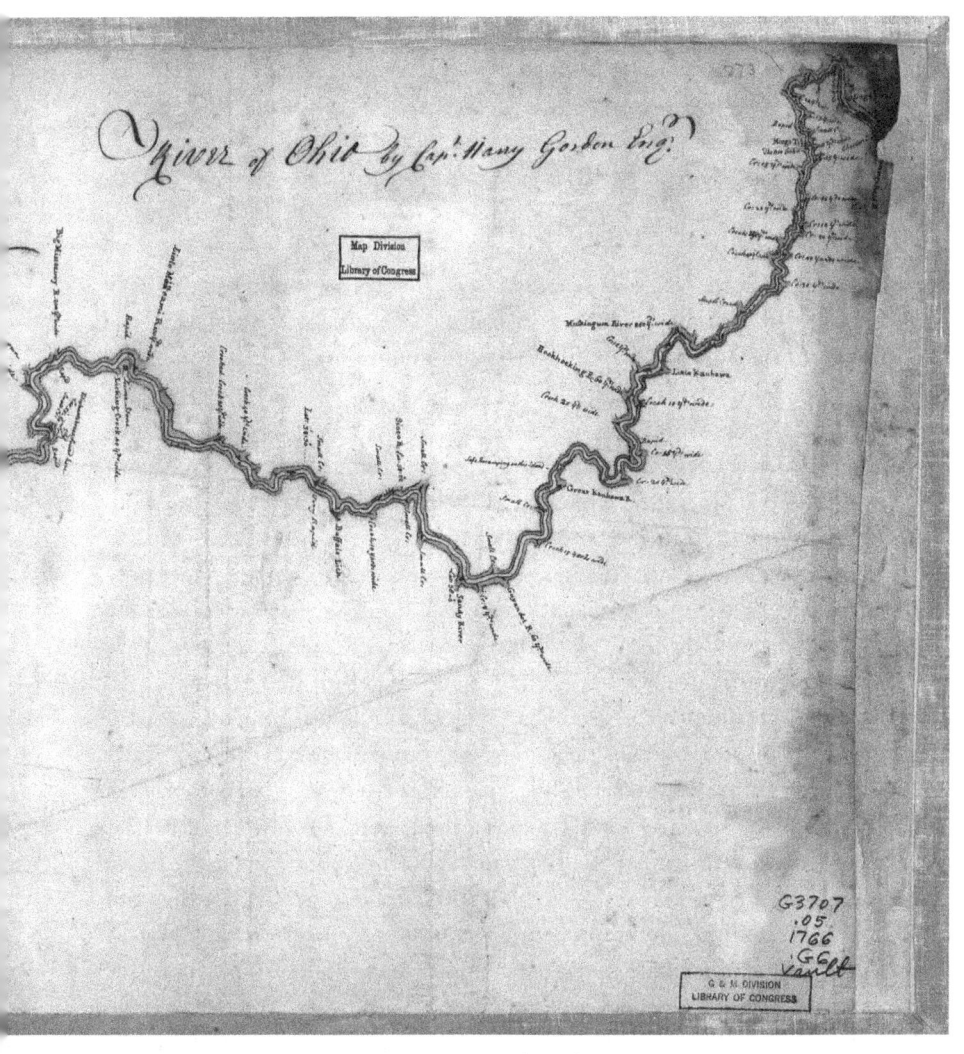

FIGURE 40. Harry Gordon, *River of Ohio* (1766). Courtesy of Library of Congress.

asserted that "we are a poor People dependent upon the Woods for our Support, and without the means of redressing ourselves but by Violence."[8]

In the follow-up meeting in September 1766, Kittagusta responded to newly installed governor of South Carolina Charles Greville Montagu that his people were unable to "attend at the fixing of the Boundary Line before the Spring" because they had suffered a terrible outbreak.

When I got up this morning I could hear nothing but the cries of women and children for the loss of their relations, in the evenings there are nothing to be seen but smoak and houses on fire, the dwellings of the deceased; I never remember to see any sickness like the present, except the small Pox, and if we should attempt to go to run the Line, we might have been taken sick in the woods, and die, as several of our people have already been served, who attempted to escape this Devil of a disorder.

He was concerned that Virginia had yet to reach agreement on the boundary that he had proposed. He warmly anticipated "Virginia will agree to settle the Line on the back of their Country, so as to make a final conclusion of the whole at once."[9]

Acting upon these requests, Alexander Cameron, deputy commissary for Indian Affairs for the Cherokee nation, organized a survey party including "the Prince of Chote, Jud's Friend [Usteneka], Tiptoe Emy and the Wolf, with thirty young men." The Ani'-Yun-wiya "blazed the trees . . . and made the Boundary very clear and strong as they term it."[10] The survey made note of the presence of white settlements near the boundary and decried one plantation within Native country, despite Governor Bull's directive to leave the area. The Ani'-Yun-wiya were "chagrined" that Bull had not provided presents in recognition of the land that they had ceded to South Carolina. Mindful of this diplomatic faux pas, Cameron moved quickly to distribute both ammunition and presents. He also requisitioned medals to memorialize "our friendship," a move meant to dissuade them from Muscogee entreaties to align and make war against the English. Cameron reported that he had a letter from a Mr. Taylor "from over the hills that the rogue Mankiller, and his Brother Trennilitah are employed as Ambassadors between the Mortar (chief) of the Muscogee, and Oconostota; and that the Mortar engages to reinforce the Cherokee with 700 on one day's warning, provided they will go to Virginia and fall on the back settlements."[11] The move apparently had its desired effect. In September Kittagusta responded to the news that the Muscogee and the Chahta were at war with the rejoinder: "The Creeks loved war a long time and thought there was no people that could cope with them; . . . for our part we are tired of War."[12]

Cameron reported that the Ani'-Yun-wiya "proposed" running the boundary in a "straight" line to Colonel Chiswell's mines. They intended to cede their lands to Virginia south of Chiswell's mines, even "that part of their Hunting Ground [which] lies 40 miles eastward of where they now nominate their boundary; but they do not love disputing with the White People concerning a trifle, therefore they made them a present of it."[13] This favorable negotiation offered the opportunity "for carrying on an extensive Trade and supplying them on the most reasonable terms possible by building and fixing a large store at the great Island on [Holston]." The Ani'-Yun-wiya contended they could reach out to the Ohio country nations to engage in commerce at this entrepôt, but Cameron thought this expectation "too Sanguine."[14]

The Ani'-Yun-wiya continued to express their outrage at Virginia for not hanging the murderers of their people. This failing had only fueled the Muscogee efforts to turn the Ani'-Yun-wiya against the English. In addition, Oconostota and Oukanaekah

> want to see the Great King, and seem extremely desirous to embark
> from Virginia, and were they to solicit our Governor and Council for
> leave (as they seem inclined to do) they would undoubtedly obtain it
> . . . ; for there are none of the murderers, that killed a party of their
> People, yet apprehended, neither can they without imminent danger,
> for the whole body of Crackers, to a man, have unanimously declared,
> publickly, that they will espouse their cause at the expense of their
> lives, so that Proclamations and great rewards answer no purpose. And
> should these head men be allowed to take a voyage, the expence of con-
> ducting them to, and from England, would not exceed the premiums
> offered for bringing the other villains to justice.[15]

To help stave off this animosity, Cameron recommended Virginia's sending Oconostota, the great warrior of Chota, and Oukanaekah, the Little Car-penter, as another Ani'-Yun-wiya embassy to England. In the meantime Vir-ginia should assuage their grief by sending "large presents for the Relations of the murdered." If not, Oconostota and Oukanaekah "will leave no stone unturned to effect it."[16]

At the same time, they registered their displeasure at the English sup-plying "the Northward nations with hatchets which are very Sharp and have been lifted up against White as well as Red Men in our Nation."[17] They have "attacked us this year in all parts of our Country in greater Numbers and more frequent than we have ever known."[18] They also disclaimed any respon-sibility for the murders of white people in Virginia's backcountry. Lamenting these deaths, they cast the blame on "rogues" from northward nations.

> The woods have been full of the Northward Indians all this summer,
> and it is more likely it was done by them than by any of our People as
> we always give them good Talks; but we cannot be answerable for the
> acts of rogues, whom you Know will not at all times listen to our in-
> junctions, and especially when they are out in the woods and meet with
> the White men hunting on their ground. But you may depend upon it,
> that we shall never hide anything of that kind from you, when it comes

to our ears, and we promise to make a diligent search of any such acts, in order to suppress them if possible.[19]

In 1767 the Southern Department began working out an agreeable boundary between the southern colonies and Native country that would conform with the Proclamation of 1763. Running the line from the Floridas to Chiswell's lead mines in southwestern Virginia, the project ran into a stumbling block when Virginia began pressing for the line westward at the mouth of the Tennessee rather than at the of the mouth of the Great Kanawha, drawing the Ani'-Yun-wiya into the conflict. Certainly, the Ohio, Loyal Land, and Greenbrier companies of Virginia pressed for this concession west of the proclamation line, where they claimed 1.3 million acres in the Ohio Valley and hundreds of thousands of acres along the Ohio, Holston, Clinch, and Greenbriar Rivers. The appointments of Dr. Thomas Walker of the Loyal Company and Gen. Andrew Lewis of the Greenbriar Company to represent Virginia in the negotiations with the Ani'-Yun-wiya betray the department's intentions.

Superintendent Stuart exchanged diplomatic "talks and messages" with "the great Council of the Cherokee Nation assembled at Chota," where they came to consensus and agreed to cede lands to the Crown. At Hard Labor, South Carolina, the Ani'-Yun-wiya and the British representatives met on October 17, 1768, to certify the cession of lands "lying within the Province" of South Carolina, North Carolina, and Virginia. This treaty detailed the boundary between the Ani'-Yun-wiya and the southern colonies, reaffirmed the terms of the Treaty of Augusta of 1763, and restricted the Crown's "white subjects" from settling in Ani'-Yun-wiya country and the Ani'-Yun-wiya from intruding on the ceded land. The "dividing line" for Virginia included

> all the lands formerly claimed by and belonging to said Nation of Indians, lying within the province of Virginia, to the Eastward of the line already described, as far as Chiswell's Mine as well to the Eastward of a line to be marked by Deputies from said Nation of Cherokee, in Conjunction with the Superintendent of the Southern District or His Deputy and certain Commissioners to be appointed by the aforesaid province of Virginia, running in a straight line from Chiswell's Mine on the great Conhoway aforesaid to the confluence of said River with the New River where the Boundary Line behind the Northern District terminates.

In an "earnest desire of removing as far as possible all Cause of Dispute" arising from "white inhabitants . . . encroachments" on "reserved" Ani'-Yun-wiya land, Stuart, on behalf of the Dominion of Virginia, offered the Ani'-Yun-wiya "a Valuable Consideration in various Sorts of Goods."[20]

Sir William Johnson hosted a major conference with the Native nations at Fort Stanwix, New York, in 1768, a decade after Easton, with the goal of establishing a new Indian boundary line and reopening trans-Appalachian settlement.[21] In addition to the Ohio Company, the Loyal Company and the Greenbriar Company coveted Native land presumably off-limits because of the Proclamation of 1763. Dr. Walker of the Loyal Company served himself and his company's interests first in the treaty negotiations at Fort Stanwix.

By recognizing the Virginia boundary at the confluence of the Ohio and Kanawha Rivers to the mouth of the Kanawha River at Point Pleasant, the treaty not only opened the land to western settlement but also curtailed Haudenosaunee claims there. Walker continued to represent Virginia as its commissioner at the treaty negotiations at Fort Stanwix, which were scheduled to convene on October 24. His commission, signed by President John Blair of Virginia, stated that his mission was "to settle a Boundary Line between this Colony, and the Colonies of Pennsylvania and Maryland and the several Nations of Indians concerned." Sir William Johnson hosted the congress with the Haudenosaunee and their tributaries and representatives from New Jersey, Pennsylvania, and Virginia, along with "sundry Gents: from different Colonies." Eight hundred Native people had already arrived by early October, their number growing daily to twenty-two hundred by the eve of the meeting. All told, over a period of seven weeks, Johnson hosted about thirty-two hundred members of the "the Mohawks, Oneidas, Onondagoes, Senecas, Cayugas, Tuscororas, Coghnowagos, Onoghguagos, Tutuloes, Shawanese, Delawares, Mingoes of Ohio, Nanticokes, Conoys, Chughnuts, Schoras, and Orisca." Johnson had intelligence that the uninvited Susquehanna were nearby. Governor William Franklin of New York reported that all of the camps sported an "uncommon sobriety and good humour" during the negotiations. Each of the Six Nations had several chiefs representing their interests. Among the tributaries, Chief Benevissica spoke for the Shawnee and Chiefs Killbuck and Turtleheart represented the Lenape.[22]

After two days of the ceremony of condolence, the congress got to business on the third day. After pleading the renewal of the Covenant Chain by "strengthening it and rubbing off any rust which it may have contracted that it may appear bright to all Nations as a proof of our love and Friendship," Johnson addressed the issue at hand: the Crown had "signified" in 1765 its desire to firm up the boundary line between the colonies and Native country. After hearing that the rationale for setting the boundary was to prevent the encroachment on Native land, Conoghquieson, spokesperson for the Haudenosaunee, said in general to the assembled, but in particular to

the tributary nations, that "the several Nations might look towards the Onondagas who would appoint him a time and place for taking the matter into
consideration."[23]

Asserting a claim of ancient conquest—"We begin on the Ohio at the
mouth of the Cherokee River which is now our just right"—the Haudenosaunee said of the cession:

> The extent of it to the Southward which we find is no further than
> Kanawha River. Now Brother, you, who know all our affairs, must be
> sensible that our Rights go much farther to the Southward and that
> we have a very good and clear Title to the Lands as far as the Cherokee
> River which we can not allow to be right of any other Indians without
> doing wrong to our Posterity and acting unworthy [to] those Warriors
> who fought and conquered it. We therefore expect this our Right will
> be considered.

Johnson responded: "We have heard what you said and shall answer it. In
the first place I acknowledge to have heard of your claim to the Southward
before this time. The King does not deny your claims. He is not thoroughly
acquainted with the exact extent of them and finding that they may be liable
to some dispute with the Southern Indians, he being an enemy to strife directed the Line to be run in the manner he thought least liable to it."[24]

In a clear effort to curry favor with the British and discredit the Shaw-
nee, the next night, Saturday, October 28, "several of the Chiefs" came to
Johnson's quarters in secret with "Intelligence and Belts" gathered from the
Shawnee.

> According to the old agreement subsisting between the several Indian
> Nations, they were all to unite and attack the English as soon as the
> latter became formidable to them. That several of the Nations to the
> South and West greatly alarmed at the Power and increase of the Eng-
> lish and irritated at the ill treatment they had met with had expressed
> a desire to meet the rest to deliberate on what was to be done. That the
> Spaniards and French had for a long time urged them to take up arms
> and given them repeated assurances of a powerfull assistance That they
> had now called them to a meeting at the Mississippi near the mouth of
> the Ohio for that purpose.[25]

The Haudenosaunee and the British agreed on boundaries at the expense
of the Shawnee, Lenape, and the Seneca-Cayuga, with a caveat: "We do
now on this on behalf and in the name of all our Warriors of every Nation,

condition that all our Warriors shall have the liberty of hunting throughout the Country as they have no other means of subsistance and as your people have not the same occasions or inclinations—That the White people be restricted from hunting on our side of the Line to prevent contensions between us."[26] Then, to the chagrin of the Ohio nations, the vexation of the Ani'-Yun-wiya, and the delight of the British, the Haudenosaunee offered their concession:

> We begin on the Ohio at the mouth of the Cherokee River which is now our just right, and from thence we give up on the South side of Ohio to Kittanning above Fort Pitt, from thence a direct Line to the nearest Fork of the West Branch of Susquehanna thence through the Allegany Mountains along the south side of the said West Branch till we come opposite to the mouth of the Creek called Tiadaghton thence across the Nest Branch & along the East side of that Creek and along the ridge of Burnets Hills to a Creek called Awandae thence down the same to the East Branch of the Susquehanna, and across the same and up the East side of that River to Oswegy, from thence Eastward to Delaware River, and up that River to opposite where Trinaderha falls into Susquehanna, thence to Trienaderha and up the West side thereof and its West Branches to the Head thereof thence by a straight Line to the mouth of Canada Creek where it itself into Wood Creek at the end of the long carrying place beyond Fort Stanwix.[27]

The full deed of concession accepted this offer that "ALL that Tract of Land situate in North America at the Back of the British Settlements bounded by a Line which we have now agreed upon and do hereby establish as the Boundary between us and the British Colonies in America" but carried it "beyond Fort Stanwix and extending Eastward from every part of the said Line as far as the Lands formerly purchased so as to comprehend the whole of the Lands between the said Line and the purchased Lands or settlements, except what is within the Province of Pennsylvania." This land cession was exchanged for "consideration of a valuable Present of the several articles in use amongst Indians which together with a large sums of money amounts in the whole to the sum of Ten thousand four Hundred and Sixty pounds seven shillings and three pence sterling to us now delivered and paid by Sir William Johnson Baronet His Majestys sole Agent and superintendent of Indian affairs for the Northern department of America."[28] George Croghan in his deposition remembered that at General Council assembled at Fort Stanwix in November 1768 the Six Nations sold to Sir William Johnson, then superintendent for Indian Affairs, all the lands lying between the mountains and the Ohio, as far down as the mouth of the Cherokee River, declaring "that Country Belonged to them, they having conquered the Nations who formerly resided [there]."[29]

The sachems and chiefs signing the Treaty of Fort Stanwix included signatories from each of the Six Nations but excluded the representatives of the Shawnee, the Lenape, and the Seneca-Cayuga, an assertion both of their tributary status and of Haudenosaunee proprietary rights.

The *Virginia Gazette* heralded the treaty in its December 1, 1768, edition.

> The Six Nations and all their tributaries have granted a vast extent of country to his Majesty, and to the proprietaries of Pennsylvania, and settled an advantageous boundary line between their hunting country and this, and the other colonies to the southward, as far as the Cherokee river, for which they received the most valuable present in goods and dollars that was ever given at any conference since the settlement of America. . . . It is therefore earnestly to be hoped that this grand cession and boundary will be rightly improved as they will undoubtedly secure the future tranquility of these colonies and be productive of lasting commercial advantages to them and Great Britain.

Although the *Gazette* concluded that the "the Sachems and Warriours departed from the congress in a very happy disposition of mind from a firm persuasion that his Majesty will gratify them in their just and reasonable expectations," that sentiment could not apply to all nations in attendance, particularly the Shawnee, Lenape, and Seneca-Cayuga.[30]

Conscious of the dissension of the Shawnee and Lenape, Johnson felt compelled to speak to them directly:

> I am not ignorant that this has happened and I have good intelligence that there are people who have been lately deceiving some of you with stories of Revolutions in American affairs and of French Fleets and armies, . . . Be assured, Brothers, that those who were able to conquer Canada, and drive their enemies out of their country, will always have it in their power to defeat their future projects. . . . I likewise desire you to remember all your engagements with the English to observe the treaty of Peace with the Cherokee, to avoid any irregularities on the Frontiers and pay due regard to the Boundary Line now made, & to make all your People acquainted with it, and to keep the Roads and Waters open and free whereby you will enjoy the benefits of Peace and Commerce, the esteem of the King of Great Britain and the friendship of all his subjects and I desire you will remember and often repeat my words.[31]

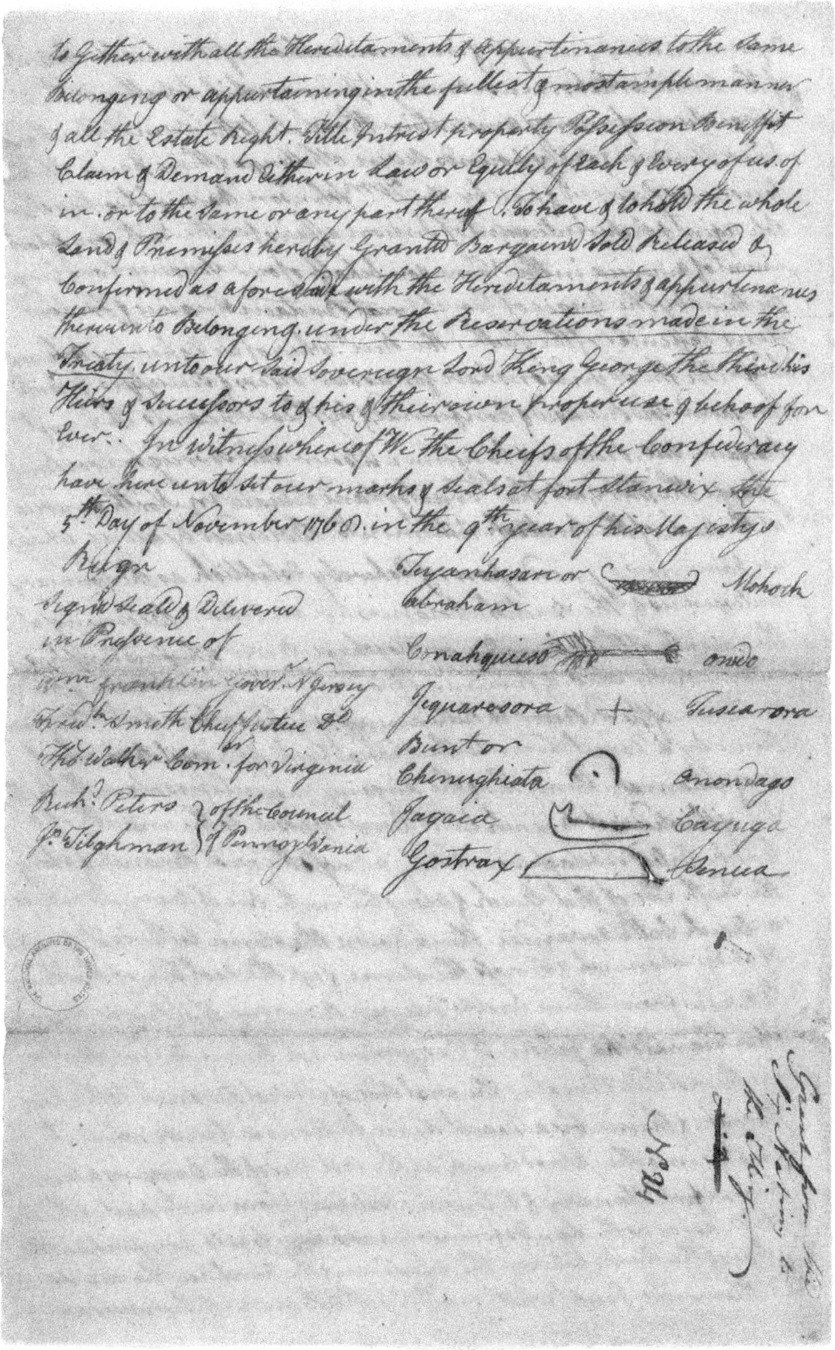
to Gether with all the Hereditaments & appurtenances to the same
belonging or appurtaining in the fullest & most ample manner
& all the Estate Right, Title Interest property Possession Benefit
Claim & Demand either in Law or Equity of each & every of us of
in. or to the same or any part thereof. To have & to hold the whole
Land & Premises hereby Granted Bargained Sold Released &
Confirmed as aforesaid with the Hereditaments & appurtenances
thereunto Belonging, under the Reservations made in the
Treaty, unto our said Sovereign Lord King George the Third his
Heirs & Successors to & his & their own proper use & behoof for
ever. In witness whereof We the Chiefs of the Confederacy
have here unto set our marks & seals at fort Stanwix the
5th Day of November 1768. in the 9th year of his Majesty's
Reign

Sign'd Seal'd & Delivered in Presence of
Wm Franklin Govr. N Jersey
Fred. Smith Chief Justice Do.
Thos Walker Comr. for Virginia
Richd. Peters } of the Council
Jas. Tilghman } of Pennsylvania

Tyanhasare or Abraham — Mohock
Conahquieso — Oneido
Sequaresora + Tuscarora
Bunt or Chenughiata — Onondago
Tagaia — Cayuga
Gostrax — Seneca

FIGURE 41. Signature page for the Treaty of Fort Stanwix, signed by the sachems for each of the Six Nations on November 5, 1768. Manuscript copy, National Archives.

The Haudenosaunee negotiations also put into play the Native country in the region north of the Ohio River that the speculators called Indiana, much to the discontent of the Myaamia, Lenape, Shawnee, Potawatomi, and Illinois. In light of the Treaty of Fort Stanwix, Pennsylvania merchants, calling themselves the "Suffering Traders," put in an application to William Johnson for compensation for deprecations made in 1763 by the Shawnee, Lenape, and Wyandot, "Dependents, and Tributaries of the Six United Nations." The traders claimed these three nations did "most unjustly and violently seize upon and appropriate to their own use the Merchandize and Effects of Several of your Memorialist." They assessed the damage sustained at "£85916,10-8."

The aggrieved merchants had earlier secured a deed from the Haudenosaunee to "Indiana, a tract of country on the river Ohio" for reparations and the right-of-way through the country. The tract began at Ah-wa-ga or Owego, an Onondaga and Cayuga town "on the east branch of Susquehanna River, thence down the east side of the river to Shamokin [or Fort Augusta], and running up the west branch of Susquehanna, on the south side thereof, and from thence to Kittaning [Kittanning], or Adigo on the Ohio, thence along and down the Ohio to the Cherokee River, and up the same to its head, on this side." They asserted that the Haudenosaunee, "the true and absolute owners and Proprietors of the Lands," granted to them

> all that Tract of Land, Beginning at the Southerly side of the mouth of the Little Kanawha Creek, where it empties itself into the River Ohio, and running from thence South East to the Laurell Hill, thence along the Laurell Hill, until its strikes the River Monongahela, thence down the stream of the said River Monongahela, according to the several courses thereof to the Southern Boundary Line of the Province of Pennsylvania, thence Westerly along the Course of the said Province Boundary Line as far as the same shall extend, and from thence, by the same course to the River Ohio—Thence down the said River Ohio according to the several courses thereof to the place of Beginning.[32]

The Commissioners for Collecting Evidence on behalf of the Commonwealth of Virginia, against the several Persons pretending to claim Lands within the Territory and Limits thereof under Deeds or Purchases from Indians examined George Morgan, agent for the Indiana Company. He said that he had given "an authenticated Copy of their Grant from the Six Nations" to John Harvie Esq., one of the commissioners appointed to take depositions in the fall of 1776. He also emphasized that Dr. Thomas Walker, one of the commissioners for Virginia at the Treaty of Fort Stanwix, was a "subscribing witness" to the signing of the Indiana grant.[33] Col. William Crawford said that he made his "first acquaintance" with Ohio country in 1758, then an officer in Virginia's service during the war. He noted that between then and 1765 "many settlements" were made on the public roads with the permission of "several commanding officers at Fort Pitt." He himself in the spring of that year made "some Improvements on the West Side of the Allegheny Mountains" and settled there permanently the following spring.[34]

Other settlers, perhaps as many as three hundred, followed suit in the succeeding years, some within the Indiana Company claims and others within Croghan's, none securing permission from the commanding officers at Fort Pitt. Colonel Dorsey issued several of these grants totaling upward of two thousand acres, which Thomas Lewis of Augusta County had surveyed, "none of which Entries were made before the years 1775." Crawford's settlement was never within the confines of the Indiana Company grant, which he reckoned the condition to be "nineteen-twentieth very bad." Crawford said that Croghan's grants are "thickly settled," but "few settlements" were made in the Indiana grants, "except on the Monongahela River and Middle Island Creek." Virginia had commissioned only "three surveys by Warrants or Orders by the Council of Virginia with Col. Croghan's Grants, but a number were made by virtue of Warrants from the Government of Pennsylvania." Settling illegally westward of the Alleghany Mountains, "people continued to emigrate to this Country very fast."[35]

In 1756 Maj. Edward Ward, who then commanded the First Pennsylvania Regiment under the command of Col. John Armstrong, prosecuted an attack and destroyed the Lenape town of Kittanning on the southeast shore of the Allegheny River, killing a "small number." The remainder abandoned the region and "never after took possession by renewing their settlements," but rather "they removed further to the Westward."[36] Nevertheless, the English did not take possession, because "it was judged expedient, by the Commanding officer, to retreat in a few Hours."[37] Thomas Girty was captured by a party principally of Lenape and was confined at Kittanning "till it was destroyed by the English." He also remembered that the Lenape resettled on the other side of the river and never returned. The Lenape moved their town across the Allegheny River and also "never returned," said Girty. He was informed that "it is not Customary for Indians to Resettle a Town, after being Destroyed by an Enemy, or Deserted on any other Occasion."[38] Indeed, the Treaty of Fort Stanwix put the nations of Ohio—the Shawnee, Lenape, Seneca-Cayuga, and Myaamia—on a collision course with not only expanding settler colonialism but also the nations from the west: the Odawa, Wyandot, and Chippewa. Provoked by surveyors, speculators, and squatters, these nations began to confederate. In a bid toward nativism, the Shawnee began forming alliances with the Ohio nations in a bid that historian Michael Witgen calls "the first explicitly 'pan-tribal' Native social movement," perhaps influenced by veterans of Pontiac's War who had migrated east. Oddly, they even sent a war belt to Onondaga, seeking an alliance with the Haudenosaunee, who had sold them out in the first place, which was promptly rejected.[39]

At the Treaty of Fort Stanwix in 1768, the Haudenosaunee sold "all the lands lying between the mountains and the Ohio, as low down as the mouth of the Cherokee River." Croghan said he had never heard anyone challenge the proprietary rights of the Haudenosaunee "until a few years ago, when a Deputation of the Six Nations going to the Cherokee Country, informed him that the Cherokee has Set up a claim to it, and said that they the Six Nations had no right to sell it, and that they were then going to Cherokee Country in order to settle the matter." He learned on their return, some going to Pittsburg and others to New York, that "the Cherokee acknowledged in Public Council the right of the Six Nations to the aforesaid County to have been good."[40]

On behalf of Virginia, Superintendent Stuart began to treat with the Ani'-Yun-wiya on May 13, 1769, to determine the boundary line running from the western bounds of North Carolina westerly through the Holsteins River "Straight to the Confluence" of the Kanawha and the Ohio Rivers. On October 18, 1770, the Ani'-Yun-wiya, for an unspecified "Valuable Consideration in various Sorts of Goods," ceded to Virginia their country west of "the Cherokee Hunting grounds," and six miles east and north of Long Island to the Holstein River and from there "in a Straight Course to the Confluence" of the Great Kanawha and Ohio Rivers.[41]

The treaty also put into jeopardy the Native land south of the Ohio country, which the Ani'-Yun-wiya contested, coveted by both the Loyal and Greenbrier Companies. The land companies' ravenous desire for the headwaters of the Cinch River and the mouth of the Cherokee [Tennessee] even put Kentucky in jeopardy of land speculation. Rather than finding agreement and quelling the tension between the Native occupants and Virginia settlers, the Treaty of Fort Stanwix confounded Indigenous expectations and excited settler avarice, escalating tension in the borderlands. Forcing an additional conference, Virginia and the Ani'-Yun-wiya continued negotiations at Lochaber, South Carolina, in October 1770. In the treaty agreement, the Ani'-Yun-wiya ceded additional territory westward to the Kentucky River and the Holston River, finally terminating the Haudenosaunee claims to the land but not those of the Shawnee, who continued to press their sovereignty.[42]

The opening of Native country following the treaties of Hard Labor and Fort Stanwix revived the land bounty movement. Dinwiddie's proclamation of February 19, 1754, had promised land bounties to the officers of the Virginia regiment. The Proclamation of 1763 effectively postponed their promised land. Prompted by the opening of Ohio, George Washington convened with his former officers in Fredericksburg in August 1770. He not only advertised their land bounty claims in the *Virginia Gazette* but also solicited support for them from Governor Norborne Berkeley, baron de Botetourt, and the council. The council moved to honor the officers who had served prior to the Battle at Great Meadows, allocating two hundred thousand acres on the Monongahela to the Great Kanawha.[43] In the fall of 1770, Washington began to scout the land along the Ohio and Kanawha Rivers. He triangulated out the location in Indigenous terms such as Wheeling (Wee-lunk) and Mingo Town. He was keen to give the Native place-names, sometimes explaining their provenance. He learned that Cut Creek referenced a people cut off and deported by the Haudenosaunee and Pipe Creek alluded to the stones Native people found there and used for making pipes. He pinpointed potentially productive soil, noting the "appearance of good land, . . . a bottom of exceedingly rich land," and "some bottoms of very good land." He even noted the absence of waterways strong enough to generate "mill seats."[44]

Because the Proclamation of 1763 was reputed to restrain access across the Alleghenies, President William Nelson, acting as governor, said to the king's minister that he would not oppose the crown's prerogative. "However, his successor, Governor Dunmore, not only coveted these western lands but also challenged Pennsylvania's access to them. He granted "his friend" Dr. John Connolly four thousand acres in Fincastle at the Falls of Ohio. Under this guise in 1772, Connolly became both zealous advocate and point man willing to pursue Dunmore's ambition in Native country with alacrity. Even though during the French and Indian War he served as a surgeon's mate under British command, his grant was reputedly at the time "said to be Irregularly Issued."[45] Curiously, in September 1772, Connolly promoted Ohio to George Washington: "It is astonishing to me that notwithstanding your Colony of Virginia is honored with a number of spirited and enterprising Gentlemen, *you* have so long neglected an Acquaintance with the true value of this Western Country" (emphasis added). Suggesting that enslaved people with "proper Managers" could "advantageously" cultivate tobacco and render you a "very great emolument, . . . I am at this present acquainted with large Bodies of Land unappropriated, and excellently adapted to that purpose, open to a Market by a very good, at least tolerable Navigation for Boats of any Burden."[46] Perhaps after learning Washington's experience with Ohio, Connolly in June 1773 asked him "to acquaint me what expectation I might have in procuring a Right to two thousand Acres of Land from the Government of Virginia, by Virtue of his Majesty's Proclamation, being entitled thereto as a Staff-Officer."[47] "Notwithstanding the Proclamation so late as

December 1773," Dunmore and the council, "by direction from the Crown, Issued Patents for lands in that Countrey, to the Officers and Soldiers of the last War, According to the Kings."[48]

Acting on "some disagreeable intelligence" that settlers "upon the Ohio, near Wheeling and Yellow Creek" had committed "deprecations . . . upon several Indian parties" downriver from Fort Pitt, Arthur St. Clair, assistant to Gov. John Penn of Pennsylvania for border relations, reached out to the applicable chiefs. He directed his message to "King Custologa [Custaloga], Captains White Eyes, Pipe, and such other Chiefs as were most contiguous to this place." He asked them for their "immediate attendance at this place" to discuss "some things of importance to communicate to you, which intimately concerns the welfare of us both."[49] On May 6, 1774, he also sent this message by Koquethagechton (aka Captain George White Eyes), a Lenape chief, to give to the Shawnee and Lenape chiefs. Koquethagechton, who had promised to do his utmost to mend the relations, returned three weeks later with ten white people who had been held hostage by the Lenape. The Lenape indicated to Koquethagechton that "they are not inclined for war" and would encourage the Shawnee "to preserve the lives of the traders" in their custody. The Shawnee chief Hardman sent a response to Croghan's talk by Koquethagechton. He said that the Shawnee were all warriors and "will not listen to us until they have satisfaction of us for what injuries they have received from the Virginians."[50]

Koquethagechton also reported that the family of Logan, a Seneca-Cayuga chief, had been murdered in the attack near Yellow Creek. Logan had since "raised a party to cut down the Shawanese Town traders at the Canoe Bottom, on Hockhocking Creek, where they were pressing their peltry." Were these the same traders in Shawnee custody, for whose protection Koquethagechton had pleaded? "We hope they are still alive," prayed Devereux Smith, who operated outpost in Native county, "and if it be so they have a chance to come in, if the outrageous behaviour of the Virginians do not prevent them." Smith presumed that Logan was responsible for an assault on a family farm that took place at Muddy Creek where it drains into the Monongahela River. Around May 20 Smith assigned blame to a party of both Shawnee and Seneca-Cayuga for a murder near Newcomer's Town and another at Wheeling.[51]

Understandably, the settlers on the Cinch River were frightened. Capt. Daniel Smith found that they were "much more fearful of the Indians than I expected to find them. The late Reports alarm'd them so much that 4 families in my neighborhood mov'd over to Holston before I heard of their Setting off, they went in Such haste that they left all their Stock and greatest part of their Household Furniture." When they returned to retrieve some of their belongings after hearing that it was safe to do so, Smith persuaded them to remain.[52] "The Virginians in this part of the country seem determined to make war with the Indians at any rate. Connolly has embodied upwards of one hundred men and will have this fort in good order in a short time. He is gathering in all the provisions he can possibly get from the country, which, he says, will be paid for by the Government of Virginia."[53]

On May 25, 1774, the Haudenosaunee and the Lenape responded to the condolence speeches presented to them by Captain Koquethagechton. They expressed their satisfaction with the speed undertaken by the white people in dealing with "the late disturbances which have happened between our young men." The Haudenosaunee were now ready to renew their "ancient friendship" and return to peace. They had spoken to their grandchildren the Shawnee and counseled them to restrain their young people. Since the white people have agreed to open the road in the trade negotiations "our young men may be permitted to continue their trade as usual. Those white people who are in our towns to the number of eleven, you will see in a few days."

The Shawnee speaker next responded to the condolence talks sent to them. Unlike the Haudenosaunee and the Lenape, they accused Dr. Connolly; George Croghan, the deputy Indian agent for the Crown; and his assistant Alexander McKee, son of Thomas, of lying to them. Now they held out hope that what they would hear "will be more confined to truth than what we usually hear from the white people. It is you who are frequently passing up and down the Ohio and making settlements upon it and as you have informed us that your wise people have met together to consult upon this matter, we desire you to be strong and consider it well." "Yet even as you ask us to believe you, we see your warriors have collected together at sundry places upon this river, . . . building forts. . . . Our people at the Lower Towns have no Chiefs among them, but are all warriors, and are also preparing themselves to be in readiness, that they may be better able to hear what you have to say. . . . We have reason to expect that ours will take the same advice when we require it, that is, when we have heard from the Governour of Virginia."[54]

Dunmore responded by calling out the militias not to curb settler behavior but to check marauders, supposed to be the Lenape and the Shawnee, on the borders of the settlements of Augusta, Botetourt, and Fincastle. They were to attack the Native towns and either "drive off or extirpate" them. He left Williamsburg on July 10 to host a conference with the Ohio nations to negotiate the terms of peace.[55] By August 25 reports of settler discontent in the backcountry so exasperated Dunmore that he pressed Colonel Preston and Colonel Lewis each to raise one thousand troops.[56] They would engage the "united tribes" of Shawnee, Lenape, Seneca-Cayuga, Ojibwe, and "many

FIGURE 42. Felix Renick, *A Map of the Ancient Indian Towns on the Pickaway Plain Illustrating a Sketch of the Country*, 1846. Courtesy of Osher Map Library.

other Nations, in number not less than eight hundred, and by many thought to be a thousand," approximately three quarters of a mile from their camp. These efforts ultimately resulted in the Battle at Point Pleasant, located at the mouth of the Great Kanawha, on October 10. Witnesses gave details of the ferocity of the fighting. The warfare lasted from dawn to noon and left three colonels dead.[57]

A participant writing from Staunton after the battle said, "They soon made our men retreat about one quarter of a mile, when a reinforcement coming up, they continued fighting till noon, and were never above twenty yards apart, often within six, and sometimes close together tomahawking one another. The Indians then began to fall back, but continued fighting at a distance till night came on and parted them." He estimated the Virginia casualties "upwards of fifty men killed, and ninety wounded." He could not determine the Native casualties because they were "continually carrying them off and throwing them into the River [to avoid scalping]; but from the tracks of blood, the number must have been great." The Virginians counted among their spoils "upwards of twenty scalps, eighty blankets, about forty guns, and a great many tomahawks."[58]

CHAPTER 23

The Bloody Ground Would Be Dark, and Difficult to Settle It

Patrick Henry remembered that early in 1774 William Byrd III said to him that the Ani'-Yun-wiya had offered him a tract of land some years earlier. After their conversation on the topic together with John Page, they agreed to send William Kennedy to the Ani'-Yun-wiya nation to see whether they would part with "some of their Land, on the Waters [of] their own Rivers in Virginia, to Convey the same to them and not for the State." Col. William Christian also would be "a partner if the scheme succeeded." Christian, who had three warrants from Lord Dunmore for three thousand acres "located near the Falls of Ohio and on the Salt River in the County of Kentucky," remembered that in 1774 he had joined with Byrd, Page, and Henry, all of Virginia, in approaching the Ani'-Yun-wiya about these lands on the Holston and Clinch Rivers and in Powell's Valley. With this scheme in mind, they appointed Kennedy to go to the Ani'-Yun-wiya nation and "sound the temper for a meeting and treaty for that purpose." On his return Kennedy said to Byrd that "some of the chiefs" were willing to treat.[1]

Virginia focused intently on Kentucky. Dr. Thomas Walker and Gen. Andrew Lewis, representing both their land companies' and the Dominion's interests, had negotiated with the Haudenosaunee at Fort Stanwix for land on the north side of Kentucky. Following up this acquisition, Virginia commissioned Col. John Donelson to survey the bounds of the agreement. After running the line from "the Long Island, on Holstein, to the mouth of the great Kanawha," he realized that the Haudenosaunee still laid claim to an "extensive tract of excellent country" on the north side of the Kentucky River, which the settlers of the Clinch and Holstein valleys coveted. After haggling with the Haudenosaunee, Donelson agreed to a purchase price of "five hundred pounds, specie" and extended his boundary "up the Ohio, to the mouth of Great Kanawha." However, Virginia refused to confirm the deal.[2]

Before they could "treat on the subject," the "Troubles with Great Britain" had caused Henry to enter the "patriotic" continental service. After his decision he disclaimed any interest in Native country for three reasons: "the enormous extent . . . of the bounds" of the country involved, the "disputes [which] had arisen on the Subject of these purchases," and "the sovereignty and right to Disposal . . . would be claimed by the American States."[3]

Nonetheless, Judge Richard Henderson's activity "had drawn the attention" of Virginia back to Kentucky. Colonel Henderson of North Carolina had negotiated with the Ani'-Yun-wiya at Watauga in March 1775 the purchase of the land on the south side of the Kentucky River for "six thousand pounds, specie." Henderson's purchase "alarmed" Virginia. The Dominion disputed the acquisition, agreed to the terms of Donelson's contract, and "rewarded him with a tract of land, at the mouth of Green River, to the amount of two hundred thousand acres; and the state of North Carolina gave him the like quantity in Powel's Valley."[4]

To smooth out the relations with Virginia, shortly after Henderson and Company's "supposed purchase" of Ani'-Yun-wiya land in March 1775, Judge Henderson reached out with "a great number of messages" offering a "Distant and Plain Hint" that Henry should partner with them. Henry "uniformly refused and plainly declared his Strongest Disapprobation of their whole proceedings, giving as a Reason, that the People of Virginia had a right to the back Country derived from their Charter and the Blood and Treasure they expended on that account."[5] Henry's rationale in refusing Henderson's proposal likely led him, now as governor of the Commonwealth, to launch the "Commissioners for Collecting Evidence on behalf of the Commonwealth of Virginia, against the several Persons pretending to claim Lands within the Territory and Limits thereof under Deeds or Purchases from Indians." From these depositions, memorials, and letters collected by the commissioners, which did not include any Native testimony, it is possible to ferret out what happened at the Sycamore Shoals of the Watauga River in March 1775.

Judge Henderson had advertised on Christmas Day 1774 his proposal for settling lands "to be purchased . . . on the Branches of the Mississippi River from the Ani'-Yun-wiya." His plan included bounties for security, incentives for settlement, and inducements for manufacturers. His first order of business planned the recruitment of a fifty-man militia under officers to protect the settlement from Native attack, offering each soldier a bounty of 500 acres and three pounds sterling for their service until November 1. Then he offered every settler who plants a crop of corn and professes to be "ready with their Lives and Fortunes to defend, protect and support each other in their mutual interests and advantages against the Savages," the opportunity for patenting 500 acres for himself and 250 acres for each tithable taxable member of the household for the cost of 20 shillings sterling per hundred acres. To sweeten the deal, he offered a prize of 500 acres to the person either raising the "greatest" numbers of ears of corn or bringing the "greatest" flock of sheep. Finally, he offered grants of land to artificers who open an ironworks, a saltworks, sawmill, or a "Great Mill." Demonstrating what he valued most in founding a settlement, he offered the foundry owner 5,000 acres and the salt manufacturer 1,000 acres, or twice as many as the other industries. All of the land grants were to be issued without encumbrances except an annual quitrent of two shillings sterling per one hundred acres.[6]

By February 22, 1775, Henderson said he had "the greatest reason to believe" that his company would soon acquire "a large Tract of Country lying on the Kentucky, Cumberland and other waters of the Ohio and Tenisee Rivers." Referencing his proposal for settling the land, he discouraged squatters from rushing into the territory, for a "promiscuous and diffused settlement would only endanger their lives." Rather, "to prevent unthinking and inconsiderate persons from attempting to settle the said Lands in any diffused or scattered manner," he said that the "first adventurers" should settle in a town during the spring, select the land they wish to buy during the year, and for those who chose to quitclaim their town properties, then the appraised value would be paid by the buyers.[7] Henderson had good reason to be concerned about scattered settlements. If settlers could survive Native attacks, squatters could homestead the country without going through his company by evoking the "ancient cultivation law."[8]

William Farrar was one of the vendors at the Sycamore Shoals conference on the Watauga River. He supplied beef for the support of about one thousand Ani'-Yun-wiya in attendance during the March 1775 conference. Chiefs Oconostota, Oukanaekah, and "all the other Chiefs" convened the council at the invitation of Richard Henderson of the Transylvania Company. Henderson expended at "great expense . . . a great Quantity of Beeves, flour, Corn, Rum and other necessarys to a very great amount." He counted "about thousand in all counting big and little; and about one half of them were men." He understood that there was not "anymore . . . than one principal man behind called Judges Friend [Usteneka], who . . . had sent word that the other Chiefs agreed to, he would abide by."[9] Charles Robertson, a trustee for Transylvania Company, whose "tract of land accounted to be within the Chartered Boundary of the Commonwealth of Virginia," said he "heard every Public Talk, that was delivered by the Parties." He believed the negotiations were "held fairly and openly" and that both Henderson and the Native chiefs had "present the white men and Indian Half Breeds who understood both Languages, as a check upon the Chief Interpreter, lest he should mistranslate, or leave out, through Forgetfulness any Part of what either Party should speak."[10]

On day one, Tsiyu Gansi-ni [Dragging Canoe], son of Oukanaekah and his favorite wife, Nionne Ollie (Tame Doe), proposed to sell to Henderson the land above Kentucky upon the northeast side or above the New River.[11] Henderson refused the offer, because "the state of Virginia had already

FIGURE 43. Lunette depicting the Treaty of Sycamore Shoals painted by Thomas Gilbert White. Creative Commons.

bought it and it was not that land he wished to purchase, [but the land] on the southside of Kentucky."[12] Rather, he wanted the land from the "mouth of the Kentucky River some distance down the Ohio."[13]

Appearing unwilling to sell that land, Ani'-Yun-wiya suggested that Henderson "return home and they would look to [the Virginians for] the price of land, which they sold them above Kantuckey. They also said to Henderson that the "Country which he wanted was of great service to them as hunting Ground and they looked upon their Cattle or game in it, to be as beneficial as Tame Cattle to the white People."[14] Instead, the Ani'-Yun-wiya offered up "Some Lands which they said Col. Donelson had agreed to give them for 500 pounds."

Henderson said that it was "not worth his while to talk about buying that only." He offered to purchase "lands lying from the Mouth of the Great Kanawha, down the Ohio to the Mouth of Tenesse." He then asked "if it was their land." After "some private, or low talk among themselves and afterwards," they said yes, "the lands were theirs." If theirs, Henderson said, then "he had goods there to give them for it."[15] He had "a House full of Goods for them and be at ye greater Expense for Beaves and rum to entertain them upon."

Tsiyu Gansi-ni said that "there was bad People both of his Nation and the Whites—that there was a dark cloud over that Country—He could not vouch that his own Countrymen would not hurt him, but was afraid the Northern Indians would—that it was good to have the path clean and clear." "Stamping his feet on the ground," Tsiyu Gansi-ni said, "We will give you from this place, pointing towards Kentucky."[16]

Henderson then asked what "about the land between them and his?" He "had bought the land on Kentucky from them, yet [had no] path to it."[17] Tsiyu Gansi-ni said that "he had all of the country from there to the Kentucky purchase, for a path."[18] Henderson said that he "did not want to walk upon their Land, to his Country—that he had got more goods and ammunition—that he wanted a path to his Country."[19] Houghton said that "the manner of the Indians pointing, he understood they gave up the Path, Col. Henderson had asked for."[20]

Tsiyu Gansi-ni "stamped on the ground, as he was speaking of the Nation,—Lands Northward of the Holston and on this side of Cumberland Mountain." He said that "it was the bloody Ground, and would be dark, and difficult to settle it."[21] Although Tsiyu Gansi-ni's statement is often interpreted as a prophetic curse, in truth the land was called "the Low, Dark, and Bloody Lands" around the time of his birth. He was born in the vicinity of the Red and Cumberland Rivers about 1731, the year of the battle at the site called the "dark and bloody lands." The site was likely memorialized as sacred ground because the Haudenosaunee defeated and killed about twelve hundred Cotawpes and Ani'-Yun-wiya there.[22] John Filson, who first came to the region in 1767, wrote that the Ani'-Yun-wiya name Ka-ten-ta-teh, for what became Kentucky meant the "Dark and Bloody Ground, and sometimes the Middle Ground. . . . This region was formerly claimed by various tribes of Indians; whose title, if they had any, originated in such a manner, as to render it doubtful which ought to possess it: Hence this fertile spot became an object of contention, a theatre of war, from which it was properly denominated the Bloody-Grounds."[23]

The Ani'-Yun-wiya again offered to sell him the land on the north side of the Kentucky River, but Henderson again refused: "He would not have that land, as it was already claimed by Virginians, and if he could not get the lands he asked for he would keep his Goods." Hearing this, Tsiyu Gansi-ni' "went out displeased," because "the white people wanted too much of their Hunting Grounds."[24] He "got angry and withdrew himself from the Conference." The other chiefs followed his lead, and the conference broke up for the day. One of the attendants told John Williams, one of Henderson's partners, that Tsiyu Gansi-ni's "passion" was not a dealbreaker, for "some of the headmen might still be got to sign the Deed privately."

John Reid, representing Virginia, did not recall "anything of consequence" discussed over the next couple of days of haggling.[25] Henderson again asked for his initial land proposal. The chiefs appeared to be "inclined to let . . . Henderson have some of the land" but felt the goods offered insufficient and asked that he give them consideration later. Henderson said that "he would give them the Keys to the House in which they lay, and he could promise them no more." The Ani'-Yun-wiya agreed to sell him "the land as far as the Cumberland River." Henderson countered that he wanted the Cumberland and the "Waters of the Cumberland River." The Ani'-Yun-wiya agreed with a caveat: these "were their Hunting Grounds, and to their children who were then growing up might have reason to complain, if they sold that land." James Robinson, a representative of the Transylvania Company, said this was a "frequently" used refrain from the time they began entertaining the sale of land below the Kentucky River. The other caveat attributed by others solely to Tsiyu Gansi-ni was the veiled threat: "it was a Bloody Country, and if he went to it, they would not hold him by the hand any longer, and he must do it as his own Risque, and must not blame them if anything happened to him."[26]

When the Ani'-Yun-wiya appeared in compliance with the proposals, Henderson said, "there was Land between them and his Country—He did not love to walk upon their land. That he had more Goods, Guns, and Ammunition, which they had not yet seen." Henderson also said, "if they did not choose to take them, they would still be friends." The Ani'-Yun-wiya "appeared to be satisfied."[27] On day four "a deed was produced, and read, and Interpreted Sentence by Sentence to the Indians."[28]

The Ani'-Yun-wiya balked when Henderson produced "eight or nine" deeds, saying there were that many partners and each should have a deed "lest they be destroyed by fire or water." They' relaxed when he presented the first deed to Oconostota. Still Henderson refused to read aloud the boundaries until after the deeds were signed, which Reid thought "not generous to get a people to sign a Deed, who did not know what was in it."[29] When Oconostota and Oukanaekah, the Raven Warrior, were about to sign, John Vann [aka Joseph Vann], the interpreter, "took them by the hand and stop'd them from signing . . . and told them to take care of what they were about." If they signed the deed, understand they were "to clear him and not blame him afterwards for it."

Henderson addressed the problem of John Vann the interpreter. "More men" than Vann understood the Ani'-Yun-wiya language "whom he understood were to take notice, that either party said was fairly translated."[30] Charles Robertson, "acting as a Trustee," also noted that Henderson presented "eight or nine" deeds to the Ani'-Yun-wiya, "who were told that the Reason of their being so many, was that there was so many different Partners in the Company, and each must have one for fear one should be destroyed and that everyone might know where his land was." Only one of them was read to the Ani'-Yun-wiya, for they allegedly "were all alike word for word," and the Ani'-Yun-wiya "said they did not want them read." Robertson did not know how many Native signatories signed the deeds, but he "understood it was done by Consent of the whole, as he did not hear any Particular one make an objection."[31] Apparently he was unaware, as Reid also noted, that the young warriors "appeared to be much dissatisfied upon the Division of the Goods and set off the same night the Deeds should have been signed." One of them said he had "received only one shirt for his part, who said he had sold the land, and he could have killed more deer in one day then would have bought such a shirt."[32]

The next evening after the signing of the deeds, Reid and Richard Pearis visited the Native camps. "They found the Chiefs almost all drunk." After Pearis told Oconostota's wife "that the Chiefs had given a Deed for the Lands upon this River, she appeared to be very Uneasy and went away . . . to acquaint some of the Chiefs with it." She apparently got their attention, for the next morning Reid and Pearis found several sachems at Oconostota's tent "marking out the sundry Water Courses, which he took to be the Holstein River" and its tributaries. Pearis asked them if they had sold off the water courses to Henderson, and they replied that "they had not, nor would they." Later that day the Ani'-Yun-wiya returned to the site where the conference was held "to inform Henderson that they had not sold the Lands upon these waters and had only allowed him a path through them to pass to Kentucky." Henderson then proposed that the Ani'-Yun-wiya "allow him a small distance on each side of the path for hunting, to support the people on their way to and from Kentucky." Reid did not know if the Ani'-Yun-wiya assented to the right-of way for hunting proposition.[33]

If the Ani'-Yun-wiya did in the end agree to sell to Henderson and company the land that they wanted, the deponents were ambiguous about the proceedings. Wilson believed that the negotiations were conducted in good order; the chiefs were sober in their deliberations and "appeared to be satisfied with the Goods given Them for the Land."[34] Lowry did not know the boundaries. Neither did he recall any deed given by the Ani'-Yun-wiya for it, nor any "valuable consideration" exchanged for the path; the goods were for the Kentucky purchase, but he did not hear mention of an eastern boundary to the Kentucky purchase.[35] Samuel Wilson, who was "present at all the public conferences," said that he did not understand the contention that the land was "claimed by other nations," likely made in reference to Tsiyu Gansi-ni's statement, because the Ani'-Yun-wiya "sold them as the proprietors."[36]

Nevertheless, Charles Robertson, "acting as a Trustee," was displeased because Tsiyu Gansi-ni's actions and words nullified the Watauga tract, which he planned to purchase "in conjunction with said Henderson."[37] He understood that this nullification meant that "the lands in Carter's Valley which border on Clinch Mountain, quite to the Ohio, [were] then given up." If he were to make the purchase then he had to go through Henderson, which was why he was displeased. He was not privy to any deeds "being signed on these last-mentioned lands," though he learned later that Henderson did make a deed for "all the Land from Watauga quite to the Ohio."[38] Robertson said he never heard read "any other bounds to the Indians than what was in the deed. . . . [He] heard there had been some claim to this Country by the Northward Indians, but these Indians said it was their Land and what they would so sell it."[39] He also witnessed Oconostota and Oukanaekah both sign a deed over to Henderson "certain lands ling upon the South Side of the Kentucky, but he does not know the boundary lines."[40] Although did not recall the "whole of the Boundary," Thomas Houghton believed the negotiations Henderson made were in good faith and understood by the Ani'-Yun-wiya. He believed that "it joined the Ohio, and in them was mentioned something about the Head Springs of Kentucky, and . . . of Cumberland, and that 'tis his opinion it was to keep the dividing Ridge between Cumberland and Tennessee."[41]

William Christian, self-proclaimed "evangelist of Almighty God," said on June 3, 1777, that he had three warrants from Lord Dunmore for three thousand acres "located near the Falls of Ohio and on the Salt River in the County of Kentucky as appears by the Platts." His understanding was that with the Donelson's line, Virginia "in effect ceded the land lying below the line upon the waters of the Clinch and Holston and Powell's Valley to the Cherokee."[42] Robinson said he thought the boundaries delimited in the deed "were from the mouth of the Kentucky River, up to the same Donelson's Line, thence along the s^dline to perhaps Cumberland Mountain, thence to the South Branch of the Cumberland River, including Cumberland and the waters of Cumberland to the Ohio, thence to the Ohio to the Beginning."[43]

Later that winter Robinson saw Vann, who told him that Henderson and Company "claimed more land than the Indians had given a Deed for." Vann said the company "claimed the land in Tenese, to within ten miles of the Ani'-Yun-wiya towns." Robinson said he had not heard directly from the Ani'-Yun-wiya "whether they were satisfied or dissatisfied with the settlement." Isaac Thomas had told him that the Ani'-Yun-wiya "deny'd altogether" selling John Carter "any lands . . . below the north Fork of the Holstein." He also heard Oconostota deny selling land, which he witnessed sold in the deed. He said that Oukanaekah told him they added "the land where they then stood" to the Kentucky purchase in exchange for a path, but he could "not recollect . . . the extent of country on both sides of the path."[44] The Ani'-Yun-wiya were considerably indebted to John Carter. Carter sought a deed in lieu of payment owed to him for goods already disbursed. Henderson offered to buy out Carter's "spoiled books" for "goods to the value of Two Thousand weight of leather" in exchange for the path to the Kentucky purchase, to which the Ani'-Yun-wiya agreed.[45] Robertson not only saw the storehouse goods and the "last mentioned" goods, guns, and ammunition; he also saw others delivered and divided and saw papers destroyed, said to be "Carter's Book of Accounts against the Indians," which Carter said was for more than six hundred pounds.[46]

Although Isaac Shelby said he had "made several entries of land" from Henderson's land office, he did not believe that he had any in the disputed territory between the Commonwealth of Virginia and Henderson. He was present at the treaty meeting held at Watauga in March 1775. He heard the deeds read to the Ani'-Yun-wiya and believed they understood the terms of agreement from the interpreters. He also had heard at Great Island in 1777, on the Holton River, which the Ani'-Yun-wiya held sacred, either Oconostota or Chief Tassel of the Overhill Ani'-Yun-wiya say that since they had signed the deed with Henderson, "he was afraid to sign one, and that Mr. Henderson, ever since he had signed the Paper, deprived him of the privilege of catching even crawfish on the land."[47]

CHAPTER 24

The Virginians Have Taken Away All Their Lands

John Stuart and William Bartram met in Charleston during a period of intense partisan pressure. After hearing Bartram's plans to visit Native country, Superintendent Stuart proposed that he attend the congress of nations in Ani'-Yun-wiya country, where delegates from the Ani'-Yun-wiya, Muscogee, and "other nations" would convene later in the spring. He promised him "friendship and protection" from the Ani'-Yun-wiya during his passage. By the end of April, they had both left Charleston, Bartram directly through South Carolina to Ani'-Yun-wiya country and Stuart in a roundabout through Florida. Bartram first stopped to consult with Stuart's aide Alexander Cameron at his Lochaber Plantation, where the treaty of 1770 had set the boundary line between the Ani'-Yun-wiya, North Carolina, and Virginia. As deputy commissary for Indian Affairs for the Ani'-Yun-wiya nation, Cameron was uniquely qualified to advise Bartram about his expedition. On May 15, 1776, after five days waiting out "uncommonly wet, almost daily showers of rain and frequently attended with tremendous thunder," Bartram set out on his expedition.[1]

After traveling forty-five miles, Bartram arrived at Sinica [also called Isunigu, Seneca, Esseneca] on the east bank of the Keowee River, "a new town rebuilt" after the Ani'-Yun-wiya defeat in the Anglo–Cherokee War of 1761. Although the council house and most of the five hundred residents were located on the west bank, "the chief's house, with those of the traders, and some Indian dwellings are seated on the ascent of the heights on the opposite shore." Sinica could muster up one hundred warriors. After a sixteen-mile jaunt through the high forest, he next stopped at Prince George Keowee. He found Keowee not only a "most charming" vale but also "almost impregnable," because it was blessed with "adjacent heights [that] are naturally so formed and disposed."[2] He learned from "some old traders" that the vale was once densely peopled by the Ani'-Yun-wiya, memorialized by several Native mounds.[3] Here Bartram meditated. He lamented feeling "abandoned" and "dejected," for he was far away from home and at a great distance from the white settlements.

> It is true, here were some of my own colour, yet they were strangers, and though friendly and hospitable, their manners and customs of living so

different from what I had been accustomed to, administered but little
to my consolation: some hundred miles yet to travel, the savage vindictive inhabitants lately ill-treated by the frontier Virginians, blood being
spilt between them and the injury not yet wiped away by formal treaty;
the Cherokee extremely jealous of white people travelling about their
mountains, especially if they should be seen peeping in amongst the
rocks or digging up their earth.[4]

After following a trading path, Bartram's uneasiness at Keowee portended his arrival at an Ani'-Yun-wiya burial grounds,

> being covered with stones or fragments of rocks, and very large, smooth
> pebbles of various shapes and sizes, some of ten- or fifteen-pounds
> weight: I observed on each side of the road many vast heaps of these
> stones. . . . At this place was fought a bloody and decisive battle be-
> tween the Indians and the Carolinians, under the conduct of general
> Middleton, when a great number of Ani'-Yun-wiya warriors were slain,
> which shook their power, terrified and humbled them, insomuch that
> they deserted most of their settlements in the low countries, and be-
> took themselves to the mountains as less accessible to the regular forces
> of the white people.[5]

After leaving the burial grounds, Bartram set off for Cowee, where he
stayed at the house of the "chief trader" Mr. Galahan for a couple of days
exploring the environs of this branch of the lower Tennessee River. Unable
to secure a guide for the Overhill towns, Bartram set off on his own "against
the advice of the traders; the Overhill Indians being in an ill humour with
the whites, in consequence of some late skirmishes between them and the
frontier Virginians, most of the Overhill traders having left the nation."[6]
After crossing a "large branch" of the Tennessee River, Bartram observed
an Ani'-Yun-wiya band on horseback moving quickly downhill toward them.
He recognized the leader, whom he had seen at the Augusta conference in
1763: Oukanaekah, "a man of remarkable small stature, slender, and deli-
cate frame." Oukanaekah greeted them and introduced himself. After they
exchanged pleasantries, Oukanaekah recognized "him to the tribe of white
men, of Pennsylvania, who esteem themselves brothers and friends to the red
men, but particularly so to the Cherokee." Oukanaekah asked about John
Stuart. Bartram was quick to say he had seen him in Charleston and that he
was well. Stuart had endorsed his expedition and provided him with letters
of reference to the Ani'-Yun-wiya for their friendship and protection. After
assuring Bartram of his security, Oukanaekah left him and continued his

journey heading for Charleston. Although Bartram persisted in his journey heading toward the Overhill towns, he soon realized the terrain was such that he could not safely traverse it to Overhills in time to attend the congress as Stuart recommended, before a treaty was confirmed, which he anticipated would be "late in June."[7]

On his return he stopped again at Cowee, a town banking both sides of the Little Tennessee River with one hundred houses. He observed:

> The Cherokee construct their habitations on . . . but one oblong four square building, of one story high; the materials consisting of logs or trunks of trees, stripped of their bark, notched at their ends, fixed one upon another, and afterwards plaistered well, both inside and out, with clay well-tempered with dry grass, and the whole covered or roofed with the bark of the Chestnut tree or long broad shingles. This building is however partitioned transversely, forming three apartments, which communicate with each other by inside doors; each house or habitation has besides a little conical house, covered with dirt, which is called the winter or hot-house; this stands a few yards distance from the mansion-house, opposite the front door.

He also noted that their council house could hold up to one hundred people and rested on a foundation of an ancient mound.[8]

During his visit he and the "white traders" were treated to a "grand festival." He witnessed the rehearsal for "the ball-play dance," scheduled against another town the next day. The people assembled and listened to an elderly praise singer recount the past exploits of the athletes, urging them to victory. The musicians followed, "both vocal and instrumental," accompanying "a company of girls, hand in hand, dressed in clean white robes and ornamented with beads, bracelets and a profusion of gay ribbands." They sang and undulated for about a quarter of an hour before the whooping young men burst onto the scene, rackets in hand. "Well dressed, painted and ornamented with silver bracelets, gorgets, and wampum, neatly ornamented with moccasins and high waving plumes in their diadems," they "formed themselves in a semicircular rank also, in front of the girls, when these changed their order." He described their dance as "something singular and diverting in their step and motions, and I imagine not to be learned to exactness but with great attention and perseverance."[9]

Leaving Ani'-Yun-wiya country, Bartram prepared to journey to Muscogee country. On June 22 he left from Fort Charlotte, crossed into Georgia, and advanced on a "great trading path from Augusta to the Creek nation." He planned to rendezvous in Mobile with the leader of a "company of adventurers," venturing to West Florida through the vast territories of the Creeks.[10] Meanwhile, instead of going directly to Ani'-Yun-wiya country, Superintendent Stuart took a circuitous southwestern route. After arriving in West Florida with arms and ammunition for the Ani'-Yun-wiya and the Muscogee, Stuart learned that Tsiyu Gansi-ni was in Mobile. He was keen to meet him there, because he had had no contact with the Ani'-Yun-wiya for several months. Tsiyu Gansi-ni was just as inquisitive: What was the cause of the conflict within the colonies? Why could they no longer get their arms and ammunition from Georgia and South Carolina? Tsiyu Gansi-ni revealed that the Ani'-Yun-wiya were "under very great apprehensions and uneasiness" with the Virginia settlers' encroaching on their land. "He said that they were almost surrounded by the White People, that they had but a small spot of ground left for them to stand upon and that it seemed to be the Intention of the White People to destroy them from being a people."[11]

Stuart tried to explain the civil crisis confronting the colonies and to re-assure him that the distress it had caused was contrary to the Crown's Native policy. Although the trade had ceased, he had come with arms and ammu-nition, both for the hunt and for their security. "I told him that I was sorry for the Encroachments that were made on their Lands by the Virginians but that they were made contrary to the Kings Orders." Nevertheless, "I put him in mind that they themselves were to blame for making private Bar-gains for their Lands. . . . They had frequently been told not to suffer any person to settle nor even to hunt beyond the Boundary Line which was run by Mr. Cameron to divide them from the White People and to prevent any future Quarrels." Alluding to the Watauga settlement, Tsiyu Gansi-ni said that he had played no role in making those bargains. Making a generational statement, he said if "some of their Old Men who he said were too old to hunt and who by their Poverty had been induced to sell their Land," then he "had a great many young fellows that would support him and that were determined to have their Land."[12]

Over the next three weeks, Stuart tried to supply the Ani'-Yun-wiya with ammunition by going through either the Muscogee or the Chikashsha', but he was thwarted by swollen rivers, contravening winds against the sails of their sloops, and "parties of Choctaw out against the Creeks."[13] Desperate to placate the Ani'-Yun-wiya, he "borrowed" thirty horses at Mobile to carry the ammunition directly to them. After a "tedious journey" through the inclement weather, he met a long-suffering Tsiyu Gansi-ni surrounded by eighty warriors on the Tennessee River. The Ani'-Yun-wiya expressed their concern that the English planned to build a fort at the mouth of the Watauga River and their desire to drive off the settlers who had been in the region for seven years. Stuart wanted to disabuse the Ani'-Yun-wiya of the belief that they could seize the goods and burn the houses of hunters and squatters on their land. He warned them that there would be consequences. "Although I wished to see those People off their Land, I did not wish to see Blood spilt, that there were many poor people among them who thought that they lived on Lands fairly purchased."[14]

Ani'-Yun-wiya delegates returned "here lately from the Lower Towns, who had been at Fort Charlot[te] at the congress with Commissioners from Virginia and Carolina, . . . informed us that they were assured by the Commissioners that the Congress intended to order the people off who were settled on their lands without loss of time."[15] They also advised them to disregard Cameron, "to be good Friends to the Inhabitants of Watauga, and to leave a Road to pass and to repass to their Country from Virginia."[16] The Ani'-Yun-wiya now admitted that, yes, "some of the people from the Valley and a few from the Lower Towns" had gone to the congress at Fort Charlotte, desiring presents, but they had been rebuffed and were now the "jest of the Nation."[17]

The Ani'-Yun-wiya complained that the Watauga settlers had not only insulted them but also had threatened to kill Cameron. A few days later Stuart met with the "headmen from the different parts of the Nation," assembled at Chota. He gestured that the present of ammunition would "enable them to hunt and to supply their families" in lieu of the supply that the rebels in Georgia and South Carolina had shut down. The Crown asked them to remain loyal and "other paths . . . would be open for their Trade."[18] The Ani'-Yun-wiya thanked Stuart for his concern and promised to protect both him and Cameron while in their country. Although "they did not like to spill the blood of the white people but if they attempted to carry away their people who lived among them they could not avoid it." They derisively referenced the Fort Charlotte participants and then talked about the main topic, the settlements. They said that they had been misled into negotiating away their land at Watauga and Nonatluchky. When they blazed the boundary with Cameron, the white settlers on their side of the line were "ordered to remove off but they begged as their crops were then on the ground that they might be allowed to reap them and that they would certainly remove the Spring following." Some left, but others stayed and leased the land. Now they "pretend" they had purchased the land.[19]

Stuart sent an express to the settlers at Watauga and Nonaluchky reporting Ani'-Yun-wiya's intentions. Sensing the "great danger" threatening the settlers residing on the Ani'-Yun-wiya "side [of] the Boundary line," especially at Watauga and Nonatluchky, Stuart and Cameron on May 7, 1776, wrote to them: "We have lately found a general discontent among the Indians particularly among the Young people on account of the new Settlements." Stuart reported that he had told the headmen of the Ani'-Yun-wiya nation meeting in congress that he had "perceived" this anger and would assist the settlers in removing to a location "more favourable to industrious White people." For this discretion, "we begged that their young Fellows might be restrained from Committing any acts of Violence." Stuart and Cameron proposed resettling them in West Florida, offering "immediate grants of Land for them in a Climate and Situation much better suited to industrious white people than where you now live." The Ani'-Yun-wiya had agreed to allow them twenty days to relocate; otherwise they would be exposed to a "Mercyless and enraged Enemy, . . . [who] never will acknowledge your claim."[20]

Letters in reply signed by John Carter and Rev. Aaron Pinson, both Virginians, pledged their loyalty to the Crown and their intention for the settlers to remove from Native country. On behalf of the settlers, Carter responded on the following day to Stuart and Cameron's express. Couching his rhetoric in Native terms, he expressed the settlers' concern that the Ani'-Yun-wiya, with whom they had shared "the long Chain of Friendship and their brotherly Love to us," now "are a Mind to destroy Our innocent Women and Children if possible and likewise ourselves." He expressed how surprised they were: that "they should now want to wash their hands of us is amazing when they have for a long Time been in Peace with us." Calling the "warning" given to them by Stuart and Cameron "laudable," he credited the British agents with being "the material Instruments of our Brothers not shedding innocent Blood." Shifting his rhetoric from terms of Native diplomacy to the terms of transaction, Carter said the settlers comprehended both their relations with the Ani'-Yun-wiya and with the Crown as a contractual dispute. They not only adhered to the "contract" made with the Ani'-Yun-wiya, unless it violated the law, but also hoped the "great contract" with the Mother Country "may be clearly solved." Only then were they willing to relinquish their claim to the land. They countered that the demand to vacate did not give them enough time to comply and asked for a "longer respite." They asked for a quick response to this request and where they might seek refuge.[21]

Taking exception to the reference to Great Britain, Stuart and Cameron said to Carter and the Watauga settlers on May 23, 1776, that the Ani'-Yun-wiya claim to the land had nothing to do with the imperial crisis. The current colonial situation was admittedly grave, he conceded, but the "discontent of the young fellows is not at all new." Their dissension may have previously been internal—"to have made bad blood among themselves; but Now they seem unanimously resolved to recover their lands." They had focused their efforts on the Watauga and Nonatluchky settlements, not other settlers on the Ani'-Yun-wiya side of the boundary: "all that they want (they say) is their land and that they are determined to have [it]."[22]

On the same day, Stuart and Cameron responded to Aaron Pinson and the Nonatluchky settlers that after receiving his letter, the letter from the Watauga settlers, and the "Talk from Mr. Brown to the Raven," they immediately convened the Native people and shared their correspondence. They said that "the Notice we gave of the intention" of the Native people was toward the settlers in "general without any regard to their Political Principles, for howsoever different Our Opinions may be from any of the Inhabitants we Could never have forgiven Ourselves if by Omitting to inform you of what Came to Our knowledge of the Intention of the Indians, if we had suffered innocent women and Children to fall a Sacrifice." The Crown's recommendation for moving to West Florida was "for those only who by the present unhappy situation of affairs are forced to abandon" their homes for new settlements. On the other hand, if the man accompanying Isaac Thomas reflected the attitude of the settlers and they were not inclined to immigrate to West Florida, then he "can inform you of the indulgence that the Indians have given you through our intercession." "We venture to Recommend it to you as a very fit Country for poor people."[23]

Stuart later learned from Thomas, a Virginia trader who had long lived with the Ani'-Yun-wiya, that the letter read to the settlers "was very different from the original, and that it was sent to one of the Committees in Virginia [Fincastle]." Thomas also said that "Penson had not signed his letter, but his name was affixed to it by the desire of one Patrick Brown and sent in a Talk to the Raven in the same handwriting, expressing his surprize that he should deny his claim to the Lands on which he was settled, the Boundaries of which he and the Carpenter had marked, and enumerated the different articles he had given in payment." The Ani'-Yun-wiya responded and said they had leased the land in question and had additionally received as a reparation "for the Deer and Buffaloe they had destroyed, For the Houses they had built on their hunting Grounds and the Fields they had planted and for the Grass that their Horses and Cattle had eat; that they had drove away all their Deer and Buffaloe, and that now they were obliged to go a great way to look for victuals for their Families."[24]

Stuart and Cameron concurred that gifting the Ani'-Yun-wiya with ammunition was the only way to keep them in check and out of reach of the rebels, who planned a commissary for recruiting them. They also thought it wise "to assemble all the White People in the Nation and to tender to them the Oath of Allegiance." They proceeded with caution when reporting the insurgency developing in the colonies. They hesitated to tell the settlers despite their inquisitiveness that "it was reported at Augusta that Mr. Walker intended to come into the Overhills from Virginia with about 800 or 900 Men."[25]

When "a Deputation of fourteen Indians" from the northern nations with an Ani'-Yun-wiya fellow as interpreter arrived at Chota, the young warriors grew "impatient and . . . apprehensive." These deputies consisted of representatives from the Mohawk, the Odawa, the Nantucas, and the Shawnee and a "small boy" from Lenape. Dressed in "all black," the deputies reported on their seventy-day trek and the turbulence of the countryside. Passing through what once were Shawnee and Lenape hunting grounds, they saw that what was once replete with deer, bear, and buffalo now was "thickly inhabited and the people all in arms."

> They said that they had got all the Northern Tribes to assist them to take Satisfaction and that the French have supplied them with a great quantity of Ammunition and Arms and Provisions and have promised to support them; that they told them that the King's Troops would soon fall on their Enemies towards the Sea and if they united and fell on them on this side they would find them nothing; That now all Nations of Indians were at peace with one another. That they had sent messengers to the Outbacks to the Tribes there to secure their friendship, and that they would not trouble the Cherokee anymore.[26]

The Ani'-Yun-wiya and their new northward allies had difficulty apprehending the civil war developing in the colonies. "They did not believe the White People were at War, although they pretended so." Their apprehension made them wary of Stuart's promise to remove the settlers from their country.

> They told us that they were apprehensive that our Messenger had been stopped and that there was something bad intended against their Nation; that they wished to get the assistance of the Creeks in case of an army coming against them . . . they did not want any of the White people among them to go to any of the Settlements at this time for fear of their giving Intelligence of the Northern Indians being among them. They told us that the French who had promised to assist the Northern Tribes had told them that the reason of the People of Great Britain's quarreling with the People of America was because the Rebells were always making Encroachment on the Indians and oppressing them, But that the French and the King's People would assist each other against the Rebells.[27]

The Ani'-Yun-wiya and their allies braced for war. They were "determined to take all White People out of the Nation that were obnoxious to them." Stuart felt obliged to share intelligence with them, which "currently reported that 900 men were to be sent into the Nation from Virginia." When the northern nations returned for the grand talk at Chota, they were greeted with the "standard of war . . . the Flag Staff and Posts of the Town House were painted black and red." The assembled Ani'-Yun-wiya deputies all wore black, setting them apart from Usteneka and two or three others, perhaps by their attire and expression of indecision. A Mohawk spokesman representing the Six Nations opened the meeting by offering a belt of purple wampum with white beads. He said "the Long Knife had without any provocation come into one of their Towns and murdered their people and the son of their Great Beloved Man." He presented the belt to Tsiyu Gansi-ni. The Odawa delegate offered a white belt with purple symbols. He

> expressed their desire of confirming a lasting bond of true friendship with all their red Brethren they were almost constantly at war one Nation against another, and reduced by degrees, while their common enemies were taking the advantage of their situation; that they were willing and they hoped every Nation would be the same to drop all their former quarrels and to join in one common cause, and that although the Trade to their Nation and all the other Northern Nations had been stopped, that their friends, the French in Canada, had found means to supply them and would assist them.

He presented the belt to Tsiyu Gansi-ni.[28]

The Shawnee delegate, reputedly a French partisan, gave the concluding remarks. Not to be outdone by the others, he offered a "War Belt about 9 feet long and six inches wide of purple Wampum strewed over with vermilion." After enumerating the grievances his people had suffered,

> he complained particularly of the Virginians who after having taken away all their Lands and cruelly and treacherously treated some of their people, had unjustly brought war upon their Nation and destroyed many of their people; that in a very few years their Nation from being a great people were now reduced to a handful; that their Nation possessed Lands almost to the Sea Shore and that the red people who were once Masters of the whole Country hardly possessed ground enough to stand on that the Lands where but lately they hunted close to their Nations were thickly inhabited and covered with Forts and armed men; that wherever a Fort appeared in their neighbourhood, they might depend there would soon be Towns and Settlements; that it was plain, there was an intention to extirpate them, and that he thought it better to die like men than to diminish away by inches.[29]

He presented the belt to Tsiyu Gansi-ni. After a few minutes, Coskuah [aka Abraham, Old Abram], "the headman of Chilhowie, who had lived long in the Mohawk Nation and whose wife had constantly lived in Sir William Johnson's house," took the belt from Tsiyu Gansi-ni and sang "the war song and all the Northern Indians joined in the chorus." The deputies looked to Stuart and Cameron and the other white people present and motioned that they should take up the belt. They declined, and Stuart said to them the quiet part out loud: they "did not understand our written Talks and we did not understand their Beads." He cautioned them to recognize that "the Virginians when they were not above half the number that they are at present had withstood the French and the combined Force of all the Indian Nations when they were twice as numerous as they are at present and that now they are in Arms ready to go against the King's forces."[30]

Oukanaekah, the Raven of Chota, said to the assembly "that they would consider of their Talks before they gave them a full answer and a meeting was appointed next day at Settico [Tellico]."[31] At the meeting at Tellico two days later, the northern deputies assured Stuart of their alliance with the "King's friends." They said that the British and the French had acted in concert to help them reclaim their possessions taken by the rebels.

On the following day, Tsiyu Gansi-ni met with all the delegates and the traders convened at Cameron's house. After reminding the white attendees that they "considered their White People to be the same with themselves," they would not demand that they join them in going to war, but at least they supply them with goods and ammunition. Cameron would remain among them as an adviser. Stuart put Tsiyu Gansi-ni on the spot by making him acknowledge before the headmen the sole cause of the war. The deputies said to the white men that they were returning homeward without meeting the Muscogee. They had sent "Messengers with Belts and that they desired the Lower Creeks to assist the Lower Cherokee."[32] On June 7, 1776, the *Virginia Gazette* published a "copy of a letter addressed [to] frontier inhabitants, by Mr. Stuart, the British superintendent of Indian Affairs in the southern district, which was delivered the 18th of May last, by a messenger sent by him expressly for that purpose." After hearing the Native displeasure with the Watauga and Nolichucky settlements, Stuart warned the settlers that "you are under great apprehensions" and advised them to come to the Ani'-Yun-wiya nation for security. "As soon as they arrive at the Cherokee nation, by repairing to the king's standard, [they] shall find protection, and their families and estates be secure from all danger." To this end they must sign a loyalty oath to the Crown and pledge that "they are ready and willing, whenever called upon, to appear in arms in defence of the British rights in

America." He promised to protect them by landing a British troop at West Florida, marching it through Muscogee country to Chikashsha' country, collecting "500 warriors from each nation" en route to "the Cherokee (who have also promised their assistance) then take possession of the frontiers of North Carolina and Virginia."[33]

Isaac Thomas returned to Chota bearing an "enclosed talk" from the Committee of Fincastle. These talking points painted Native country as a highly militarized zone, which so "exasperated" the Native delegates that Stuart lost faith in his "ability to restrain them." The report alleged a series of events meant to provoke them: six thousand militiamen were marching to Native country from Virginia and North Carolina; Watauga settlers had built forts and, along with Nonatluchky settlers, pledged neutrality; a Virginia trader had gone to the Shawnee and the Lenape and proposed taking two hundred hostages from each of them "as security for the behavior of the rest." Fincastle exaggerated the Native initiative against North Carolina and Virginia "in order to engage their [the settlers'] assistance against the Cherokee." It warned them that the Shawnee chief Cornstalk and fourteen Shawnee warriors had joined the Ani'-Yun-wiya and would attack the settlers on Henderson's purchase. It also stated a British troop was marching from Pensacola to converge with five hundred warriors each from the Muscogee, Chahta, and Chikashsha'. They along with "all the Ani'-Yun-wiya Nation were immediately to fall on the Frontiers of Virginia and North Carolina."[34]

If Stuart was unaware of the lower towns' attacks on South Carolina two days earlier, he was certainly mindful of the deceitful rendition of his letters. Because these forgeries contained "horrid falsehoods" and had been "very industriously circulated," he enclosed "Duplicates of all my Correspondence" with the Watauga and Nonatluchky settlers in his letter from Toqua, June 28, 1776, to Edward Wilkinson, appointed commissioner of peace for the Ani'-Yun-wiya District ten years earlier. These falsehoods and "the Talk sent them by one of the Virginia Committee has only served to exasperate them, And I am informed and have Reason to believe, that many of the Members are concerned in the Lands." "I send them and Isaac Thomas's Oath, in hopes that You will endeavor to expose and bring to Justice those Villains that can be capable of Forgery in Order to involve the Settlements of Virginia and North Carolina in an unjust War with the Indians, in Support of a Set of People who we are credibly informed have endeavored to defraud them of a Country much larger than Carolina." Not only had he and Cameron "done all in our Power to prevent their going to drive the People off their Lands in hopes that we could get them to go off quietly; "till at Last we had it hinted that they believed all the White People had combined to deprive them of

FIGURE 44. Bernard Romans, *A General Map of the southern British Colonies . . . with the Neighboring Indian Countries, from the Modern Surveys of Engineer de Brahm, Capt. Collet, Mouzon, 1776.* South Caroliniana Library Map Collection, Courtesy of University of South Carolina, Columbia.

their Lands and to destroy them from being a Nation." "I can assure you of One Serious Truth, that the Cherokee are not alone in the Resolution to free themselves from the unjust Incroachment of their Neighbours."[35]

In addition to the false flags alleged in the Fincastle intelligence, Stuart said that his letter had been forged in a campaign of misinformation, placing the Ani'-Yun-wiya firmly in the loyalist camp and seeking to unify the backcountry against the British. Of the letter Stuart allegedly wrote to the Watauga settlers, "threatening the Frontiers of North Carolina and Virginia," Andrew Williamson and Edward Wilkinson carped, "if there was an Indian war it would be occasioned by that letter."[36] Still hopeful that "a war might yet be prevented," Stuart used these conflicting references to the Shawnee to undermine the Ani'-Yun-wiya's faith in this potential ally. Adhering to the proposition that they were "being deceived" by the Shawnee, the Ani'-Yun-wiya began "to entertain some doubts about them" and decided to table their answer to the Committee of Fincastle the full twenty days allotted for their response. At the same time, Usteneka, "the Great Warrior of the Nation, had yet to give his opinion and they would be obliged to abide by whatever he should determine, whether Peace or War."[37]

"It was in vain to talk any more of Peace," Stuart said of the Ani'-Yun-wiya: "All that could now be done was to give them strict charge not to pass the Boundary Line, not to injure any of the King's faithful subjects, not to kill any women and children, and to stop hostilities when you should desire it notwithstanding any promises to the contrary given to the Shawnese." The Ani'-Yun-wiya agreed to these terms, relented from their call to war, and admitted they had been "rash." They had foolhardily been persuaded by the addresses of the northward nations, moved by the inuendo against Cameron and Stuart, and angered by the "cruelty" to William Johnson's son. They pledged their allegiances to the Crown and blamed Tsiyu Gansi-ni "as the cause of their beginning [warfare] before they received your Orders."[38]

The Ani'-Yun-wiya appeared "inclinable" to protect the white settlers in their midst. They planned to invite the settlers at Nonatluchky to seek refuge in their nation under a white flag. To achieve this end, they authorized Capt. Nathaniel Gist to deliver this offer to the settlement. Gist selected four Virginians who knew the woods to accompany him. They ran away on the eve of their planned departure. The white settlers among the Ani'-Yun-wiya now believed their only security rested with the Ani'-Yun-wiya. The "greatest part" of the Ani'-Yun-wiya nation "set out very much dejected" and escorted the white settlers to Overhill and the Middle Settlements. Some others accompanied Stuart when he left Chota for Muscogee country on July 12, unbeknownst to him a week after the Declaration of Independence. When he arrived, he said to the Muscogee that the Ani'-Yun-wiya had sought their alliance, but he advised them of the Crown's directive to stand down. The Muscogee said they would stay home and wait for further orders. The British continued to supply the Ani'-Yun-wiya with a hundred-horse load of ammunition and presents, warning that if they injured the settlers, ignored Cameron, or "listen" to the Shawnee, this would be their "last supply."[39]

The Ani'-Yun-wiya finally selected a date for the Great Warrior's pronouncement on the timing of the war. Although an attack could take place a month or two later, the lower towns launched their attack on the "Settlements of Carolina" on June 26, 1776. The entry of Capt. James McCall's detachment of militia and rangers into the lower towns with a warrant to arrest Cameron precipitated the Ani'-Yun-wiya's attacking them. The Ani'-Yun-wiya killed four of the militia and captured McCall. If provoked by the intrusion of South Carolina troops into the lower towns in search of Cameron, they had already decided on this "rash step" immediately following the return of their deputies from the congress with the northward nations. They were also influenced by what their deputies learned from the "private talk" of a warrior of Tellico and Ninituca, his relation, which they sent to Tukeesee, the Terrapin and the son of Oconostota. They resented the Terrapin "being very active in getting Ninituca's Brother, who was his Kinsman, put to death, as satisfaction for the Murder of a white man in Virginia."[40]

This attack on McCall's troop combined with the forged Stuart letter published in the *Virginia Gazette* and circulated to the Fincastle committee and Continental Congress, along with Dunmore's proclamation offering freedom to enslaved Africans who joined British forces, likely prompted Thomas Jefferson, a Virginian, to pen the twenty-seventh grievance against George III in the Declaration of Independence: "He has excited domestic insurrections amongst us, and has endeavored to bring on the inhabitants of our frontiers, the merciless Indian Savages whose known rule of warfare, is an undistinguished destruction of all ages, sexes, and conditions."

This final grievance punctuated a century of Virginia colonialism, precipitated the triple threat of incursion, insurrection, and invasion, and projected an American nationalism that propelled both the continued enslavement of Africans and the conquest of Native country.

Notes

Introduction

1. Wood, "Changing Population of the Colonial South"; J. F. Lee, "What Is a Hunting Ground?" 314–15; Sleeper-Smith, *Indigenous Prosperity and American Conquest*, 47–52.
2. Native Land Digital, https://native-land.ca/.; Native Land Digital is an interactive app that allows the user to locate historic Indigenous territories. "About the Appalachian Region," Appalachian Regional Commission, https://www.arc.gov/about-the-appalachian-region/.
3. Wulf, "Vast Early America."
4. Okihiro, *Third World Studies*, 142.
5. Ibid., 143.
6. Ibid., 144.
7. Witgen, *Infinity of Nations*, 18–19. See also Witgen, "Rethinking Colonial History as Continental History," 529; Iliffe, *Honour in African History*.
8. DuVal, *Native Ground*, 72–73.

Chapter 1. By a Swan, They Signify the English

1. Lederer, *Discoveries of John Lederer*, 4.
2. Ibid., foreword, 1–2.
3. Following the Third Anglo-Powhatan War, Governor Berkeley put into place what became the "recurrent mode of the tributary system," writes historian Kristalyn Shefveland. "The creation of boundaries and reservations served . . . both as forms of control over the Indigenous peoples and . . . as a buffer between interior Indians and their specter of the paramount chieftaincy." Shefveland, *Anglo-Native Virginia*, 16–17, 23.
4. Lederer, Discoveries of John Lederer, 6–8; Shefveland, *Anglo-Native Virginia*, 39–40.
5. Washburn, *Virginia under Charles I and Cromwell*, 55.
6. Schmidt, *Divided Dominion*, 154.
7. Lederer, *Discoveries of John Lederer*, 1–8. J. Jones, "Anglo-Siouan Relations on Virginia's Piedmont Frontier," 34–35; Kristalyn Shefveland, "Indian Enslavement in Virginia," *Encyclopedia Virginia*, https://encyclopediavirginia.org/entries/indian-enslavement-in-virginia.
8. Ibid., 9.
9. Ibid. 10. Harris was killed near the falls of the James River in the summer of 1678 trying repel an incursion of a Northern nation, likely the Seneca.
10. Lederer, *Discoveries of John Lederer in Three Several Marches*, 13.
11. Ibid., 12.
12. Ibid., 14.
13. Hatfield, *Atlantic Virginia*, 25; Ryland, "Pamunkey Neck," 323; Hoffman, "Observations on Certain Ancient Tribes of the Northern Appalachian Province," 195, 220.

14. Lederer, *Discoveries of John Lederer*, 14–; Shefveland, *Anglo-Native Virginia*, 30–31.
15. Cf. Everett, "'They Shalbe Slaves for Their Lives,'" 73–74.
16. Shefveland, *Anglo-Native Virginia*, 17, 38–40.
17. Alexander, "Indian Vocabulary from Fort Christanna," 309.
18. Lederer, *Discoveries of John Lederer*, 15–16. The Eno (Oenock) may have split from the Wyanoke, who remained in Virginia. Speck, "Siouan Tribes of the Carolinas," 216; Simpkins, "Aboriginal Intersite Settlement System Change," 275.
19. Lederer, *Discoveries of John Lederer*, 19.
20. Lederer, *Discoveries of John Lederer*, 14–18; Wilson, "Study of the Late Prehistoric, and Historic Indians of the Carolinas and Virginia Piedmont," 83–84.
21. Lederer, *Discoveries of John Lederer*, ii, 20–23.
22. Ibid., 26–27; Juricek, "Westo Indians," 137; Catawba (also known as Issa, Iswa, Ushery, Ysa, Usi, Esau, Esaugh, Esaw). "Carolina Indians in 1700," Native American Net Roots, December 1, 2013, http://nativeamericannetroots.net/diary/1609.
23. The expedition has erroneously been called the Batts and Fallam Expedition. Briceland, Alan, and *Dictionary of Virginia Biography*. "Thomas Batte (fl. 1630s–1690s)" *Encyclopedia Virginia*. Virginia Humanities, https://encyclopediavirginia.org/entries/batte-thomas-fl-1630s-1690s. Shefveland, *Anglo-Native Virginia*, 17, 48.
24. "Journal from Virginia beyond the Appalachian Mountains," 238–39; Lederer, *Discoveries of John Lederer*, 13, 26; J. Jones, "Anglo-Siouan Relations on Virginia's Piedmont Frontier," 76n46.
25. "The Iroquois name Tutelo, Totero, or Todirich-roone, in its various forms, although commonly used by the English to designate a particular tribe, was really the generic Iroquois term for all the Siouan tribes of Virginia and Carolina, including even the Catawba"; "The Saponi and Tutelo Indians," Access Genealogy, https://accessgenealogy.com/north-Carolina/the-saponi-and-tutelo-indians.htm. See also Glanville and Mays, "Where Was Totera Town?" 38.
26. Summers L., C.B. Coale, and Bickley, eds. "Batts and Fallam Expedition of 1671." In Annals of Southwest Virginia, 1769–1800, 1–7. Abingdon, Va: L. P. Summers, 1929. Shefveland, *Anglo-Native Virginia*, 48; Byrd, Byrd, and Byrd, *Correspondence of the Three William Byrds*, 1: 3.
27. "Journal from Virginia beyond the Appalachian Mountains," 238–39.
28. Ibid., 239n.
29. "Batts and Fallam Expedition of 1671," 6.
30. Warren, *Worlds the Shawnees Made*, 69. "The Tomahittan's principal towns lay west of the Appalachians, somewhere in eastern Tennessee or northern Alabama. . . . The Tomahittan might have represented aa multilingual, coalescent community that ultimately migrated to the Coosa River" (ibid.).
31. Davis, "Travels of James Needham and Gabriel Arthur," 45.
32. Ibid., 45–46.
33. Ibid., 34–35.
34. Ibid., 35–36.
35. Ibid., 37–38.
36. Ibid., 38.
37. Ibid., 38–39.
38. Ibid., 39.
39. Ibid., 40.
40. Ibid., 40–41; Briceland, *Westward from Virginia*, 166.
41. Davis, "Travels of James Needham and Gabriel Arthur," 41–42.

42. Ibid., 42.
43. Ibid., 42–43.

Chapter 2. Flights of Pigeons, Their Length No Visible End

1. Richter, "Rediscovered Links in the Covenant Chain," 57–65; Eid, "Ojibwa-Iroquois War," 309.
2. Colden, *History of the Five Indian Nations of Canada*, 27.
3. Ibid.
4. Daniel K. Richter, "War and Culture: The Iroquois Experience," *William and Mary Quarterly* 40, no. 4 (1983): 532n17.
5. Jemison, *Narrative of the Life*, 46.
6. Ryland, "Pamunkey Neck," 322–24; s.v. "Mattaponi Tribe," *Encyclopedia Virginia*, December 7, 2020. https://encyclopediavirginia.org/entries/mattaponi-tribe.
7. Ryland, "Pamunkey Neck," 323. See Mattaponi Indian Tribe, et al. v. Commonwealth of Virginia, record no. 000509, March 2, 2001.
8. Woodard, *High Plains Sappony*, 20; Glanville and Mays, "Where Was Totera Town?," 35.
9. Richter, "Rediscovered Links in the Covenant Chain," 57–58; Indigenous Values Initiative, "Guswentha." Rediscovered Links in the Covenant Chain
10. Quoted in Richter, Ibid., 57–58; Indigenous Values Initiative, "Guswentha"; Vest, "From Nansemond to Monacan," 784.
11. Colden, *History of the Five Indian Nations of Canada*, 26.
12. Sleeper-Smith, *Indigenous Prosperity and American Conquest*, 72–73.
13. Richter, "Rediscovered Links in the Covenant Chain," 59.
14. Rice, "Bacon's Rebellion in Indian Country," 733. Richter says the Haudenosaunee never conquered the Susquehannock; Richter, "Rediscovered Links in the Covenant Chain," 66n49.
15. "The Case of Wahanganoche; an Excerpt from the Journals of the House of Burgesses of Virginia (1662)," *Encyclopedia Virginia*, https://encyclopediavirginia .org/entries/the-case-of-wahanganoche-an-excerpt-from-the-journals-of-the -house-of-burgesses-of-virginia-1662/; William Deyo, "History of the Patawomeck," Secretary of the Commonwealth, https://www.commonwealth.virginia .gov/virginia-indians/state-recognized-tribes/patawomeck-tribe/.
16. Virginia Council et al., *Minutes of the Council*, 116–17.
17. "History," Patawomeck Indian Tribe of Virginia, https://patawomeckindiantribe ofvirginia.wordpress.com/history; Brendan Wolfe, "Patawomeck Tribe," *Encyclopedia Virginia*, https://encyclopediavirginia.org/entries/patawomeck-tribe/.
18. Mathew, *Beginning, Progress, and Conclusion of Bacon's Rebellion in Virginia*.
19. Kruer, "Bloody Minds and Peoples Undone," 406; Parent, *Foul Means*, 21–22.
20. Mathew, *Beginning, Progress, and Conclusion of Bacon's Rebellion in Virginia*.
21. Ibid.
22. Ibid.; Rice, "Bacon's Rebellion in Indian Country," 733, 736–37; Kruer, "Bloody Minds and Peoples Undone," 417–21.
23. Mathew, *Beginning, Progress, and Conclusion of Bacon's Rebellion in Virginia*.
24. Rice, "Bacon's Rebellion in Indian Country," 738–40; Vest, "From Nansemond to Monacan," 783.
25. Parent, *Foul Means*, 21–22.
26. *Articles of Peace between the Most Serene and Mighty Prince Charles II . . . and Several Indian Kings and Queens, &c. Concluded the 29th day of May 1677* (London:

John Bill, Christopher Barker, Thomas Newcomb, and Henry Hills, 1677). *Articles of Peace* (1677), Encyclopedia Virginia, Virginia Humanities https:// encyclopediavirginia.org/entries/articles-of-peace-1677/.

27. *Articles of Peace*; Articles of Peace (1677), *Encyclopedia Virginia*, Virginia Humanities https://encyclopediavirginia.org/entries/articles-of-peace-1677/.

Chapter 3. New Incursions Were So Troublesome

1. Colden, *History of the Five Indian Nations of Canada*, 24–25. Gallatin, *Synopsis of the Indian Tribes*, 55–56.
2. Colden, *History of the Five Indian Nations of Canada*, 28; Kemper, "Early Westward Movement of Virginia," 131n11; Gallatin, *Synopsis of the Indian Tribes*, 55–56.
3. Colden, *History of the Five Indian Nations of Canada*, 35.
4. Livingston, *Livingston Indian Records*, 55–56; Kruer, *Time of Anarchy*, 188.
5. Hinke, "Report of the Journey of Francis Louis Michel," 30, 30n49. When Michel wrote "'Col. Bornn'" the name he "probably intended was Col. William Byrd, who owned much land on Falling Creek, though he lived at the site of the present Richmond. He received no such grant as Michel describes, but in April 1679 the General Assembly granted him a tract of land five miles long and three miles wide lying on both sides of James River at the falls, on condition that he kept fifty armed men there as settlers." Jay Hansford C. Vest reconciles the presence of the Monacan in the region by drawing on Monacan oral tradition along with Michel's account. Vest, "Crossing Paths."
6. *EJCCV*, 1: 52; Woodard, *High Plains Sappony*, 21.
7. *EJCCV*, 1: 53–54; "Mattaponi Tribe," *Encyclopedia Virginia*.
8. *EJCCV*, 1: 53; "Mattaponi Tribe"; Malone, "Changing Military Technology," 56.
9. *EJCCV*, 1: 54.
10. Byrd, Byrd, and Byrd, *Correspondence of the Three William Byrds*, 189–90, 190n1; "Continuation of the Yarborough Family Magazine."
11. *EJCCV*, 1: 64; Vest, "From Nansemond to Monacan," 783.
12. Rhoades, *Long Knives and the Longhouse*, 41. From this contact, but certainly by about the mid-eighteenth century, Virginia began to document this usage. Native people called the Virginians "long knives," "knifemen," or "big knives"; Thwaites, *Daniel Boone*, 111n. See also *OED* s.v. "Long Knife," 2. "Frequently in plural and with capital initials. (A translation of) a name given by North American Indians to a white settler, esp. of Virginia, or a white soldier. . . . Now historical." Schenawolf, "Knives of the American Revolution."
13. Colden, *History of the Five Indian Nations of Canada*, 34–35.
14. Ibid., 35.
15. Ibid., 32.
16. Ibid., 37–38.
17. Richter, "Rediscovered Links in the Covenant Chain," 58.
18. Ibid., 64.
19. Colden, *The History of the Five Indian Nations*, 50.
20. Richter, "Rediscovered Links in the Covenant Chain," 64.
21. Colden, *History of the Five Indian Nations of Canada*, 32.
22. William Byrd I to Thomas Grendon, [April 29, 1684], Byrd, Byrd, and Byrd, *Correspondence of the Three William Byrds*, 4, 16–17.
23. Colden, *History of the Five Indian Nations of Canada*, 51.
24. Richter, "Rediscovered Links in the Covenant Chain," 59–60.

25. *EJCCV*, 1: 71.

26. Richter, "Rediscovered Links in the Covenant Chain," 59–60, 63, 66.

27. Colden, *History of the Five Indian Nations of Canada*, 51–53.

28. Byrd, Byrd, and Byrd, *Correspondence of the Three William Byrds*, 61; Deloria, *Playing Indian*; Green, "Tribe Called Wannabee," 34–35.

29. "A letter from the Revd Mr. John Clayton, (afterwards Dean of Kildare in Ireland) to Dr. Grew, in answer to several queries relating to Virginia, sent to him by that learned gentleman, A. D. 1687. Communicated by the Right Reverend Father in God Robert Lord Bishop of Corke, to John Earl of Egmont, F. R. S.," Philosophical Transactions of the Royal Society of London. Volume 41, Issue 454, Oct 1739, 161. In Clayton, *Reverend John Clayton*, 21–39. Jay Hansford C. Vest indicates that the rattlesnake root cure was known to the Monacan people and noted by Beverly in his *Present State of Virginia* (1705); Vest, "From Nansemond to Monacan," 167–68. The assumption that Native men were beardless or without facial hair also offered a stereotype. Chavers, *Racism in Indian Country*, 20.

30. William Byrd II to Dr. Hans Sloane, Virginia, April 20, 1706, in Byrd, Byrd, and Byrd, *Correspondence of the Three William Byrds*, 260.

31. William Byrd I to Perry and Lane, Virginia, June 16, 1688; William Byrd I to Hon. Charles Howard June 16, 1688, Ibid., 82–83.

32. William Byrd I to Francis Howard, Baron Howard of Effingham, Virginia, June 10, 1689, Ibid., 107–8.

33. William Byrd I to Warham Horsmanden, Virginia July 25, 1690; William Byrd I to Daniel Horsmanden, Virginia, July 25, 1690, William Byrd I to Nordest Rand, Virginia, July 25, 1690, Ibid., 120–23.

34. William Byrd I to Effingham, Virginia, June 10, 1689, Ibid., 107–8.

35. William Byrd I to Effingham, January 23, 1691, Ibid., 145.

36. *SAL*, 3: 69; s.v. "fire hunting," *OED*: "Now historical," usually associated with Native American mode of hunting.

37. Day, "Indian as an Ecological Factor," 337.

38. H. Jones, *Present State of Virginia*, 10–11, 35; Commisso, "Land Use History," 27–28.

39. Hinke, "Report of the Journey of Francis Louis Michel," part 1, 41–42.

40. Beverley, *History and Present State of Virginia*, 2: 37, 39.

41. Thomas Jefferson to John Adams, May 27, 1813, Founders Online, National Archives, https://founders.archives.gov/documents/Jefferson/03–06–02–0138.

42. Byrd, Byrd, and Byrd, *Correspondence of the Three William Byrds*, 154.

43. Ibid., 153.

44. *JHB*, 2: 454; Feeley, "Tuscarora Trails," 49n108.

45. Byrd, Byrd, and Byrd, *Correspondence of the Three William Byrds*, 174.

46. Brizon, "Collections coloniales?," 30; Woodard, "Colonial National Historical Park"; Buck Woodard, "Appendix A: Natives in the Landscape: Images and Documents of the Seventeenth Century Virginia Indians," in *A Study of Virginia Indians and Jamestown: The First Century* (Williamsburg, Virginia: Colonial National Historical Park National Park Service U.S. Department of the Interior, 2005), https://www.nps.gov/parkhistory/online_books/jame1/moretti-langholtz/chap10.htm.; Hinke, "Report of the Journey of Francis Louis Michel," part 2, following 131. "Three Americans. Powhatan? Southern Algonquian. Original pen drawing washed with watercolor, Found Ibid. "Report of the Journey of

Francis Louis Michel from Berne, Switzerland, to Virginia, October 2, 1701–December 1, 1702." Brizon, "Collections coloniales?" 24–38.

47. Deed or Nanfan Treaty, July 19, 1701. *Iroquois Indians: A Documentary History*, 908–11, Reel 6, Newberry Library Deed from the Five Nations to the King of their Beaver Hunting Ground. [New-York Papers. Bundle, P.Q; Q 49.], https://www.sixnations.ca/LandsResources/NanFanTreaty.pdf; C. Anderson, "Rediscovering Native North America," 486; Richter, "Rediscovered Links in the Covenant Chain," 65.

48. William Byrd I to Philp Ludwell, Virginia, July 6, 1702, in Byrd, Byrd, and Byrd, *Correspondence of the Three William Byrds*, 186.

49. By persuading "the belligerents to recognize their neutral status, by deterring internal threats to that status, by employing diplomacy to minimize the potential for serious bloodshed in their territory, by offering their services as mediators, and by carefully balancing the amount of military help or hindrance they gave to either side," Jon Parmenter writes, "Iroquois people on both sides of the colonial boundary protected their neutrality and their self-determination as an independent nation." Parmenter, "After the Mourning Wars," 63.

50. Byrd, Byrd, and Byrd, *Correspondence of the Three William Byrds*, 187n3. Parmenter, "'Onenwahatirighsi Sa Gentho Skaghnughtudigh,'" 246–48.

Chapter 4. Slaves Belonging to Virginia Are amongst the Shawnee

1. Ethridge, *From Chicaza to Chickasaw*, 94–98. See Davis, "Travels of James Needham and Gabriel Arthur"; King, *Cherokee Indian Nation*, 36; Warren, *Worlds the Shawnees Made*, 58–59, 225; C. Anderson, "Rediscovering Native North America," 496.

2. A Map of the British and French Dominions in North America. With the Roads, Distances, limits, and Extent of the Settlements, Humbly Inscribed to the Right Honourable the Earl of Halifax, and other Right Honourable The Lords Commissioners for Trade & Plantations . . . (1755). John Mitchell, Thomas Kitchin, and Andrew Millar. *A map of the British and French dominions in North America, with the roads, distances, limits, and extent of the settlements, humbly inscribed to the Right Honourable the Earl of Halifax, and the other Right Honourable the Lords Commissioners for Trade & Plantations.* [London; Sold by And: Millar, 1755] Map. https://www.loc.gov/item/74693173/.

3. John Sergeant to Stephen Williams, Housatun muk [Housatonic], May 14, 1739. John Sergeant and Stephen Williams, "Letters 1739–1743," Edward E. Ayer Collection, Ayer MS 800, Newberry Library.

4. George Washington, diary entry, October 25, 1770, Founders Online, National Archives, last modified July 12, 2016, http://founders.archives.gov/documents/Washington/01-02-02-0005-0029-0021. Original source: *The Diaries of George Washington*, vol. 2, *14 January 1766–31 December 1770*, ed. Donald Jackson (Charlottesville: University Press of Virginia, 1976), 298–301 (hereafter *Diaries of George Washington*); Kemper, "Early Westward Movement of Virginia," 131n11.

5. Sleeper-Smith, *Indigenous Prosperity and American Conquest*, 69, 92–96. Historian Stephen Warren argues against the early chroniclers who contend that the Haudenosaunee had conquered the Shawnee; rather the Shawnee just lost the legal claim to sovereignty to the rival Nation. In collusion with the English, the Haudenosaunee used the written word, especially in the form of

treaties, to usurp the sovereignty of the Shawnee. Warren, *Worlds the Shawnees Made*, 225. See also Misencik and Misencik, *American Indians of the Ohio Country*, 6–12, 23–25.

6. Anderson, "Rediscovering Native North America," 489.

7. Warren, *Worlds the Shawnees Made*, 139.

8. Sergeant to Williams, May 14, 1739.

9. Lawrence Vanden Bosh, *Map of the Lower Mississippi River, Neighboring Coast, and the Country to the Southwest* (1694), Edward E. Ayer Collection, Newberry Library Special Collections; Waselkov, "Indian Maps of the Colonial Southeast," 437–39, 441, 445.

10. *Assembly Proceedings, May 26–June 11, 1697.*, 19: 574, Archives Md.; Marye, "'Patowmeck above Ye Inhabitants,'" 128.

11. Marye, "'Patowmeck above Ye Inhabitants,'" 127.

12. *Minutes of the Provincial Council of Pennsylvania*, vol. 2, 15–16; Jennings, "Constitutional Evolution of the Covenant Chain," 90.

13. Bushnell, "Account of Lamhatty," 568–69.

14. Ibid.

15. Ibid., 569.

16. Hazard, *Colonial Records of Pennsylvania*, 534, 574; Jennings, "Constitutional Evolution of the Covenant Chain," 91–92; Bedell et al., "River and Mountain, War and Peace," 21–24, 35, 36–37; Warren, *Worlds the Shawnees Made*, 10, 163–64; Charles A. Hanna, *Wilderness Trail*, 153.

17. Bedell et al., "River and Mountain, War and Peace," 36, 38.

18. Parent, *Foul Means*, 163–65.

19. "Ratified Treaty #1: The Great Treaty of 1722 between the Five Nations, the Mahicans, and the Colonies of New York, Virginia, and Pennsylvania," in O'Callaghan et al., *Documents Relative to the Colonial History of the State of New York*, 5: 657–81.

20. Minutes of the Provincial Council of Pennsylvania, vol. 3, 226–27; Bedell et al., "River and Mountain, War and Peace," 40.

21. Acts Not Previously Printed, Assembly Proceedings, 1714–1726. 36: 585–86, Archives Md.

22. Assembly Proceedings, May 26–June 11, 1697, 19: 574, Archives Md. If eighty buckskins seem underpriced for an enslaved African, Michel noted in 1702 that "a deer skin would have cost me a dollar, a basket half a dollar. . . . My rifle was valued at twelve skins. . . . In England a deerskin is valued at more than two dollars." Hinke, "Report of the Journey of Francis Louis Michel," part 2, 134. In 1716 South Carolina valued a raw buckskin weighing 1.5 pounds at five shillings per skin. Lapham, *Hunting for Hides*, 12.

23. *Proceedings of the Council of Maryland, 1722.*, 25: 394–95, Archives Md.

24. Assembly Proceedings, October 6–November 6, 1725, 35: 200–201, Archives Md.

25. *Proceedings of the Council of Maryland, 1725*, 125: 442–43, Archives Md.

26. Assembly Proceedings, October 6–November 6, 1725, 35: 206, Archives Md.

27. Assembly Proceedings, July 12–25, 1726, 35: 506, Archives Md.

28. Ibid.

29. The Upper House, Acts Not Previously Printed, Assembly Proceedings, 1714–1726. 36: 583, Archives Md.

30. Acts Not Previously Printed, Assembly Proceedings, 1714–1726. 36: 585–86.

31. Quoted in Hofstra, *Planting of New Virginia*, 104.

32. Guzy, "1736 Survey of the Potomac River," 28; Peter Jefferson and Robert Brooke, *A Map of the northern neck in Virginia, according to an actual survey begun in the year MDCCXXXVI and ended in the year MDCCXLVI. Drawn by Peter Jefferson and Robert Brooke, Surveyors. Receiv'd Aug'st ye 10th 1747 with Sir Wm. Gooch's letter to ye Board of Trade, dated the 10th of June 1747*, PRO, CO 700, Virginia 11; Darlington Digital Library, University of Pittsburgh, https://digital.library.pitt.edu/islandora/object/pitt:DARMAP0629. Journal from Virginia beyond the Appalachian Mountains," 239n; Marye, "'Patowmeck above Ye Inhabitants.'"

33. Sergeant to Williams, May 14, 1739; Aron, "Pigs and Hunters," 186n22; Grumet et al., *Beyond Manhattan*, 38–39.

34. Sleeper-Smith, *Indigenous Prosperity and American Conquest*, 6–7, 17, 20–22, 24, 70; Hofstra, *Planting of New Virginia*, 51; "Historic Perrysburg—Great Black Swamp."

35. Hofstra, *Planting of New Virginia*, 105; Sleeper-Smith, *Indigenous Prosperity and American Conquest*, 126; Feight, "Lower Shawnee Town and Céloron's Expedition."

Chapter 5. Securing the Peace of the Country against the Indians

1. *EJCCV*, 1: 136.
2. *EJCCV*, 2: 41.
3. *EJCCV*, 3: 45.
4. *JHB*, 4: 49, 74, 369.
5. *EJCCV*, 2: 380–81; *EJCCV*, 3: 45; *JHB*, 4: 52.
6. *JHB*, 4: 49, 74, 359.
7. The attack on the Rowley family documented is in the Richmond County Order Book no. 3, 1699–1704, 373–84 (1704) Library of Virginia, Interlibrary Loan transcript; Lozier, "Nicer Red," 49.
8. Newton, *Revolutionary Suicide*; Ghaemi, "Revolutionary Suicide."
9. *EJCCV*, 1: 136.
10. *EJCCV*, 2: 385.
11. *EJCCV*, 3: 159–61; Robinson, "Legal Status of the Indian in Colonial Virginia," 252; Schwarz, *Twice Condemned*, 17, 53, 85, 98; Tyler and Chitwood, "Justice in Colonial Virginia," 213–14; Rankin, "Criminal Trial Proceedings in the General Court of Colonial Virginia," 57–59; Morgan, *Hegemony of the Law*, 111–12; Parent, *Foul Means*, 125–26.
12. *EJCCV*, 2: 389–90.
13. Goetz, "Nanziatticos and the Violence of the Archive," 47, 49.
14. Ibid., 50; Morgan, "Sold into Slavery," 171.
15. *EJCCV*, 2: 396–98.
16. It may seem anachronistic to use the term *genocide*, which was not coined until 1944, in the context of the eighteenth century, but the English had already threatened in 1686 "to cut [the Haudenosaunee] off Root and Branch." Colden, *History of the Five Indian Nations of Canada*, 51–53. The UN definition of genocide includes acts committed "with intent to destroy, in whole or in part, a national, ethnical, racial or religious group: . . . killing members of the group; causing serious bodily or mental harm to members of the group; deliberately inflicting on the group conditions of life calculated to bring about its physical destruction in whole or in part; imposing measures intended to prevent births within the group;

and forcibly transferring children of the group to another group." United Nations Office on Genocide Prevention, https://www.un.org/en/genocide-prevention/definition. All five elements were present in the Nanziattico genocide.

17. *SAL*, 2: 218–19.
18. *JHB*, 4: 25, 94, 97–98; Goetz, "Nanziatticos and the Violence of the Archive," 50, 52. Unfortunately, no copy of the act is extant.
19. *EJCCV*, 3: 12, 20, 50.
20. Ibid.
21. *JHB*, 4: 94.
22. *EJCCV*, 3: 98.
23. Hening, *Statutes at Large*, 2: 475, 479–80.
24. Ibid., 3: 453.
25. *EJCCV*, 3: 5–6.
26. Goetz, "Nanziatticos and the Violence of the Archive," 53–55, 57–58. Although Goetz argues that the English names were given to the children by the councilors, Rountree contends that by the mid-seventeenth century Native people began using English names. By the turn of the century, it was not unusual for elders to use English first names, even if they maintained their Native names as surnames. Rountree, "Personal Names by Early Virginia Indians."
27. *JHB*, 4: 88, 92; *EJCCV*, 2: 453.
28. *EJCCV*, 3: 101.
29. Rountree, "Termination and Dispersal of the Nottoway Indians," 194.
30. *EJCCV*, 3: 13; *JHB*, 4: xxvi, 96.
31. *EJCCV*, 3: 45.
32. *EJCCV*, 3: 98; Strachey, *Dictionary of Powhatan*, 5; T. D. Stewart, "Archeological Exploration of Patawomeke," 6, 84; "Native American Burial Sites in Virginia," Virginia Places, http://www.virginiaplaces.org/population/natamergraveyards.html.
33. *JHB*, 4: 103, 115.
34. *EJCCV*, 3: 241; Virginia Governor's Council, "Order."
35. *EJCCV*, 3: 136.
36. Ludwell and Harrison, "Journal of the Proceedings," 739–40.
37. Exam. of ye Wyanoke Indian Women y' live at ye Nottoway, September 22, 1710, DVNCBC, "Indians of Southern Virginia," pt. 2, 4.
38. Ibid.
39. Ibid.
40. "The Exam: of Great Peter," September 23, 1710, DVNCBC, "Indians of Southern Virginia," pt. 2, 5–6.
41. Ludwell and Harrison, "Journal of the Proceedings," 740.
42. Deposition of Henry Briggs, DVNCBC, "Indians of Southern Virginia," pt. 1, 349–50; Rountree, "Termination and Dispersal of the Nottoway Indians," 194.
43. "The Exam: of Great Peter, ye Great man of ye Nansemond Indians, aged above 60," July 23, 1711, DVNCBC, "Indians of Southern Virginia," pt. 2, 5–6; Simpkins, "Aboriginal Intersite Settlement System Change," 273.
44. Deposition of Henry Briggs.
45. Nansemond Town-"Examination Nick Majr and Several Old of the Maherin Indians, Aged as We Suppose about Sixty Years," May 22, 1711, DVNCBC, "Indians of Southern Virginia," pt. 2, 5–6.

46. Nansemond Town-SS: Nick Majr and other old man of the Maheerink Indians, aged as we suppose about sixty years, May 22, 1711, DVNCBC, "Indians of Southern Virginia," pt. 2, 10.

47. "Prince George County -SS: Thomas Wynn, Gent., aged fifty years," November 12, 1707, DVNCBC, "Indians of Southern Virginia," pt. 1, 341–42.

48. May 28, 1709. Deposition of Benjamin Harrison in Regard to Indian Affairs, 1707, "Colonial Letters, &c.," *VMHB* 5, no. 1 (1897): 47–50; Simpkins, "Aboriginal Intersite Settlement System Change," 273–74, 384.

49. Ibid.

50. Testimony of Francis Tomes (age 77), September 27, 1710, North Carolina, *DVNCBC*, "Indians of Southern Virginia," pt. 2, 2–4.

51. Ibid.

52. Testimony of Robert Bolling (age 61), Thomas Wynn (age 50), and James Thweat (age 64), November 12, 1707, Prince George County-SS, DVNCBC, "Indians of Southern Virginia," pt. 1, 340–43.

53. Ludwell and Harrison, "Journal of the Proceedings," 745.

54. Byrd, Tinling, and Wright, *Secret Diary of William Byrd of Westover*, 319.

Chapter 6. Without Making the Tuscarora Acquainted

1. Feeley, "Tuscarora Trails," 81–82.

2. *EJCCV*, 2: 351–52, 381–82.

3. *EJCCV*, 2: 390–91.

4. *EJCCV*, 2: 402, 405.

5. *EJCCV*, 3: 147, 156, 158.

6. *EJCCV*, 3: 159–61; Robinson, "Legal Status of the Indian in Colonial Virginia," 252; Schwarz, *Twice Condemned*, 17, 85, 98; Tyler and Chitwood, "Justice in Colonial Virginia," 213–14; Rankin, "Criminal Trial Proceedings in the General Court of Colonial Virginia," 57–59.

7. *EJCCV*, 3: 160–61, 163–65.

8. Ibid., 173

9. Ibid., 3–174.

10. Ibid.,171, 182, 185, 190.

11. Ibid.,199–200.

12. Ibid.,202.

13. Byrd, Tinling, and Wright, *Secret Diary of William Byrd of Westover*, 7, 25.

14. *EJCCV*, 3: 220.

15. "Memorial from the Virginia Indian Company," CO 5/1318, pt. 1, April 24, 1717, 33; Lt. Governor Spotswood to the Council of Trade and Plantation, Virginia, January 27, 1715. CSPC, 28: 71–90, 188. M. G. Lawson, "Act for the Better Regulation of the Indian Trade."

16. Alexander Spotswood to the Earl of Dartmouth, September 14, 1713, OLAS, 2: 34.

17. Todd and Goebel, *Baron Christoph von Graffenried*, 47.

18. Graffenried, "Narrative by Christoph von Graffenried," 909.

19. Ibid., 913 J. Russell Snapp, "Graffenried, Christoph, Baron von (1661–1743)," *American National Biography*, https://www.anb.org/display/10.1093/anb/9780198606697 .001.0001/anb-9780198606697-e-0100336.

20. Graffenried, "Narrative by Christoph von Graffenried," 920.

21. Alexander Spotswood to Lord Dartmouth, July 15, 1711, Virginia, OLAS, 1: 78.

22. Alexander Spotswood to the LCTP, Kiquotan, July 28, 1711, *OLAS*, 1: 105.

23. Graffenried, "Narrative by Christoph von Graffenried," 921–22.

24. Ibid., 922–23.

25. J. Lawson, *New Voyage to Carolina*, 88.

26. Graffenried, "Narrative by Christoph von Graffenried," 926.

27. Ibid., 927.

28. Ibid., 928.

29. Ibid., 929.

30. Ibid., 932.

31. Ibid., 933.

32. Ibid., 935.

33. Ibid., 935–36.

34. *EJCCV*, 3: 284–85.

35. Alexander Spotswood to the Council of Trade, Virginia, October 15, 1711, *OLAS*, 1: 117–18.

36. Parramore, "Tuscarora Ascendancy," *North Carolina Historical Review* 59, no. 4 (1982): 323–24.

37. Berlin, "From Creole to African," 253n5, 254n8, 255–67.

38. Parramore, "Tuscarora Ascendancy," 323–24.

39. *EJCCV*, 3: 285–86.

40. Beverley, *History and Present State of Virginia*, 23–24.

41. Alexander Spotswood to the Council of Trade, Virginia, November 17, 1711, *OLAS*, 1: 121–23; Alexander Spotswood to the Bishop of London, Virginia, November 11, 1711, Virginia, *OLAS*, 1: 127.

42. Alexander Spotswood to Lord Dartmouth, November 11, 1711, *OLAS*, 1: 121–22; Alexander Spotswood to the Bishop of London, 1: 126–27.

43. William Byrd II, diary entry, October 21, 1711, "The Diary of William Byrd II of Virginia, 1709–1712," *Becoming American: The British Atlantic Colonies, 1690–1763*, National Humanities Center. https://nationalhumanitiescenter.org/pds/becomingamer/economies/text5/williambyrddiary.pdf.

44. *EJCCV*, 1: 815.

45. Alexander Spotswood to Lord Dartmouth, Virginia, November 11, 1711, *OLAS*, 1: 123–25.

46. Alexander Spotswood to LCTP, Virginia, December 28, 1711, *OLAS*, 1: 129–30.

47. Graffenried, "Narrative by Christoph von Graffenried," 938–39.

48. Ibid., 939–40.

49. Ibid., 923–24.

50. Ibid., 924–25. Graffenried wrote to Governor Hyde on October 23, 1711, how he had escaped ritual torture and execution at the hands of the Tuscarora.

51. Ibid., 948.

52. Ibid., 947, 949–50, 956.

53. Alexander Spotswood to the Council of Trade, Virginia, February 8, 1711 [1712], *OLAS*, 1: 141–42.

54. Ibid., 142–43; Alexander Spotswood to the Sec'y of State [the Earl of Nottingham], Virginia, February 8, 1711 [1712], *OLAS*, 1: 144–46.

55. Alexander Spotswood to the Council of Trade, Virginia, May 8, 1712, *OLAS*, 1: 152; Todd and Goebel, *Baron Christoph von Graffenried*, 88–89, 391n57.

56. J. Barnwell, "Tuscarora Expedition," 30.

57. Alexander Spotswood to Your Excellency, February 27, 1711 [1712], Preston Davis Collection, 1560–1903, folder 15 (259), Wilson Special Collections Library, University of North Carolina.

58. J. Barnwell, "Tuscarora Expedition," 37.

59. Ibid., 45; Dove Williamson, ca. 1711, Wills, vol. 54, 1694–1704; vol. 55, 1711–1718, Charleston, SC, Ancestry Library. https://www.ancestrylibrary.com/search /collections/9080/records/.

60. J. Barnwell, "Tuscarora Expedition," 42, 46, 54; Tibbetts, "Carolina's Gold Coast"; La Vere, "Of Fortifications and Fire," 372. La Vere interprets Harry's feats as stemming less from his African background and more from the possibility that he had worked on South Carolina military fortifications. Georgiou, "Archaeologists Uncover American Slaves' Engineering Feats Underwater."

61. J. Barnwell, "Tuscarora Expedition," 52–53.

62. "North Carolina Resolutions against Bay River Indians, Tuscaroras and Their Allies"; See *North Carolina Colonial Record*, 2nd ser, vol. 7, 1711–1712 for original. Robert J. Cain, ed. The Colonial Records of North Carolina (Second Series) Volume VII: Records of the Executive Council 1664–1734. Raleigh: The North Carolina State Division of Archives and History, 1984, 8–10.

63. J. Barnwell, "Tuscarora Expedition," 38.

64. Byrd, diary entry, March 16, 1712.

65. Alexander Spotswood to Lord Dartmouth, Virginia, May 8, 1712, *OLAS*, 1: 146–48.

66. J. Barnwell, "Tuscarora Expedition," 35.

67. Alexander Spotswood to the Council of Trade, Virginia, May 8, 1712, *OLAS*, 1: 170–71.

68. Alexander Spotswood to the Bishop of London, Virginia, May 8, 1712, *OLAS*, 1: 156–57. By the spring of 1713, the number of tributary children at the college had increased to seventeen. Alexander Spotswood to the Bishop of London, Virginia, March 13, 1713, *OLAS*, 2: 64.

69. Alexander Spotswood to the Council of Trade, Virginia, July 26, 1712, *OLAS*, 1: 167.

70. Alexander Spotswood to the Bishop of London, Virginia, July 26, 1712, *OLAS*, 1: 175. Alexander Spotswood to the Bishop of London, Virginia, May 8, 1712, *OLAS*, 1.

71. Alexander Spotswood to the Bishop of London, Virginia, January 27, 1715, *OLAS*, 2: 91.

72. Alexander Spotswood to the Council of Trade, Virginia, July 26, 1712, *OLAS*, 1: 167.

73. Ibid., 169–70.

74. Alexander Spotswood to Col. Nehemiah Blakiston, Virginia, May 8, 1712, *OLAS*, 1: 160.

75. Alexander Spotswood to the Council of Trade, Virginia, July 26, 1712, *OLAS*, 1: 169.

76. Alexander Spotswood to Mr. Blathwayt, Virginia, May 8, 1712, *OLAS*, 1: 157–58.

77. J. Barnwell, "Tuscarora Expedition," 36; J. W. Barnwell, "Second Tuscarora Expedition"; Ewen, Whyte, and Davis, "Archaeology of North Carolina," 10–31.

78. *EJCCV*, 3: 333.

79. Ibid.

Chapter 7. The White Men Would Come and Fetch the Yamasees in One Night

1. *EJCCV*, 3: 177; Buchner, "Yuchi Indians."
2. "Memorial from the Virginia Indian Company," 33.
3. *JHB*, 4: 178.
4. Ibid., 203.
5. Byrd, Tinling, and Wright, *Secret Diary of William Byrd*, 49.
6. *JHB*, 4: 242.
7. Alexander Spotswood to the Council of Trade, December 15, 1710, *OLAS*, 1: 42.
8. Alexander Spotswood to LCTP, Virginia, September 5, 1711, *OLAS*, 1: 110.
9. Alexander Spotswood to LCTP, Virginia, December 15, 1710, *OLAS*, 1: 40–41.
10. Alexander Spotswood Directed to the hon'ble Edw'd Hide, Esq'r, Gov'r of North Carolina in Council, December 24, 1710, *OLAS*, 1: 45.
11. Alexander Spotswood to the Council of Trade, Virginia, May 8, 1712, *OLAS*, 1: 172.
12. Alexander Spotswood to the Council of Trade, Virginia, July 26, 1712, *OLAS*, 1: 167.
13. Ramsey, "'Something Cloudy in Their Looks,'" 57.
14. Alexander Spotswood to the Board of Trade, February 1, 1719 [1720], *OLAS*, 2: 331–32; Ramsey, "'Something Cloudy in Their Looks,'" 72, 72n53; Barker, "Pryce Hughes, Colony Planner," 303–5, 310–12.
15. America and West Indies, July 1715, *CSPC*, 28: 1–15.
16. Report by Charles Craven, "Endorsed, Referred to the Board of Trade," "America and West Indies: July 1715, 1–15," *CSPC*, 28: 1–15.
17. Worth, "Yamassee Origins and the Development of the Carolina-Florida Frontier," 4.
18. Quoted in Beck, *Chiefdoms, Collapse, and Coalescence*, 213.
19. Ramsey, *Yamasee War*, 228; Ramsey; "'Something Cloudy in Their Looks,'" 69.
20. Letter of Capt. Jonathan St. Lo and enclosure, July 12, 1715, Admiralty Office, 1: 2451, British Public Record Office, London; Published in Ramsey, *Yamasee War*, 228.
21. Report by Charles Craven.
22. See William Byrd II's contribution to "Journal, July 1715: Journal Book R," in *Journals of the Board of Trade and Plantations*, vol. 3, *March 1715–October 1718*, ed. K. H. Ledward (London: His Majesty's Stationery Office, 1924), 49–65. *British History Online British History Online*. http://www.british-history.ac.uk /jrnl-trade-plantations/vol3/pp49–65.
23. Ibid.
24. Byrd, Byrd, and Byrd, *Correspondence of the Three William Byrds*, 1: 288–89.
25. Ramsey, "'Something Cloudy in Their Looks,'" 70.
26. Reports of Mr. Byrd and Mr. Crawley, "Journal, August 1715: Journal Book R," in *Journals of the Board of Trade and Plantations*, 3: 65–76, *British History Online*. http://www.british-history.ac.uk/jrnl-trade-plantations/vol3/pp65–76, 2023. Ramsey called sexual abuse "the most corrosive form of misconduct perpetrated by Englishmen in Indian territory. . . . The corrosive effects of gender-specific violence on Anglo-Indian exchange relations . . . did their damage selectively, depending on tribal affiliation and the specific clans or lineages involved, and always within the simultaneous context of positive influences for other native

women and their kinship networks." Ramsey, "'Something Cloudy in Their Looks,'" 51–52.

27. Reports of Byrd and Crawley.

28. "Memorial Relating to Assistance Given by Virginia to South Carolina in the Indian War," June 21, 1717, 25, CO 5/1318, National Archives, Kew.pt. 1; "Journal, June 1717: Journal Book S," in *Journals of the Board of Trade and Plantations*, 3: 238–244, *British History Online*, http://www.british-history.ac.uk/jrnl-trade -plantations/vol3/pp238–244; CO_5_1318_PART1_008, National Archives, Kew. Alexander Spotswood to Col. Nehemiah Blakiston, April 16, 1717, *OLAS*, 2: 242.

29. Alexander Spotswood to the Board of Trade, February 1, 1719 [1720], *OLAS*, 2: 331; Smyth, "Natchez Diaspora," 40.

30. Alexander Spotswood to the Board of Trade, February 1, 1719 [1720], *OLAS*, 2: 332.

31. *EJCCV*, 4: 1721–1739, 1–2; Beck, *Chiefdoms, Collapse, and Coalescence*, 234; Tim St. Onge, "Celebrating Native American Cartography: The Catawba Deerskin Map," *Library of Congress Blogs*, November 30, 2016, https://blogs.loc.gov/maps/2016 /11/celebrating-native-american-cartography-the-catawba-deerskin-map/.

32. *EJCCV*, 3: 554–55.

33. *EJCCV*, 4: 2.

34. Chambers, "Cherokee Origin for the 'Catawba' Deerskin Map," 213–14.

35. St. Jean, "Trading Paths: Mapping," 769–71; St. Jean, "Trading Paths: Chickasaw Diplomacy," 19–21; Featherling, "Horses, Culture, and Trade," 59–60.

36. Hunter and Salley, "George Hunter's Map of the Cherokee Country and the Path Thereto in 1730."

37. Oliphant, *Peace and War on the Anglo-Cherokee Frontier*, 1–2; Wood, "Changing Population of the Colonial South," 72.

38. Byrd, Byrd, and Byrd, *Correspondence of the Three William Byrds*, 1: 619–20.

Chapter 8. A New Method for Bringing the Indians under a Regulation

1. Parent, *Foul Means*, 162.

2. Alexander Spotswood to the Council of Trade, July 26, 1712, *OLAS*, 1: 167–72; Alexander Spotswood to the Council of Trade, October 15, 1712, Virginia, *OLAS*, 2: 1–2.

3. Byrd, *Histories of the Dividing Line*, 116, 118; McDowell, *Journals of the Commissioners of the Indian Trade*, 80. The commissioners also proposed building a "small Factory" for trading purposes. See Richter, "War and Culture," 557–58; Richter, *Ordeal of the Longhouse*, 238–40; Axtell, *Invasion Within*, 191, 262; Parent, *Foul Means*, 172.

4. Alexander Spotswood to the Earl of Dartmouth, May 15, 1713, Virginia, *OLAS*, 2: 18–19.

5. *EJCCV*, 3: 363.

6. Ibid.

7. Ibid., 364.

8. Alexander Spotswood to Lord Dartmouth, July 26, 1712, Virginia, *OLAS*, 1: 173

9. Alexander Spotswood to LCTP, October 24, 1710, Virginia, *OLAS*, 1: 25.

10. Alexander Spotswood to the hon'ble Edw'd Hide, Esq'r, Gov'r of North Carolina in Council, December 24, 1710, *OLAS*, 1: 47–48.

11. Ibid.

12. *EJCCV*, 3: 364, 367.

13. *EJCCV*, 3: 365.

14. *EJCCV*, 3: 368.

15. Alexander Spotswood to the Council of Trade and Plantation, Virginia, July 26, 1712, *OLAS*, 1: 100; Alexander Spotswood to the Council of Trade and Plantation, Virginia, January 27, 1715; *CSPC*, 28: 71–90; the document number M. G. Lawson, "Act for the Better Regulation of the Indian Trade."

16. Alexander Spotswood to the Council of Trade and Plantation, January 27, 1715; M. G. Lawson, "Act for the Better Regulation of the Indian Trade."

17. Alexander Spotswood to LCTP, July 21, 1714, *OLAS*, 2: 70.

18. Alexander Spotswood to LCTP, March 28, 1715, Virginia, *OLAS*, 2: 108–9.

19. Fontaine et al., *Memoirs of a Huguenot Family*, 98.

20. *EJCCV*, 3: 367–68.

21. Ibid.

22. Ibid., 3: 365–66, 368.

23. "Memorial from the Virginia Indian Company," 33.

24. Alexander Spotswood to the Bishop of London, January 27, 1715, Virginia, *OLAS*, 2: 88–90.

25. "Memorial from the Virginia Indian Company," CO 5/1318, pt. 1, April 24, 1717, 33; Lt. Governor Spotswood to the Council of Trade and Plantation, January 27, 1715, Virginia. *CSPC*, 28: 71–90. M. G. Lawson, "Act for the Better Regulation of the Indian Trade."

26. Alexander Spotswood to LCTP, January 27, 1715,Virginia, *OLAS*, 2: 94; M. G. Lawson, "Act for the Better Regulation of the Indian Trade."

27. Fontaine et al., *Memoirs of a Huguenot Family*, 96, 155.

28. Ibid., 85.

29. "A significant remnant of the Algonquians, such as the Pochicks, were present on the reservation. This finding acts to affirm the amalgamation of these Algonquian Pochick-Nansemond among the Siouan Saponi"; Jay Hansford C. Vest. "From Nansemond to Monacan: The Legacy of the Pochick-Nansemond among the Bear Mountain Monacan." *American Indian Quarterly* 27, no. 3/4 (2003), 792.

30. Alexander Spotswood to LCTP, Virginia, June 4, 1715, *OLAS*, 2: 113; Alexander Spotswood to LCTP, Virginia, February 16, 1715 [1716], *OLAS*, 2: 141.

31. Alexander Spotswood to the Bishop of London, Virginia, October 26, 1715, *OLAS*, 2: 138.

32. Fontaine et al., *Memoirs of a Huguenot Family*, 91, 98.

33. Alexander Spotswood to LCTP, Virginia, June 4, 1715, *OLAS*, 2: 113; Spotswood to LCTP, Virginia, February 7, 1715 [1716], *OLAS*, 2: 198–99.

34. Fontaine et al., *Memoirs of a Huguenot Family*, 98.

35. Alexander Spotswood to the Bishop of London, Virginia, January 27, 1715, *OLAS*, 2: 88–90; Spotswood to LCTP, Virginia, February 16,1715 [1716], *OLAS*, 2: 141; Alexander Spotswood to LCTP, Virginia, February 16, 1715 [1716], *OLAS*, 2: 197.

36. Fontaine et al., *Memoirs of a Huguenot Family*, 96.

37. Ibid.

38. Ibid., 99.

39. Alexander Spotswood to LCTP, February 16, 1715 [1716], *OLAS*, 2: 141.

40. Alexander Spotswood to Mr. Secretary Methuen, Virginia, May 30, 1717, *OLAS*, 2: 251; Spotswood to LCTP, Virginia, August 29, 1717, *OLAS*, 2: 257–58.

41. "A memorial from several Virginia merchants, relating to the Act passed there, for preventing frauds in tobacco payments, and the Act relating to the Indian Trade," May 10, 1717, *Journals of the Board of Trade and Plantations*, 3: 226–37.
42. "Memorial from the Virginia Indian Company," 34; Lozier, "Nicer Red," 49–50.
43. Ibid., 44.
44. Ibid., 34.
45. Ibid., 45.
46. Alexander Spotswood to the Board of Trade, August 14, 1718, *OLAS*, 2: 296–97.
47. Alexander Spotswood to the Board of Trade, June 24, 1718, Virginia, *OLAS*, 2: 282.
48. Alexander Spotswood to the Board of Trade, September 27, 1718, *OLAS*, 2: 302–3.
49. Alexander Spotswood to the Board of Trade, June 24, 1718.
50. Kemper, "Early Westward Movement of Virginia" 1–2.
51. Byrd, "Westover Manuscripts," 89.
52. Ibid., 36, 88–89; *EJCCV*, 3: 397; Kemper, "Early Westward Movement of Virginia," 1n1; Sleeper-Smith, *Indigenous Prosperity and American Conquest*, 246; Woodard, Moretti-Langholtz, and Hasselbacher, *High Plains Sappony*, 25–28; Alexander, "Indian Vocabulary from Fort Christanna," 309.
53. *EJCCV*, 4: 269; Kemper, "Early Westward Movement of Virginia," 2n.1; Alexander, "Indian Vocabulary from Fort Christanna," 306.
54. Byrd, "Westover Manuscripts," 34–36.
55. James Logan to unknown recipient, December 20, 1736, presented at a council held in the Council Chamber, July 23, 1742, Archives Md., 28: 271–72.

Chapter 9. Remembrance of These Things Is Faithfully Preserved

1. Ganter, "'Make Your Minds Perfectly Easy,'" 126–28.
2. *Treaty of Friendship Held with the Chiefs of the Six Nations*, 7.
3. August 26, 1732. *Minutes of the Provincial Council of Pennsylvania*, 1840, 3: 476; *Treaty of Friendship Held with the Chiefs of the Six Nations*, 8.
4. Ibid., 11.
5. Ibid.
6. John Sergeant to Stephen Williams, Housatun muk [Housatonic], May 14, 1739, "Letters 1739–1743," Newberry Library.
7. Charles A. Hanna, *Wilderness Trail*, 1: 19–20. Peter Chartier may have been the son of the French trader Martin Chartier and Opessa's daughter. Bedell et al., "River and Mountain, War and Peace," 35.
8. *Treaty of Friendship Held with the Chiefs of the Six Nations*, 11.
9. Ibid., 14.
10. Ibid., 7.
11. Ibid., 12.
12. Proceedings of the Council of Maryland, 1732–1753, 28: 271–72, Archives Md.
13. Ibid., Logan to unknown recipient.
14. America and West Indies: December 1738, *CSPC*, vol. 44 (1738), ed. K. G. Davies (London: Her Majesty's Stationery Office, 1969), 256–76, *British History Online*. http://www.british history.ac.uk/cal state papers/colonial/america west indies /vol44/pp256 276; Board of Trade to Gooch, Whitehall, August 7, 1740, PRO, CO 5/1366, 329–31 (M-230, SR 845), VCRP.
15. America and West Indies: December 1738; *British History Online*. Board of Trade to Gooch, August 7, 1740.

16. Philip Livingston Jr. to Laurens Claese Van der Volgen, March 6, 1738, Att a meeting of the Com:rs of Indian Affairs att Albany the 6:th Mar. 1737/8. Records of the Commissioners of Indian Affairs 1723–1748 © Ann H. Hunter 2021 https://albanyindiancommissioners.com/translations-of-dutch-entries/.

17. Instructions from the Commissioners of the Indian Affairs for Corn.s Verplank, March 6, 1738, Ibid.

18. America and West Indies: September 1738, *CSPC*, vol. 44 (1738), ed. K. G. Davies (London: Her Majesty's Stationery Office, 1969), 206–20, *British History Online*. http://www.british-history.ac.uk/cal-state-papers/colonial/america-west-indies/vol44/. Gooch's account collaborates Samuel Kercheval's informants, who recollected that several locations in the northern Shenandoah Valley had become killing fields after a 1734 series of attacks by northern nations, especially the Lenni Lenape, and Catawba counterattacks. Kercheval, *History of the Valley of Virginia*, 35–37.

19. Council of Trade and Plantations to Lieut.-Governor William Gooch, Whitehall, December 21, 1738); America and West Indies: December 1738, *CSPC*, vol. 44 (1738). *British History Online*.

20. America and West Indies: December 1738, *CSPC*, vol. 44 (1738); Board of Trade to William Gooch, Whitehall, August 7, 1740, PRO, CO 5/1366, 329–31 (M-230, SR 845), VCRP.

21. *Treaty of Friendship Held with the Chiefs of the Six Nations*, 8–11; Grumet et al., *Beyond Manhattan*, 80. See also Gipson, *Moravian Indian Mission on White River*.

22. *Treaty of Friendship Held with the Chiefs of the Six Nations*, 10.

23. Ibid., 13–14.

24. Ibid., 13.

25. "By the Honourable George Thomas, Esq; Lieutenant Governor and Commander in Chief of the Province of Pennsylvania and the Counties of New-Castle, Kent and Sussex upon Delaware. A Proclamation" (Philadelphia, 1742), Library of Congress, https://www.loc.gov/resource/rbpe.14100800/?st=gallery.

26. Charlevoix, Caxton Club, and Kellogg, *Journal of a Voyage to North America*, 50.

27. *Treaty of Friendship Held with the Chiefs of the Six Nations*, 21–22. The Haudenosaunee around 1725 had lambasted the Lenni Lenape for not joining with the Shawnee in attacking the English, characterizing them "as women for the future and not as men." Quoted in Hofstra, *Planting of New Virginia*, 104.

28. *Treaty, Held at the Town of Lancaster*, 24. "It was not uncommon for Indians to invoke the term 'female' and the characteristics and roles associated with it in a derogatory manner to shame males." Merritt, "Metaphor, Meaning, and Mis understanding," 78.

29. Proceedings of the Council of Maryland, 1742, 28: 272–73, Archives Md.

30. *Treaty, Held at the Town of Lancaster*, 4–5; Thomson, *Enquiry into the Causes of the Alienation*, 50.

Chapter 10. Exposing Ourselves to All Manner of Hardships

1. Hofstra, "'Extention of His Majesties Dominions,'" 1305.

2. William Beverley to unknown recipient, April 30, 1732, in Palmer et al., *Calendar of Virginia State Papers*, 217–18.

3. William Gooch to Board of Trade, May 24, 1734, CO 5/1323, Colonial Office Papers, "Letters from William Gooch," Correspondence, National Archives, Kew, Hofstra, "'Extention of His Majesties Dominions,'" 1301.

4. William Beverley, Virginia, to Capt. James Patton, Kircubright (Kirkcudbright), Scotland, August 8, 1737, in Ford, "Some Letters of William Beverley," 226–27; Guzy, "1736 Survey of the Potomac River," 27.
5. William Beverley, Virginia, to John Fairfield (Barbados) Augst 25, 1738, in Ford, "Some Letters of William Beverley," 228n1.
6. Bartram quoted in Hofstra, "'Extention of His Majesties Dominions,'" 1303; Hofstra, *Planting of New Virginia*, 24.
7. William Gooch to Board of Trade, August 26, 1741, CO 5/1325.
8. William Beverley, Virginia, to Lord Fairfax, London, June 14, 1738, in Ford, "Some Letters of William Beverley," 227.
9. William Beverley, Virginia, to Lord Fairfax, London, May 18, 1739, in Ford, "Some Letters of William Beverley," 228–29.
10. William Beverley, Blanfield, Virginia, to Lord Fairfax, Leeds Castle, Kent, July 3, 1742, in Ford, "Some Letters of William Beverley," 230; *SAL*, 5: 207.
11. William Beverley, Virginia, to Chr Smyth, merchant, London, March 10, 1741, in Ford, "Some Letters of William Beverley," 229.
12. William Beverley, Virginia, to Chr Smyth, merchant, London, August 9, 1742, in Ford, "Some Letters of William Beverley," 230. Although he failed to secure the secretary's appointment, Beverley continued in the House of Burgesses (1736–40, 1742–49) and joined the Council of State ten years later, where he served from 1752 until 1756.
13. William Beverley, Williamsburg, to Lord Fairfax, Leeds Castle, Kent, April 20, 1743, in Ford, "Some Letters of William Beverley," 231.
14. Fairfax Harrison, "Virginians on the Ohio and the Mississippi," 204–5.
15. Ibid., 212.
16. Ibid., 207.
17. Ibid., 207, 213, 215.

Chapter 11. Invasions, Incursions, and Insurrections

1. Parent, *Foul Means*, 159–61.
2. Ibid., 166–67.
3. Jemison, *Narrative of the Life*, 114–15; DuVal, *Native Ground*, 95–96.] The Cotawpes were likely the Quapaw or Ogáxpa people. O-ga-xpa in the Dhegiha language meant the "the down-stream people," so called because their ancestors went down the Mississippi, while the Omahas, Ponca, Osages, and Kansa went up that stream, after leaving the mouth of the Ohio River. "The Ogáxpa or Kwapas have been called Shappas, Shapahas, Kapahas, Quappas, Quapaws, etc. They were also known in early colonial days as the Akansa or Arkansa (Kanza)"; "Origin of Tribal Name," Quapaw Tribe official website, https://www.quapawtribe.com/401/Tribal-Name; J. F. Lee, *Masters of the Middle Waters*, 9–10.
4. Governor Clark to the Lords of Trade, May 24, 1739, CO 5/1094, part 1, National Archives, Kew; "Lieut-Governor George Clarke to Commissioners for Trade and Plantations, enclosing small map of the country taken, I suppose, from M. E. De Lisle's [1718 Carte de la Louisiane]," New York, May 24, 1739; America and West Indies: May 1739, *CSPC*, vol. 45 (1739), ed. K. G. Davies (London: Her Majesty's Stationery Office, 1994), 90–111, ., http://www.british-history.ac.uk/cal-state-papers/colonial/america-west-indies/vol45/pp90–111; C. Anderson, "Rediscovering Native North America," 484–85.

5. Carl Van Doren, Julian P. Boyd, and Historical Society of Pennsylvania, *Indian Treaties Printed by Benjamin Franklin, 1736–1762* (Ulan Press, 2012), 21, 45.

6. M. M. Smith, *Stono*, 5, 13–15. Peter H. Wood says Oglethorpe was the likely author of "Account of the Negroe Insurrection in South Carolina." "Anatomy of a Revolt," Ibid., 70n9

7. Ibid., 14.

8. Ibid., 16–17.

9. Ibid., 15.

10. Boston, Oct. 22. By a Vessel from Cape Fear, *Virginia Gazette*, January 4, 1740.

11. Account of HM's revenue of 25 per hogshead arising within Virginia, October 25, 1738, to April 25, 1739 [CO 5/1324, ff. 170–77d], America and West Indies: August 1739, *CSPC*, vol. 45 (1739), ed. K. G. Davies (London: Her Majesty's Stationery Office, 1994), 153–74, *British History Online*. http://www.britishhistory.ac.uk/calstatepapers/colonial/americawestindies/vol45/pp153174.

12. America and West Indies: August 1739, *CSPC*, vol. 45 (1739). *British History Online*.

13. William Bull, Governor of South Carolina, to the Royal Council, October 5, 1739, South Carolina Department of Archives and History, Columbia.

14. William Gooch to the LCTP, August 29, 1740, PRO, CO 5/1325, ff. 2–3 (ff. 18–29) (M-242, SR 788), VCRP; *JHB*, 6: xxviii, 301–3; *SAL*, 4: 310–22, 5: 92–94; Parent, *Foul Means*, 170–71.

15. William Gooch to Secretary of State, Virginia, May 2, 1740, PRO, CO 5/1337, ff. 226–27 (M-246, SR 245), VCRP.

16. William Gooch to Secretary of State, July 28, 1742, PRO, CO 5/1337, ff. 265–66 (M246, SR 245), VCRP.

Chapter 12. Several Nations of Our Indians

1. Samuel Ogle to William Gooch, Annapolis, MD, July 14, 1742, PRO, CO 5/1337, ff. 275–76 (M-246, SR 245), VCRP.

2. Proceedings of the Council of Maryland, 1742. 28: 259–60, Archives Md.

3. Ibid., 28: 266.

4. Ibid., 28: 266–67.

5. Ibid., 28: 263.

6. Ibid., 28: 266.

7. Ibid., 28: 263.

8. Ibid., 28: 266.

9. Ibid., 28: 266.

10. Ibid., 28: 266–67.

11. Ibid., 28: 264.

12. Ibid., 28: 268.

13. Ibid., 28: 269.

14. Ibid., 28: 267–68.

15. Ibid., 28: 269.

16. Ibid.

17. Ibid., 28: 274.

18. Assembly Proceedings, May 1–June 4, 1744, 42: 652, Archives Md.

19. James Logan to unknown recipient.

Chapter 13. Skirmish in the Back Parts of Virginia

1. William Gooch to Secretary of State, July 28, 1742, PRO, CO 5/1337, ff. 265–66 (M-246, SR 245), VCRP.

2. Samuel Ogle to the Board of Trade, May 17, 1743, CO, 5/655, f. 218., VCRP.

3. William Gooch to the Board of Trade, July 31, 1742, PRO, CO 5/1325 (M-242, SR 788), VCRP.

4. "Journal, August 1743: Volume 51," in *Journals of the Board of Trade and Plantations*, vol. 8, *January 1742–December 1749*, ed. K. H. Ledward (London: His Majesty's Stationery Office, 1931), 79–81, *British History Online*. http://www.british-history.ac.uk/jrnl-trade-plantations/vol8/pp79–81; *Indian Treaties Printed by Benjamin Franklin*, 41, 46.

5. James Patten (Patton) to Governor Gooch, October 23, 1742 [duplicate February 14, 1742/43], PRO, CO, 5/1325 (M-242, SR 788), York County Records.

6. Governor Gooch to Board of Trade, February 14, 1743, PRO, CO 5/1325 (M-242, SR 788), York County Records.

7. *Minutes of the Provincial Council of Pennsylvania*, 4: 464–65; Hofstra, *Planting of New Virginia*, 19, 49; Merrell, *Into the American Woods*, 168–75.

8. *Minutes of the Provincial Council of Pennsylvania*, 4: 464–66.

9. Deposition of Thomas McKee of Lancaster County, January 24, 1742/43, *Minutes of the Provincial Council of Pennsylvania*, 4: 630–33.

10. *Minutes of the Provincial Council of Pennsylvania*, 4: 631.

11. Ibid., 4: 632.

12. Ibid.

13. Ibid., 4: 632–33.

14. "A Journal of the Proceedings of Conrad Weiser [manuscript]: On His Journey to Ohio with a Message & Present from the Government of Pensilvania to the Indians There," August 11–October 2, 1748, manuscript, Ayer MS 3200, Edward E. Ayer Collection, Newberry Library; William A. Hunter, "Swatana," in *Dictionary of Canadian Biography*, vol. 3 (Toronto: University of Toronto/Université Laval, 2003–), http://www.biographi.ca/en/bio/swatana_3E.html.

15. *Minutes of the Provincial Council of Pennsylvania*, 4: 649.

16. Ibid., 4: 650.

17. Berkeley and Berkeley, *Correspondence of John Bartram*, 219.

18. Bartram and Kalm, *Observations on the Inhabitants*; "Conrad Weiser's Report of His Journey to Onondago on the Affairs of Virginia, in Obedience to the Orders of the Governor in Council, 13 June, 1743, Delivered to the Governor the 1st September," *Minutes of the Provincial Council of Pennsylvania*, 4: 660–69.

19. *Minutes of the Provincial Council of Pennsylvania*, 4: 660–69. Cf. Goetzmann, "John Bartram's Travel to Onondaga in Context," 102–3.

20. June 25, 1744, Lancaster, *Indian Treaties Printed by Benjamin Franklin*, 45.

21. *Treaty, Held at the Town of Lancaster*, 6.

22. Ibid., 24.

23. Ibid., 20.

24. *Treaty, Held at the Town of Lancaster*, 15–16; Charles A. Hanna, *Wilderness Trail*; Fenton, *Great Law and the Longhouse*, 428–29.

25. *Treaty, Held at the Town of Lancaster*, 23.

26. Ibid., 24, 31; C. Anderson, "Rediscovering Native North America," 497.

27. Thomson, *Enquiry into the Causes of the Alienation*, 52–53; Nash, "When We Were Young," 13–15.

28. Samuel Ogle to the Board of Trade, May 17, 1743, CO 5/655, f. 218. VCRP.
29. September 14, 1744, *JHB*, 7: 91.
30. *Virginia Gazette*, December 5, 1745.
31. *Virginia Gazette*, October 10, 1745.
32. "Governor George Clinton in New York," June 6–July 11, 1746, Ayer MS 633, Edward E. Ayer Collection, Newberry Library.
33. Ibid.
34. Berkeley and Berkeley, *Correspondence of John Bartram*, 283.
35. "Act 39: An Act for Making Provision against Invasions and Insurrections," *SAL*, October 1748, 6: 112–14.

Chapter 14. The Rich Back Lands

1. *EJCCV*, 4: 355.
2. George Washington to John Posey, June 24, 1767, Founders Online, National Archives, https://founders.archives.gov/documents/Washington/02–08–02–0001. Original source: W. W. Abbot and Dorothy Twohig, eds., *The Papers of George Washington, Colonial Series*, vol. 8, *24 June 1767–25 December 1771* (Charlottesville: University Press of Virginia, 1993), 1–4 (hereafter *George Washington Papers*).
3. William Beverley, Williamsburg, to Lord Fairfax, Leeds Castle, Kent, April 20, 1743, in Ford, "Some Letters of William Beverley," 231; Glanville and Mays, "William Beverley, James Patton, and the Settling of the Shenandoah Valley"; Brent Tarter, "John Robinson (1705-1766)," *Dictionary of Virginia Biography*, https://encyclopediavirginia.org/entries/robinson-john-1705-1766/.
4. George Washington to William Crawford, September 17, 1767, Founders Online, National Archives, https://founders.archives.gov/documents/Washington/02–08–02–0020. Original source: *Papers of George Washington*, 8: 26–32. See also *EJCCV*, 5: 231n6. Jeanne A. Calhoun, "Thomas Lee of Stratford, 1690–1750, Founder of a Virginia Dynasty," paper presented to the Robert E. Lee Memorial Association, August 1989, http://www.stratfordhall.org/collections-research /staff-research/thomas-lee-of-stratford-1690–1750/#6.
5. Del Papa, "Royal Proclamation of 1763," 409–10; Stephen G. Smith, "Loyal Company," *The West Virginia Encyclopedia*, https://www.wvencyclopedia.org /print/Article/1462.
6. Order of the Committee of Council, "referring to the Lords of Trade the petition of John Hanbury to the Lords of Trade the petition of John Hanbury et al., incorporators of the Ohio Company," February 9, 1748–49, B T, Vol. 20 reprinted in Fernow, *Ohio Valley in Colonial Days*, 250–51; February 14, 1749. Journal, February 1749: Volume 57, in *Journals of the Board of Trade and Plantations: Volume 8, January 1742-December 1749*, ed. K H Ledward (London, 1931), *British History Online*, https://www.british-history.ac.uk/jrnl-trade-plantations /vol8/pp377–387. *JHB*, 7: 76.
7. Deposition of George Croghan, February 27, 1777, in Palmer et al., *Calendar of Virginia State Papers and Other Manuscripts*, 276–77.
8. Order of the Committee of Council; reprinted in Fernow, *Ohio Valley in Colonial Days*, 250–51; *JHB*, 7: 76.
9. *JHB*, 7: 76.
10. *Treaty of Friendship Held with the Chiefs of the Six Nations*, 8; Carter, "Allummapees, King of the Delawares at Shamokin"; Thomson, *Enquiry into the Causes of*

the *Alienation*, 53; Misencik and Misencik, *American Indians of the Ohio Country*, 14–17; D. Miller, "Wyandot, Shawnee, and African American Resistance," 35.

11. Misencik and Misencik, *American Indians of the Ohio Country*, 17, 23; Charles A. Hanna, *Wilderness Trail*, 21–22, 161; Ironstrack, "Crooked Trail to Pickawillany." See also Hurt, *Ohio Frontier*; s.v. "Shawnee," *New World Encyclopedia*, https://www.newworldencyclopedia.org/p/index.php?title=Shawnee&oldid=1026678.

12. George Washington, diary, October 22, 1770, Founders Online, National Archives, last modified June 29, 2017, http://founders.archives.gov/documents/Washington/01–02–02–0005–0029–0018 (original source: *Diaries of George Washington*, 2: 295–97); Sleeper-Smith, *Indigenous Prosperity and American Conquest*, 7.

13. Deposition of Maj. Edward Ward, March 10, 1777, Pittsburg, in Palmer et al., *Calendar of Virginia State Papers and Other Manuscripts*, 277.

14. As editor James E. Seaver notes, "That town, according to the geographical description given by Mrs. Jemison, must have stood at the mouth of Indian Cross creek, which is about 76 miles by water, below Pittsburgh; or at the mouth of Indian Short creek, 87 miles below Pittsburgh, where the town of Warren now stands: But at which of those places I am unable to determine." Jemison, *Narrative of the Life*, 51n.

15. Ibid., 48–50.

16. Ibid., 55.

17. Order of the Committee of Council; reprinted in Fernow, *Ohio Valley in Colonial Days*, 249.

18. Ibid.

19. Board of Trade to William Gooch, March 4, 1749, PRO, CO 5/1366, 439–44. M230, SR 845; reprinted in Fernow, *Ohio Valley in Colonial Days*, 250–59; Commissioners for Trade and Plantations, report to the Committee of the Privy Council for Plantation Affairs, September 2, 1748, PRO, CO 5/1335, ff. 239–44 (M-245, SR 798) VCRP.

20. Letter from Col. Thomas Lee, President of the Council of Virginia, to the Lords of Trade, October 18, 1749, B T, Va Vol. 20; reprinted in Fernow, *Ohio Valley in Colonial Days*, 258; *Memoirs of the Principal Transactions of the Last War between the English and French*.

21. Washington quoted in Royster, *Fabulous History of the Dismal Swamp Company*, 21, 40–43; Parent, *Foul Means*, 53–54.

22. Norona, "Joshua Fry's Report on the Back Settlements of Virginia," 26.

23. Zontine, "Dr. Thomas Walker."

24. Lee, Carey, and Jones, *Water in Kentucky*, 29; Walker, "Journal of Doctor Thomas Walker," 8.

25. Walker, "Journal of Doctor Thomas Walker," 12.

26. Ibid., 13, 17, 18, 22.

27. Nyland, "Doctor Thomas Walker," 19, 22–23; Kincaid, *Wilderness Road*, 32; Hartley, *Life of Daniel Boone*, 36.

28. Walker, "Journal of Doctor Thomas Walker," 15–16.

29. Mills, "Dr. Thomas Walker State Park"; Walker, "Journal of Doctor Thomas Walker," 17.

30. Sapp, *Native Americans State by State*, 118; Nyland, "Doctor Thomas Walker," 24.

31. Walker, "Journal of Doctor Thomas Walker," 17.

32. Ibid., 19, 23. OED s.v. "shifted": "change one's clothing or dress in fresh under-clothing, now obsolete."
33. Ibid.; Tayac, "Ancestors Speaking"; Ronan, "'Kicked About,'" 4.
34. Hantman, *Monacan Millennium*, 54, 56–60, 65.
35. Jefferson, *Notes on the State of Virginia*, 103–6.
36. Harry Innes to Thomas Jefferson, July 8, 1790, Founders Online, National Archives, https://founders.archives.gov/documents/Jefferson/01-17-02-0008. Original source: *The Papers of Thomas Jefferson*, vol. 17, *6 July–3 November 1790*, ed. Julian P. Boyd (Princeton, NJ: Princeton University Press, 1965), 20.
37. Thomas Jefferson to Harry Innes, March 7, 1791, Founders Online, National Archives, https://founders.archives.gov/documents/Jefferson/01-19-02-0119 –0006. Original source: *The Papers of Thomas Jefferson*, vol. 19, *24 January–31 March 1791*, ed. Julian P. Boyd (Princeton, NJ: Princeton University Press, 1974), 521–22. Art historian and Native American studies scholar Kristine K. Ronan in 2012 "reidentified" a pair of stone busts, which Jefferson had received around the turn of the century at Monticello, one male and the other female, from an African American to Indigenous American provenance. Excavated at Palmyra on the Tennessee-Kentucky border, where "Native-made mounds were built singly and were relatively evenly spaced, suggesting small village patterns," she identified them as "Mississippian Culture (800–1600 CE) funerary pairs." Ronan surmises the black-pigmented but fully completed "female kneeling (sometimes with a delineated skirt line around her legs)" is comparable to the "kneeling woman" found in the same region. Ronan, "'Kicked About,'" 2.
38. Nash, "When We Were Young," 47.

Chapter 15. Buy Land and Contract for the Settling Thereof

1. *American Husbandry*, 229–30.
2. George Montagu-Dunk, Second Earl of Halifax, to Col. [Thomas] Lee, White-hall, September 1, 1750, Custis-Lee Family Papers, 1700–circa 1928, Library of Congress. See Thomas Lee to Board of Trade, May 11, 1750, "Journal, June 1750: Volume 58," in *Journals of the Board of Trade and Plantations: Volume 9, January 1750-December 1753*, ed. K H Ledward (London, 1932), *British History Online*, https://www.british-history.ac.uk/jrnl-trade-plantations/vol9/pp79–85.
3. "A Narrative of the Late Massacres, [30 January? 1764]," Founders Online, National Archives, https://founders.archives.gov/documents/Franklin/01-11-02 –0012. Original source: *The Papers of Benjamin Franklin*, vol. 11, *January 1 through December 31, 1764*, ed. Leonard W. Labaree (New Haven, CT: Yale University Press, 1967), 42–69 (hereafter *Papers of Benjamin Franklin*).
4. The instructions given to Gist by the Committee of the Ohio Company are included in "Expedition of Christopher Gist, 1750–1751: Gist's Journal for the Honorable Robert Dinwiddie, Esquire, Governor and Commander of Virginia," in *Annals of Southwest Virginia, 1769–1800*, ed. Lewis Preston Summers (Abingdon, VA: Overmountain, 1992), 27–57; Ellis, "Ohio Company," 129–31.
5. John Tayloe to Richard Lee, 1750, Richard Bland Lee Papers, 1700–1825, ser. 1, Custis-Lee Family Papers, 1700–circa 1928, Library of Congress.
6. "Orders and Resolutions of the Ohio Company and the Committee of the Company," May 21–24, 1751, in Mulkearn, *George Mercer Papers*, 174–75.
7. Mulkearn, *George Mercer Papers*, enclosure opposite 72, 225–26, 472–73n60, 643n666; Taliaferro, "Fry and Jefferson Revisited."

8. Ellis, "Ohio Company." "The oldest list of the members of the Ohio Company, found by Mr. M. M. Jones, of Utica, New York, is as follows: John Hanbury, Thomas Lee, Thomas Nelson, Thomas Cresap, William Thornton, William Nimmo, Daniel Cresap, John Carlisle, Lawrence Washington, Augustine Washington, George Fairfax, Jacob Giles, Nathaniel Chapman, James Wardrop, John Tayloe, Presley Thornton, Philip Ludwell Lee, Gawin Corbin, Rev. James Scott. The company was limited to twenty subscribers, and the capital subscribed was £4,000"; Evans, A "Topping People," 96.

9. Mulkearn, George Mercer Papers, 226.

10. "Journal from Virginia beyond the Appalachian Mountains," 239n.

11. American Husbandry, 229–30; Koontz, Virginia Frontier, 154.

12. F. Anderson, Crucible of War, 18

13. Jortner, Gods of Prophetstown, 17; William A. Hunter, "Tanaghrisson," in Dictionary of Canadian Biography, vol. 3 (Toronto: University of Toronto/Université Laval, 1974), http://www.biographi.ca/en/bio/tanaghrisson_3E.html. See A journal of the proceedings of Conrad Weiser [manuscript]: on his journey to Ohio with a message & present from the government of Pensilvania to the Indians there, 1748 Aug. 11–Oct. 2, Weiser, Conrad (1696–1760)11 August 1748–02 October 1748." Ayer MS 3200, Newberry Library.

14. "Céloron Plate," Virginia Museum of History and Culture, https://virginiahistory .org/learn/celoron-plate.

15. Céloron de Blainville, Bonnecamps, and Gallup, Céloron Expedition to the Ohio Country, 50–53.

16. Bernholz and O'Grady, "Indians of the Northern and Southern Districts of North America."

17. Parmenter, "After the Mourning Wars," 63.

18. Deposition of George Croghan, February 27, 1777, in Palmer et al., Calendar of Virginia State Papers and Other Manuscripts, 1: 276–77.

19. Christopher Gist's First and Second Journals, September 11, 1750–March 29, 1752, pt. 1, 15–16, in the George Mercer Papers Relating to the Ohio Company of Virginia, Darlington Memorial Library, University of Pittsburgh.

20. Dunk Halifax to Col. [Thomas] Lee; "Treaty of Logg's Town," 168; Trent, Goodman, and Dinwiddie, Journal of Captain William Trent, 44.

21. "Treaty of Logg's Town," 168.

22. Ibid., 174.

23. Report to Governor Dinwiddie, Twightwees Town, June 21, 1752, in JHB, 8: 509.

24. Misencik and Misencik, American Indians of the Ohio Country, 23.; s.v. "Orontony," Dictionary of Canadian Biography, vol. 3, http://www.biographi.ca/en/bio/orontony _3E.html.

25. JHB, 8: 511.

26. "Journal from the Ohio to the Twightwees and Back in June 1752," CO 5/1327, pt. 2, June 21, 1752–August 4, 1752, National Archives, Kew.

27. Trent, Goodman, and Dinwiddie, Journal of Captain William Trent, 86–88; "Journal from the Ohio to the Twightwees and Back."

28. See "Journal, August 1753: Volume 61," in Journals of the Board of Trade and Plantations, vol. 9, January 1750–December 1753, ed. K. H. Ledward (London: His Majesty's Stationery Office, 1932), 451–52, British History Online, http://www .british history.ac.uk/jrnl trade plantations/vol9/pp. 451–452.

Chapter 16. This Country Belongs to Virginia

1. "The answer Sir William Gooch to the queries," June 10, 1747, CO 5/1326, 211–12 (479–80), National Archives, Kew.
2. Ibid.
3. *Virginia Gazette*, Hunter, August 16, 1751.
4. Grier, "Staging the Cherokee Othello."
5. Robert Dinwiddie to the Board of Trade, December 10, 1752, Correspondence, CO 5/1327, National Archives, Kew, pt. 2.
6. Oliphant, *Peace and War on the Anglo-Cherokee Frontier*, 12–13.
7. M. A. Stewart, "William Gerard de Brahm's 1757 Map," 526, 534n5.
8. Governor Robert Dinwiddie to the "Emperor, Sachems, Warriors of the great Nation of the Cherokees," May 31, 1753, "Governor Dinwiddie's letters to the Cherokee Indians," Correspondence, CO 5/1327, National Archives, Kew.
9. Brock, *Official Records of Robert Dinwiddie*, 1: 388–89.
10. Hantman, *Monacan Millennium*, 51, 65–67, 152–55, 169.
11. "Report from Governor Dinwiddie on the Present State of Virginia, Transmitted the Lords Commissioners for Trade and Plantations," January 1755, Brock, *Official Records of Robert Dinwiddie*, 1: 388.
12. "The draught of a representation to his Majesty upon an Act passed in Virginia in 1752, having been prepared pursuant to the minutes of the 28th of May, was agreed to and ordered to be transcribed." "Journal, June 1754: Volume 61, Part 2," in *Journals of the Board of Trade and Plantations*, vol. 10, *January 1754–December 1758*, ed. K. H. Ledward (London: His Majesty's Stationery Office, 1933), 45–54, *British History Online*. http://www.british history.ac.uk/jrnl trade plantations /vol10/pp45 54.
13. Edney, "John Mitchell's Map of North America," 70; Taliaferro, "Fry and Jefferson Revisited."
14. Taliaferro, "Fry and Jefferson Revisited," n33; Edney, "John Mitchell's Map of North America," 72.
15. Loyal Land Company Transaction (1752), Papers of Walker, his son, Francis Walker, and the Walker and Page families, 1742–1886, accession no. 3098, Special Collections, University of Virginia Library, University of Virginia, Charlottesville.
16. Fontaine et al., *Memoirs of a Huguenot Family*, 342.
17. Wooldridge, *Mapping Virginia*, 110.
18. Robert de Vaugondy, *Carte de la Virginie et du Maryland* (1755), Robert De Vaugondy, Gilles, Joshua Fry, Peter Jefferson, and E Haussard. *Carte de la Virginie et du Maryland*. [Paris, ca. 1757] Map. https://www.loc.gov/item/74692500.
19. George-Louis Le Rouge *Essay du cours de l'Oyo avec les Forts François et Anglois, tiré de la Carte Angloise* (1755), accession no. 1988–420, Colonial Williamsburg, https://emuseum.history.org/objects/31685/.
20. Nyland, "Doctor Thomas Walker," 24–25; Wooldridge, *Mapping Virginia*, 111–13; Henderson, "Dr. Thomas Walker and the Loyal Company of Virginia," 91; C. Anderson, "Rediscovering Native North America," 493–94.
21. Taliaferro, "Fry and Jefferson Revisited"; Nyland, "Doctor Thomas Walker," 24–25; Wooldridge, *Mapping Virginia*, 111–13; Henderson, "Dr. Thomas Walker and the Loyal Company of Virginia," 91.
22. Mitchell, *New and Complete History of the British Empire in America*, 3: 195, quoted in Carrier, "Dr. John Mitchell," 210.

Chapter 17. Commencement of the French Hostilities

1. Smith, Livingstone, and Scott, *Review of the Military Operations in North-America*, 8.
2. Michael Ray, "French and Indian War," *Encyclopedia Britannica*, https://www .britannica.com/event/French-and-Indian-War.
3. Trudel, "Jumoville Affair," 355.
4. Treaty of Carlisle, November 1, 1753, Founders Online, National Archives, https:// founders.archives.gov/documents/Franklin/01–05–02–0026. Original source: *Papers of Benjamin Franklin*, 5: 84–107.
5. Ibid.
6. Smith, Livingstone, and Scott, *Review of the Military Operations in North-America*, 8.
7. Treaty of Carlisle.
8. See "Memorandum: Preliminary Conference with the Indians," September 26, 1753, Founders Online, National Archives, https://founders.archives.gov/documents /Franklin/01–05–02–0019. Original source: *Papers of Benjamin Franklin*, 5: 64–66.
9. Treaty of Carlisle.
10. Ibid.
11. Ibid.
12. Smith, Livingstone, and Scott, *Review of the Military Operations in North-America*, 8.
13. George Washington, "Journey to the French Commandant: Narrative," Founders Online, National Archives, http://founders.archives.gov/documents/Washington /01–01–02–0003–0002 (last modified June 29, 2017). Original source: *Diaries of George Washington*, 1: 130–61.
14. Ibid.
15. Boucher, *View of the Causes*, 29.
16. Washington, "Journey to the French Commandant."
17. Ibid.
18. Ibid.
19. Mulkearn, *George Mercer Papers*, 70–71, 105.
20. Robert Dinwiddie to the Commander in Chief of the French Forces on the River Ohio, Williamsburg, Virginia, October 31, 1753, CO 5/1328, 45–46, "Letters Relating to French Movements on the Ohio River," National Archives, Kew.
21. Smith, Livingstone, and Scott, *Review of the Military Operations in North-America*, 8.
22. Washington, "Journey to the French Commandant." Editors' note 63 suggests that this is probably a reference to the massacre of the family of Robert Foyles, "his wife and 5 children," who were killed on the Monongahela rather than the Great Kanawha.
23. Smith, Livingstone, and Scott, *Review of the Military Operations in North-America*, 10.
24. Lieutenant Governor, Robert Dinwiddie, Williamsburg, to James Hamilton, January 29, 1754, Ayer MS 952, Edward E. Ayer Collection, Newberry Library.
25. *SAL*, 7: 661–62.
26. "Message of Governor Dinwiddie to the Council and Burgesses, February 14, 1754," Brock *Official Records of Robert Dinwiddie*, 1, 73–75.
27. Ibid., 75.
28. Message of Governor Dinwiddie to the House of Burgesses; ibid., 75–76.
29. Ibid., Brock, 119.
30. Deposition of Maj. Edward Ward, 277.

31. George Washington, "Expedition to the Ohio, 1754: Narrative," Founders Online, National Archives, https://founders.archives.gov/documents/Washington /01–01–02–0004–0002. Original source: *Diaries of George Washington*, 1: 174–210.

32. Ibid.

33. Deposition of Maj. Edward Ward, 277.

34. "Expedition to the Ohio, 1754: Narrative."

35. Brock *Official Records of Robert Dinwiddie*, 1: 256.

36. George Washington to Robert Dinwiddie, May 29, 1754, Founders Online, National Archives, https://founders.archives.gov/documents/Washington/02–01 –02–0054. Original source: *Papers of George Washington*, 1: 107–15.

37. Brock *Official Records of Robert Dinwiddie*, 1: 216.

38. George Washington to Robert Dinwiddie, May 29, 1754, Founders Online, National Archives, https://founders.archives.gov/documents/Washington/02–01 –02–0054. Original source: *Papers of George Washington*, 1: 107–15.

39. Preston, "When Young George Washington Started a War."

40. Ibid.

41. "I., 19 July 1754," *Founders Online*, National Archives, https://founders.archives .gov/documents/Washington/02–01–02–0076–0002. Original source: *The Papers of George Washington*, Colonial Series, vol. 1, *7 July 1748–14 August 1755*, ed. W. W. Abbot. Charlottesville: University Press of Virginia, 1983, pp. 159–164. https://founders.archives.gov/documents/Washington/02–01–02–0076–0002.

42. Smith, Livingstone, and Scott, *Review of the Military Operations in North-America*, 16.

43. Ibid., 11.

44. Deposition of Maj. Edward Ward, in Palmer et al., *Calendar of Virginia State Papers and Other Manuscripts*, 1: 277.

45. Thomson, *Enquiry into the Causes of the Alienation*, 80–81; *Minutes of the Provincial Council of Pennsylvania*, vol. 3 (1840), 152.

46. *Minutes of the Provincial Council of Pennsylvania*, vol. 3 (1840), 151–52; Lengel, "Treating American Indians as 'Slaves,'" 41.

Chapter 18. Defend Our Lands and Hinder the French

1. "The Speech of the Honorable Robert Dinwiddie, Esq; His Majesty's Lieutenant-Governor, and Commander in Chief, of the Colony and Dominion of Virginia, at the Prorogation of the General Assembly." *Early American Imprints*, 1st ser., no. 40723 (filmed).

2. *SAL*, 6: 453–68. William Fairfax to George Washington, June 28, 1755, Founders Online, National Archives, https://founders.archives.gov/documents/Washington /02–01–02–0159. Original source: *Papers of George Washington*, 1: 316–19.

3. Trimble, "Christopher Gist and Settlement on the Monongahela," 18–21.

4. Maj. Gen. Edward Braddock orderly books, Ayer MS 103, Edward E. Ayer Collection, Newberry Library.

5. Smith, Livingstone, and Scott, *Review of the Military Operations in North-America*, 27.

6. Braddock orderly books.

7. Chegeree. *Map of the Country about the Mississippi* (ca. 1755), https://www.loc .gov/item/74695023/. Anderson, "Rediscovering Native North America," 494.

8. "Expedition to the Ohio, 1754: Narrative"; Bond, "Captivity of Charles Stuart," 63.

9. Smith, Livingstone, and Scott, *Review of the Military Operations in North-America*, 30–31.

10. Ibid., 31.

11. Ibid., 33.

12. Berkeley and Berkeley, *Correspondence of John Bartram*, 386–87.

13. Smith, Livingstone, and Scott, *Review of the Military Operations in North-America*, 32.

14. "Remarks, 1787–1788," Founders Online, National Archives, https://founders .archives.gov/documents/Washington/04–05–02–0463–0002. Original source: *Papers of George Washington*, 5: 515–26.

15. *Minutes of the Provincial Council of Pennsylvania*, vol. 3 (1840), 589.

16. Smith, Livingstone, and Scott, *Review of the Military Operations in North-America*, 68.

17. Ibid.,103–4.

18. Ibid., 68–69.

19. Ibid., 89; Thomson, *Enquiry into the Causes of the Alienation*, 47.

20. Bond, "Captivity of Charles Stuart," 64.

21. Deposition of Joseph Nicholas, February 27, 1777, in Palmer et al., *Calendar of Virginia State Papers and Other Manuscripts*, 1: 282.

22. Merrell, "'I Desire All That I Have Said,'" 806.

23. Bond, "Captivity of Charles Stuart," 64.

24. Ibid., 61–62, 65.

25. Deposition of Simon Girty, February 27, 1777, in Palmer et al., *Calendar of Virginia State Papers and Other Manuscripts*, 1: 280.

26. Jemison, *Narrative of the Life*, 33.

27. Ibid., 41.

28. Ibid., 47. Jemison, *Narrative of the Life*.

29. Ibid., 44–45, 52.

30. Brock *Official Records of Robert Dinwiddie*, 2: 101–2.

31. Ibid., 180, 306, 538. Baker-Crothers, *Virginia and the French and Indian War*, 104.

32. *JHB*, 8: 297–99.

33. George Washington to Robert Dinwiddie, July 18, 1755, Founders Online, National Archives, https://founders.archives.gov/documents/Washington/02–01 –02–0168. Original source: *Papers of George Washington*, 1: 339–42.

Chapter 19. Assure Them of a Right to the Lands

1. For transcripts see Merrell, "Easton Treaty Texts," 24 h. archived at the Wayback Machine, https://web.archive.org/web/20150803164636/https://oieahc.wm .edu/wmq/Oct06/merrell_final.pdfMerrell, "'I Desire All That I Have Said,'" 778n1, 823.

2. Thomson, *Enquiry into the Causes of the Alienation*, 47.

3. Richter, "Rediscovered Links in the Covenant Chain," 64, 64n45.

4. Eid, "Ojibwa-Iroquois War," 309.

5. J. Miller, "Delaware as Women," 510–13; Merritt, "Metaphor, Meaning, and Misunderstanding," 77–78; Boose, "Scolding Brides and Bridling Scolds," 204.

6. Merrell, "'I Desire All That I Have Said,'" 808; Merrell, "Easton Treaty Texts," 12, 20, 27.

7. Smith, Livingstone, and Scott, *Review of the Military Operations in North-America,* 17–18.

8. Thomson, *Enquiry into the Causes of the Alienation,* 4.

9. "Friendly Association," Digital Paxton: Digital Collection, Critical Edition, and Teaching Platform, http://digitalpaxton.org/works/digital-paxton/friendly -association.

10. *Minutes of a Treaty Held at Easton.*

11. Ibid., 18.

12. Ibid., 19.

13. Ibid., 22.

14. Joseph Ball to Mr. Charles Goore, merchant in Liverpool, Westham, September 21, 1758, Joseph Ball Letterbook, 1744–1759, p. 188. Colonial Wiliamsburg Foundation.

15. *Minutes of a Treaty Held at Easton,* 28.

16. Thomson, *Enquiry into the Causes of the Alienation,* 47–48; *Minutes of a Treaty Held at Easton,* 24, 33; "Charles Thomson," University Archives and Records Center, https://archives.upenn.edu/exhibits/penn-people/biography/charles-thomson.

17. *Minutes of a Treaty Held at Easton,* 23.

Chapter 20. Experience Has Taught Them Wisdom

1. Fontaine et al., *Memoirs of a Huguenot Family,* 406–7.

2. Smith, Livingstone, and Scott, *Review of the Military Operations in North-America,* 89.

3. Extract from letter of William Allason, Rappahannock to William Walker, Antigua, November 8, 1757, in D. R. Anderson, "Important Letters from the Papers of William Allason," 121.

4. Fontaine et al., *Memoirs of a Huguenot Family,* 431–36.

5. Brock *Official Records of Robert Dinwiddie,* 3: 267–68.

6. Ibid., 3: 273.

7. Byrd, Byrd, and Byrd, *Correspondence of the Three William Byrds,* 2: 619–20.

8. Virginia, *Treaty Held with the Catawba and Cherokee Indians,* xii.

9. Ibid., 2–3.

10. Ibid., 4.

11. Brock *Official Records of Robert Dinwiddie,* 3: 268.

12. *Treaty Held with the Catawba and Cherokee Indians,* xiii–xiv.

13. Ibid., 11–13.

14. Ibid., 14.

15. Charles Pinckney to the Lords Commissioners for Trade and Plantations, June 27, 1754, "Letters concerning frontier fortifications and agriculture," CO 5/375, National Archives, Kew.

16. Smith, Livingstone, and Scott, *Review of the Military Operations in North-America,* 89.

17. Pinckney to the LCPT.

18. Oliphant, *Peace and War on the Anglo-Cherokee Frontier,* 21; Hamer, "Anglo-French Rivalry in the Cherokee Country," 305–6, 307, 309; D. M. Wood, "'I Have Now Made a Path to Virginia,'" 35, 39.

19. Oliphant, *Peace and War on the Anglo-Cherokee Frontier,* 17, 20–21.

20. Hamer, "Anglo-French Rivalry in the Cherokee Country," 312–13.

21. Oliphant, *Peace and War on the Anglo-Cherokee Frontier,* 32–33.

22. *SAL*, 7: 116.

23. Oliphant, *Peace and War on the Anglo-Cherokee Frontier*, 321–22.

24. Ibid., 37–38.

25. Byrd, Byrd, and Byrd, *Correspondence of the Three William Byrds*, 2: 656.

26. John Blair, president of the Virginia Council, to Captain Abraham Bosomworth, Williamsburg, April 8, 1758, Abercrombie box 3, AB 132. Huntington Library (HL).

27. Bosomworth to Abercromby, Williamsburg, April 8, 1758, Abercrombie box 3, AB 132, HL.

28. John Forbes to James Abercromby, April 20, 1758, New York, Abercromby Papers, AB box 4, 175, HL. Forbes enclosed a letter from the Lower Cherokee to the Mohawk, which he asked Abercromby to please forward to William Johnson.

29. Ibid.

30. Message from Cherokee chiefs Techtama and Homwhyowa or the Wolf King, two Chiefs of the Cherokees, to the Delaware Indians and Their chief, Teedyuscung, as Interpreted, June 20, 1758, VAULT box Ayer MS 877, Edward E. Ayer Collection, Newberry Library.

31. Forbes to Abercromby, September 1758, Abercromby Papers, box 13, AB 709, 9. See remainder of the document in photo.

32. Hamer, "Fort Loudon in the Cherokee War," 442–43; *SAL*, 7: 165, 241.

33. Palmer et al., *Calendar of Virginia State Papers and Other Manuscripts*, 1: 277.

34. Burnaby, *Travels through the Middle Settlements in North-America*, 90–91.

35. William Bull to LCTP, Charles Town, May 8, 1760, "Letters from William Bull to the Lords Commissioners, concerning the Cherokee War," Correspondence, CO 5/377, pt. 1, 1760, National Archives, Kew.

36. Military Commission Granted to Chief Okana-Stoté of the Cherokee by Governor Louis Billouart, Chevalier de Kerlérec, National ArchivesCatalog.,. https://catalog.archives.gov/id/6924937.

37. Attakullakulla, Cherokee Chief, Speech to William Byrd, July 17, 1761, *George Washington Papers*, series 4, *General Correspondence*, https://www.loc.gov/item/mgw443099/.

38. Ibid.

39. Ibid.

40. J De Brahm, *Report of the General Survey in the Southern District of North America*, 109.

41. Timberlake, *Memoirs of Lieut. Henry Timberlake*, 33–34.

42. Ibid., 34–35.

43. Thomas Boone to Francis Fauquier, February 16, 1762, *EJCCV*, 6: 210.

44. Francis Fauquier to LCTP, May 1, 1762, Correspondence, CO 5/1330, 123. The National Archives, Kew. Boulware, "Effect of the Seven Years' War on the Cherokee Nation," 421.

45. Timberlake had observed thirty captives, poorly fed and clothed. Fauquier to LCTP; Timberlake, *Memoirs of Lieut. Henry Timberlake*, 52, 59, 152.

46. Earl of Halifax to the Board, February 1, 1765, "Journal, February 1765: Volume 72," in *Journals of the Board of Trade and Plantations*, vol. 12, *January 1764–December 1767*, ed. K. H. Ledward (London: His Majesty's Stationery Office, 1936), 143–53, *British History Online*, http://www.british history.ac.uk/jrnl trade plantations/vol12/pp143–153.

Chapter 21. Convert Them into Free Men, Useful Subjects, and Good Christians

1. The Memorial of the Virginia Indian Company To the Honorable Alexander Spotswood [FP XIV 254- 257. See Library of Virginia General Correspondence, Virginia Lambeth Palace Library Class Fulham Palace Papers, Vol. 11–14.
2. Del Papa, "Royal Proclamation of 1763," 406–9.
3. Palmer et al., *Calendar of Virginia State Papers and Other Manuscript*, 1: 278.
4. Ibid., 1: 277; Henry Bouquet to [General Jeffrey Amherst], August 5, 1763, Ibid., August 6,1763, CO 5/63, National Archives, Kew. https://explorepahistory.com /odocument.php?docId=1-4-56 "Henry Bouquet," Bushy Run Battlefield, https:// bushyrunbattlefield.com/henry-bouquet/.
5. "George Mercer," George Washington's Valley Forge, https://www.mountvernon .org/library/digitalhistory/digital-encyclopedia/article/george-mercer/.
6. Mulkearn, *George Mercer Papers*, 175.
7. D. R. Anderson, "Important Letters from the Papers of William Allason," 130–31.
8. William Fleming to Francis Fauquier, Staunton, VA, July 26, 1763, Draper Collection, State Historical Society of Wisconsin.
9. McCulloh, *Miscellaneous Representations Relative to Our Concerns in America*, 4–7.
10. Berkeley and Berkeley, *Correspondence of John Bartram*, 578–79.
11. McCulloh, *Miscellaneous Representations Relative to Our Concerns in America*, 10–12.
12. "Read a letter from the Lieutenant Governor of Virginia, dated Williamsburg, November 30th, 1761," "Journal, April 1762: Volume 69," Virginia.fo. 113 in *Journals of the Board of Trade and Plantation*. https://www.british-history.ac.uk/jrnl -trade-plantations/vol11/pp268–276.
13. "Minutes of the Southern Congress at Augusta, Georgia," *CSRNC*, 11: 170, https://docsouth.unc.edu/csr/index.php/document/csr11–0084.
14. Bartram, *Travels through North and South Carolina*, 485–86.
15. "Minutes of the Southern Congress at Augusta," 185–88.
16. Ibid., 190.
17. Ibid., 196–98.
18. Ibid., 199–203.
19. Berland et al., *Commonplace Book of William Byrd II of Westover*, 235; W. D. Jordan, "American Chiaroscuro," 198–99.
20. "Thomas Jefferson's Argument in *Howell v. Netherland* (1770)," *Encyclopedia Virginia* https://encyclopediavirginia.org/primary-documents/thomas-jeffersons -argument-in-howell-v-netherland-1770.
21. Fontaine et al., *Memoirs of a Huguenot Family*, 349.
22. Berkeley and Berkeley, *Correspondence of John Bartram*, 432.
23. Fontaine et al., *Memoirs of a Huguenot Family*, 349.
24. Boucher, *View of the Causes*, 31–32.
25. "Report on the Colony by Francis Fauquier for Lords Commissioners of Trade and Foreign Plantations [Board of Trade]: Sunday, 30 January 1763," CO 5/1330, 261–262, National Archives, Kew, org.wake.idm.oclc.org/10.13051/ee:doc /fauqfrVH0021009a1d/.
26. Carrier, "Dr. John Mitchell," 204.
27. Bartram and Kalm, *Observations on the Inhabitants*, viii.
28. Berkeley and Berkeley, *Correspondence of John Bartram*, 622.
29. Smith, *Theory of Moral Sentiments*, 312; Boucher, *View of the Causes*, 9.
30. Boucher, *View of the Causes*, 35.

31. Jemison, *Narrative of the Life*, 56.

32. Boucher, *View of the Causes*, 31–32.

33. "'N.N.': First Reply to Vindex Patriae, [28 December 1765]," Founders Online, National Archives, https://founders.archives.gov/documents/Franklin/01-12-02-0204. Original source: *Papers of Benjamin Franklin*, 12: 413–16.

34. "'Pacificus Secundus': Reply to ',' 2 January 1766," Founders Online, National Archives, https://founders.archives.gov/documents/Franklin/01-13-02-0002.). Original source: *Papers of Benjamin Franklin*, 13: 4–6.

35. "Narrative of the Late Massacres."

36. A. Lee, *Essay in Vindication of the Continental Colonies of America*, 144.

37. Smith, *Theory of Moral Sentiments*, 316.

38. MacMaster, "Arthur Lee's 'Address on Slavery,'" 144n15. Cf. Klein, "Adam Smith's 1759 Rebuke of the Slave Trade," 93, 96n6. Klein neither credits Lee with authorship of *An Essay in Vindication*, nor interprets "refuse of the jails of Europe" as referring to Virginians but rather considers it a general allusion to slave traders.

39. Lee, *Essay in Vindication of the Continental Colonies of America*, 29. Emphasis added.

Chapter 22. It Is You Who Are Frequently Passing Up and Down the Ohio, and Making Settlements Upon It

1. George Washington to John Posey, June 24, 1767.

2. George Washington to William Crawford Mount Vernon, VA, September 21, 1767, 1–5. Washington, George. *George Washington Papers, Series 5, Financial Papers: Copybook of Letters and Invoices, -1775. /1775*, 1767. Manuscript/Mixed Material. https://www.loc.gov/item/mgw500004/.

3. John Mercer to George Mercer, December 22, 1767–January 28, 1768, in Mulkearn, *George Mercer Papers*, 212.

4. "Journal, August 1765: Volume 72," in *Journals of the Board of Trade and Plantations*, vol. 12, *January 1764–December 1767*, ed. K. H. Ledward (London: His Majesty's Stationery Office, 1936), 189–97, *British History Online*. http://www.british history.ac.uk/jrnl trade plantations/vol12/pp189–197.

5. "Letter from Francis Fauquier," Correspondence, CO 5/1331, 1765National Archives, Kew.

6. Ibid.

7. Francis Fauquier, Lieutenant Governor of Virginia, to the Board, June 14, 1765, "Documents Concerning the Murder of Cherokee Indians," CO 5/1331, 1765, National Archives, Kew.

8. "Speech of the Cherokee Chief Kittagusta to Indian Agent Alexander Cameron and Engisn George Price, Fort Prince George," May 8, 1766, William L. Clements Library, University of Michigan, https://clements.umich.edu/exhibit/american-encounters/nah-case-8/kittagusta-speech-1766/.

9. Address by Kittagusta to Charles Greville Montagu, September 22, 1766, 7: 256–57, https://docsouth.unc.edu/csr/index.php/document/csr07–0137.

10. Alexander Cameron to John Stuart, May 10, 1766, Fort Prince George, 7: 207, America and West Indies, vol. 269, British Public Records Office, London.

11. Ibid., 7: 208–10.

12. Address by Kittagusta to Charles Greville Montagu.

13. Alexander Cameron to John Stuart.

14. Ibid., 210–11.

15. Ibid., 210.

16. Ibid., 211.

17. "Speech of the Cherokee Chief Kittagusta to Indian Agent Alexander Cameron and Engisn George Price."

18. Ibid.

19. Address by Kittagusta to [Charles Greville Montagu].

20. Treaty of Hard Labor, in William Laurence Saunders, ed., *The Colonial Records of North Carolina*, vol. 6 (Raleigh: P. M. Hale, State Printer, 1886–90), 851–55, http://jeffersonswest.unl.edu/archive/view_doc.php?id=jef.00089.

21. Del Papa, "Royal Proclamation of 1763," 406–9.

22. "Ratified Treaty # 7 Treaty of Fort Stanwix, or The Grant from the Six Nations to the King and Agreement of Boundary—Six Nations, Shawnee, Delaware, Mingoes of Ohio, 1768," in O'Callaghan et al., *Documents Relative to the Colonial History of the State of New York*, 8: 112–13.

23. Ibid., 118–19.

24. Ibid., 121, 127.

25. Ibid., 123.

26. Ibid., 127.

27. Ibid.

28. Ibid., 136.

29. Palmer et al., *Calendar of Virginia State Papers and Other Manuscripts*, 276–77.

30. *Virginia Gazette*, December 1, 1768, Caption: New York, November 17, HIS Excellency William Franklin, Esq; Governour of New Jersey, the Hon. Frederick Smyth, Esq; Chief Justice of New Jersey, Thomas Walker, Esq; Commissioner from Virginia, and the Rev. Mr. Peters, and James Tilghman, Esq; of the Council of Pennsylvania, with several other Gentlemen, returned here a few days ago from Fort Stanwix, where they have been attending the congress held by Sir William Johnson, Bart. with the Six United Nations and their tributaries.

31. "Ratified Treaty # 7 Treaty of Fort Stanwix," 131.

32. "The Memorial of the Proprietors of a Tract of Land on the Ohio called Indiana," October 1, 1776, in Palmer et al., *Calendar of Virginia State Papers and Other Manuscripts*, 1: 273, The Deposition of George Croghan Esquire, taken before Abraham Hite and James Wood, February 27, 1777, Ibid., 277, http://archive.org/details/calendarvirgini12palmgoog; Wharton and Bancroft, *View of the Title to Indiana*, 12; Kingman, *Owego*.

33. Deposition of George Morgan, agent for the Indiana Company, March 10, 1777, Pittsburg, in Palmer et al., *Calendar of Virginia State Papers and Other Manuscripts*, 277.

34. Deposition of Col. William Crawford, February 27, 1777, in Palmer et al., *Calendar of Virginia State Papers and Other Manuscripts*, 280.

35. Ibid., 281–83.

36. Deposition of George Morgan, 277.

37. Ibid.

38. Deposition of Simon Girty, in Palmer et al., *Calendar of Virginia State Papers and Other Manuscripts*, 280.

39. Calloway, "'We Have Always Been the Frontier,'" 40; Witgen, *Infinity of Nations*, 218–19.

40. Deposition of George Croghan, 276–77.

41. "Treaty of Lochaber, 1770," *Virginia Magazine of History and Biography* 9 (1902): 360–64, http://jeffersonswest.unl.edu/archive/view_doc.php?id=jef.00091.

42. Billington, "Fort Stanwix Treaty of 1768," 183, 185, 190–93; Robert T. Anderson, "Treaty of Hard Labor," *e-WV: The West Virginia Encyclopedia*, November 21, 2023, https://www.wvencyclopedia.org/articles/768; Robert T. Anderson, "Treaty of Lochaber," *e-WV: The West Virginia Encyclopedia*, January 25, 2021; "Treaties of Fort Stanwix North," *Encyclopaedia Britannica*, https://www.britannica.com/event/Treaties-of-Fort-Stanwix.

43. George Washington, diary, July 30, 1770, Founders Online, National Archives, https://founders.archives.gov/documents/Washington/01–02–02–0005–0018 –0030. Original source: *Diaries of George Washington*, 2: 256–57.

44. Journal of George Washington written during an expedition along the Ohio and Kanawha Rivers, http://www.wvculture.org/history/settlement/washington journal1770.html. "Remarks & Occurrs. in October [1770]," *Founders Online*, National Archives, https://founders.archives.gov/documents/Washington/01–02 –02–0005–0029. Original source: *The Diaries of George Washington*, vol. 2, *14 January 1766–31 December 1770*, ed. Donald Jackson. Charlottesville: University Press of Virginia, 1976, 286–307.

45. Burton, "John Connolly, a Tory of the Revolution," 95.

46. John Connolly to George Washington, September 18, 1772, Founders Online, National Archives, http://founders.archives.gov/documents/Washington/02 09 02 0074, ver. 2013 12 27. Original source: *The Papers of George Washington*, 9: 95–99.

47. John Connolly to George Washington, June 29, 1773, Founders Online, National Archives, https://founders.archives.gov/documents/Washington/02–09 –02–0188. Original source: *Papers of George Washington*, 9: 245–51, n. 6.

48. Edmund Pendleton to Joseph Jones, February 10, 1781, *EE*, pendedVH0010328a1c; Confirmed: see note 45 above Burton, "John Connolly, a Tory of the Revolution," 95.

49. "Extracts from Mr. McKee's Journal of Indian Transactions, Message to King Custologa, Captains White Eyes, Pipe, and Other Chiefs," May 1, 1774, S4-V1-P03-sp12-D0028, American Archives, VI: 475, Northern Illinois University Digital Library.

50. Letter from Devereux Smith to Dr. Smith, June 10, 1774, Pittsburgh, S4-V1-P03-sp12-D0021, American Archives, VI: 468–69, Northern Illinois University Digital Library.

51. Ibid.

52. Capt. Daniel Smith to Col. William Preston, Castle's Woods, March 22, 1774, [3QQI5]. *DHDW*, 2–3. The *DHDW* is listed as the abbreviation for Reuben Gold Thwaites et al., Documentary History of Dunmore's War, 1774 [Draper Series; v. 1] (Madison: Wisconsin historical society, 1905), https://catalog.hathitrust.org /Record/001691128.

53. Letter from Devereux Smith to Dr. Smith, June 10, 1774, Pittsburgh, S4-V1-P03-sp12-D0021, American Archives, VI: 468–69, Northern Illinois University Digital Library.

54. Answer of the Delawares to the Condolence Speeches, Answer of the Shawanese to the Condolence Speeches, May 25, 1774, S4-V1-P03-sp12-D0036, American Archives, VI: 479–80, Northern Illinois University Digital Library.

55. Express at Williamsburg, with intelligence of skirmishes with the Indians, Williamsburg, July 14, 1774, S4-V1-P03-sp15-D0038, American Archives, VI: 536–37, Northern Illinois University Digital Library.

56. Express at Williamsburg, from Pittsylvania County, Williamsburg, August 25, 1774, S4-V1-P03-sp25-D0001, American Archives, VI: 737, Northern Illinois University Digital Library; letter from Fredericksburg, VA, September 14, 1774, S4-V1-P03-sp25-D0060, American Archives, VI: 787, Northern Illinois University Digital Library.

57. Letter from the Camp, on Point Pleasant, October 17, 1774, S4-V1-P03-sp38-D0015, American Archives, VI: 1016, Northern Illinois University Digital Archive.

58. Extract of a Letter from Staunton, in Virginia, 4 November 1774, S4-V1-P03-sp38-D0016, American Archives, VI: 1017, Northern Illinois University Digital Archive.

Chapter 23. The Bloody Ground Would Be Dark, and Difficult to Settle It

1. Deposition of Patrick Henry, Esq., June 4, 1777, in Palmer et al., *Calendar of Virginia State Papers and Other Manuscripts*, I: 289; Deposition of William Christian, Evangelist of Almighty God, June 3, 1777, in Palmer et al., *Calendar of Virginia State Papers and Other Manuscripts*, I: 288.

2. Filson and Royster, "Discovery, Settlement and Present State of Kentucke," 8–9.

3. The Deposition of Patrick Henry, Esq.; Deposition of William Christian.

4. Filson and Royster, "Discovery, Settlement and Present State of Kentucke," 8–9.

5. Deposition of Patrick Henry.

6. Advertisement by Richard Henderson and the Transylvania Company concerning settlement of the Transylvania Colony, December 25, 1774–February 22, 1775, *CSRNC*, 9: 1129–31, https://docsouth.unc.edu/csr/index.php/document/csr09-0354. [British Public Record Office, America and West Indies, North Carolina, no. 222.]

7. Proposal of Richard Henderson, February 22, 1775, ibid.

8. Aron, "Pioneers and Profiteers," 181.

9. Deposition of William Farrar, July 4, 1776, in Palmer et al., *Calendar of Virginia State Papers and Other Manuscripts*, I: 272–73.

10. Deposition of Charles Robertson, October 3, 1777, in Palmer et al., *Calendar of Virginia State Papers and Other Manuscripts*, I: 291.

11. Deposition of John Lowry, etc., on behalf of the Commonwealth [of Virginia], Washington Court House, April 16, 1777, in Palmer et al., *Calendar of Virginia State Papers and Other Manuscripts*, I: 283–84.

12. Deposition of John Reid, etc., on behalf of the Commonwealth [of Virginia], Washington Court House, April 16, 1777, in Palmer et al., *Calendar of Virginia State Papers and Other Manuscripts*, I: 284–85.

13. Deposition of James Robinson, in behalf of Richard Henderson and Co., April 16, 1777, in Palmer et al., *Calendar of Virginia State Papers and Other Manuscripts*, I: 285–87.

14. Deposition of John Lowry.

15. Deposition of James Robinson.

16. Deposition of Charles Robertson, I: 292.

17. Deposition of John Lowry.

18. Ibid.

19. Deposition of Thomas Houghton, October 3, 1777, in Palmer et al., *Calendar of Virginia State Papers and Other Manuscripts,* 1: 290.
20. Ibid.
21. Deposition of Samuel Wilson, April 15, 1777, in Palmer et al., *Calendar of Virginia State Papers and Other Manuscripts,* 1: 282–83; Deposition of Charles Robertson.
22. See above chapter 11.
23. Filson and Royster, "Discovery, Settlement and Present State of Kentucke," 7, 9. Nila Annadurai, "Land of Tomorrow, Dark and Bloody Ground," The Harvard Advocate, Spring 2021, https://theharvardadvocate.com/content/land-of -tomorrow-dark-and-bloody-ground.
24. Deposition of John Reid.
25. Ibid.
26. Deposition of James Robinson.
27. Deposition of Charles Robertson, 1: 291.
28. Deposition of James Robinson.
29. Deposition of John Reid.
30. Deposition of Thomas Houghton.
31. Deposition of Charles Robertson, 291.
32. Deposition of John Reid.
33. Ibid.
34. Deposition of Samuel Wilson.
35. Deposition of John Lowry.
36. Deposition of Samuel Wilson
37. Deposition of Charles Robertson, 1: 292.
38. Ibid.
39. Ibid.
40. Deposition of Samuel Wilson.
41. Deposition of Charles Robertson.
42. Deposition of William Christian; Henderson, "Treaty of Long Island of Holston," 104.
43. Deposition of James Robinson.
44. Ibid.
45. Ibid.
46. Deposition of Charles Robertson, 1: 292.
47. Deposition of Isaac Shelby, etc., December 3, 1777, in Palmer et al., *Calendar of Virginia State Papers and Other Manuscripts,* 1: 296.

Chapter 24. The Virginians Have Taken Away All Their Lands

1. Bartram, *Travels through North and South Carolina,* 326–28.
2. Ibid., 330.
3. Ibid., 333–32.
4. Ibid., 331.
5. Ibid., 348.
6. Ibid., 359.
7. Ibid., 364–65, 485.
8. Ibid., 366–67.
9. Ibid., 370.
10. Ibid., 366.

11. Henry Stuart, "Account of His Proceedings with the Cherokee Indians about Going against the Whites," August 25, 1776, in Saunders, *Colonial Records of North Carolina*, 764.

12. Ibid.

13. Ibid., 765.

14. Ibid.

15. Henry Stuart and Alexander Cameron to John Carter, Toqua, May 23, 1776, in Hamer, "Correspondence of Henry Stuart and Alexander Cameron with the Wataugans," 456.

16. Stuart, "Proceedings with the Cherokee Indians," 766.

17. Ibid., 768.

18. Ibid., 766–67.

19. Ibid., 768.

20. Henry Stuart and Alexander Cameron to the Inhabitants of Watauga and Nonatluchly Toqua in the Cherokee Nation, May 7, 1776, in Hamer, "Correspondence of Henry Stuart and Alexander Cameron," 453.

21. John Carter to Henry Stuart and Alexander Cameron, May 13, 1776, Ibid., 454–55.

22. Henry Stuart and Alexander Cameron to John Carter, Toqua, May 23, 1776, Ibid., 455.

23. Henry Stuart and Alexander Cameron to Aaron Penson, Toqua, May 23, 1776, Ibid., 456.

24. Stuart, "Proceedings with the Cherokee Indians," 769–70.

25. Ibid., 771–72.

26. Ibid., 773–74.

27. Ibid., 774–75.

28. Ibid., 777.

29. Ibid., 777–78.

30. Ibid., 779.

31. Ibid.

32. Ibid., 781.

33. *VAG*, 3, June 7, 1776.

34. Stuart, "Proceedings with the Cherokee Indians," 782.

35. Henry Stuart to Edward Wilkinson, Toqua, June 28, 1776, in Hamer, "Correspondence of Henry Stuart and Alexander Cameron," 458.

36. Stuart, "Proceedings with the Cherokee Indians," 783.

37. Ibid., 782–83.

38. Ibid., 784.

39. Ibid., 785.

40. Ibid., 783; Gordon, *South Carolina and the American Revolution*, 47.

Bibliography

Alexander, Edward P. "An Indian Vocabulary from Fort Christanna, 1716." *Virginia Magazine of History and Biography* 79, no. 3 (July 1971): 303–13.

American Husbandry: Containing an Account of the Soil, Climate, Production and Agriculture, of the British Colonies in North-America and the West-Indies; With Observations on the Advantages and Disadvantages of Settling in Them, Compared with Great Britain and Ireland. London: Bew, 1775.

Anderson, Chad. "Rediscovering Native North America: Settlements, Maps, and Empires in the Eastern Woodlands." *Early American Studies: An Interdisciplinary Journal* 14, no. 3 (2016): 478–505.

Anderson, D. R., ed. "Important Letters from the Papers of William Allason, Merchant of Falmouth, Virginia." Richmond College Historical Papers 2, no. 1 (June 1917): 118–75.

Anderson, Fred. *The Crucible of War: The Seven Years' War and the Fate of Empire in British North America, 1754–1766.* New York: Knopf, 2000.

Annadurai, Nila. "Land of Tomorrow, Dark and Bloody Ground." *The Harvard Advocate,* Spring 2021. https://theharvardadvocate.com/content/land-of-tomorrow -dark-and-bloody-ground.

Appalachian Regional Commission. "About the Appalachian Region." 2024. https:// www.arc.gov/about-the-appalachian-region/.

"Archives of Maryland Online." https://msa.maryland.gov/megafile/msa/speccol /sc2900/sc2908/html/volumes.html.

Aron, Stephen. "Pigs and Hunters: 'Rights in the Woods' on the Trans-Appalachian Frontier." In *Contact Points, American Frontiers from the Mohawk Valley to the Mississippi, 1750–1830,* edited by Andrew R. L. Cayton and Fredrika J. Teute, 175–204. Chapel Hill: University of North Carolina Press, 1996.

Aron, Stephen. "Pioneers and Profiteers: Land Speculation and the Homestead Ethic in Frontier Kentucky." *Western Historical Quarterly* 23, no. 2 (May 1992): 179–98.

Articles of Peace between the Most Serene and Mighty Prince Charles II . . . and Several Indian Kings and Queens, &c. Concluded the 29th day of May 1677. London: John Bill, Christopher Barker, Thomas Newcomb, and Henry Hills, 1677.

Axtell, James. *The Invasion Within: The Contest of Cultures in Colonial North America.* New York: Oxford University Press, 1985.

Baker-Crothers, Hayes. *Virginia and the French and Indian War.* Chicago, Illinois: University of Chicago Press, 1928.

Barker, Eirlys M. "Pryce Hughes, Colony Planner, of Charles Town and Wales." *South Carolina Historical Magazine* 95, no. 4 (1994): 302–13.

Barnwell, John. "The Tuscarora Expedition: Letters of Colonel John Barnwell." *South Carolina Historical and Genealogical Magazine* 9, no. 1 (1908): 28–54.

Bartram, John, and Pehr Kalm. *Observations on the Inhabitants, Climate, Soil, Rivers, Productions, Animals, and Other Matters Worthy of Note: Made by Mr. John*

Bartram, in His Travels from Pensilvania to Onondago, Oswego and the Lake Ontario, in Canada: To Which Is Annex'd, a Curious Account of the Cataracts at Niagara. London: Printed for J. Whiston and B. White, in Fleet-Street, 1751. http://archive.org/details/gpl_489946.

Barnwell, Joseph W. "The Second Tuscarora Expedition." *South Carolina Historical and Genealogical Magazine* 10, no. 1 (1909): 33–48.

Bartram, William. *Travels through North and South Carolina, Georgia, East and West Florida, the Cherokee Country, the Extensive Territories of the Muscogulges or Creek Confederacy, and the Country of the Chactaws.* 1st ed. Philadelphia: James & Johnson, 1791.

Beck, Robin. *Chiefdoms, Collapse, and Coalescence in the Early American South.* Illustrated ed. Cambridge: Cambridge University Press, 2013.

Bedell, John, Jason Shellenhamer, Charles Lee Decker, and Stuart Fiedel. "River and Mountain, War and Peace." Final Report Louis Berger Group, Washington, DC: National Park Service, 2011.

Berkeley, Edmund, and Dorothy Smith Berkeley, eds. *The Correspondence of John Bartram, 1734–1777.* Gainesville: University Press of Florida, 1992.

Berland, Kevin Joel, Jan Kirsten Gilliam, and Kenneth A. Lockridge, eds. *The Commonplace Book of William Byrd II of Westover.* Chapel Hill: Omohundro Institute and University of North Carolina Press, 2001.

Berlin, Ira. "From Creole to African: Atlantic Creoles and the Origins of African-American Society in Mainland North America." *William and Mary Quarterly* 53, no. 2 (1996): 251–88.

Bernholz, Charles D., and Brian T. O'Grady. "The Indians of the Northern and Southern Districts of North America: Levenshtein Comparisons of the Tribe Lists from the 1764 'Plan for the Future Management of Indian Affairs.'" American Indian Treaties Portal, http://treatiesportal.unl.edu/planof1764/.

Beverley, Robert. *The History and Present State of Virginia, in Four Parts. I. The History of the First Settlement of Virginia, and the Government Thereof, to the Present Time. II. The Natural Productions and Conveniencies of the Country, Suited to Trade and Improvement. III. The Native Indians, Their Religion, Laws, and Customs, in War and Peace. IV. The Present State of the Country, as to the Polity of the Government, and the Improvements of the Land. By a Native and Inhabitant of the Place.* London: R. Parker, 1705.

Billington, Ray A. "The Fort Stanwix Treaty of 1768." *New York History* 25, no. 2 (1944): 182–94.

Bond, Beverly W. "The Captivity of Charles Stuart, 1755–57." *Mississippi Valley Historical Review* 13, no. 1 (1926): 58–81.

Boose, Lynda E. "Scolding Brides and Bridling Scolds: Taming the Woman's Unruly Member." *Shakespeare Quarterly* 42, no. 2 (1991): 179–213.

Boucher, Jonathan. *A View of the Causes and Consequences of the American Revolution; in Thirteen Discourses Preached in North America between the Years 1763 and 1775: With an Historical Preface.* London: G. G. & J. Robinson, 1797.

Boulware, Tyler. "The Effect of the Seven Years' War on the Cherokee Nation." *Early American Studies: An Interdisciplinary Journal* 5, no. 2 (2007), 395-426.

Briceland, Alan Vance. *Westward from Virginia: The Exploration of the Virginia-Carolina Frontier, 1650–1710.* Charlottesville: University Press of Virginia, 1987.

Brizon, Claire. "Collections coloniales? L'implication de la Suisse dans le processus d'expansion coloniale européen au siècle des Lumières." *TSANTSA—Journal of the Swiss Anthropological Association* 24 (May 2019), 24-38. Brock, R. A., ed. *The*

Official Letters of Alexander Spotswood, Lieutenant-Governor of the Colony of Virginia, 1710–1722. Richmond: Virginia Historical Society. https://digital.library.pitt.edu/islandora/object/pitt:31735054779560.

Brock, R. A., ed. *The Official Records of Robert Dinwiddie, Lieutenant-Governor of the Colony of Virginia, 1751–1758.* Vol. I. Collections of the Virginia Historical Society, New Series. Richmond: Virginia Historical Society, 1883.

Buchner, C. Andrew. "Yuchi Indians." In *Tennessee Encyclopedia.* https://tennesseeencyclopedia.net/entries/yuchi-indians/.

Burnaby, Andrew. *Travels through the Middle Settlements in North-America, in the Years 1759 and 1760. With Observations upon the State of the Colonies. By the Rev. Andrew Burnaby, A.M. Vicar of Greenwich.* London: Printed for T. Payne, 1775. Eighteenth Century Collections Online, https://link.gale.com/apps/doc/CB0126276878/ECCO?u=nclivewfuy&sid=bookmark-ECCO&xid=adcf95f9&pg=98.

Burton, Clarence Monroe. "John Connolly, a Tory of the Revolution." *Proceedings of the American Antiquarian Society* 20, pt. 1 (October 1909), 70–105.

Bushnell, David I. "The Account of Lamhatty." *American Anthropologist* 10, no. 4 (1908): 568–74.

Byrd, William, I, William Byrd II, and William Byrd III. *The Correspondence of the Three William Byrds of Westover, Virginia, 1684-1776:* Volumes 1 and 2. Edited by Marion Tinling. Charlottesville: Published for the Virginia Historical Society [by] the University Press of Virginia, 1977.

Byrd, William, II. Histories of the Dividing Line betwixt Virginia and North Carolina. Edited by William K. Boyd. 1929; reprint, New York, 1967.

Byrd, William, II. "William Byrd, 1674–1744. The Westover Manuscripts: Containing the History of the Dividing Line betwixt Virginia and North Carolina; A Journey to the Land of Eden, A.D. 1733; and A Progress to the Mines. Written from 1728 to 1736, and Now First Published." Edmund Ruffin, ed., Petersburg: Printed by Edmund and Julian C. Ruffin, 1841.

Byrd, William, Marion Tinling, and Louis B. Wright. *The Secret Diary of William Byrd of Westover, 1709–1712.* Richmond, VA: Dietz, 1941.

Calloway, Colin G. "'We Have Always Been the Frontier': The American Revolution in Shawnee Country." *American Indian Quarterly* 16, no. 1 (1992): 39–52.

Carrier, Lyman. "Dr. John Mitchell, Naturalist, Cartographer, and Historian." *Agricultural History Society Papers* 1 (1921): 199–219.

Carter, John H. "Allummapees, King of the Delawares at Shamokin." In *Early Events in the Susquehanna Valley: A Collection of the Writings and Addresses as Presented by John H. Carter Before This Society.* Northumberland, PA: Northumberland County Historical Society, 1981.

Cain, Robert J. ed. *The Colonial Records of North Carolina (Second Series) Volume VII: Records of the Executive Council 1664-1734.* Raleigh: North Carolina State Division of Archives and History, 1984.

Céloron de Blainville, Pierre-Joseph, Joseph-Pierre Bonnecamps, and Andrew Gallup. *The Céloron Expedition to the Ohio Country, 1749: The Reports of Pierre-Joseph Céloron and Father Bonnecamps.* Bowie, MD: Heritage Books, 1997.

Chambers, Ian. "A Cherokee Origin for the 'Catawba' Deerskin Map (c. 1721)." *Imago Mundi* 65, no. 2 (2013): 207–16.

Charlevoix, Pierre Francois Xavier de, Caxton Club, and Louise Phelps Kellogg. *Journal of a Voyage to North America.* Chicago: Caxton Club, 1923. http://archive.org/details/journalofvoyageto2char.

Chavers, Dean. *Racism in Indian Country.* New York: Lang, 2009.

Clayton, John. "A letter from the Revd Mr. John Clayton, (afterwards Dean of Kildare in Ireland) to Dr. Grew, in answer to several queries relating to Virginia, sent to him by that learned gentleman, A. D. 1687. Communicated by the Right Reverend Father in God Robert Lord Bishop of Corke, to John Earl of Egmont, F. R. S.," *Philosophical Transactions of the Royal Society of London* 41, no. 454 (Oct 1739): 143–62.

Clayton, John. *The Reverend John Clayton: A Parson with a Scientific Mind; His Scientific Writings and Other Related Papers.* Charlottesville: Published for the Virginia Historical Society by University Press of Virginia, 1965.

Colden, Cadwallader. *The History of the Five Indian Nations of Canada Which Are Dependent on the Province of New York.* Vol. 1. New York: Barnes, 1904.

"Colonial Letters, &c." *Virginia Magazine of History and Biography* 5, no. 1 (July 1897): 42–53.

"Colonial National Historical Park: A Study of Virginia Indians and Jamestown-The First Century (Chapter 10)." https://npshistory.com/publications/jame/moretti-langholtz/chap10.htm.

Commisso, Michael. "Land Use History for Cedar Creek and Belle Grove National Historical Park." Boston: Olmsted Center for Landscape Preservation, 2007.

"The Continuation of the Yarborough Family Magazine." *Yarborough Family Magazine* 6, no. 2 (n.d.): 23–25.

Davis, R. P. Stephen, Jr. "The Travels of James Needham and Gabriel Arthur through Virginia, North Carolina, and Beyond, 1673–1674 (Contained in a Letter from Abraham Wood to John Richards, August 22, 1674)." *Southern Indian Studies* 39 (1990): 31–55.

Day, Gordon M. "The Indian as an Ecological Factor in the Northeastern Forest." *Ecology* 34, no. 2 (1953): 329–46.

De Brahm, John Gerar William. *Report of the General Survey in the Southern District of North America. South Carolina Tricentennial Commission.* Tricentennial Edition, no. 3. Columbia: University of South Carolina Press, 1971.

Deed or Nanfan Treaty, July 19, 1701. Iroquois Indians: A Documentary History, 908–11, Reel 6, Newberry Library Deed from the Five Nations to the King of their Beaver Hunting Ground. [New-York Papers. Bundle, P.Q; Q 49.]. https://www.sixnations.ca/LandsResources/NanFanTreaty.pdf.

Deloria, Philip J. *Playing Indian.* New Haven, CT: Yale University Press, 1999.

Del Papa, Eugene, M. "The Royal Proclamation of 1763: Its Effect upon Virginia Land Companies." *Virginia Magazine of History and Biography* 83, no. 4 (Oct 1975): 406–11.

DuVal, Kathleen. *The Native Ground: Indians and Colonists in the Heart of the Continent.* Philadelphia: University of Pennsylvania Press, 2007.

Editor. "North Carolina Resolutions against Bay River Indians, Tuscaroras and Their Allies." Coastal Carolina Indian Center (blog), December 15, 2011. https://www.coastalcarolinaindians.com/.

Edney, Matthew H. "John Mitchell's Map of North America (1755): A Study of the Use and Publication of Official Maps in Eighteenth-Century Britain." *Imago Mundi* 60, no. 1 (2008): 63–85.

Eid, Leroy V. "The Ojibwa-Iroquois War: The War the Five Nations Did Not Win." *Ethnohistory* 26, no. 4 (1979): 279–324.

Ellis, Thomas H. "The Ohio Company." *William and Mary Quarterly* 5, no. 2 (1896): 129–31.

Ethridge, Robbie. *From Chicaza to Chickasaw: The European Invasion and the Trans-formation of the Mississippian World, 1540–1715*. Chapel Hill: University of North Carolina Press, 2010.

Evans, Emory G. A *"Topping People": The Rise and Decline of Virginia's Old Political Elite, 1680–1790*. Charlottesville: University of Virginia Press, 2009.

Everett, C. S. "'They Shalbe Slaves for Their Lives': Indian Slavery in Colonial Virginia." In *Indian Slavery in Colonial America*, edited by Alan Gallay, 67–108. Lincoln: University of Nebraska Press, 2015.

Ewen, Charles R., Thomas R. Whyte, and R. P. Stephen Davis, eds. "The Archaeology of North Carolina: Three Archaeological Symposia." *North Carolina Agricultural Council Publication* 30. 2011. https://www.rla.unc.edu/ncac/publications/ncac30/Front.pdf.

Featherling, Jacob. "Horses, Culture, and Trade: The Impact of the Horse on South-eastern Native Nations, 1650–1830." MA thesis, University of Southern Missis-sippi, 2019.

Feeley, Stephen. "Tuscarora Trails: Indian Migrations, War, and Constructions of Colonial Frontiers." PhD diss., College of William and Mary, 2007.

Feight, Andrew Lee. "Lower Shawnee Town & Céloron's Expedition of 1749." *Scioto Historical*, https://sciotohistorical.org/items/show/35.

Fenton, William N. *The Great Law and the Longhouse: A Political History of the Iroquois Confederacy*. Norman: University of Oklahoma Press, 2010.

Fernow, Berthold. *The Ohio Valley in Colonial Days*. Albany, NY: Munsell, 1890. http://archive.org/details/ohiovalleyincoloo1fern.

Filson, John, and Paul Royster, ed. "The Discovery, Settlement and Present State of Kentucke (1784): An Online Electronic Text Edition." n.d., https://digitalcommons.unl.edu/cgi/viewcontent.cgi?article=1002&context=etas.

Fontaine, James, James Maury, John Fontaine, Ann Maury, and France. *Memoirs of a Huguenot Family*. New York: Putnam, 1853.

Ford, Worthington Chauncey, ed. "Some Letters of William Beverley." *William and Mary Quarterly* 3, no. 4 (1895): 223–39.

Gallatin, Albert. *A Synopsis of the Indian Tribes within the United States East of the Rocky Mountains, and in the British and Russian Possessions in North America*. Cambridge, MA: American Antiquarian Society, 1836. Zea E-Books in American Studies 16. http://digitalcommons.unl.edu/zeaamericanstudies/16.

Ganter, Granville. "'Make Your Minds Perfectly Easy': Sagoyewatha and the Great Law of the Handenosaunee." *Early American Literature* 44, no. 1 (2009): 121–46.

Georgiou, Aristos. "Archaeologists Uncover American Slaves' Engineering Feats Underwater." *Newsweek*, March 1, 2024. https://www.newsweek.com/.

Ghaemi, Nassir. "Revolutionary Suicide: The Lesson of Black Panther Huey Newton about Suicide." *Psychology Today*, August 30, 2010. https://www.psychologytoday.com/us/blog/.

Gipson, L. H., ed. *The Moravian Indian Mission on White River: Diaries and Letters, May 5, 1799, to November 12, 1806*. Indianapolis: Indiana Historical Bureau, 1938.

Glanville, Jim, and Ryan Mays. "Where Was Totera Town?" *Historical Society of Western Virginia Journal* 20, no. 1 (2012): 31–43.

Glanville, Jim, and Ryan Mays. "William Beverley, James Patton, and the Settling of the Shenandoah Valley." Tappahannock, Virginia 55 (November 2010), https://ecmhs.org/wp-content/uploads/2021/02/bulletin-vol-55.pdf.

Goetz, Rebecca Anne. "The Nanziatticos and the Violence of the Archive: Land and Native Enslavement in Colonial Virginia." *Journal of Southern History* 85, no. 1 (2019): 33–61.

Goetzmann, William H. "John Bartram's Travel to Onondaga in Context," 97–106. In *America's Curious Botanist: A Tercentennial Reappraisal of John Bartram*, edited by Nancy Hoffmann and John C. Van Horne. Philadelphia: American Philosophical Society, 2004.

Gordon, John W. *South Carolina and the American Revolution: A Battlefield History.* Columbia: University of South Carolina Press, 2002.

Graffenried, Christoph von. "Narrative by Christoph von Graffenried Concerning His Voyage to North Carolina and the Founding of New Bern." *Colonial and State Records of North Carolina* 1 (1708): 905–86.

Green, Rayna. "The Tribe Called Wannabee: Playing Indian in America and Europe." *Folklore* 99, no. 1 (1988): 30–55.

Grier, Miles P. "Staging the Cherokee Othello: An Imperial Economy of Indian Watching." *William and Mary Quarterly* 73, no. 1 (2016): 73–106.

Grumet, Robert Steven, and Raymond Whritenour. *A Gazetteer of Delaware Indian History Reflected in Modern-Day Place Names.* Albany: New York State Education Department, 2014.

Guzy, Dan. "The 1736 Survey of the Potomac River." *Virginia Magazine of History and Biography* 122, no. 1 (2014): 2–39.

Hamer, Philip M. "Anglo-French Rivalry in the Cherokee Country, 1754–1757." *North Carolina Historical Review* 2, no. 3 (1925): 303–22.

Hamer, Philip M. "Correspondence of Henry Stuart and Alexander Cameron with the Wataugans." *Mississippi Valley Historical Review* 17, no. 3 (1930): 451–59.

Hamer, Philip M. "Fort Loudon in the Cherokee War 1758–1761." *North Carolina Historical Review* 2, no. 4 (1925): 442–58.

Hanna, Charles A. *The Wilderness Trail; or, The Ventures and Adventures of the Pennsylvania Traders on the Allegheny Path, with Some New Annals of the Old West, and the Records of Some Strong Men and Some Bad Ones.* Vol. 1. New York: Putnam, 1911. http://archive.org/details/wildernesstrail00hann.

Hantman, Jeffey L. *Monacan Millennium: A Collaborative Archaeology and History of a Virginia Indian People.* Charlottesville: University of Virginia Press, 2018.

Harrison, Fairfax. "The Virginians on the Ohio and the Mississippi in 1742." *Virginia Magazine of History and Biography* 30, no. 2 (1922): 203–22.

Hartley, Cecil B. *Life of Daniel Boone, the Great Western Hunter and Pioneer, . . . to Which Is Added His Autobiography Complete, as Dictated by Himself, Etc.* Philadelphia: J. E. Potter, 1865.

Hatfield, April Lee. *Atlantic Virginia: Intercolonial Relations in the Seventeenth Century.* Philadelphia: University of Pennsylvania Press, 2004.

Hazard, Samuel, ed. *Colonial Records of Pennsylvania.* Harrisburg, PA: Fenn, 1852.

Henderson, Archibald. "Dr. Thomas Walker and the Loyal Company of Virginia." *Proceedings of the American Antiquarian Society* 41, pt. 1 (April 1931): 77–178.

Hederson, Archibald. "The Treaty of Long Island of Holston, July 1777." *North Carolina Historical Review* 8, no. 1 (1931): 55–116.

Hening, William Waller, ed., *The Statutes at Large; Being a Collection of All the Laws of Virginia, from the First Session of the Legislature, in the Year 1619. Published Pursuant to an Act of the General Assembly of Virginia, Passed on the Fifth Day of February*

One Thousand Eight Hundred and Eight. Richmond: Printed by and for Samuel
Pleasants, junior, printer to the commonwealth, 1809, http://archive.org/details
/statutesatlargebo2virg.

Hinke, Wm. J. "Report of the Journey of Francis Louis Michel from Berne, Switzerland, to Virginia, October 2, 1701–December 1, 1702." *Virginia Magazine of History and Biography* 24, no. 1 (1916): 1–43.

Hinke, Wm. J. "Report of the Journey of Francis Louis Michel from Berne, Switzerland, to Virginia, October 2, 1701–December 1, 1702, Part II." *Virginia Magazine
of History and Biography* 24, no. 2 (1916): 113–41.

Hinke, Wm. J. "Report of the Journey of Francis Louis Michel from Berne, Switzerland, to Virginia, October 2, 1701-December 1, 1702, Part III." *Virginia Magazine
of History and Biography* 24, no. 3 (1916): 275–303.

"Historic Perrysburg—Great Black Swamp." https://www.historicperrysburg.org
/_files/ugd/41e4be_bd559c76a0f64b68aedfaabe3cce7622.pdf.

Hoffman, Bernard G. "Observations on Certain Ancient Tribes of the Northern
Appalachian Province." *Smithsonian Institution Bureau of American Ethnology* 191,
no. 70 (1964), 191–246.

Hofstra, Warren R. "'The Extention of His Majesties Dominions': The Virginia
Backcountry and the Reconfiguration of Imperial Frontiers." Journal of American History 84, no. 4 (1998): 1281–1312.

Hofstra, Warren R. *The Planting of New Virginia: Settlement and Landscape in the
Shenandoah Valley.* Baltimore, MD: Johns Hopkins University Press, 2004.

Hunter, George, and A. S. Salley. "George Hunter's Map of the Cherokee Country
and the Path Thereto in 1730," 1917. https://dc.statelibrary.sc.gov/handle/10827
/7842.

Hurt, R. Douglas. *The Ohio Frontier: Crucible of the Old Northwest, 1720–1830.*
Bloomington: Indiana University Press, 1996.

Iliffe, John. *Honour in African History.* Cambridge: Cambridge University Press, 2004.

"The Indians of Southern Virginia, 1650–1711: Depositions in the Virginia and
North Carolina Boundary Case." *Virginia Magazine of History and Biography* 7,
no. 4 (1900): 1–11.

"The Indians of Southern Virginia, 1650–1711: Depositions in the Virginia and
North Carolina Boundary Case (Concluded)." *Virginia Magazine of History and
Biography* 8, no. 1 (1900): 1–11.

Indigenous Values Initiative. "Guswentha: Two Row Wampum Belt." https://
indigenousvalues.org/decolonization/guswentha-two-row-wampum-belt/.

Ironstrack, George. "The Crooked Trail to Pickawillany (1747–1752)." *Aacimotaati-
iyankwi,* April 19, 2012, https://aacimotaatiiyankwi.org/2012/04/19/.

Jefferson, Thomas. *Notes on the State of Virginia.* Philadelphia: Prichard & Hall,
1788.

Jemison, Mary. *A Narrative of the Life of Mrs. Mary Jemison, Who Was Taken by the
Indians, in the Year of 1755, When Only about Twelve Years of Age, and Who Has
Continued to Reside amongst Them to the Present Time . . . and Other Entertaining
Matter. Edited by James E. Seaver. Introduction by Allen W. Trelease.* New York:
Corinth Book, 1824.

Jennings, Francis. "The Constitutional Evolution of the Covenant Chain." *Proceedings
of the American Philosophical Society* 115, no. 2 (1971): 88–96.

Jones, Hugh. *The Present State of Virginia.* London: Alvord, 1865.

Jones, Joseph. "Anglo-Siouan Relations on Virginia's Piedmont Frontier, 1607–1732." MA thesis, College of William and Mary, 1989.

Jordan, Winthrop D. "American Chiaroscuro: The Status and Definition of Mulattoes in the British Colonies." *William and Mary Quarterly* 19, no. 2 (April 1962): 183–200.

Jortner, Adam. *The Gods of Prophetstown: The Battle of Tippecanoe and the Holy War.* Oxford: Oxford University Press, 2011.

"A Journal from Virginia beyond the Appalachian Mountains in Septr., 1671, Sent to the Royal Society by Mr. Clayton, and Read Aug. 1, 1688, before the Said Society." *William and Mary Quarterly* 15, no. 4 (1907): 235–41.

Kemper, Charles E. "The Early Westward Movement of Virginia, 1722–1734. As Shown by the Proceedings of the Colonial Council." *Virginia Magazine of History and Biography* 13, no. 1 (1905): 1–16.

"The Early Westward Movement of Virginia, 1722–1734. As Shown by the Proceedings of the Colonial Council (Continued)." *Virginia Magazine of History and Biography* 13, no. 2 (1905): 113–38.

Kercheval, Samuel. A History of the Valley of Virginia. Strasburg, VA: Shenandoah, 1925.

Kincaid, Robert Lee. *The Wilderness Road.* Harrogate, TN: Lincoln Memorial University Press, 1955.

King, Duane H. *The Cherokee Indian Nation: A Troubled History.* Knoxville: University of Tennessee Press, 2005.

Kingman, Leroy Wilson. *Owego: Some Account of the Early Settlement of the Village in Tioga County, N.Y., Called Ah-wa-ga by the Indians, Which Name Was Corrupted by Gradual Evolution into Owago, Owego, Owegy, and finally Owego.* Owego, NY: Owego Gazette, 1907.

Klein, Daniel B. "Adam Smith's 1759 Rebuke of the Slave Trade." *SSRN Electronic Journal* 25, no. 1 (Summer 2020): 91–98.

Koontz, Louis K. *The Virginia Frontier, 1754–1763.* Baltimore, MD: Johns Hopkins Press, 1925.

Kruer, Matthew. "Bloody Minds and Peoples Undone: Emotion, Family, and Political Order in the Susquehannock-Virginia War." *William and Mary Quarterly* 74, no. 3 (2017): 401–36.

Kruer, Matthew. *Time of Anarchy: Indigenous Power and the Crisis of Colonialism in Early America.* Cambridge, MA: Harvard University Press, 2022.

Lapham, Heather A. *Hunting for Hides: Deerskins, Status, and Cultural Change in the Protohistoric Appalachians.* Tuscaloosa: University of Alabama Press, 2006.

La Vere, David. "Of Fortifications and Fire: The Tuscarora Response to the Barnwell and Moore Expeditions during North Carolina's Tuscarora War, 1712 and 1713." *North Carolina Historical Review* 94, no. 4 (2017), 363–90.

Lawson, John. *A New Voyage to Carolina; Containing the Exact Description and Natural History of That Country: Together with the Present State Thereof. And a Journal of a Thousand Miles, Travel'd Thro' Several Nations of Indians. Giving a Particular Account of Their Customs, Manners, &c.*

Lawson, Murray G. "An Act for the Better Regulation of the Indian Trade, 1714." *Virginia Magazine of History and Biography* 55, no. 4 (1947): 329–32.

Lederer, John. *The Discoveries of John Lederer in Three Several Marches from Virginia to the West of Carolina and Other Parts of the Continent Begun in March, 1669 and Ended in September, 1670: Together with a General Map of the Whole Territory*

Which He Traversed / Collected and Translated out of Latine from His Discourse and Writings, by Sir William Talbot, Baronet. London: Samuel Heyrick, at Grays-Inne-gate in Holborn, 1672.

Lee, Arthur. *An Essay in Vindication of the Continental Colonies of America, from a Censure of Mr. Adam Smith in His Theory of Moral Sentiments: With Some Reflections on Slavery in General.* Printed for the author, 1764.

Lee, Brian D., Daniel I. Carey, and Alice L. Jones. *Water in Kentucky: Natural History, Communities, and Conservation.* Lexington: University Press of Kentucky, 2017.

Lee, Jacob F. *Masters of the Middle Waters: Indian Nations and Colonial Ambitions along the Mississippi.* Cambridge, MA: Belknap Press of Harvard University Press, 2019.

Lee, Jacob F. "What Is a Hunting Ground? Reflections on Indigenous Kentucky." *Register of the Kentucky Historical Society* 121, no. 4 (2023): 305–19.

Lengel, Edward G. "Treating American Indians as 'Slaves,' 'Dogs,' and Unwanted Allies: George Washington, Edward Braddock, and the Influence of Ethnocentrism and Diplomatic Pragmatism in Ohio Valley Military Relations, 1753–1755." In *A Companion to George Washington,* edited by Edward G. Lengel, 32–52. Hoboken, NJ: Wiley-Blackwell, 2012.

"Letters Relating to French Movements on the Ohio River." Correspondence, CO 5/1328 1753/10/31, National Archives, Kew.

Livingston, Robert. *The Livingston Indian Records 1666–1723.* Edited by Lawrence H. Leder. Gettysburg: Pennsylvania Historical Association, 1956.

Lozier, Jean-François. "A Nicer Red: The Exchange and Use of Vermilion in Early America." *Eighteenth-Century Studies* 51, no. 1 (2017): 45–61.

Ludwell, Philip, and Nathaniel Harrison. "A Journal of the Proceedings of Philip Ludwell and Nathaniel Harrison Commissioners Appointed for Settling the Boundarys between Her Majesty's Colony and Dominion of Virginia and the Province of Carolina." *Colonial and State Records of North Carolina,* 1, no. 400 (April 18, 1710): 735–46.

MacMaster, Richard K. "Arthur Lee's 'Address on Slavery': An Aspect of Virginia's Struggle to End the Slave Trade, 1765–1774." *Virginia Magazine of History and Biography,* April 1, 1972, 141–57.

Malone, Patrick M. "Changing Military Technology among the Indians of Southern New England, 1600–1677." *American Quarterly* 25, no. 1 (1973).

Marye, William B. "'Patowmeck above Ye Inhabitants': A Commentary on the Subject of an Old Map, Part Two." *Maryland Historical Magazine* 30 (1906): 126–33.

Mathew, Thomas. *The Beginning, Progress, and Conclusion of Bacon's Rebellion in Virginia, in the Years 1675 and 1676.* Washington, DC: Peter Force, 1835. Thomas Jefferson Papers, 1606–1827, Library of Congress. https://www.loc.gov/collections/thomas-jefferson-papers/articles-and-essays/virginia-records-1606-to-1737/beginning-progress-and-conclusion-of-bacons-rebellion/.

McCulloh, Henry. *Miscellaneous Representations Relative to Our Concerns in America: Submitted in 1761 to the Earl of Bute.* London: Harding, 1905. http://archive.org/details/miscellaneousrepoomccuuoft.

McDowell, W. L., ed. *Journals of the Commissioners of the Indian Trade: September 20, 1710– August 29, 1718, Colonial Records of South Carolina,* 2d ser. Columbia, SC: The Indian Books, 1955.

McIlwaine, H. R., and John Pendleton Kennedy, eds. *Journals of the House of Burgesses of Virginia*. 15 vols. Richmond, VA: Colonial Press, E. Waddey, 1905–1915. https://catalog.hathitrust.org/Record/009792681.

Memoirs of the Principal Transactions of the Last War between the English and French in North America. From the Commencement of It in 1744, to the . . . Treaty at Aix la Chapelle. Containing in Particular an Account of the Importance of Nova Scotia or Acadie, and the island Of Cape Breton to Both Nations. 3rd ed. London: Green & Russell, 1758.

Merrell, James H, ed. "Easton Treaty Texts July and November 1756." *William and Mary Quarterly* 63, no. 4 (2006): 1–99.

Merrell, James H. "'I Desire All That I Have Said . . . May Be Taken down Aright': Revisiting Teedyuscung's 1756 Treaty Council Speeches." *William and Mary Quarterly* 3rd ser., 63, no. 4 (2006): 777–826.

Merrell, James H. *Into the American Woods: Negotiators on the Pennsylvania Frontier.* New York: Norton, 1999.

Merritt, Jane T. "Metaphor, Meaning, and Misunderstanding: Language and Power on the Pennsylvania Frontier." In *Contact Points: American Frontiers from the Mohawk Valley to the Mississippi, 1750–1830,* edited by Andrew R. L. Clayton and Frederika J. Teute, 60–87. Chapel Hill: University of North Carolina Press, 1998.

Miller, Diane. "Wyandot, Shawnee, and African American Resistance to Slavery in Ohio and Kansas." PhD dissertation, University of Nebraska, 2019. https://digitalcommons.unl.edu/historydiss/94.

Miller, Jay. "The Delaware as Women: A Symbolic Solution." *American Ethnologist* 1, no. 3 (1974): 507–14.

Mills, Jarrod. "Dr. Thomas Walker State Park a Tribute to First Log Cabin Built in Ky." *Corbin (KY) Times-Tribune,* February 16, 2021. https://www.thetimestribune.com/news/local_news/.

The Minutes of a Treaty Held at Easton, in Pennsylvania, in October 1758. By the Lieutenant Governor of Pennsylvania, and the Governor of New-Jersey; with the Chief Sachems and Warriors of the Mohawks, Oneydos, Onondagas, Cayugas, Senecas, Tuscaroras, Tuteloes, Nanticokes and Conoys, Chugnuts, Delawares, Unamies, Mohickons, Minisinks, and Wapings. Woodbridge, NJ: James Parker, 1758, http://name.umdl.umich.edu/N06429.0001.001.

Minutes of the Provincial Council of Pennsylvania: From the Organization to the Termination of the Proprietary Government. [Mar. 10, 1683–Sept. 27, 1775]. Vol. 3. J. Severns, 1840.

Minutes of the Provincial Council of Pennsylvania: From the Organization to the Termination of the Proprietary Government. [Mar. 10, 1683–Sept. 27, 1775]. Vol. 2. J. Severns, 1852.

"Minutes of the Southern Congress at Augusta, Georgia Georgia; North Carolina; Cherokee Indian Nation; Catawba Indian Nation; Et Al. October 1, 1763–November 21, 1763." CSRNC 11, 156–207.

Misencik, Paul R., and Sally E. Misencik. *American Indians of the Ohio Country in the Eighteenth Century.* Jefferson, NC: McFarland, 2020.

Morgan, Gwenda. *The Hegemony of the Law: Richmond County, Virginia, 1692–1776.* New York: Garland, 1989.

Mitchell, John, Kitchin, Thomas, and Millar, Andrew. *A map of the British and French dominions in North America, with the roads, distances, limits, and extent of the settlements, humbly inscribed to the Right Honourable the Earl of Halifax, and the other*

Right Honourable the Lords Commissioners for Trade & Plantations. [London; Sold by And: Millar, 1755] Map. https://www.loc.gov/item/74693173/.

Morgan, Gwenda. "Sold into Slavery: In Retribution against the Nanziattico Indians." *Virginia Calvacade* 33, no. 4 (1984): 168–73.

Mulkearn, Lois. *George Mercer Papers: Relating to the Ohio Company of Virginia*. Pittsburgh, PA: University of Pittsburgh Press, 1954.

Nash, Gary B. "When We Were Young: The American Philosophical Society in the 18th Century." Proceedings of the American Philosophical Society 163, no. 1 (March 2019): 10–50.

Newton, Huey P., and Blake, J. Herman. *Revolutionary Suicide*. New York: Harcourt Brace Jovanovich, 1973.

Norona, Delf. "Joshua Fry's Report on the Back Settlements of Virginia (May 8, 1751)." *Virginia Magazine of History and Biography*, January 1, 1948, 22–41.

Nyland, Keith Ryan. "Doctor Thomas Walker (1715–1794): Explorer, Physician, Statesman, Surveyor and Planter of Virginia and Kentucky." PhD diss., Ohio State University, 1971.

O'Callaghan, E. B., et al., eds. *Documents Relative to the Colonial History of the State of New York*. Albany, NY: Weed, Parsons, 1853–87.

Okihiro, Gary Y. *Third World Studies: Theorizing Liberation*. Durham, NC: Duke University Press, 2016.

Oliphant, John Stuart. *Peace and War on the Anglo-Cherokee Frontier, 1756–63*. Baton Rouge: Louisiana State University Press, 2001.

Palmer, William Pitt, Sherwin McRae, Raleigh Edward Colston, and Henry W. Flournoy. *Calendar of Virginia State Papers and Other Manuscripts*. Vol. 1. Richmond: Walker, 1875.

Parent, Anthony S. *Foul Means: The Formation of a Slave Society in Virginia, 1660–1740*. Chapel Hill: University of North Carolina Press, 2003.

Parmenter, Jon W. "After the Mourning Wars: The Iroquois as Allies in Colonial North American Campaigns, 1676–1760." *William and Mary Quarterly* 64, no. 1 (2007): 39–76.

Parmenter, Jon W. "'Onenwahatirighsi Sa Gentho Skaghnughtudigh': Reassessing Haudenosaunee Relations with the Albany Commissioners of Indian Affairs, 1723–1755," 235–83. In *English Atlantics Revisited: Essays Honouring Ian K. Steele*, edited by Nancy L. Rhoden, 246–48. Montreal: McGill-Queen's University Press, 2007.

Parramore, Thomas C. "The Tuscarora Ascendancy." *North Carolina Historical Review* 59, no. 4 (1982): 307–26.

Preston, David. "When Young George Washington Started a War." *Smithsonian Magazine*, October 2019. https://www.smithsonianmag.com/history/.

Preston, Summers L., C.B. Coale, and Bickley, eds. "Batts and Fallam Expedition of 1671." In *Annals of Southwest Virginia, 1769-1800*. Abingdon, VA: L. P. Summers, 1929: 1–7.

Ramsey, William L. "'Something Cloudy in Their Looks': The Origins of the Yamasee War Reconsidered." *Journal of American History* 90, no. 1 (2003): 44–75.

Ramsey, William L. *The Yamasee War: A Study of Culture, Economy, and Conflict in the Colonial South*. Lincoln: University of Nebraska Press, 2008.

Rankin, Hugh F. "Criminal Trial Proceedings in the General Court of Colonial Virginia." *Virginia Magazine of History and Biography* 72, no. 1 (1964): 50–74.

Rhoades, Matthew L. *Long Knives and the Longhouse: Anglo-Iroquois Politics and the Expansion of Colonial Virginia.* Madison: Fairleigh Dickinson University Press, 2010.

Rice, J. D. "Bacon's Rebellion in Indian Country." *Journal of American History* 101, no. 3 (December 2014): 726–50.

Richter, Daniel K. *The Ordeal of the Longhouse: The Peoples of the Iroquois League in the Era of European Colonization.* Chapel Hill: University of North Carolina Press, 1992.

Richter, Daniel K. "Rediscovered Links in the Covenant Chain: Previously Unpublished Transcripts of New York Indian Treaty Minutes, 1677–1691." *Proceedings of the American Antiquarian Society* 92, no. 1 (1982): 43–85.

Richter, Daniel K. "War and Culture: The Iroquois Experience." *William and Mary Quarterly* 3rd ser., 40, no. 4 (1983): 528–59.

Robinson, W. Stitt. "The Legal Status of the Indian in Colonial Virginia." *Virginia Magazine of History and Biography* 61, no. 3 (1953): 247–59.

Ronan, Kristine K. "'Kicked About': Native Culture at Thomas Jefferson's Monticello." *Panorama: Journal of the Association of Historians of American Art* 3, no. 2 (Fall 2017): 1-7. https://journalpanorama.org/article/native-culture-at-monticello/.

Rountree, Helen C. "Personal Names by Early Virginia Indians, Uses of." In *Encyclopedia Virginia*, December 7, 2020. https://encyclopediavirginia.org/entries/.

Rountree, Helen C. "The Termination and Dispersal of the Nottoway Indians of Virginia." *Virginia Magazine of History and Biography* 95, no. 2 (April 1987): 193–214.

Royster, Charles. *The Fabulous History of the Dismal Swamp Company: A Story of George Washington's Times.* New York: Alfred A. Knopf, 1999.

Ryland, Elizabeth Hawes. "Pamunkey Neck: The Birth of a Virginia County." *Virginia Magazine of History and Biography* 50, no. 4 (October 1942): 321–33.

St. Jean, Wendy. "Trading Paths: Chickasaw Diplomacy in the Greater Southeast, 1690s–1790s." PhD diss., University of Connecticut, 2004.

St. Jean, Wendy. "Trading Paths: Mapping Chickasaw History in the Eighteenth Century." *American Indian Quarterly* 27, no. 3/4 (2003): 758–80.

Sapp, Rick. *Native Americans State by State.* New York: Chartwell, 2018.

Saunders, William L., ed. *The Colonial Records of North Carolina* Vol. 10. Raleigh, NC: Josephus Daniels, 1890.

Schenawolf, Harry. "Knives of the American Revolution." *Revolutionary War Journal* (blog), October 29, 2020. https://www.revolutionarywarjournal.com/knives-of-the-american-revolution/.

Schmidt, Ethan A. *The Divided Dominion: Social Conflict and Indian Hatred in Early Virginia.* Boulder: University Press of Colorado, 2015.

Schwarz, Philip J. *Twice Condemned: Slaves and the Criminal Laws of Virginia, 1705–1865.* Baton Rouge: Louisiana State University Press, 1988.

Shefveland, Kristalyn Marie. *Anglo-Native Virginia: Trade, Conversion, and Indian Slavery in the Old Dominion, 1646–1722.* Athens: University of Georgia Press, 2016.

Simpkins, Daniel L. "Aboriginal Intersite Settlement System Change in the Northereaster North Carolina Piedmont during the Contact Period." PhD diss., University of North Carolina at Chapel Hill, 1992.

Sleeper-Smith, Susan. *Indigenous Prosperity and American Conquest: Indian Women of the Ohio River Valley, 1690–1792.* Chapel Hill, NC: Omohundro Institute of Early American History and Culture, 2018.

Smith, Adam. *The Theory of Moral Sentiments*. London: A. Millar, 1761.

Smith, Mark M., ed. *Stono: Documenting and Interpreting a Southern Slave Revolt*. Columbia: University of South Carolina Press, 2005.

Smith, William, William Livingstone, and John Morin Scott. *A Review of the Military Operations in North-America, from the Commencement of the French Hostilities on the Frontiers of Virginia in 1753, to the Surrender of Oswego, on the 14th of August, 1756: Interspersed with Various Observations, Characters, and Anecdotes; Necessary to Give More Light into the Conduct of American Transactions in General; and More Especially into the Political Management of Affairs in New York: In a Letter to a Nobleman*. London: R. and J. Dodsley, 1757.

Smyth, Edward Noel. "The Natchez Diaspora: A History of Indigenous Displacement and Survival in the Atlantic World." PhD diss., University of California, Santa Cruz, 2016.

Speck, Frank G. "Siouan Tribes of the Carolinas as Known from Catawba, Tutelo, and Documentary Sources." *American Anthropologist* 37, no. 2 (1935): 201–25.

Stewart, Mart A. "William Gerard de Brahm's 1757 Map of South Carolina and Georgia." *Environmental History* 16, no. 3 (2011): 523–35.

Stewart, T. Dale. "Archeological Exploration of Patawomeke: The Indian Town Site (44St2) Ancestral to the One (44Stl) Visited in 1608 by Captain John Smith." *Smithsonian Contributions to Anthropology* no. 36 (1992): iv–96.

Strachey, William. *A Dictionary of Powhatan. American Language Reprints 8*. Southampton, PA: Evolution, 1999.

Taliaferro, Henry. "Fry and Jefferson Revisited." *Journal of Early Southern Decorative Arts* 39 (2018). http://www.mesdajournal.org/2013/fry-jefferson-revisited/.

Tayac, Gabriella (Piscataway). "Ancestors Speaking: Objects and Cultural Sovereignty in Native America." Distinguished Speaker Series, UCLA/Getty Conservation of Archaeological and Ethnographic Materials, March 5, 2021.

Thomson, Charles. *An Enquiry into the Causes of the Alienation of the Delaware and Shawanese Indians from the British Interest: And into the Measures Taken for Recovering Their Friendship: Extracted from the Public Treaties, and Other Authentic Papers Relating to the Transactions of the Government of Pensilvania and the Said Indians, for near Forty Years, and Explained by a Map of the Country: Together with the Remarkable Journal of Christian Frederic Post, by Whose Negotiations, among the Indians on the Ohio, They Were Withdrawn from the Interest of the French, Who Thereupon Abandoned the Fort and Country: With Notes by the Editor Explaining Sundry Indian Customs, &c*. London: Printed for J. Wilkie, 1759.

Thwaites, Reuben Gold. *Daniel Boone*. New York: Appleton, 1902.

Thwaites, Reuben Gold, Louise Phelps Kellogg, Sons of the American Revolution, and State Historical Society of Wisconsin. *Documentary History of Dunmore's War, 1774*. Madison: Wisconsin Historical Society, 1905.

Tibbetts, John H. "Carolina's Gold Coast: The Culture of Rice and Slavery." *Coastal Heritage Magazine* 28, no. 1 (Winter 2014). https://www.scseagrant.org/.

Timberlake, Henry. *The Memoirs of Lieut. Henry Timberlake (Who Accompanied the Three Cherokee Indians to England in the Year 1762) Containing Whatever He Observed Remarkable, or Worthy of Public Notice, during His Travels to and from That Nation; Wherein the Country, Government, Genius, and Customs of the Inhabitants, Are Authentically Described. Also the Principal Occurrences during Their Residence in London. Illustrated with an Accurate Map of Their Over-Hill Settlement, and a Curious Secret Journal, Taken by the Indians Out of the Pocket of a Frenchman They*

Had Killed. London: Printed for the author, 1765. https://www.gutenberg.org/files
     /65256/65256-h/65256-h.htm.

Todd, Vincent H., and Julius Goebel, eds. *Baron Christoph von Graffenried, 1661–1743*.
     Translated by Vincent H. Todd and Julius Goebel. Raleigh, NC: Edwards &
     Broughton, 1920. https://docsouth.unc.edu/nc/graffenried/graffenried.html.

*A Treaty, Held at the Town of Lancaster, in Pennsylvania, by the Honourable the
     Lieutenant-Governor of the Province, and the Honourable the Commissioners
     for the Provinces of Virginia and Maryland, with the Indians of the Six Nations,
     in June 1744.*

A Treaty of Friendship Held with the Chiefs of the Six Nations, at Philadelphia,
     in September and October, 1736. Philadelphia: Benjamin Franklin, 1737. http://
     name.umdl.umich.edu/N03399.0001.001.

"The Treaty of Logg's Town, 1752. Commission, Instructions, &c., Journal of Virginia
     Commissioners, and Text of Treaty." *Virginia Magazine of History and Biography*
     13, no. 2 (1905): 143–74.

Trent, William, Alfred Thomas Goodman, and Robert Dinwiddie. *Journal of Cap-
     tain William Trent from Logstown to Pickawillany, A.D. 1752: Now Published for
     the First Time from a Copy in the Archives of the Western Reserve Historical Society,
     Cleveland, Ohio, Together with Letters of Governor Robert Dinwiddie; an Historical
     Notice of the Miami Confederacy of Indians ; a Sketch of the English Post at Picka-
     willany, with a Short Biography of Captain Trent, and Other Papers Never before
     Printed*. Cincinnati: William Dodge, 1871.

Trimble, David B. "Christopher Gist and Settlement on the Monongahela, 1752–1754."
     Virginia Magazine of History and Biography 63, no. 1 (1955): 15–27.

Trudel, Marcel. "The Jumoville Affair." Translated by Donald H. Kent. *Pennsylvania
     History: A Journal of Mid-Atlantic Studies* 21, no. 4 (1954): 351–81.

Tyler, Lyon Gardiner, Review of Oliver Perry Chitwood. "Justice in Colonial Virginia."
     American Historical Review 11, no. 2 (January 1906): 406–8.

Van Doren, Carl, Julian P. Boyd, and Historical Society of Pennsylvania. *Indian
     Treaties Printed by Benjamin Franklin, 1736–1762*. Ulan Press, 2012.

Vest, Jay Hansford C. "Crossing Paths: Intersections between Louis Michel and
     Monacan Oral Traditions." *Native South* 2 (2009): 163–74.

Vest, Jay Hansford C. "From Nansemond to Monacan: The Legacy of the Pochick-
     Nansemond among the Bear Mountain Monacan." *American Indian Quarterly* 27,
     no. 3 (2003): 781–806.

*Virginia. A Treaty Held with the Catawba and Cherokee Indians, at the Catawba-Town
     and Broad-River, in the Months of February and March 1756. By Virtue of a Commis-
     sion Granted by the Honorable Robert Dinwiddie, Esquire, His Majesty's Lieutenant-
     Governor, and Commander in Chief of the Colony and Dominion of Virginia, to the
     Honorable Peter Randolph and William Byrd, Esquires, Members of His Majesty's
     Council of the Said Colony*. Published by Order of the Governor.

Virginia Governor's Council. "Order by the [Virginia Governor's Council] Concern-
     ing the North Carolina/Virginia Boundary," 1706. https://docsouth.unc.edu/csr
     /index.php/document/csr01-0335.

Virginia Council, Virginia General Court, H. R. McIlwaine, and Virginia State
     Library. *Minutes of the Council and General Court of Colonial Virginia, 1622–1632,
     1670–1676, with Notes and Excerpts from Original Council and General Court Rec-
     ords, into 1683, Now Lost*. Richmond: Colonial Press, 1924.

Virginia Council, Virginia State Library, and H. R. McIlwaine. *Executive Journals of the Council of Colonial Virginia*. 6 vols. Richmond: Davis Bottom, 1925.

Walker, Thomas. "Journal of Doctor Thomas Walker—1749–1750." In *Annals of Southwest Virginia, 1769–1800*, edited by Lewis Preston Summers, 8–26. Abingdon, VA, 1929. http://hdl.handle.net/2027/uva.x000213451.

Warren, Stephen. *The Worlds the Shawnees Made: Migration and Violence in Early America*. Chapel Hill: University of North Carolina Press, 2013.

Waselkov, Gregory A. "Indian Maps of the Colonial Southeast." In *Powhatan's Mantle*, edited by Peter H. Wood, Gregory A. Waselkove, and M. Thomas Hatley, 435–49. Lincoln: University of Nebraska Press, 2006.

Waselkov, Gregory A., Peter H. Wood, and M. Thomas Hatley, eds. *Powhatan's Mantle: Indians in the Colonial Southeast*. Revised and expanded ed. Lincoln: University of Nebraska Press, 2006.

Washburn, Wilcomb E. *Virginia under Charles I and Cromwell, 1625–1660*. Williamsburg: Virginia 350th Anniversary Celebration Corp., 1957.

Wharton, Samuel, and Edward Bancroft. *View of the Title to Indiana, a Tract of Country on the River Ohio. Containing Indian Conferences at Johnson-Hall, in May, 1765—The Deed of the Six Nations to the Proprietors of Indiana—The Minutes of the Congress at Fort Stanwix, in October and November, 1768—The Deed of the Indians, Settling the Boundary Line between the English and Indians Lands—and the Opinion of Counsel on the Title of the Proprietors of Indiana*. Evans Early American Imprint Collection. Philadelphia: Styner & Cist, 1765.

Wilson, Jack Hubert. "A Study of the Late Prehistoric, and Historic Indians of the Carolinas and Virginia Piedmont: Structure, Process, and Ecology." PhD diss., University of North Carolina, 1983.

Witgen, Michael. *An Infinity of Nations: How the Native New World Shaped Early North America*. Philadelphia: University of Pennsylvania Press, 2012.

Witgen, Michael. "Rethinking Colonial History as Continental History." *William and Mary Quarterly* 69, no. 3 (2012): 527–30.

Wood, Douglas McClure. "'I Have Now Made a Path to Virginia': Outacite Ostenaco and the Cherokee-Virginia Alliance in the French and Indian War." *West Virginia History: A Journal of Regional Studies* 2, no. 2 (2008): 31–60.

Wood, Peter H. "The Changing Population of the Colonial South: An Overview by Race and Region, 1685–1790." In *Powhatan's Mantle*, edited by Peter H. Wood, Gregory A. Waselkove, and M. Thomas Hatley, 58–62. Lincoln: University of Nebraska Press, 2006.

Wood, Peter H. "Anatomy of a Revolt." In *Stono: Documenting and Interpreting a Southern Slave Revolt*, edited by Mark M. Smith, 59–72. Columbia: University of South Carolina Press, 2005.

Woodard, Buck. "Appendix A: Natives in the Landscape: Images and Documents of the Seventeenth Century Virginia Indians." In *A Study of Virginia Indians and Jamestown: The First Century*. Williamsburg, Virginia: Colonial National Historical Park National Park Service US Department of the Interior, 2005. https://www.nps.gov/parkhistory/online_books/jame1/moretti-langholtz/chap10.htm.

Woodard, Buck, Danielle Moretti-Langholtz, and Stephanie Hasselbacher. *The High Plains Sappony of Person County, North Carolina and Halifax County, Virginia; Sites of Significance in the Christie Indian Settlement: Churches, Schools, and General Store*. College of William and Mary Anthropological

Research Report Series 5 / Commonwealth of Virginia Research Report Series 21, 2017. 081_High_Plains_Sappony_NCVA_Christie_Indian_Settlement_2017 _WM_report.pdf.

Wooldridge, William C. *Mapping Virginia: From the Age of Exploration to the Civil War.* Charlottesville: University of Virginia Press, 2012.

Worth, John E. "Yamassee Origins and the Development of the Carolina-Florida Frontier." Fifth annual conference of the Omohundro Institute of Early American History and Culture, June 12, 1999, Austin, Texas.

Wulf, Karin. "Vast Early America: Three Simple Words for a Complex Reality." Omohundro Institute of Early American History and Culture. February 6, 2019. https://oieahc.wm.edu/publications/blog/.

Zontine, Patricia. "Dr. Thomas Walker." Lucy Meriwether Lewis Marks. https:// www.monticello.org/sites/library/exhibits/lucymarks/lucymarks/bios /drthomaswalker.html.

Index